DATE DUE

DEMCO 38-296

ALSO BY LESLEY DOWNER

On the Narrow Road

THE BROTHERS

THE
BROTHERS

The Hidden World of Japan's Richest Family

LESLEY DOWNER

RANDOM HOUSE
NEW YORK

For my father and for Kojo

Library of Congress Cataloging-in-Publication Data
Downer, Lesley.
    The brothers : the hidden world of Japan's richest family / Lesley
    Downer. — 1st ed.
        p.   cm.
    Includes bibliographical references and index.
    ISBN 0-679-42554-3
    1. Tsutsumi family. 2. Tsutsumi, Yasujiro, 1889–1964.
    3. Tsutsumi, Seiji. 4. Tsutsumi, Yoshiaki, 1934– .
    5. Executives—Japan—Biography. 6. Businessmen—Japan—Biography.
    7. Conglomerate corporations—Japan—History—20th century.
    I. Title. II. Title: Tsutsumi family, a saga of modern Japan.
    CT1837.5.T78D69 1995
    338.8´87179006852—dc20   94-41340

Manufactured in the United States of America
on acid-free paper
98765432
First U.S. Edition

Talking about business—you have to go right to the gates of prison. You go right there but you don't go inside. That's the way to do it. If you once go inside you've had it. But if you don't get close to jail you won't achieve anything.

YASUJIRO TSUTSUMI

My father received his grandfather's seventy-four years of experience. Add to that his own seventy-five years and you have one hundred fifty years. When you add my age, fifty, to that one hundred fifty, that makes two hundred years of experience. That is the power of the Seibu Railways Group. We have three people's ways of thinking. If you look at this, you'll understand what a secure foundation my business has.

YOSHIAKI TSUTSUMI

I thought I had managed to dodge the pitfalls of submersion in the environment Father had created. But the dark clouds of his acts relentlessly followed me, even as I tried to drive them away. I'd heard that on moonlit nights a purple ring, like that given off by luminous moss, can be seen behind soldiers who ate human flesh to survive during the war. I wondered if Father had continually run with such a nimbus behind him. I suspect that all leaders are unable to escape this kind of fate. . . . I sometimes think that the one thing I can do is make sure never to forget that I too am burdened with a purple nimbus.

TAKASHI TSUJII (SEIJI TSUTSUMI)

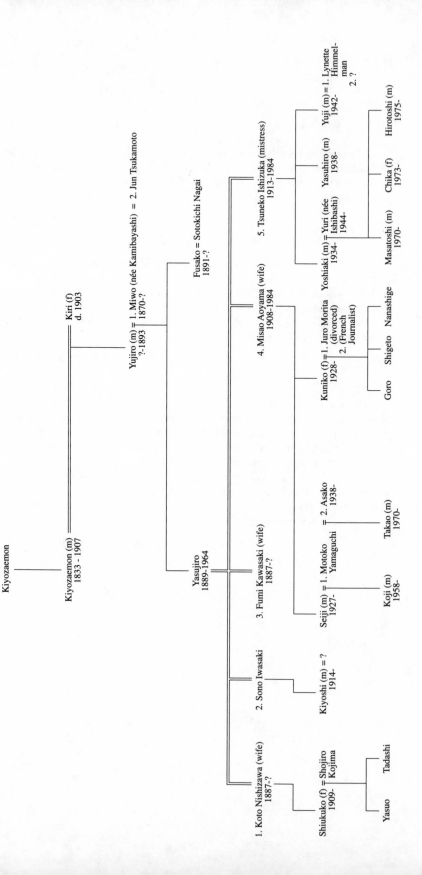

Kiyozaemon

Kiyozaemon

Kiyozaemon (m)
1833 - 1907

Kiri (f)
d. 1903

Yujiro (m) = 1. Miwo (née Kamibayashi) = 2. Jun Tsukamoto
?-1893   1870-?

Fusako = Sotokichi Nagai
1891-?

Yasujiro
1889-1964

1. Koto Nishizawa (wife)
1887-?

2. Sono Iwasaki

3. Fumi Kawasaki (wife)
1887-?

4. Misao Aoyama (wife)
1908-1984

5. Tsuneko Ishizuka (mistress)
1913-1984

Shiukuko (f) = Shojiro
1909-   Kojima

Kiyoshi (m) = ?
1914-

Seiji (m) = 1. Motoko
1927-   Yamaguchi
         = 2. Asako
            1938-

Kuniko (f) = 1. Juro Morita
1928-   (divorced)
           2. (French
              Journalist)

Yoshiaki (m) = Yuri (née
1934-   Ishibashi)
              1944-

Yasuhiro (m)
1938-

Yuji (m) = 1. Lynette
1942-   Himmel-
           man
           2. ?

Yasuo   Tadashi

Koji (m)
1958-

Takao (m)
1970-

Goro   Shigeto   Nanashige

Masatoshi (m)
1970-

Chika (f)
1973-

Hirotoshi (m)
1975-

Acknowledgments

Many people provided help and support during the writing of this book, and I am very grateful to all of them.

My thanks first of all to the various members of the Tsutsumi family who were willing to offer help and cooperation. Seiji, Yoshiaki, Kuniko and Yuji Tsutsumi all agreed to meet me, provided introductions and gave me access to people I would otherwise not have been able to meet.

I am indebted to Sir Terence Conran, who kindly provided an introduction to Seiji Tsutsumi. Thanks also to Jeremy Hardie, Sue Henny, Graham McCallum, Chris McDonald, Sir Peter Parker and Ben Thorne, all of whom made strenuous efforts to help me obtain the vital introductions.

Within the Saison Group, I would like to thank Etsuko Miyairi, executive assistant to Seiji Tsutsumi; Seiichi Mizuno, president of Seibu department stores; Toshio Takeuchi, president of Credit Saison; and the many other people who provided help and information. Hiroyuki Nishibe, now retired, and Katsutoshi Ozaki, working on the history of Saison, gave generously of their time and memories. Thanks also to Yasuo Fukumoto, of the Inter-Continental Hotels in the U.K., who followed the progress of this book with an interested though detached eye.

Within Kokudo, the public relations department opened many doors for me. I am indebted too to public relations director Nozomi Kawakami and manager Masaaki Mori of the Seibu Lions.

Kasuke Hoshino provided hospitality and companionship in Karuizawa, where I would also like to thank Kaoru Iwata and his family, Masao Ezawa (in Nagano), Ichiro Koido, Matsuki Nakajima and Nobuo Tsuchiya.

Many thanks to the following, who kindly agreed to interviews or otherwise gave invaluable help: Michio Akiyama, Mike Allen of Barclays de Zoete Wedd, Professor Eiichi Aoki of Tokyo Gakugei University, Jeffrey Archer, Setsu Asakura, Mrs. Aso, Arseny Besher, Martine Bouché, Alan Catling, David Coleridge, Rodney Fitch, Sakumi Hagiwara, Sir Ralph Halpern, Takajiro Hamada, Bill Hersey, Kumiko Hirano, Ryuichi Ishida, Eiko Ishioka, Matsuko Ishizuka, Kunio Kamibayashi, Shizue Kato, Alex Kinmont of Morgan Stanley, Michihisa Kitashirakawa, Kazuko Koike, Mrs. Kosugi of the Tsutsumi house in Shimoyagi, Bernard Krisher, Tsuji Masuda, Michio Nagai, Tokuya Nagai, Bruce Osborne, Keiko Ruwhiu, Yumiko Shimatsu, Takayuki Suzuki of Merrill Lynch, Akiko Takahashi, Kumiko Takase of BZW, Takashi Takatsu of Teikoku Databank, Torao Takazawa, Hideo Totsuka, Hiroshi Tsuruoka, Wedda Uyeda, Joy Walbert of Baring Securities, Michael Williams, Colin Woodhead, Ganri Yamashita, Takashi Yokota of Dentsu, Soichiro Yoshida, Toshiro Yoshie, Kunihiko Yoshimeki, Eitaro Yoshioka, Dr. Tsunehiko Yui.

Certain people spoke to me on condition that I do not reveal their names: special thanks to them. Of the many books in Japanese on the Tsutsumi family, Naoki Inose's seminal *Mikado no Shozo* (Portrait of the Emperor) provided inspiration.

Several Japanese journalists have made a specialty of following the family's fortunes and kindly shared their knowledge with me. In particular I should like to thank Toshiaki Kaminogo, and also Koki Eikawa, Gentaro Taniguchi, Yasuo Hariki, Eiji Oshita, Hideki Otsuka and Yasunori Tateishi. Special thanks also to Tatsuya Iwase.

Of the journalistic community thanks to: Kozo Abe of *Yukan Fuji,* Soichiro Arai, Yasuo Fujigane of *Toyo Keizai,* Nagaharu Hayabusa of the *Asahi Shimbun,* Seigo Kimata of *Shukan Bunshun,* Hiroshi Kusano, Yonosuke Miki, Mineo Noda, Makoto Sadaka, Yoichi Clark Shimatsu of the *Japan Times,* Gregory Starr, Henry Scott Stokes, Takao Toshikawa of *Insideline,* Robert Whiting and Karel von Wolferen. John Roberts gave me much time and help and provided access to his extensive collection of materials on Japan.

Without the help of my research assistants, it would have been impossible to write this book. Chieko Tsuneoka proved expert at working out what I was looking for and finding it for me, provided accurate and efficient translations and continues to ply me with material on the family to this day. Itsuko Sugawara, Ann Hesugi and Shiho Sakamoto also provided invaluable help.

All my friends, both in Japan and the UK, have been extremely understanding and supportive. Special thanks to those in Tokyo who ensured I had a roof over my head: Carol Potter, Yuriko Kuchiki and Neil Gross, Nizam Hamid, Margaret Scott and Ben Rauch, Sho and Sachiko Ojima, Harriet and Stephen Cohen, and Annie Cousin and Kazuto in Kamakura.

Simon and Takako Prentis were my Japanese-language consultants in London, and Takako provided the calligraphy for the cover. I am indebted to Professor Arthur Stockwin of the Nissan Institute, Oxford, who very kindly looked over the text, though of course any mistakes therein are entirely my own responsibility.

My publishers, both in Britain and the United States, have been enormously enthusiastic and supportive. My thanks to Jonathan Burnham and everyone at Chatto & Windus; to Ann Godoff and the staff at Random House; and to my agent, Gill Coleridge.

And, lastly, thanks to Kojo, for being there, reading the first draft, and providing sunshine.

Author's Note

Even before I began the research for this book, many people warned me against it. In Japan the name of Tsutsumi is as well known as that of the Kennedys or the Rockefellers in the West. In the same way, everyone knows a garbled version of their story—their wealth, the complexities of their private lives and the fabled hatred of one brother for the other. Yet the story has never been told in English.

Many people refused to speak to me or denied that they had any knowledge of the family. The brothers would never speak to me, they said. I would find out nothing. Worse, it might be dangerous if I probed too far. The brothers, after all, were frighteningly powerful. And in Japan big business is never far removed from the underworld.

One British ex-ambassador and old Japan hand, whom I asked for help with introductions, bellowed into the telephone, "You are sticking your head into a wasps' nest!"

At first it seemed unlikely that I would ever be able to meet the brothers themselves. Both habitually refuse interviews with the press. In the event, both responded to my overtures in characteristic fashion.

Following the usual Japanese procedure, I approached Seiji via an introduction from a leading British company chairman with whom he had business connections. He agreed to meet me. At our meeting he was charm itself. He would be a passive, not an active, participant; but I was welcome to interview him, more than once if required, and I could fax questions to him whenever I needed to, throughout the writing of the book. Once the meeting was over, however, when I approached his personal assistant to set up the first interview, I was told that he was too busy. I should fax him questions, as he had suggested. When I faxed him, my faxes went unanswered.

Yoshiaki was more straightforward. In his case, no one was willing to risk providing an introduction. There was nothing for it but to approach his public relations department. To my surprise, they were prepared to cooperate. They made their position clear. I could observe Yoshiaki, I could watch him in action, but I could not interview him. Having made their offer, they kept to it. I attended the opening of one of Yoshiaki's hotels, where I was even able to shake the great man's hand. But I was allowed no closer contact.

Unable to interview either brother, I turned to secondary sources. Both brothers instructed their assistants to provide help and introductions. I interviewed Kuniko, Seiji's younger sister, in Paris, and was able to meet old school friends of the brothers, some of the top men in both business empires, and people who had been with Seibu since the time of the founder, Yasujiro.

Some people told me less than I expected, others far more. One interviewee described each member of the family individually in a single word: "ordinary." Several who hold top positions in the various companies first asked me not to reveal their names. Then, when I agreed to this condition, they spoke with astonishing frankness, answering questions I had not asked and revealing details I had never known existed.

I visited some of the places in Japan associated with the family or with Seibu, and interviewed many people whom I searched out independently as well as those whom I met with the help of the personal assistants. I studied the books and many articles written about the family in Japanese and met the journalists who have made it their life's work to follow the family's fortunes.

I checked and double-checked my information, asking many different people about the same events and comparing their stories. I turned also to Seiji's autobiographical novels, again asking people within the company to confirm that particular stories were taken from life. I have indicated in my narrative where my stories originate in Seiji's novels.

In the end I sat down to collate the information I had, to assess both the validity of each piece of information and the reliability of my sources. Some of the information—particularly when it derived from supporters of each of the brothers—was contradictory; most people I spoke to supported either one or other of the two; and there were people who had reason to hate or fear them. All this I had to take into account.

The story I have pieced together is in no way an authorized biography. I have done the best I can to ascertain the facts, and in some cases I have had to interpret the material. But in the end there are some things that are simply unknowable.

Except where stated, the translations in this book are my own. Japanese and English are very different and a literal translation would be wooden and unnatural. I have kept the substance of the original but tried to communicate its flavor and spirit by using colloquial speech appropriate to the person and the period.

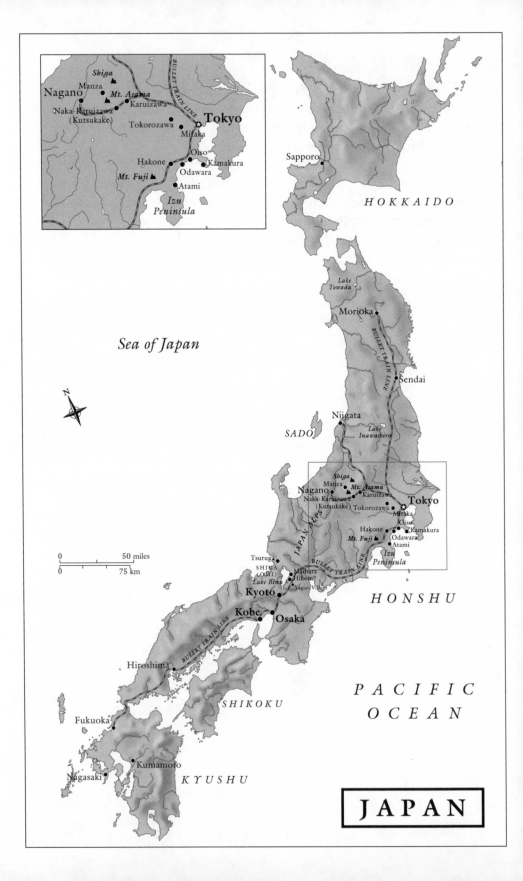

Sea of Japan

HOKKAIDO

Sapporo

Lake
Towada

Morioka

Sendai

Niigata

SADO

Lake
Inawashiro

Shiga
Manza   Mt. Asama
Nagano   Karuizawa
Naka-Karuizawa   Tokyo
(Kutsukake)   Tokorozawa
Mitaka
Oiso
Hakone   Kamakura
Odawara
Mt. Fuji   Atami
Izu
Peninsula

HONSHU

N

JAPAN ALPS

BULLET TRAIN LINE

Tsuruga
SHIGA
(OMI)
Lake Biwa
Maibara
Hikone
Yagiso Village
Kyoto
Kobe
Osaka

50 miles
75 km

Hiroshima

PACIFIC
OCEAN

SHIKOKU

Fukuoka

Kumamoto

Nagasaki

KYUSHU

JAPAN

Shiga
Manza
Nagano   Mt. Asama
              Karuizawa
Naka-Karuizawa
(Kutsukake)   Tokorozawa   Tokyo
Mitaka
Oiso
Hakone   Kamakura
Odawara
Mt. Fuji   Atami
Izu
Peninsula

BULLET TRAIN LINE

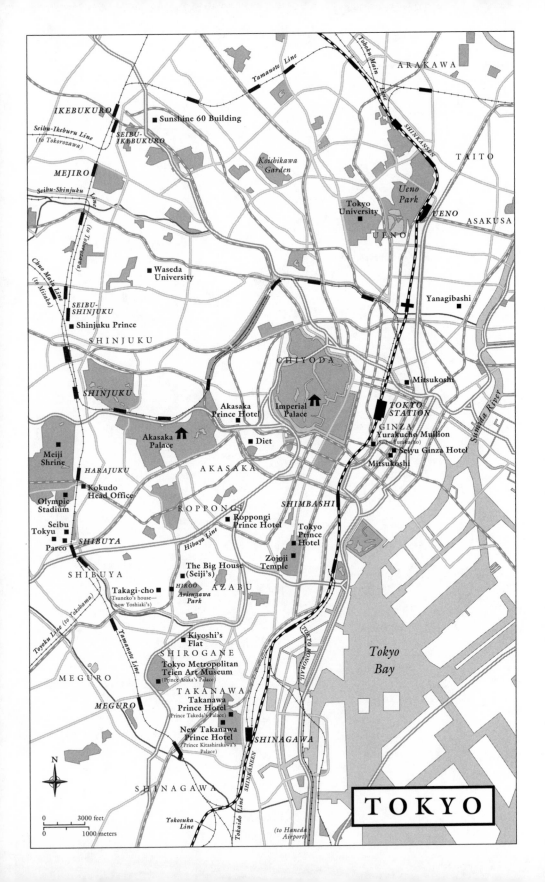

Contents

Prologue

The Dawn Ceremony

The first limousines swept up to the cemetery gates well before dawn. There were two guards there, one in a trench coat, one in an anorak, rubbing their hands and stamping their feet, their breath turning to steam in the freezing January air. They checked the occupants, spoke rapidly into their walkie-talkies, and the gates swung open.

It was the early hours of New Year's Day, 1993—though it could have been practically any of the last thirty years. The ritual never changed. And many of the men who took part were the same year after year.

The cemetery, one of the largest in Japan, covered an entire hill just outside the venerable city of Kamakura, about 25 miles from Tokyo. At that hour it was silent and empty. The ten thousand tombs, arranged in terraces along the slopes, were hidden in the darkness.

But at the very top lights flickered. Figures ran to and fro carrying torches or patrolled the perimeter of the area. Groups of men, all in formal black suits, hurried up the steps, past the shadowy outline of a temple, and disappeared inside a large marquee. It glowed mysteriously, an oblong of light against the black sky.

One limousine was still to come. The guards straightened their ties nervously. The gates were already open as it swept by. Along the road and on the hilltop there was a flutter of bowing.

Six o'clock. To the east the sky was tinted a shade of dark apricot, with black clouds rushing upward away from the rising sun. From the great bronze bell on the hilltop came a dull reverberation, booming out across the countryside. The echo hung in the air, then faded. The bell sounded again, then again, six times in all. Then there was silence, except for the rustling of the pine trees on the hillside.

Inside the marquee the men stood stiffly in ranks, waiting for the ceremony to begin. It was bitterly cold. A few bare lightbulbs cast a cold light. Paraffin heaters sputtered out more fumes than warmth. From time to time the sides of the tent flapped in a sudden wind.

There was a mood of solemn intensity. Everyone was silent. Everyone felt the significance of this ceremony that they were about to take part in, when they gathered together from all corners of Japan to make their vows for the coming year. Assembled were the leading members of one of the country's largest and most powerful business empires. It was a business that encompassed land, railways, golf courses, ski resorts, hotels, recreation facilities. Unlike the great Japanese business empires of the prewar years such as Mitsui and Mitsubishi, which were founded on manufacturing, this was a business for the new age, for the last years of the century, when the Japanese had leisure and were looking for ways to enjoy it. It was a business that had made its way by reshaping the face of Japan, carving golf courses and ski runs out of the hills and fields, turning wild land to profit.

The different companies within the group had many names. The core company of the whole group went by the grand title of Kokudo Keikaku, which in English translates as National Land Planning. But most people thought of the company still by the name it had been given by its founder: Seibu.

That morning five or six hundred top executives from every company within the group crowded into the tent—directors, managing directors, vice presidents, presidents. They were arranged by company in blocks and within each company by rank, with the most senior members at the front.

In front of them was the traditional New Year's decoration, an elaborate arrangement of round white rice cakes with pine branches and red and white diamonds of folded paper, set on a red table. Beyond that shallow steps led up to a low gate.

From where they stood none of the men could see what was beyond the gate. But they all knew. All of them, as fresh young recruits to the company, had come here, most of them many times, to sweep the path and clear the leaves from the lawns, and to pay their respects to the dead founder.

At the top of the steps, commanding the entire hill, was a tomb, splendid and spacious enough to house an emperor. It was vast and flat, carpeted with white pebbles. In the middle was a tombstone of black granite, carrying the simple inscription: "Yasujiro Tsutsumi's tomb."

Everyone felt the power of the old man imbuing the atmosphere. He was spiritually present among them.

As the last stroke of six sounded, the crowd parted and a burly figure strode through. Like the others, he was dressed in black, though his suit was distinguished by its fine tailoring and the quality of the fabric. He stepped up to the tomb and, as each of the men had done when they entered the tent, clapped his hands twice and bowed.

"Happy New Year, Father, Happy New Year," he intoned. His voice was surprisingly high-pitched for such a burly frame.

Yoshiaki Tsutsumi was a heavyset man, broad-shouldered and in the prime of health. He was approaching sixty but he carried himself like a young man, his back very straight, his shoulders thrown back. His hair was jet-black still, and glossy. From some angles his face was handsome, from others ugly; it was a strong, angular face, a face that could not be ignored. His enemies spoke of his *geta*-face after the blunt wooden clogs that workmen wear. He had a large, generous mouth with a jutting lower lip, piercing eyes that missed nothing and a ruthless thrust to his square jaw. The corners of his mouth were turned down in an expression of steely determination.

Now he turned to face the assembled crowd. Framed against the grave behind him, with its vases of flowers and New Year's decorations, he addressed them in the gruff tones of a feudal lord admonishing his men.

His speech was brief, a mere seven or eight minutes. Each year it was much the same: Last year had been tough, this year would be tougher. With Japan's economy entering a recession, they would have to work harder than ever before.

"Even if you're a section chief with Seibu Real Estate, you'll be transferred to the hotels if your performance is bad," he thundered. "There you start with washing dishes. That's the sort of determination I want you to have! Even if you're near retirement, you can quit right now if you don't have commitment and ability!"[1]

Then he outlined the projects for the year to come. There were new hotels planned, to be designed by the top architects in the country, new golf courses and ski resorts, and building developments abroad. Every year the assembled executives were taken by surprise. But they all had complete faith in their leader.

Few people doubted that Yoshiaki Tsutsumi was one of the most powerful men in the country. But although he wielded power, he did not like to be seen to wield it. He preferred to operate from behind the scenes. He was famous for his network of connections. His friends included the current prime minister, previous prime ministers and those mysterious figures who were the real power brokers in the country. He was not indebted to them; they were indebted to him. No matter which faction or which party happened to be in power, Yoshiaki could always be certain of wielding influence.

The secret of his power was his legendary wealth. According to *Forbes,* the American business magazine, he was the richest man in the world—richer than the Rockefellers, the Rothschilds, the Gettys. His riches were exceeded only by those of royalty—the sultan of Brunei, the queen of England. For four years running he had headed *Forbes*'s list of the world's billionaires. In 1993 he was to top the list again, with private assets variously assessed at $9 or $22 billion. No one knew the full extent of his wealth. His companies were not listed and their accounts were a closely guarded secret.

The business was one of Japan's great success stories. Yoshiaki's companies owned one sixth of all the land in Japan; and their land holdings increased every year. They owned the largest luxury hotel chain in the country with more than sixty hotels. You could live in a Seibu apartment, travel to work on Seibu Railways, stay at a Seibu-owned Prince hotel and go on holiday to one of Seibu's resorts, which dominated all the country's best ski slopes. Each year, even when the country's economy was threatened by recession, new hotels and new resort developments opened. Each year more of the countryside of Japan was replaced by golf courses and ski resorts.

As all the men gathered that morning in the marquee knew, the empire had been founded not by the man standing before them but by his father. Many of them had been with Seibu long enough to remember the gruff old man with his coarse country accent. Many of their fathers before them had worked for Seibu. They had been there in the hard days when the old man was building the empire from nothing. Yoshiaki never claimed to be anything more than the son of his father. He was simply performing the duty expected of a good son. He was carrying on the business that had been left to him.

The sides of the tent creaked and flapped in the icy wind.

"This year too let's do our best!" boomed the burly man standing on the steps of the tomb. The six hundred men stood silent and unmoving, their heads bowed.

Yoshiaki turned to face his father's grave. An assistant hurried forward to place a red-lacquered saucer in his hands, brimming with warm sake. In unison with the company presidents lined up behind him he raised the cup in both hands and bowed his head to salute the old man in his grave.

"Happy New Year, Father!" he intoned.

The red saucers full of the warm, intoxicating liquor passed back down the line, from presidents to vice presidents to managing directors to directors to managers, all the way down to section chiefs. Each in turn raised the cup in homage to the grave and the man who lay in it.

Minutes later Yoshiaki was gone. Amid another flurry of bowing the limousine glided off down the hill. In the marquee the men relaxed, laughing and chatting, toasting one another again and again to welcome in the New Year.

Six-thirty. The great bell tolled again, a single stroke echoing across the valley to the surrounding hills. The sky was a shade of pale turquoise.

Far away on the horizon to the west a phantasm appeared. At first it was no more than a hint. Then, as the sun rose higher, the shape became clearer and clearer. It could be seen only from the very top of the hill, where the old man's tomb lay: Mount Fuji, so perfect in its symmetry that it brought tears to the eyes.

Beyond Fuji, a mere shadow receding on the horizon, were the corrugated hills of Hakone, the place the old man had loved best. And there, across a vista of tombstones as far as the eye could see, was the sea, glistening pearly in the dawn light.

The old man who lay at the center of all this had led a life that was far from neat and orderly. For all the grand ceremony that surrounded him now, his life had been wild and fiery, driven by unbridled ambition and passion. And he had left behind him a legacy of disorder.

Yasujiro Tsutsumi was a man of the Meiji era, born toward the end of the last century, during the reign of Emperor Meiji. Like the great entrepreneurs of Victorian England, he had risen from nothing to carve out an empire for himself with little regard for all the people who had to be trampled underfoot along the way. He had been born the son of a farmer, in a small village surrounded by rice fields. By the end of his life he was one of the most powerful entrepreneurs in the land and a leading political figure, ex-Speaker of the House of Representatives, the friend and mentor of prime ministers. He had toured the world as the representative of his country. He had hobnobbed with Eisenhower and Nixon, Nehru and Macmillan and been invited to Kennedy's inauguration.

But in Japan he was remembered above all for his voracious sexual appetite. He had seven acknowledged children, of whom three could be called legitimate. No one knew how many others he had fathered. Some put the figure at fifty, some at a hundred. Wherever you turned in Seibu, it was said, there was a drop of the old man. As for the mothers of those children, even Yasujiro himself would probably not have known who they all were.

And therein lay the roots of the trouble that followed after his death.

That morning at the hilltop cemetery, besides directors and managing directors, vice presidents and presidents, there were others observing the dawn ceremony. Family members, who saw one another only on that one day of the year, had gathered there. Standing in a corner was a small, sharp-featured old man, who looked remarkably like the dead founder: Kiyoshi, Yasujiro's eldest son. Another of the sons, the reserved Yasuhiro, was there every year, even though he was on bad terms with Yoshiaki.

There was one notable absence. The best-known member of the family was not there.

It was a decade since Seiji Tsutsumi had last been seen at the dawn ceremony. Each year he sent a representative to place flowers on the old man's grave, but he himself stayed away. Rumor had it that he never communicated in any way with his half brother Yoshiaki.

Seiji was the elder of the two and the legitimate son of their father, yet he had inherited nothing but a tiny fragment of the old man's fortune. With that he had built his own empire, not of land and wealth but of taste and style. He was something of a legend in Japan. While Yoshiaki was rich, Seiji was influential. To most people the name Seibu meant not Yoshiaki's empire of land, hotels, golf courses and ski resorts but Seiji's department stores. Almost single-handedly he had brought glamour and luxury into Japanese life. The Seibu department stores epitomized the new Japan, the Japan of the economic miracle.

A complex, rather mysterious figure, Seiji was one of Japan's most flamboyant businessmen, but he was also a literary man, who wrote under the pen name of Takashi Tsujii and had won awards for his poetry and novels. He was a man of many faces and many talents.

But why was he not at the dawn ceremony and why had he not inherited his father's wealth? Though they themselves did all they could to conceal it, rumors abounded of an unbridgeable rift between the two brothers. It was the dark secret behind the glittering façade of their wealth and success.

The dispute could only be explained by going back to the roots of the two empires, to the man who had begun it all and now lay entombed at the top of the mountain—Yasujiro Tsutsumi. The story begins more than a century ago, in a small village in central Japan.

I

The Patriarch

I

The Beginning
Omi 1889–1907

I lost my father at the age of five and had to part with my mother, and tasted the grief of parting at that time. Later I was brought up by my grandparents with their love. But before I came of age my grandparents died. After that my life has risen and fallen—it still continues today. Literally it's a seventy years' history of struggle.　YASUJIRO TSUTSUMI
Thirty Years of Struggle

One wintry day in 1893, in mountain country deep in central Japan, a woman was hurrying along the dirt track that led through the fields away from the village of Yagiso. In her arms she carried a small girl; a little boy ran behind her, grabbing at the skirts of her kimono. A man strode a few paces ahead, carrying the woman's belongings bundled in a dark-blue cloth.

As she walked, she wept. Her head was covered with a thick cotton traveling scarf. From time to time she turned to look back at the dark walls and straw roofs of Yagiso village. In the distance the huddle of houses was like an island in the middle of the sea of rice fields, spreading in flat brown furrows to the snow-covered mountains on the horizon. The sky was blue but the air was icy.

She was a slight, pretty woman, a country girl, just twenty-four years old, dressed in an indigo-blue kimono and padded cotton jacket, shuffling along on wooden *geta* clogs. Under the scarf her long black hair was swept into a knot. When a strand escaped and fell over her face, she reached up and pushed it back into place. Her hands were already red and rough from work.

The little group did not have far to go. A few minutes from the village, they came to a stream with a flimsy wooden bridge across it. The grass that lined the banks was withered and dry. Here the woman set the little girl down. On the other side the path wound away toward the hills.

As she walked she had been pondering the best course to take. Should she take the children with her? But when she saw the stream she knew she had no choice.

"Come, you're good children," she said gently. "Run back home now. Go back to Grandma and Granddad and do what they say. Then you'll grow up good children. Good-bye now."

The children clung to her, wailing loudly.

"Very well. Come with me to the bridge. We'll say good-bye there."[1]

Hand in hand the two children—Yasujiro Tsutsumi and his sister, Fusako—stood at the end of the bridge, watching and waving. The man, then the woman, crossed and walked away; the two figures grew smaller and smaller in the distance until they turned a corner and disappeared. The children watched and waited a while longer, then, sobbing, turned and scuttled back up the path to the village.

Yasujiro was four when his mother left him at the end of the bridge. To the end of his days he never forgot that desolate moment when he stood, abandoned, watching her walk away. It was an experience that was to shape the whole of his life.

Yasujiro Tsutsumi was born on a wintry March day in 1889. In Yagiso village a bitter wind whistled across the parched brown earth and snow lingered on the distant mountains. There was no electricity in those days and precious little heating, just the odd charcoal brazier to warm your hands by. Every year the farmers kept a weather eye out for the changes in the shapes and patterns that the melting snow made on the mountainsides. When a certain shape appeared—a bird or a deer or a circle—it was a sign that it was time to plant out the rice seedlings. It was knowledge that had been passed down for generations.

In the world outside, enormous changes were taking place. In Europe and the United States, the very landscape was being transformed by the Industrial Revolution. Pitheads, factories and smoking chimneys sprouted across the countryside. Trains trundled through the fields, in the cities electric lights glowed and telephones and cameras had been invented.

But Japan remained sealed against change until 1853, when the American commodore Matthew Perry and his steam warships appeared in Tokyo Bay. Their mission was to force the shogun to open his country to trade and exchange. They also brought with them the first breath of the new world.

In the thirty-six years that passed since then, the country changed with astonishing speed. But nearly all the changes were restricted to the great cities, to Tokyo and Osaka. In Yagiso village, deep in the countryside, life continued much as it had for the last thousand years. Only one development brought the promise of change. In 1889, the year that Yasujiro was born, the railway was completed linking Shimbashi station, the main Tokyo terminal, with Osaka and Kobe. It followed the route of the old Tokaido highway and passed not far from Yagiso village, only a couple of hours' walk away.

Yagiso was like a thousand farming villages all over Japan, a cluster of steep-roofed, thatched farmhouses divided by rutted dirt paths, with a patchwork of rice fields all around. In the summer everything was green, in the winter brown, until the snow fell, when it all turned white.

One of the largest houses in the village belonged to Kiyozaemon (or Saezaemon) Tsutsumi, Yasujiro's grandfather and the patriarch of the family. It was a ramshackle house roofed with *kaya* grass, and had a stout storehouse with fireproof earthen walls where they kept the valuables. Opposite was the village temple, Renshoji. Kiyozaemon's name is listed in the records there. He was a village elder and one of the three leaders of the parish, a respected member of the community.

Yasujiro's great-grandfather, another Kiyozaemon (in the traditional way, the given name was passed down from generation to generation), had died young. As a result the family fortunes had declined. Although the younger Kiyozaemon owned some of the fields that surrounded the village, it was not enough to support him and his family. So he became a linen trader. He bought supplies of linen thread, then tramped across the fields to the mountains that rose at the edge of the plain. There he climbed from one village to the next, setting up a network of young women to weave his thread into cloth. At the same time that he delivered the thread he would collect the finished cloth and take it away to sell it. Gradually this grew into a thriving business.

As for Yasujiro's grandmother, Kiri, she was a small, dry woman, nut-brown and wrinkled from years of working in the fields. Her one pleasure was to sit back and puff on her pipe. Kiri had come from a family that owned a kimono shop in the neighboring village of Noto-gawa. When the time came for her son to marry, she decided he should take a daughter of the Kamibayashi family who were running the shop.

These were well-off people from the northern island of Hokkaido, where they had a herring farm. Their nineteen-year-old daughter, Miwo, was a pretty, rather spoiled girl, who was used to good living; but in those days marriage was a matter for the family, not the individual, to decide. Miwo went off docilely enough to become a bride of the Tsutsumi family and live in the family farmhouse.

It was there—or rather, in a small shed behind the house, in the traditional way—that Yasujiro was born, on March 7, 1889. It was the year of the ox, according to the Japanese calendar, and the twenty-second year of the reign of Emperor Meiji. Two years later the young couple had another child, a daughter whom they called Fusako.

Yasujiro's father, Yujiro, was a handsome young man, hardworking and popular in the village. At one point he served as the village headman. As for the little boy, playing and wrestling with his friends on the dirt paths between the houses, he seemed destined for an uneventful life. No doubt he would follow in his father's and grandfather's footsteps, take on the family name of Kiyozaemon and inherit the house and fields.

But when Yasujiro was a tough little boy of four, something happened that changed everything. Old Kiyozaemon was then sixty, a sturdy old man, wrinkled like a walnut. Off for a few days' holiday, he went first to Tokyo for a little sightseeing, then on to a spa on the Japan Sea coast to take the waters. On his way back he stopped by at the home of a relative.

There was a telegram waiting for him there. "Yujiro seriously ill. Return immediately," it read.

He rushed back on the next train. In those days the 450 miles took nearly twenty-four hours.

By the time he got back it was too late. Yujiro, his only son, was dying. He had contracted typhoid fever.

They moved the sick man into a separate room near the store-house. Some of Yasujiro's earliest memories were of the sickroom and the pungent smell of the carbolic acid used to disinfect it. He remembered the warmth of his mother's body as she held him and his little sister in her arms to say good-bye to their father.

It was September 30, 1893, when Yujiro was cremated and his ashes placed in an urn in Renshoji temple. People said it was as if the light of the village had gone out. But for little Yasujiro, what happened next was more terrible still.

Not long after the funeral—a matter of weeks—his mother took him on her lap and told him that she was going to leave. She was going back to Notogawa, where her family ran the kimono shop. He would be able to come and visit her there. He was to be a good boy, she said, to take care of his little sister and obey his grandparents.

A few days later her brother arrived from Hokkaido to take her away.

Throughout his life Yasujiro pondered why his mother left. In his memoirs he put forward a couple of explanations. Perhaps, he wrote, it was his grandparents' kindness. They felt sorry for the young girl, widowed at the age of twenty-four, and sent her away to find a new husband. Or perhaps she was a willful, selfish girl, having grown up in luxury, and his grandparents could not control her.[2]

To the end of his life he never forgot the pain she had caused him. Once, when she was an old woman, he took his family to visit her. In the car on the way home afterward he said grimly, "That was not a good woman."[3]

But there was another story about why she left, a story that Yasujiro never knew.

More than twenty years after Yasujiro himself was dead and gone, in 1987, an article came out that caused a sensation. It was written by an old cousin of Yasujiro's, a man called Kunio Kamibayashi.

Kamibayashi was the son of the very same brother who had come to take Miwo away from the Tsutsumi house in Yagiso village. He was born ten years after those dramatic events, in 1903, but no doubt his father told him the tale.

In his youth Yasujiro visited his uncle in Hokkaido. He grew fond of this young cousin of his. When Kamibayashi grew up, Yasujiro sent for him and gave him a job in his company in Tokyo. There

Kamibayashi saw many things. He had sharp eyes and sharp ears. But, loyal to the cousin who had helped him out, he kept his counsel.

The years passed. Yasujiro died and his sons Seiji and Yoshiaki took over his business empire. The wealth and power of the Tsutsumi dynasty grew and grew. In the 1980s books began to come out, telling the story of the family. All mentioned the faithless mother, who had deserted her children to go off and marry another man.

Finally old Kamibayashi decided it was time to speak out. Yasujiro was long since dead and gone, and Kamibayashi himself was eighty-four. He wanted to tell his story before he died. Besides, he needed the money. He called the editor of a magazine called *Shukan Bunshun*. The editor listened with interest.

"My Tsutsumi Family—the Secret of Blood" was packed with scandalous allegations. Everyone read it; everyone was aghast. That month *Shukan Bunshun* sold an extra fifty thousand copies. Yoshiaki Tsutsumi was so outraged that he canceled all his companies' advertising with the magazine's publisher for a year. The publisher lost ¥100 million ($690,000) in advertising revenues. Seiji Tsutsumi, though, showed a characteristic sense of style; perhaps he was rather tickled by the whole affair. The Saison Group, his rival empire, didn't just continue its advertising, it also sent several cases of excellent wine to *Shukan Bunshun*. "I don't know why," the editor mused.

But no one denied the truth of the contents; and no inexplicable accidents happened to old Kamibayashi.

Old-timers in the companies say that perhaps 70 percent of Kamibayashi's allegations are true. Some are clearly invention; there are references to ghosts and dreams. And some things Kamibayashi may have simply forgotten.

As for the old cousin himself, at ninety-one Kamibayashi was still alive and thriving, living alone in the suburbs of Tokyo. At first sight he was a tiny, frail old man with thick white hair and parchment skin covered in a network of wrinkles, who peered through half-closed eyes and gripped his companion's arm to steady him as he walked. But when he spoke he revealed an almost frightening determination. His story was watertight. But most of all he wanted to talk of Yasujiro's sexual exploits, and did so with unseemly zest.

Most of Kamibayashi's allegations concerned events later in Yasujiro's life. It was only at the very end of his article that he wrote of his aunt, Yasujiro's mother. He began by saying that he had no grudge against Yasujiro or the Tsutsumi family. He was a great admirer of Yasujiro. His cousin was a hero, a giant among men. But, like all heroes, he was flawed.

> There was a devilish side to him too. You could say he had a fault. In my opinion that fault led to the present "dispute" between the Tsutsumi brothers. As to the fault, in the older generation [Yasujiro]'s case it was "lust." They say heroes love sex, but in this case it was precisely that that was the root of the present "dispute."[4]

Finally he wrote that he had a story to tell that even Yujiro himself did not know. It had to do with his mother.

Everyone who speaks of Yasujiro always says that it was the loss of his mother that was "the root of his insatiable sexual appetite." But, Kamibayashi wrote, no one knew the whole story. In fact the womanizing did not begin with Yasujiro. The family's blood had been tainted for generations.

That was why his aunt Miwo had been forced to leave; it was because of the old grandfather, Kiyozaemon.

> Actually this is how it was. Yasujiro's mother, Miwo, was my father's sister. According to what I heard from my father, Miwo's father-in-law [Yasujiro's] grandfather in fact, after his father, Yujiro, died, repeatedly tried to seduce Miwo, so she ran away. There's no mistaking that she ran away to her brother's place in Hokkaido as quickly as she could. At that time it was really difficult to get to Hokkaido. And after that Miwo could never forget Yasujiro and his little sister, and could never feel easy in her mind; certainly as a mother Miwo did not do wrong.
>
> The problems in the blood of the Tsutsumi family may still become worse and worse.[5]

Like Yasujiro after him, Grandfather Kiyozaemon was a womanizer. Time and time again he tried to lay hands on Miwo, until she was forced to telegraph her brother in Hokkaido to ask him to take her away. Kamibayashi made only one small correction to his original story. She did not return to Hokkaido; she went back to the family kimono shop in Notogawa.

Thus at the tender age of four (five by the Japanese way of reckoning), Yasujiro was left alone with his little sister, without a mother or a father. Instead he lived with his grandparents in the big house with the thatched roof and earthen-walled storehouse in Yagiso village.

Yasujiro grew up devoted to his grandfather. In his memoirs he has little to say about his grandmother, except that she liked her pipe. One of his chores was to clean it out with a stalk of rice.

It was his grandfather who was his taskmaster and mentor. There was no one now but the little boy to take over the family house and the family name. The gruff old man took it upon himself to make sure that his grandson grew up imbued with all the precepts and values proper to a farmer. Every day, as farmers still do in Japan, they rose at three or four in the morning. Grandfather Kiyozaemon also taught the child the overriding importance of land. Without land, a farmer had nothing.

While other grandparents spoiled their grandchildren, Kiyozaemon had to be mother and father as well as grandfather to young Yasujiro. An old-fashioned man, he was determined to train his unruly grandson, to pass on all the knowledge he had acquired in his sixty years of experience and to make him a worthy successor to the Tsutsumi name. There was little warmth and gaiety in the Tsutsumi household, but many beatings and angry words.

In those days each of the provinces of Japan was almost like a separate country. It took hours to travel just to the next province; not many years had passed since nearly all journeys were made on foot. When the traveler arrived he was liable to find himself in an alien place with strange food, a strange way of speaking and strange habits.

Yagiso village was in the province of Omi, almost exactly in the center of Japan. Not far away was Lake Biwa, shaped like the *biwa*, the Japanese lute, and the natural heart of the country. It was around Lake Biwa that some of the first inhabitants of Japan had settled, thousands of years before. To the south of the lake they built their capitals, first Nara and then Kyoto. For centuries, Kyoto remained the capital, and even after the shoguns established their base in Tokyo, people still thought of it as that. Most of the men of Omi dreamed of one day setting up business in Kyoto.

Proverbially the men of Omi were famous for one thing: their single-minded pursuit of money. When people spoke of Omi, they spoke of Omi *shōnin*—Omi merchants. It was said that the women of

Omi soothed their children to sleep by telling them tales of local heroes who had gone to the big city to be merchants and had come home rich men. Like Kiyozaemon with his linen business, most people in Omi were not content simply to farm. They also did business, plying back and forth across the lake with their wares. Many of the country's great merchant families originated in Omi: the Mitsuis, the Toyotas, the founders of the great department stores, the founder of C. Itoh, and many others.

There was another name for the men of Omi: Omi *dorobo*, Omi robbers. Gullible farmers complained that they cheated them or forced unwanted wares on them, then charged them high rates of interest. They were ruthless in their pursuit of money—but they loved their homeland. No matter how far the Omi merchant roamed in search of wealth, no matter how many women he collected along the way, he always kept a wife and family in Omi; and in the end he always returned.

In later years many things changed. Even the name of the province was changed, from Omi to Shiga. But the myth of the Omi merchant remained. Many people said that the greatest Omi merchant of them all was Yasujiro Tsutsumi.

No one doubted that the Tsutsumis came from Omi, but some people questioned where they came from before that. Once the family became rich and powerful, the rumor quickly spread that their ancestors were Korean. Despite all attempts at liberalization, in modern Japan being Korean is still a stigma. The Koreans have suffered oppression for generations. Most do their best to conceal their origins.

There was the name itself. The word *tsutsumi* means "riverbank." Unlike most Japanese surnames, which are written with two characters, it is written with only one. Then there was the mystery surrounding the family's history. Most families can trace their ancestry back through three generations. In the Tsutsumis' case, no one knew anything about the family before Grandfather Kiyozaemon.

Certainly there were records. In Renshoji temple the family records go back as far as 1755, but it is well known that in prewar days diligent scribes invented long genealogies for men who had achieved fame. It would not do for a great man to have a short family tree. What excited suspicion was the lack of stories and memories.

There was also a strange lack of an extended family. In Japan most people are bound into an inescapable web of aunts, uncles, cousins, great-aunts and great-uncles, all living close at hand. It is only in recent years that the system has begun to break down. In Yasujiro's case, there were only his grandfather and grandmother on his father's side—no aunts, no uncles, no cousins.

It all seemed to suggest that Kiyozaemon, or his father before him, had been the first in the family to live in Yagiso village. Where had they come from? In the time of the shoguns Japanese were prohibited by law from moving from their villages. One explanation might be that they had somehow arrived from Korea.

With his usual panache, Seiji Tsutsumi confronted the rumor head-on. On several occasions, when he was in Korea on business, he mentioned that his ancestors might have originated there.

The company's spokespeople found a way to take the sting out of the tale. When asked if the family was Korean, their answer was that they are—but then, so is everyone else in Shiga (modern Omi). In about A.D. 500 there was a huge migration of people from Shiragi in Korea to the Japanese heartland, around Lake Biwa. The imperial family itself was part of that migration. And the name Shiragi was later transmuted to Shiga. The Omi merchants, in fact, derived their skill and cunning from the fact that they originated in Korea. It was a skillful way to bypass the real issue.

Yasujiro himself had no doubts about his origins. He wished he knew more about his ancestors, he wrote, but at least he could be sure of one thing: "they were of the Yamato race"—Japanese, in other words.[6]

In 1902, at the age of thirteen, Yasujiro completed his primary school education. His marks were good and he was offered a place at the middle school in Hikone, the nearest large town. Grandfather Kiyozaemon was extremely worried. The old man was sure that if he loosened the reins for one minute his grandson would turn wild; and besides, in a bustling town like Hikone, who knew what kinds of vice there might be? Undoubtedly there were geisha houses and all kinds of terrible people.

"I've brought you up so carefully till now," he said, scowling. "If you go off to a rough place like Hikone and turn delinquent, it will be terrible. If that happens, it will be the end of the Tsutsumi family."[7]

By now the boy had quite a reputation in the village for being a roughneck. The one person he respected was his grandfather.

"What shall I do?" he asked.

"I want you to stay here and be a peasant."[8]

So Yasujiro stayed in Yagiso village. Kiyozaemon was nearly seventy. It was time for young Yasujiro to take over as the head of the household. He had to grow up quickly, and took his duties seriously. Every day, well before the sun rose, while the stars were still glimmering in the sky, he shouldered his tools and tramped along the dark earthen paths between the houses out to the fields.

Yet he had not been to school for nothing. He realized that hard work was not enough. All the villagers worked hard, they were all stooped and gnarled from a life of hard work. But they all used the same antiquated farming methods and no matter how hard they worked, every year the rice crop was poor.

What was needed was study. Study, in fact, might be the way to escape from the narrow world of the village, with its grinding poverty. So Yasujiro began to read books on agriculture. Night after night, when everyone else was asleep, the night light would still be flickering in the ramshackle farmhouse. The old men of the village muttered to one another, "That one will do well when he grows up."

Finally he worked it out. Modern farmers, he discovered, used phosphate fertilizer, whereas the local villagers did not. He asked the farmers around the village where he could find it, but none of them knew. Word was going around at the time of a trade fair, the Fifth Industrial Exposition, to be held in Osaka. There undoubtedly he would find phosphate fertilizer.

In 1903, when he was fourteen, he packed a few belongings and set off for Osaka. Grandfather Kiyozaemon's stern old heart must have sunk. If the little town of Hikone was a den of vice, heaven knew what the boy could get into in the huge city of Osaka. The journey— about sixty-five miles—took half a day in a little wooden train carriage where the seats were lined with tatami matting. Yasujiro alighted in the big new station in Osaka and made his way to the Tennoji section of the city, to the exposition.

Osaka was a vast, smoky, overcrowded city, already one of the biggest cities in the world. To the boy from Yagiso village, it must have been a revelation. Its narrow streets and wooden houses, pressed roof to roof, extended for miles. Swaths of electric cable swung overhead; and in the distance factory chimneys pumped out black smoke. It went by the proud title of Manchester of the East. In the center of the city there were streets lined with imposing brick buildings, several stories high, such as young Yasujiro had never seen before.

Among the booths at the exposition he found what he was looking for: phosphate fertilizer. He also had a stroke of luck. It turned out that the president of the company that produced the phosphate, Osaka Chemicals, was a Shiga man himself—an Omi merchant. He would be bound to understand young Yasujiro and what he wanted. Reassured by the news, Yasujiro made an appointment with the president, Ichizaburo Abe, and went in to see him.

Behind his desk, sitting in his *hakama,* the traditional men's stiff pleated skirt, abacus at the ready, Abe stared suspiciously at the gangly, bullet-headed fourteen-year-old.

Brimming over with youthful eagerness, Yasujiro came straight to the point. His plan was rapidly swelling into a mighty ambition.

"Mr. Abe," he burst out in his high-pitched tones. His voice was barely beginning to break and he spoke in an absurdly rustic Shiga accent. "Mr. Abe. To make fertilizer you have to have phosphate. Without it you can't make it. But in Shiga they still don't use it. Let me have the exclusive rights to sell it in Shiga prefecture!"

Abe's jaw dropped. Exclusive rights?

"You mean your father . . . ?" He scowled.

"My father's dead. I have a grandfather. But it's nothing to do with him. I'm the one doing business."

Abe pondered. As a good Omi merchant, he was not going to turn down any business opportunity. Besides, this young man was from his own home region of Shiga—and he had courage.

"You're quite a lad," he grunted finally, softening. "But don't think too big. Why don't you just take back a cartload of fertilizer and see how it goes?"

Yasujiro was downcast. He had set his heart on having the exclusive sales rights, on being the man who transformed agriculture in Shiga. Still, in the end he ordered three cartloads of fertilizer and set off for home.

When it arrived he had it dumped in an outhouse and, bursting with pride, set up a big sign outside the house and on all the street corners in the village: "Osaka phosphate fertilizer, exclusive sales—

Kiyozaemon Tsutsumi." Better to use his grandfather's name, he had decided. All the villagers knew old Kiyozaemon and would be more likely to try the new product if they thought Kiyozaemon was behind it. He sat down in front of a mountain of pungent fertilizer to wait for the rush of customers.

No one came. The conservative old farmers of Yagiso village had no intention of spending their money on some unknown newfangled product. In the end Yasujiro used the fertilizer on his own fields, which had never been fed chemical fertilizer before. He planted beans, he planted clover, and his crops sprang up like magic.

The villagers cocked their heads when they saw his fields and said to one another, "Looks like Tsutsumi put a charm on those beans and that clover—and it really worked!"[9]

For four years Yasujiro worked hard on the family fields. He grew into a handsome, strong young man. He could pick up a sack of rice weighing 140 pounds and lift it high above his head, a feat that only two or three young men in the village could equal.

Finally, when he was seventeen, his grandfather relented and allowed him to continue with his studies. In those days some of the best higher education was to be found in military establishments. Yasujiro was sent off to a naval college in Kyoto for a year. When he went back to Yagiso village, he got a job in local government, in the ward office. It was 1907. And Yagiso village was becoming too small for him.

Sixty years before, when Grandfather Kiyozaemon was growing up, Japan had been a feudal country, under the rule of what was in effect a military dictatorship. For two hundred and fifty years, a quarter of a millennium, beginning in 1600, the Tokugawa shoguns had governed the country. They had established peace and order after years of civil war, but only by establishing a system of extremely tight controls.

Life in Tokugawa Japan was strictly regulated. There were four classes: the military at the top, from the highest-ranking daimyo to the humblest foot soldier; then the peasants, who performed the essential task of producing food; then the craftsmen; and merchants at the bottom. Merchants produced nothing and were regarded practically as parasites. Everything was laid down: what each class wore, what they ate, what they did, where they lived. In theory there was almost no mobility of any sort. Where you were born, there you died. What your father and grandfather had done, you did. If you were a merchant, no matter how much money you made you could never rise above your class. You could never use your wealth to move to a better area or to marry your son to a samurai's daughter.

To ensure that no subversive ideas entered and upset the delicate balance, the country was closed to foreigners and foreign contact. Foreigners were not allowed in and Japanese were not allowed out. Only one small window was left open—the port of Nagasaki, where Chinese junks brought their goods and a small Dutch trading post was established. Through this porthole, news of some of the developments transforming the outside world filtered in.

Two hundred and fifty years on, the country was ripe for change. The centuries of peace had brought prosperity and a high standard of living, at least for the wealthier classes. The merchants in particular had grown rich and frustrated at being unable to change their status. In the countryside many farmers, like Kiyozaemon, had begun to supplement their income by trading. As for the military government, it had turned into a rambling bureaucracy.

In 1853, when Kiyozaemon was twenty, Commodore Matthew Perry steamed into Tokyo Bay with his four black ships mounted with cannon. He carried a letter from the American president demanding that Japan open its doors to trade and friendship forthwith. He would return the following year for an answer, he declared, and with a much larger fleet.

The Japanese were defenseless against such force. They had no navy. There was no choice but to accede to his demands. Over the next years they were forced to submit to a series of trading treaties with the Western powers, with terms both disadvantageous and humiliating to Japan.

The shogun had proved unable to defend Japan against the Western nations. The weakness of the decaying military regime was brutally revealed. Under the slogan "Revere the emperor and expel the barbarians," hot-headed young samurai from the distant provinces of Choshu and Satsuma in the deep south of the country plotted revolt. After some years of intrigue and fighting, they led a coup d'état. The shogun was overthrown and surrendered his power. In 1868 Emperor Meiji, who was just sixteen at the time, traveled in grand procession from his traditional capital, Kyoto, to be installed as the nominal head of state in the new capital, Tokyo. But the real power lay in the hands of the southern samurai who had led the revolt.

The political revolution was over; but the real revolution was just beginning. The country's new leaders realized that there was only one way to resist the foreign powers and expel the barbarians. They had to fathom the secret of their military might. That meant studying their culture, learning their science and technology and catching up with their industrial development.

Young men steamed off on P & O liners to the West to study; Western experts were invited to Japan. Within five years after the emperor had made his historic journey down from Kyoto, the country had the beginnings of a telegraph system, its first lighthouses, a postal service, compulsory education at primary school level and Western-style law courts. It also had its first railway, the Tokyo–Yokohama line, built by a British engineer, which opened with enormous fanfare on October 12, 1872. The emperor, dressed in his full court regalia, traveled on the first train, which had been freighted over from Britain.

What had begun as a desire to beat the West at its own game quickly developed into a fascination with all things Western. The sophisticates of Tokyo adopted Western dress and Western hairstyles, ate Western food and learned Western dances. In the 1880s, when the fad for Western ways was at its height, the fashionable gathered in the Rokumeikan, the Deer Cry Pavilion, designed by the British architect Josiah Conder, for garden parties and balls. They drank Western drinks, played billiards and, above all, danced the waltz and the quadrille.

But the more serious purpose behind all these changes was not forgotten. The entire structure of the country needed to be transformed from top to bottom, honed into a modern nation state strong enough to stand up against the aggressive Western powers.

The country's leaders carefully chose the best models to emulate. The first priority was to build up the army and navy. French officers were employed to train the new Japanese conscript army while the British developed and trained the navy. The first prime minister, Hirobumi Ito, was largely responsible for drawing up the first constitution, based on the German model. And in February 1889, a month before Yasujiro was born, the first parliament, known as the Diet, was convened.

Then in 1904, while young Yasujiro was still hard at work in the fields in Yagiso village, Japan went to war with Russia. The issue was control of the Korean peninsula. The Japanese decisively won a series of battles, though there were dreadful casualties on both sides. The final blow was when the new Japanese navy succeeded in sending an entire Russian fleet to the bottom of the sea.

The battle of tiny Japan against the Russian giant was like the battle of David and Goliath. It was a message to both Japan and the world that all the hard work and modernization had paid off. Japan was now a force to be reckoned with, a highly industrialized modern nation, ready to take on any nation in the West.

It was an intoxicating time, a time of extraordinary ferment and upheaval and of dazzling opportunities. The old social structures had broken down; the new ones were still being shaped. For the first time after centuries of repression there was a chance for a young man with determination and a good dose of ruthlessness to shake off his social origins and create his own destiny. It was a time when a young man from a humble background could make his fortune.

This was the world Yasujiro Tsutsumi was about to step into.

Escape
Waseda 1907–1915

From my own experience I always say to young people: by the age of twenty you may look like an adult, but your power of judgment is still like a five-year-old child's.   YASUJIRO TSUTSUMI
My History

On April 7, 1907, when the cherry blossoms were beginning to fall along the dirt tracks and earthen lanes of Yagiso village, Grandfather Kiyozaemon died. He was seventy-four. It was the same year that Yasujiro completed his studies in Kyoto and returned to the village to work in the ward office. Old Kiyozaemon's last words to his grandson, according to Yasujiro's official biography, were: "The restoration of the Tsutsumi house is not a matter of making money. Making money is fine, but more than that—make the Tsutsumi house an honorable house!"[1]

Yasujiro never forgot those words. He was on his own now. His grandfather, who had been mother, father and companion to him, was gone. His pipe-smoking old grandmother had died a few years before. There was no extended family to fall back on, no one left but his sister, Fusako, whom he now had to take care of.

Yasujiro was eighteen when his grandfather died and a strikingly handsome young man. He had a broad, open face with delicate, very regular features, almost girlish—a small straight nose, large steady eyes and a full sensual mouth. He gazes out of photographs of the time with an air of cool assurance, his eyebrows lifted in mild disdain, the set of his mouth hinting at arrogance. Farm boy he may be, but he is ready to take on the world.

Out among the rice fields of Omi, he must have been the best-looking lad for miles around; and he quickly discovered how easy it was to bowl over women.

In Japan, then as now, sex was a far less complicated matter than it is in the West. When the first Westerners arrived in Japan, they were shocked at what to their Victorian eyes looked like moral laxity. In almost every aspect of Japanese society there are very strict rules of conduct, but they operate in a rather different way from rules in the West. In one's public life everything must be in order; but in private there is a considerable degree of freedom. Marriage is in the public domain; it is the union of two families, only to be entered upon after detailed investigation of the opposite side's financial and social standing. Sex, however, is private; and, so long as it stays that way, men, at least, may largely do as they please.

Around Yagiso village there was a standard procedure for meeting girls. In the off season when there was not much farming work to be done, any farmer with daughters of marriageable age would find himself inundated with helpers from the village, young men eager to make themselves useful, sitting around plaiting straw or carving wooden pestles. Thus relationships started up; and Yasujiro was one of the most popular.

Kiyozaemon worried, as always, about his grandson's morals and his future. He had better get married quickly, he grumbled, before he started getting involved with bad women.

In the end it was not until his grandfather was dead that Yasujiro settled down. He had been seeing a girl from out toward the mountains, a quiet girl, recall the villagers, named Koto Nishizawa. She was a couple of years older than he. Early in 1909, before his twentieth birthday, she bore him a child, a daughter whom they called Shukuko. It was another ten months before they formalized the relationship.

By then Yasujiro had been alone in the big house in Yagiso village, with only his sister, Fusako, for nearly two years. No doubt he carried on his work as a clerk in the ward office. The story has passed down among the villagers that he frittered away the money that his grandfather had left him, and that the neighbors took pity on him and used to call him in at mealtimes to make sure that he was fed. In fact he was well able to take care of himself. For those two years he was thinking hard about his future.

For most of the villagers life consisted of working the land, tilling their fields until they died. Yasujiro, however, had been to Osaka; he had studied in Kyoto. He knew that there was more to life than that. Now that his grandfather was dead, he was free. He had no intention of being stuck in this backwater for the rest of his life—he was determined to escape.

Money was the key. If only he could get money, he could do anything. Two years after Kiyozaemon's death, he mortgaged the family lands. His ancestral heritage—the house that his grandfather had toiled to build, the rice fields that his father and grandfather had dug out of the hard earth—he put into hock. The property must have been sizable, for he got ¥5,000, a large sum in those days, enough to give a young man a good start in life.

Leaving the house and land in the care of the neighbors, he packed his belongings in a simple wicker trunk, said good-bye to his friends in the village and set off at dawn one morning to walk across the fields to the station. His sister, his wife-to-be, Koto, and his two-month-old baby daughter went with him. It was the end of March 1909, and he was just twenty.

In those days there were two trains a day to Tokyo, great black steam engines that puffed through the countryside, tugging a line of little wooden carriages behind. One left Hikone, the town that Grandfather Kiyozaemon had branded a den of vice, at 9:04 in the morning. The other left the larger junction of Maebara at 12:42. They chugged along through a landscape of woods and streams, flat brown fields and villages of thatched houses, with the occasional factory chimney pumping out smoke in the distance. By evening they were rounding the graceful flanks of Mount Fuji. The passengers craned their necks to stare up at the glistening white slopes of the legendary mountain.

Around midnight they craned their necks again to look at another legend: the shadowy portals of Shimbashi station, the Tokyo terminus. There Yasujiro and his two companions stepped onto the platform with their wicker trunks and out into the odorous Tokyo night.

Like every newcomer to Tokyo, Yasujiro must have spent his first few days in a daze of excitement, roaming the streets intoxicated with the noise, the smells, the people, the modernity and the ever-present sense of urgency and purpose.

One of the unavoidable first impressions was the smells: the smell of humanity, the smell of cooking, the smell of charcoal burning and the all-prevailing pungent smell of sewage. It wasn't until many years later that Tokyo developed sewers; in fact, in that respect it was still as primitive as Elizabethan London. Every night the sewage collectors trundled about the streets with their carts, buckets and dippers, shouting *"Owai! Owai!,"* buying up human waste to sell for fertilizer.

Then there was the noise and hurly-burly, the trams clunking and rumbling by, the street sellers singing out their wares—goldfish, tofu, sweet potatoes—and every night the sound of wood clacking on wood as the night watchman did his rounds, warning the people of Tokyo to beware of fires. For Tokyo was still largely a wooden city, prone to sudden disastrous outbreaks of fire. Most of the houses were very low, only one story, squashed together roof against roof along roads just wide enough for a single ricksha to pass through. The roads were not paved. In the dry season, when Yasujiro arrived, there was dust everywhere, prickling between your toes, getting into your eyes, while in the rainy season, the streets turned into a sea of mud.

Above all there were the people, crowding the streets—the women mincing along in their fine silk kimonos, their hair sleekly styled in the latest modern fashion; many of the men in Western dress or with a bowler hat and rolled umbrella atop the traditional *hakama*.

Like every visitor from the provinces, Yasujiro must have gone to gawk at the Ginza, the most famous street in Japan. The very name stood for glamour, sophistication and modernity. To stroll beneath its graceful willows was like journeying to the exotic West. The street was broad enough for trams and lined with buildings made of red brick, like Western buildings. There were shops selling all manner of rare and covetable things—hats, spectacles, beef—and beer halls where dapper young men dressed in suits could sit and sip the Western brew. There were pavements, gaslights and telegraph poles that dwarfed the willow trees. Here truly the past had been left behind— this was the epitome of progress.

Yasujiro had little time to waste on sight-seeing. He had not abandoned his heritage for nothing. He had a serious purpose to accomplish. How was a young man from the country to establish himself in the great city of Tokyo? How was he to make a living? He had his ¥5,000, but that would soon disappear. He needed to find a way to make money and build a future for himself. The first step was education.

Before the Meiji Restoration, when the shoguns ruled the country, the aim of education had been to keep everyone in his place. The sons of samurai were trained in the samurai arts and the farmers needed to know only how to till the fields.

Then, after Emperor Meiji came down from Kyoto and the country began to move into the modern world, several universities were established. For an ambitious young man, the way to rise was to enter one of these. University study opened the door to practically unlimited opportunities. Only a few went to university and they automatically became the elite. Most students came from privileged backgrounds. But, in theory at least, no matter what your social class, if you had the ability and the money, you could enter.

Yasujiro took the entrance exam for the newest and most radical of the universities: Waseda. Even now it is considered a proletarian university, where talented young men from the countryside can get their start in life. Unlike the sons of the rich, who go to Keio, unlike the hardworking gray young men who go to Tokyo University and go on to form the backbone of the bureaucracy, the students of Waseda come predominantly from outside Tokyo and a large number enter politics. It is a training ground for politicians. In Yasujiro's day this was even more the case.

He passed. He was no intellectual, but he was sharp, quick-witted and burning with determination. He was accepted into the school of economics and political science.

Bursting with pride in his new Waseda uniform, he went to have his photograph taken. He had several poses done. In one he stands nonchalantly, hand on hip, in his black high-collared summer uniform, his four-cornered mortarboard perched on his head, his round face impassive, eyebrows lifted quizzically. In another he is in winter uniform, in greatcoat and military cap. The face is that of a child, plump and smooth. It is hard to imagine that he was already the father of a growing child.

Waseda in 1909 was an inspiring place to be. Yasujiro had landed in exactly the right place at the right time. It was new; it had been founded less than thirty years earlier, in 1881. It was small; there were fewer than two thousand students. As they strode the wooden corridors of the modern Western-style buildings that made up the campus or engaged in passionate political discussion under the spreading trees, the young men (it was only men in Waseda in those days) felt that they were shapers of the new age. And all to a man were devoted to the founder, the crusty, charismatic Marquis Shigenobu Okuma.

At that time Okuma was in his seventies. He had been one of the most radical political figures of his day and was still famous for his conversation and his powers of oratory. He held court daily in his palatial mansion beside the campus. From nine in the morning the most powerful men and brilliant minds of the nation appeared at his door to pay homage, ask advice and listen to the old man's homilies. He entertained foreign potentates, the wits of the day and university principals from Europe and America, holding forth on his political views and regaling them with his theory that anyone, with a little effort, could attain the natural human life span of one hundred twenty-five years. And he invariably insisted that all should stay and partake of lunch in his magnificent dining room, which seated two hundred under the candelabra and chandeliers.

Okuma loved splendor and he loved homage. A fine-looking man with a broad forehead and sternly down-turned mouth, he was never to be seen without his stick and his Egyptian cigars. When he traveled he always had a huge retinue to accompany him and usually took over a couple of railway carriages for his own use. He was a great celebrity: people would line the streets to watch as he went by; and mayors were known to celebrate his arrival at their city by lining his route with priceless gold screens.

Born in 1838, Okuma had been at the forefront in the tempestuous years that saw the transformation of Japan from a medieval to a modern country. Like the other new leaders who took over the country after the Meiji Restoration, he was from the south. But while they all hailed from the provinces of Choshu and Satsuma, he came from the Saga region in the island of Kyushu. As a result he lacked allies and a power base.

From the very beginning he was a radical and an irritant, an outsider up against the power of the establishment. When the new constitution was being discussed, he demanded that it be based on the British parliamentary system. Hirobumi Ito, a Choshu man who was to be the first prime minister, insisted on a constitution on the German model. In the ensuing furore Okuma was pushed out of government.

Forced into inactivity, he founded Tokyo College, later to be renamed Waseda University. The overt purpose was to create an independent center of learning, where lectures would be conducted in Japanese, not in English as at the rival Tokyo University, and the focus would be on practical subjects like commerce and engineering. But a secondary aim was to make a power base for himself, to gather young disciples to stand up against his enemies who were running the country.

Okuma was soon back in politics. In 1889, when he was foreign minister, a terrorist threw a bomb into his carriage. His leg was so badly injured that it had to be amputated. When he was convalescing he uttered the famous remark "I'm glad I was injured by a progressive Western invention and not by a sword or some such old-fashioned device," and expressed sympathy for his colleague, the education minister, who had had the misfortune to be stabbed to death that same year. He added that the loss of his leg meant that there would be all the more blood to circulate to his brain.[2]

For a few brief tumultuous months in 1898 Okuma was prime minister. Once again he was forced out of power, but even from his position on the sidelines he continued to do all he could to snipe at the ruling party.

The twenty-year-old Yasujiro knew little of any of this. In his first days at Waseda he must have admired the statue of the founder, unveiled two years earlier, resplendent in formal court dress with samurai swords, "like a feudal lord," grumbled the old man's critics. But there were more pressing matters to attend to. Like any freshman, he needed to decide the important question of which clubs to join.

Almost as soon as he arrived, he went to see a judo practice session. Absorbed, he stood on the sidelines and watched this interesting sport in which small young men threw big burly ones. Then one of the senior students called out, "You—have a go yourself!"

It was the first time Yasujiro had ever seen judo, let alone try it. He was a slender youth but very strong, and proud of his strength. He let himself be fitted out with white judo kit and stepped onto the mats.

Okay! Let's go! he thought to himself. He squared up to his opponent, a pale, weak-looking young man. Should be easy to throw him, he thought. The two grappled. The next second Yasujiro was on his back on the mats, his head hurting where he had hit it. Judo was definitely interesting, he thought, as he clambered painfully to his feet. He joined the club immediately and thereafter trained assiduously every morning.[3]

Along with most of the ambitious young men at Waseda, Yasujiro was determined to go into politics. No one could fail to be infected by the mood of political ferment that filled the campus and by the proximity of the fierce old marquis who had spent his life fighting for his beliefs. Besides, Yasujiro was well aware that for a young man with no family connections, politics offered the most rapid path for advancement. As a Waseda student, there was no doubting his allegiance. He was one of Okuma's men, committed to opposing the establishment.

For the budding politician, the essential qualification was oratory—to be able to leap to one's feet, rush to the stage and make an impassioned speech on any subject whatsoever at a moment's notice. Yasujiro had a rather high-pitched reedy voice and he worked hard to make it deep and resonant. Like the Oxford Union in Britain, the Waseda Debating Society was the place where youthful politicians honed their skills. They did not stop there. According to the official history of Waseda University, "students practised oratory at lecture meetings, study meetings, and at every opportunity that presented itself."[4]

In those days, as Yasujiro writes, if you did not express fervent nationalist sentiment in your speeches at the Waseda Debating Society, your audience was liable to get bored and walk out. The Japanese were still busy absorbing Western science, industry and technology, but they were determined not to lose their cultural identity in the process. The days when aristocratic Japanese ladies wore bustles and bonnets and studied the waltz and quadrille had long since passed. "Japanese spirit and Western knowledge" was the slogan that encapsulated the required synthesis. Judo, not baseball, was the sport for idealistic young students to practice.

Like everyone else, Yasujiro was a patriot. But as a follower of Okuma, the most pressing issue was not policy abroad but matters at home. For all the veneer of Western-style government, real power still rested in the hands of the few, of Okuma's enemies, the southern samurai who had ousted the shogun decades earlier and brought about the Meiji Restoration. There was very limited suffrage; out of a population of forty million, only half a million "men of substance" had the vote. The Diet, too, had only limited powers, while the prime minister himself was installed by the aging samurai; he did not necessarily command a majority in the House. For Okuma and his young supporters, it was imperative to wrest power from the ruling clique and invest it firmly in the Diet, which represented the voice of the electorate.

Like most students, Yasujiro had little time for his studies. He was far too busy practicing judo, arguing about political issues into the small hours of the night and struggling to make money. He did, however, become acquainted with at least one of his teachers, the brilliant young professor of politics Ryutaro Nagai.

Nagai was Okuma's protégé. At the time that he met Yasujiro he had just come back from four years at Oxford, where he had been studying at Manchester College, the first Waseda student ever to do so. His subject was Gladstone; he was a fervent campaigner for social reform and universal suffrage and modeled himself on the great British statesman. He had, however, been greatly disappointed by his experiences in Oxford, where he suffered racist abuse and prejudice, and made himself unpopular by making fiery speeches denouncing British imperialism.

Eight years older than Yasujiro, he was already well known for his writing and oratory. He used his classroom as a political platform, treating his students to passionate political diatribes.

In many ways Nagai was the exact antithesis of Yasujiro. He came from a samurai family, though from the lower ranks of the samurai. He was cultured, intellectual, a thinker, an ideas man, while Yasujiro was of a practical, business bent. Both, however, were ambitious, both were profoundly involved in politics and both held radical views.

At first their relationship was teacher to student; but Nagai took to the brash young man from Omi. The two became very close: as Michio Nagai, Nagai's son, puts it, they were nearly like brothers; they loved each other very much.

This friendship was to open many doors for Yasujiro. Nagai was a favorite of Okuma's. The old man was so fond of him, in fact, that rumors circulated that Nagai was Okuma's illegitimate son. The two, it was said, even looked alike—the same broad forehead, the same handsome fleshy features.[5] The rumor was no more than a rumor. All parties involved fiercely disputed it; Mrs. Nagai was said to be particularly displeased. Still, it was thanks to Nagai that Yasujiro was introduced to the old man of Waseda himself.

Okuma too was impressed with Yasujiro. Perhaps he saw something of his own fiery youth in this ambitious country lad. Okuma, moreover, as a leading player in the political field, required limitless amounts of money. He was always short of funds. He needed people around him who were good at making money. And, for all his interest in politics, that, it seemed, was where Yasujiro's talent lay.

From his first days at Waseda, Yasujiro had set about the serious business of making money. He had a sister, a wife and a child to support. One of his first ventures was to buy stocks in a company called Goto Woolens. The textile industry was booming at the time, the government was planning to revise export and import duties and Goto Woolens looked like a company with a good future. Yasujiro took all the money he had made by mortgaging his family land and invested it in Goto Woolens, "and within half a year, my ¥5,000 had turned into ¥60,000."[6]

If ¥5,000 had been a princely sum, ¥60,000 was enough to start a couple of businesses. Yasujiro spent ¥10,000 of it on buying the rights to a third-class post office in Nihonbashi, near the Ginza, and also took over the management of an iron foundry in Shibuya, with a hundred employees. "It was hard work. I hardly ever went into the university."

He was doing well. His fees at Waseda were only ¥50 a year, the same as the average yearly wage for a construction worker. By the standards of the time he was a rich man.

One hot summer's day in July 1912, news came that sent a shudder through the entire country. The emperor Meiji was ill. In the days that followed a hush descended. People stood silently outside the palace grounds or flocked to temples to pray and burn incense. Nine days later, on July 29, he died. It was an event as momentous as the death of Queen Victoria had been a decade earlier. The Meiji era, the age of giants, of the great men who had transformed the country, was over.

The whole nation went into mourning. It was grief mingled with a kind of dread. No one knew what the next era would bring. Theaters and shops closed. On the day of the funeral the great city of Tokyo was silent except for the bustle around the railway stations. People arrived from the farthest parts of Japan to bow in silent respect as the emperor's hearse rolled by, drawn by five oxen, attended by the traditional coffin-bearers who had journeyed down from Kyoto, and followed by a seemingly endless cortege, some in ancient court costume, others in military uniform. The funeral took place at night and the body was taken by train to Kyoto to be buried in the imperial graveyard.

No doubt Yasujiro was among the crush of people who lined the route and a few months later went to watch the procession when the new emperor, the ill-fated Emperor Taisho, was crowned.

In the three years since he arrived at Waseda he had grown more confident, more aggressive, and if anything even more handsome. He had grown a mustache, which became him very well. His face had lost its childish curves and become more defined. There was a certain pugnaciousness about his broad forehead and square jaw. He was not a man who would brook any opposition.

As far as women were concerned, his attitude was strictly utilitarian: they were to be used and discarded. He favored the rough approach, and usually there was no more than token resistance. Japanese women were not in the habit of resisting men: they had been brought up to be gentle, yielding creatures. He had found a way to deal with his wife, Koto. While he was at Waseda he kept her well out of the way. As soon as possible he sent her back to her parents in the Omi mountains, together with their little daughter, Shukuko.

One of the most scandalous stories in Yasujiro's career dates from those years. Around 1913, so the story goes, Yasujiro met a pretty young girl who was a Catholic nun. He took her from her convent and raped her. She became pregnant. As a devout Catholic, she was forbidden any escape from her plight: she was prohibited from having an abortion and from committing suicide. For nine months she suffered agonies of conscience. When her time came, she hid herself in a corner of the convent and there gave birth. But the emotional torment was too great for her to bear. She went mad and died. Yasujiro named the child Kiyoshi after his grandfather, Kiyozaemon. He took him away and reared him as his son.

Chroniclers of the Tsutsumi saga leaped gleefully on this story when it first appeared. For twenty years it was part of the mythology that grew up around Yasujiro and his exploits. Great heroes, after all, were expected to have monstrous sex lives.

But then Kamibayashi, the sharp-eyed cousin from Hokkaido, published his scandalous article, "My Tsutsumi Family—the Secret of Blood." Among the misconceptions that he wished to clear up was the story of Kiyoshi's birth. It was, he revealed, pure fiction. Brutal and heartless though Yasujiro undoubtedly was, he was not a monster.

The most astonishing thing about the story was its source. It first came out in 1969, fifty-five years after the events in question, when Yasujiro was dead. It appeared in a novel called *In the Season of Roaming,* by Takashi Tsujii—Yasujiro's son Seiji, writing under a pen name. In interviews, Seiji airily dismissed all questions by saying that the novel was self-evidently fiction. But even though the characters had fictional names, all were instantly recognizable. It was the story of Seiji's own family. Many of the events recorded were verifiable from other sources. The most shocking revelations about Yasujiro's sexual appetite came from Seiji's novel, though the question of why Seiji had chosen to tell stories that could only darken his father's reputation remained unanswered.

The real story—confirmed not only by Kamibayashi but also by newspaper reports dating from before Seiji's novel—was more humdrum but almost as sad. Among the staff of the third-class post office that Yasujiro had taken over was a young woman named Sono Takahashi. She was an ordinary working girl, a clerk. Unlike the fashionable ladies of the Ginza, she wore plain kimonos and had her hair coiled into a loose knot in the traditional style. Perhaps she reminded Yasujiro of the mother he had watched walking away into the distance when he was a child.

He had an affair with her—no more than a brief fling. She became pregnant. Long before her time came he discarded her, just as his mother had discarded him. He was, after all, a married man. And if he were to marry again, it would certainly not be a post-office clerk.

When the child was born, he was named Kiyoshi and Yasujiro did the proper thing. He set up a marriage for the mother, with one of his old classmates from Yagiso village, a Mr. Iwasaki. Kiyoshi was brought up by the young couple, who went to live with Sono's parents in the countryside. Yasujiro kept an eye on his son's progress. Once he had established himself, he would in the normal way adopt him and make him his heir.[7] In fact, he had already met the woman that he intended to marry.

Marriage in Japan in those days had very little to do with love and not much to do with sex. Yasujiro was no longer the simple lad from Omi. He realized that marriage was far from being just a matter of legitimizing a random encounter. For an ambitious youth, marriage could be the key to open many doors. A girl from the Omi mountains was no longer good enough for him. He could do far better.

While Waseda was exclusively male, Okuma, the great progressive, had also founded a sister institution, Japan Women's University. It was the first institution to offer higher education to women in Japan. Among its first students was a girl who became a personal favorite of the crusty old marquis.

Fumi Kawasaki was the epitome of the modern woman. She was one of Japan's earliest bluestockings—"all brains but no body" as the sharp-eyed Kamibayashi put it; not beautiful, not sensual, but bright, full of life and very intellectual. She was rather a plain girl, and wore her hair tugged back in an unflatteringly severe style. In manner she was a bit of a schoolmistress, sharp-tongued, quick to point out other people's mistakes. But all this was overshadowed by her youthful bloom and energy.

Fumi came from an impeccable samurai background. She was born into the Kazamatsuri family, but, following Japanese custom, she had been adopted into her mother's family, the Kawasakis. The family had no sons and it therefore fell to Fumi's mother to perpetuate the Kawasaki name.

After she graduated from Japan Women's University, Okuma gave her a job in his office as a secretary. The old man, by then approaching eighty, was also involved in many publishing ventures, propagating his ideas. He took her on as a journalist on his broadsheet, *Hochi News,* and later promoted her to senior writer responsible for editorials. For a Japanese woman in the early years of this century it was an astonishing achievement.

Around 1913, Yasujiro was preparing to graduate. According to one version of events, Okuma called him into his office. Now that he was about to enter the world, he said, he needed a wife. (Obviously, Yasujiro had been successful in concealing from the old marquis that he already had one.) Taking on the role of father, Okuma proposed a match for him: with Fumi, his secretary and favorite. It was an offer that Yasujiro could not possibly refuse.

According to another story, the two lived near each other and met by chance. In any case, Fumi was exactly the kind of woman that Yasujiro had been waiting for. He was determined to go ahead with the marriage. But there were certain obstacles.

One was his wife, Koto. He divorced her as quickly as possible, on the grounds of incompatibility. In Japan it was easy for men to divorce their wives, who were after all barely more than chattels. It was practically impossible for a woman to divorce her husband.

Another was Fumi's family. They were opposed to a union with a rough young peasant who lacked a respectable ancestry and was already once married; added to which, Fumi was intended to carry on the Kawasaki name, not to take another. But the two were in love—Yasujiro with this high-class, high-powered girl, Fumi with the good-looking, forceful young man who brought a breath of air into her stuffy samurai world.

More than a year after Yasujiro's graduation, Fumi's family finally consented to the match. In April 1915 the two were married. Yasujiro sent for his six-year-old daughter, Shukuko, who came to live with them in Tokyo. Some years later he also sent for Kiyoshi. Fumi brought up the two children as her own.

Yasujiro's sister, Fusako, lived with them too. Later Nagai introduced her to his cousin Sotokichi. The two married; and thus Yasujiro and Nagai, who loved each other like brothers, cemented the bond between their two families.

With Fumi at his side, Yasujiro was ready to turn full time to the matter of making a living. She was the perfect business partner—quick, intelligent, intellectually more than his equal, and ready to help him in every possible way. But there were two factors that made the marriage less than perfect. Firstly, Fumi was very much a woman of the mind, not the body. She approached sex like a Victorian matron, as an unpleasant duty to be endured for the sake of her marriage. Secondly, she was infertile.

For Yasujiro, what had begun as youthful lust was growing into something more all-consuming. He wanted sex every day and with a different partner—a homely country woman, not a beautiful geisha. In Japanese terms this was an inexplicably perverse taste. It was a society in which practically anything was acceptable—provided it was done in the proper way, in the proper place and with the proper people. There were many women trained to give pleasure to men, with geisha at the very top of the hierarchy. Far from being prostitutes, they were high-class professional entertainers, famous for their witty conversation and skill at singing and dancing. They were ladies of the evening, not ladies of the night, though they could often be prevailed upon to become the courtesans of wealthy men. At the other end of the scale were prostitutes, young country women who had to sell their bodies to support their families. It was a job that until the Meiji Restoration had been considered an honorable and necessary one.

Yasujiro needed to thrust himself upon women and then cast them aside. It was as if he were looking eternally for his mother and then rejecting her as she had rejected him. Almost as soon as he had completed his marriage vows to Fumi he took to visiting prostitutes, nearly every day. He also wanted children. Two were not enough.

Fumi, however, was a devoted, uncomplaining wife and, like many Japanese women today, turned a blind eye to her husband's infidelity. In fact, it was something of a relief. It took the pressure off her.

The most urgent matter, in any case, was to make money. Buoyed by the success of his early business ventures, Yasujiro looked around for new areas in which to invest.

Despite Fumi's loyal help, everything he touched was a disaster. First the iron foundry, which he had taken over with the proceeds of his stock speculations in Goto Woolens, went bankrupt. The last machine he produced had been a mechanized loom for weaving linen, so he tried the linen business. But he discovered that linen thread cost more than the finished fabric. The only way to make a profit was to cheat. He gave that up too.

All this time, while he floundered from one hopeless business project to another, he was holding down a job. It was not the kind of job that was likely to make him rich, but it brought him into contact with the main events of the time; it was a good job for a budding politician. He was working for Marquis Okuma.

The first months of the reign of the new emperor, Taisho, were a time of political convulsion. The clique of aging samurai, who were the de facto rulers of the country, had wielded power through Emperor Meiji, as the symbol of authority; but after his death the whole cozy arrangement began to fall apart. Many of the old samurai had died. The military was becoming a powerful force in its own right. A couple of cabinets collapsed in disorder. Finally the elderly samurai decided to call in a man who was outside of and untainted by any of the political infighting. They turned to their old enemy, Marquis Okuma, and asked him to form a cabinet.

Okuma had used his years of retirement well, and was if anything more respected and more popular than before. When he became prime minister in April 1914, many people saw it as a sign of great hope. At last the stranglehold of the Satsuma-Choshu clique had been loosened. Perhaps the Sage of Waseda would inaugurate a Taisho Restoration as far-reaching as the Meiji Restoration had been.

Then, four months later, war broke out in Europe. Japan and Britain were allies; Japan was not bound by the terms of the treaty to enter the war, but it was too good an opportunity to miss. Japan first issued an ultimatum to Germany to remove all ships from neighboring waters, then declared war. With Germany preoccupied in Europe, the Japanese attacked and occupied all the German possessions in Asia, including the Shantung peninsula in China and several Pacific islands.

For Japan, thousands of miles away from the fighting, the war was a huge and unexpected bonanza. It gave it the chance to build up its heavy industry. The warring countries of the West provided a bottomless market for ships and munitions. And as they switched their economies onto a war footing, Japan was called upon to fulfill their needs for civilian goods too. Overseas markets in the Far East and Africa, which had always been dominated by the Western powers, now magically opened to Japan.

Industrial production soared, exports doubled, then tripled. Many companies, from the huge family-run zaibatsu to smaller manufacturing and financial concerns, made fortunes. The mood of prosperity spread to encompass the entire country.

While Europe suffered, the young men and women of Tokyo were enjoying the atmosphere of excess that was coming to characterize the Taisho era. There was a certain air, which writers of the time noticed, of fin de siècle decadence. One might as well enjoy this unexpected abundance. After all, it would not last long. It was a feeling that was to become more marked as the years went on.

Yasujiro, on the other hand, was not getting any richer. There was work to be done, a family to support, but he had still not figured out how he was going to make a living.

As soon as Yasujiro graduated, Okuma told him that he had a job for him.

Okuma's most famous publication was a magazine called *Shin-Nippon* (New Japan). It was a magazine of radical thought and debate, intended to keep progressive intellectuals of the day informed about developments in the West, as well as carrying articles by leading Japanese thinkers. Initially it was published out of Okuma's house and served as a vehicle for him and his ideas. The main contributors were Okuma himself and Nagai, who was editor in chief, but as the magazine became better known, scholars and business and political leaders were eager to write for it.

At the first editorial meeting at Okuma's house in 1911, Okuma explained his aim: "The last forty years have been a period of preparation. In the future when we enter the period of actually building the new Japan, we will have to be more and more in touch with radical trends of thinking abroad; so today we have to nurture the accurate and broad acquisition of world knowledge."[8]

Inspirational writing was all very well. But in fact *New Japan* was desperately short of money and on the brink of folding. What was needed was a hardheaded young man with a business bent to take care of the financial side of things.

So Yasujiro became the business manager. He sat at his desk in a back room in Okuma's luxurious mansion and tried to balance the books, courting advertisers and fending off representatives of corporations who came with offers of huge "donations," which Yasujiro very properly refused. It was an inspiring time for him.

Despite all Yasujiro's efforts the magazine floundered. "Our goal was 10,000 copies a month, but since unsold copies were not returned until after three months, we never had the slightest idea of how well the review was selling in any current month. And then after three months we would suddenly have heaps of unsold copies of the review returned to us!"[9] Eventually the magazine was forced to close down, not least because of Okuma's complete lack of interest in whether or not it made a profit. Power, influence, ideas and radical change were Okuma's currency. Money was for others to worry about. His protégés and admirers would always ensure that the Sage of Waseda was well enough supplied to live the life to which he was accustomed.

While Yasujiro, installed in the prime minister's residence, was struggling to keep *New Japan* afloat, events of enormous historic import were happening just a few yards away. Messengers scurried back and forth, great men arrived and departed, voices were raised, papers signed.

Japan had already taken over Korea, established a presence in Manchuria as a result of the Portsmouth Treaty that concluded the war with Russia, and occupied the German-owned provinces of China. Now, with the Western powers preoccupied in Europe, Japan saw an excellent opportunity to extend its power and influence further.

In 1915 Okuma's foreign minister drew up a list of Twenty-one Demands, which was presented to President Yuan Shih-k'ai of China. These included the right of Japanese companies to do business, own land, carry out mining and extend the Japanese-owned railway system in Manchuria and Outer Mongolia. They also required China to buy half its arms from Japan and to accept Japanese military advisers. It was a barely disguised attempt to turn China into a Japanese colony.

The last demands were utterly unacceptable. The Western powers protested strongly, and these were withdrawn. In Japan a terrorist, angered at such spinelessness, threw a bomb at Okuma's car, this time without disastrous consequences. The other demands, however, were granted. China was weak and in chaos and did not have the strength to resist. For the powerful business interests that had lobbied Okuma—the great zaibatsu, led by Mitsui and Mitsubishi—it was a resounding victory. Manchuria, Inner Mongolia, maybe at some later stage China itself, offered huge opportunities for profit.

One day Okuma called Yasujiro into his office.

"Tsutsumi," he said sternly. "I've been tough on you, but now I'm going to make you some money." He ordered everyone else out of the room and lowered his voice. "I'm the only one that knows this."

Here surely was the long-awaited break—a piece of top-secret information straight from the prime minister's lips. Yasujiro bent his head to listen.

Okuma's news was that the Japanese-owned South Manchurian Railway was going to take over the Ampo Line. It was the perfect time to buy shares in the railway, before the takeover took place.

That was a Saturday. Yasujiro hurried off to collect funds and arrange for someone to buy for him. When the stock market opened on Monday morning, however, the price jumped ¥50 almost immediately. Okuma had been mistaken. He was far from the only person who had heard the news. Everyone in the government—even their typists—knew it too. Yasujiro bought stocks anyway, but the following day the price plummeted. Once again he had suffered a loss.[10]

As for Okuma, he had been too soft on China to suit the mood of the day. In October 1916 he was forced to resign. His government was replaced by a tougher one under the general who had carried out the annexation of Korea, and Okuma returned to his life of retirement.

3

Breaking New Ground
Karuizawa 1915–1923

What kind of business can I do to contribute to mankind, to the country, to society? What is the best? What is the most ideal? In this cramped Japan where people jostle so closely, there is land where the trees have grown untouched since the age of Jimmu, where foxes and badgers live. I will develop this land!
                                        YASUJIRO TSUTSUMI
                In Noma, *The Great Yasujiro Tsutsumi*

The sun was rising over the little mountain village of Kutsukake when the overnight train from Tokyo puffed into the station. It was June 1915, the rainy season, close and steamy in Tokyo but clear and fresh up here in the hills. A few sleepy passengers clambered down, wiry farmers with corrugated brown faces, bent under enormous bundles, in baggy indigo trousers and cotton jackets, with clattery wooden *geta* on their feet. On this particular day there was one stranger among them.

It was a young man who looked so out of place that everyone turned to stare. No one ever forgot what he was wearing that day; in fact, it became part of local legend. He was not much more than a boy, and he was dressed in his student uniform—starched black linen from head to toe, with a high collar and brass buttons down the front. The finishing touch was a straw boater, set at a jaunty angle on his head.

Oblivious to their inquisitive glances, he stood looking around him for a minute, then set off at a determined pace, kicking up dust with his wooden *geta*, looking for all the world as if he knew where he was going. In fact he had no idea. He had put his last few yen into buying the ticket from Tokyo—a matter of ¥1.35. He didn't even have the return fare in his pocket.

Strangely enough, the whole foolhardy project began with the sharp-eyed cousin Kamibayashi. A few months before, Yasujiro had taken a trip to the northern island of Hokkaido to visit his uncle, the very man who had spirited away his mother all those years ago, and Kamibayashi's father.

In those days Hokkaido was real frontier country. Hardy pioneering types in search of a new life moved up there, broke up the soil and built homesteads. In this rough country, Yasujiro's uncle owned a huge ranch with acres of land. After all the years lotus-eating in Tokyo, the young man from Yagiso village was back where he came from—in the countryside.

Kamibayashi, who was a child at the time, remembered the arrival of this glamorous cousin in his sharp city outfits. He took Yasujiro to look at several farms, at the end of which the brash young cousin had this to say:

> This is all very well—but if you can't get a good crop, what do you do? You're not making any profit. If I were you, I'd use all this land in another way—make business, make a profit.
>
> It's a good thing to make use of land—take swamp and turn it into paddy fields, take moorland and make it into vegetable fields and orchards. But if you do it Uncle's way, all you'll ever do is borrow money and get into debt. I want to use land to make a profit![1]

Land—that was the answer. Land was something Yasujiro knew about. Back in Omi, where he came from, everyone knew that land was what counted. A farmer with land was a wealthy man; a farmer with none would starve. Unlike stocks and shares, which could plummet in value, or magazines, which could go bankrupt, if you had land it didn't disappear. It was an old-fashioned view in those days. Conservative old farmers clung to their land, while bright young men put their energy into business, the stock market, retailing. But Yasujiro never worried about anyone else's opinion. He had found the answer and nothing would stop him until he got what he wanted.

He had no intention of going back to farming; that wasn't his plan. First, he needed land—rough land, undeveloped land, of which there was plenty in Japan. Next, he would find a way to make money out of it—and quickly. Back in Tokyo he sat down with his great friend Nagai to talk through this latest brainstorm.

Talk was the stuff of their friendship. They didn't drink, they didn't smoke; at least in these two respects they were ascetics. Instead they talked, endlessly, into the night, hunched over green tea or steaming cups of coffee in the Café Plantan, the Café Paulista or one of the other Ginza coffee shops. Mainly Nagai talked. He argued, he ranted, he railed against the present sorry state of Japanese politics, he discussed the momentous events ripping apart the world outside and what it all meant for Japan. Now that Okuma, their friend and mentor, was in power, perhaps some of the reforms that Nagai had been crusading for all his life might be achieved: rule by the people's elected parliament rather than a small clique of aristocrats or military leaders; voting rights for all, not just the privileged middle classes; protection of the workers and the implementation of democratic values. Yasujiro listened, arguing from time to time, bringing his friend down from the clouds with some brusque remark or amusing anecdote.

Nagai was the talker, the thinker, the idealist. But to put ideals into practice you needed money; it was, as everyone said, the oil of politics. And he too had come up with an idea.

He had just come back from the hill station of Karuizawa, in the mountains to the north of Tokyo, an exhausting ten hours' train ride away. By now he was rather famous. He was an inspired orator and was often invited around the country to give lectures. He was also actively involved in politics and had been campaigning on behalf of Okuma's Progressive Party for the 1915 elections.

Karuizawa was different from anywhere else he had ever been. It was an international community, where Westerners in huge hats and parasols promenaded the streets side by side with Japanese aristocrats, and the shop signs were in English. To Nagai, it was a window to the outside world, the world of Lenin and Marx, of democracy and socialism, where ideas were being shaped and lives transformed. It reminded him of his youthful days at Oxford.

In those days only the very, very rich and foreigners—missionaries, diplomats, businessmen, teachers—even thought of taking a holiday in Japan. When they did, they went to Karuizawa.

It had started out centuries before as a way station on the Nakasendo, the highway that led across the central mountains from Tokyo to Kyoto. Travelers stayed in its inns and teahouses and enjoyed the attentions of its geisha. For the local people there was no other way to make a living. The land was useless for agriculture, covered in black volcanic ash, which drifted from the still-active cone of Mount Asama, squatting violet-blue behind the town.

Then came the railway and with it Alexander Croft-Shaw. A doughty Scottish missionary, he arrived one day in 1885 by horse-drawn train. He came to work but discovered that the mountain air was cool and fresh, a welcome relief from the heavy heat of Tokyo. Two years later he returned. He bought a silkworm shed in the nearby town of Oiwake, had it moved to Karuizawa and set it up as his summer house.

Back in Tokyo, he sang the praises of Karuizawa. English, French and German families had villas built in its cool larch forests, and so did the highest class of Japanese—politicians, businessmen, members of the Tokugawa and other leading families. Shops developed to serve their needs, ricksha drivers did flourishing business, and very soon Karuizawa became the place where everyone who was anyone went to sit out the summer.

It was an exclusive community, but Nagai was convinced that it could not remain exclusive for much longer. The progress of democracy was inexorable. The day would inevitably come when Japan would become an egalitarian society and ordinary working people would have the leisure and the money to buy villas in these larch woods.

Sitting over their fashionable coffees, the two young men plotted the bloodless revolution that would transform society. What could they do? What might be one small first step that would set the wheels in motion? For Yasujiro the answer was simple: build villas, not grand, palatial ones, but simple summer houses priced so that ordinary people could afford them. And as a by-product they might also make some money to fuel their more idealistic ventures. As it happened, Nagai knew the very place.

Thus it was that the young man in his Waseda uniform and can-can hat, as they called boaters in those days, stepped off the train at Kutsukake station at five o'clock one fine June morning. Kutsukake was just a single stop farther up the tracks from Karuizawa, a mere five minutes deeper into the mountains, yet it was like turning the clock back a few hundred years.

Yasujiro set off up the road. He passed Kutsukake's four shops, tumbledown affairs with wooden walls and stones on the roof to prevent the thatch from blowing away. There came a huddle of houses and a few fields; volcanic ash didn't blow in this direction, so people could make a meager living, farming yams and wheat. Then he was out in wild country, striding along a narrow path that cut through larch forests, scrubland and marsh. He was heading for Hoshino Spa, the only inn that was still thriving in the little village of Kutsukake.

Kutsukake had fallen on hard times. For centuries, like Karuizawa, it had been a way station on the Nakasendo, a few inns and teahouses scattered along the broad earthen highway. Then came the railway. Travelers could go much farther in a single day's journey; and those who wanted to spend a night in the area invariably chose the glamorous Western-style hotels of Karuizawa. The more Karuizawa flourished, the more Kutsukake declined. The inns and teahouses fell empty and people were forced to go back to agriculture for their living.

Only Hoshino Spa escaped the decline. It was sited on a natural hot spring and drew the sick and dying, who came to bathe in its healing waters. It was a small inn, only eight rooms, and had been founded by the redoubtable Kasuke Hoshino a generation back. His son, another Kasuke Hoshino (each generation continued the same name), was an outgoing, energetic individual of Yasujiro's age, who was mad about anything newfangled. He owned the only Model T Ford in the entire prefecture, and had had to put in a special request to the prefectural governor for a license. He was frequently to be seen jolting around the rutted roads of Kutsukake or struggling on the grass shoulders with a flat tire.

Nagai had heard that there was land for sale around Hoshino Spa, but when Yasujiro arrived, he found that it was disappointingly small—a mere fifty thousand *tsubo* (about forty acres), far from enough to set his master plan in action. However, now that he had set foot in the place he could see that it was exactly what he had been looking for: rough, untamed land, the home of badgers and foxes, overgrown with weeds.

He made the acquaintance of Hoshino, then, armed with a letter of introduction from Nagai—or, rather, from the distinguished Professor Nagai of Waseda University—went in search of the village headman.

None of the people whom Yasujiro met in Kutsukake is still alive, but their children are, and nearly everyone can recount the story of the brash youth with the Shiga accent, Waseda uniform and cancan hat. Kasuke Hoshino III, a dapper sixty-year-old in blazer, spotted tie and neatly folded pocket handkerchief, every inch the local magnate, recalls that his father was rather taken with this cocky young fellow.

"My father said he was a quite aggressive young man, very ambitious, quite an unusual character. He was a good listener, a good researcher—and once he decides, he goes straight, like an *onoshishi,* a wild boar."

While Hoshino was the village squire, Saburo Tsuchiya was the power broker. A heavy-faced man of forty-four with close-cropped, bristly hair, he was always to be seen in kimono robes and wooden *geta.* He was the local politician and had been the village chief for the last three years. According to Hoshino, "Whatever he said, everyone followed."

Over the years Tsuchiya had watched the village's decline with greater and greater alarm. The number of visitors to the inn fell to nothing; one bad harvest followed another; and to cap it all, there was talk of a new railway, to bypass Kutsukake completely. If this happened, the station, which the villagers had built at great expense only fifteen years before, would have to be closed. There was only one solution if the village was to be saved. Like Karuizawa, Kutsukake had to develop; it needed visitors, it needed capital. But the villagers didn't have the funds or the ability to bring this about themselves. What they needed, in fact, was a developer. Nevertheless, Tsuchiya was taken aback when the young man in his student uniform appeared in the earthen-floored entrance hall to his house.

Seizo, Tsuchiya's son, was fourteen at the time and never forgot the encounter. Like the proverbial wild boar, Yasujiro knew what he was after, and nothing would deflect him. He began with Nagai's letter, then followed this up with the grand statement "I am the secretary of Prime Minister Shigenobu Okuma. I'm here to buy land for a villa development, as much as possible; a million *tsubo* [815 acres] will be about right."[2]

This was a little misleading: it was true that Okuma had recommended that his two young protégés look into Kutsukake; he had just finished having a summer residence built across the hill in Karuizawa, a grandiose gable-roofed, three-story chalet, all in the Western style, with several outhouses, a lake and expansive grounds. But Yasujiro was certainly not here as his representative.

Tsuchiya sucked air through his teeth and pondered awhile. There was certainly land available. It was common land that belonged to the village. Some of it the villagers used to pasture horses and cows, and the rest was wild, covered in marsh or scrub, or forests of larch and silver birch. But was this the right person to sell it to?

Finally he decided. There was indeed some land, he said, which might be for sale, up above Hoshino Spa, about six hundred thousand *tsubo* (490 acres). However, it was for the villagers to decide whether they would sell, and for how much.

For the next few days Yasujiro explored. Every day, like any farmer's son, he was up at five. From time to time Hoshino took him in his Model T Ford; otherwise he walked, deep into the hills. The six hundred thousand *tsubo* was exactly what he needed. It was a vast tract of land that stretched from Hoshino Spa for a good mile, to a vantage point high above the village, deep in forest.

But that was not all. The whole area could be developed. There was nothing here, it was wild country—wasted, unused land. Up beyond the six hundred thousand *tsubo* there was nothing but moorland, mile upon mile of it, littered with huge chunks of black volcanic rock, right to the foot of Mount Asama. The town of Karuizawa itself was already developed; it was nearly as busy as Tokyo, with shops all along the main street and rickshas rattling up and down. But south of the station again was wild country, wetlands where the villagers kept their cows. As he walked, Yasujiro's dreams became grander and grander. Here there could be houses, here shops, here a hotel, a whole summer resort. Anything was possible. All that was needed was a little cash, but cash was the one thing he didn't have. At the end of his visit, he had to tap Tsuchiya for the ¥1.35 to get him back to Tokyo.

Tsuchiya had bad news for him. He had consulted the village and put the aspiring entrepreneur's case as favorably as possible. But while he himself might be an ally, the villagers, a bunch of conservative old farmers, didn't trust this smooth-talking young man at all. For a start he came from out of town; he wasn't one of them. Did they want a stranger buying their land and setting up in their village? Anyway, he looked too young—he even wore a student uniform—and far too poor. He had no experience of business. In addition, he was asking not for a small plot of land to build a house but for an enormous stretch, an entire hill, far bigger than the whole village. It was worth a small fortune. How on earth could such a callow youth find such a huge amount of money? All he was offering them was a gentleman's agreement.

Once again Yasujiro's grand schemes had come to nothing; or so it seemed. But he was not compared to a wild boar for nothing. A week later he was on the train again. In fact, the third-class carriage of the Tokyo–Nagano line, with its hard, green-painted wooden seats, became almost a second home for him. Week after week he took the night train from Tokyo's Ueno station. Ten hours and twenty-six tunnels later he arrived in the Karuizawa highlands and stepped out onto Kutsukake station. And at five-thirty in the morning he was sliding open Tsuchiya's heavy wooden front door.

Week after week the pair held meetings. The villagers had never seen anything like it. They gathered in Tsuchiya's twelve-mat room, the biggest in the village, and talked into the night, hunched over papers under glimmering oil lamps. Yasujiro argued, he explained, he wheedled, he wore them down. He would develop the village, he said. He could do it, he had the contacts. He would bring academics from Waseda, poets, artists, to buy summer houses here and raise the image of the place. He got to know everyone. He went to their houses, sat over tea and pickled vegetables and went through the arguments again. And he became an aficionado of Mrs. Tsuchiya's homemade miso-flavored pickles. In this way nearly three years passed.

It was 1917. In Tokyo Yasujiro and Nagai were fired by the news of the February Revolution in Russia and even more so by the Bolshevik Revolution. Nagai had left his teaching job at Waseda to run for election to the Diet. The two friends, inspired by the revolutionary changes occurring in the world outside, took up the study of Russian. Their teacher, a pastor from the Nikolai Russian Orthodox Cathedral in the hilly Kanda section of Tokyo, would visit Nagai's house two evenings a week. Nagai, who already spoke excellent English, did rather well, though Yasujiro was always hopeless at languages.

The villagers were still holding out against him; Tsuchiya, however, was a powerful ally. He was convinced that this tenacious young man would be good for the village; he would give it a future. Between them the pair whittled away at the opposition until only half the villagers remained to be convinced. It was an exciting moment: when it came to a vote, if the villagers were equally divided, Tsuchiya, as headman, would have the final say. There was a meeting planned for December 23. What was needed was a grand gesture, a *coup de théâtre,* to put all their doubts to rest.

Yasujiro went in search of cash, plenty of it, as quickly as possible. But how was he to get it? He had nothing to pawn, no banks would lend him money, he had no credibility. These, though, were all minor obstacles. He had contacts, he had charm, all that was needed was a little persuasion.

Everyone has a different story to tell about how he got the money. According to Hoshino, he borrowed it from Nagai. Kamibayashi makes Yasujiro's devoted wife, Fumi, the heroine of the story. She went to her family, apparently, and persuaded them to lend her some. It was still not enough, so she took her precious watch, which she had received on graduation, and pawned it. Without poor Fumi, writes Kamibayashi sternly, the Seibu empire wouldn't even exist.[3]

Seizo, Tsuchiya's son, has a more elaborate version. Tsuchiya's brother-in-law was a doctor and a member of the Diet for the prefecture. The family persuaded him to stand surety for Yasujiro so that he could borrow money from the bank. That was still only half of what he needed, so he and young Seizo sat down with some scissors and a pile of newspaper and cut it into pieces the size of ¥10 notes, then sandwiched them neatly with the real money and bundled up the whole lot together.[4]

By December 23 Kutsukake was bright with snow. The meeting began in the evening. Crowded into the smoky twelve-mat room around the central hearth, the villagers were ready for a fight. Once again Yasujiro made his speech in his outlandish Shiga accent. He had a vision. He was eager to develop Kutsukake, to build summer villas for cultured Tokyoites, to make it a cosmopolitan center like Karuizawa. To start with, he needed this land up above Hoshino Spa.

The villagers muttered among themselves. They had been through all this before. Supposing they let him have it for even as little as five sen (one-twentieth of a yen) per *tsubo*, six hundred thousand *tsubo* would still amount to ¥30,000 (the present-day equivalent of ¥150 million, about $1.5 million), to them an unimaginably vast sum of money. The prefectural governor himself earned no more than ¥700 a month. Voices began to be raised. "Does this Tsutsumi really have money?"

This was what Yasujiro had been waiting for. He brought out his cash, bundle after bundle of it, fat wads of notes—¥30,000, all in ¥10 notes, thirty hefty bundles. The villagers were stunned. They had never seen so much money in their lives.

When Tsuchiya put the matter to a vote, they were still evenly divided. It was for the headman to cast the deciding vote: they would sell the land to Mr. Tsutsumi, for the sum of ¥30,000.

Yasujiro was in business. At the age of twenty-eight he was a man of means. He was the owner of a magnificent stretch of land. And he also had money. No one expected that he would pay for the land straightaway; the wads of notes had just been for show.

Of course the whole thing was a trick. The stubborn old villagers had been tricked, but the leaders of the village, Tsuchiya and Hoshino, had gone along with it. They were certain that it was time for change. And Yasujiro, they felt, was the man to bring it about.

The land turned out to be a greater bargain than anyone could ever have guessed. The villagers had tramped the area and made a rough estimate of the size, but when they came to check the measurements more carefully they discovered that Yasujiro had actually purchased not six hundred thousand but eight hundred thousand *tsubo* (650 acres) of fine forested land.

Yasujiro was not about to sit back and congratulate himself. He had got what he wanted—more, in fact, than he had expected. But the real test was yet to come. He still had to make a success of it. He was under contract to build fifty villas in the next two years or he would lose the land, and his financial state was as perilous as ever. The only money he had was the borrowed ¥30,000; in fact, if Seizo's story is correct, it was only ¥15,000.

At least he was no longer on his own. He was beginning to acquire the family for which he had been looking for so long. Nagai, effectively his business partner, was a close ally; and Fumi was always there in the background, providing loyal support.

The first priority was to generate money—more, much more than he already had. The youthful entrepreneur would need to apply to the task all the wiles he had acquired over the last few years. The obvious way was to form a company to attract investment. But if Yasujiro was the president, who would risk their money? No one had ever heard of him. He needed bait, an irresistible attraction to lure investors.

He made use of his contacts. He spoke to Nagai, he spoke to the home minister, soon to be mayor of Tokyo, Shimpei Goto, and in no time found himself talking to one of the country's weightiest business figures, Kenichi Fujita. Fujita was director of innumerable companies and had a reputation as a man who put ailing firms back on their feet again. Whatever business he was involved in was guaranteed to turn a profit.

Whether it was Yasujiro's impressive contacts or his powers of persuasion, Fujita agreed to become the nominal president of the new company—Sengataki Resorts Ltd., Sengataki being the name of the area. Yasujiro set up office in Tsuchiya's house, made Tsuchiya and his relatives shareholders, and offered 50 percent of the shares to the public. Letters began arriving at Tsuchiya's house, visitors arrived from Tokyo, and very soon the old wooden safe was bulging. The shares rose in value, Yasujiro and Tsuchiya sold some, and yet more money rolled in. Within the space of a few weeks Sengataki Resorts Ltd. had a capital value of ¥250,000, over a billion yen in modern terms, about $10 million.

Yasujiro began to develop the land. He took on builders, he measured out lots of one hundred *tsubo* each (.08 acres), and soon the quiet larch and silver birch woods above Kutsukake, where badgers roamed and foxes lurked, were filled with the noise of hammering and sawing.

Yasujiro's first cottages were a far cry from the grand villas of Karuizawa, across the hill. They were modest but comfortable, small two- or three-room affairs, with a kitchen and a pleasant balcony overlooking a garden. None had bathrooms; few Japanese homes had bathrooms in those days. So Yasujiro built a public bath, half a mile above Hoshino Spa. He named it Sengataki Spa, although, as Hoshino junior is quick to point out, it wasn't natural spring water; neither was it naturally hot—it had to be heated. He also made a point of advertising the magnificent marble baths, although, as any local person will tell you, they were actually made of stone. He had wooden water pipes taken up the hill, he had holes dug into the black volcanic soil to dispose of waste, and with Hoshino he began planning a hydroelectric plant.

The next thing he needed was customers, not the privileged few who holidayed in splendor in Karuizawa but ordinary middle-class folk who could afford ¥500 (¥2.5 million, $25,000 in modern terms) or ¥1,000 for a country cottage.

The timing was perfect. World War I had ended and the age of the masses had arrived: the great new powers were America, the land of democracy, and Russia, the inspiring new socialist state. In Japan the lower orders had tasted freedom for the first time only fifty years before. Now their children's children were suddenly discovering what it meant. After centuries of being fixed within an unshakable class structure, they had freedom. They even had money, and they could spend it as crazily as they liked.

The first explosion of the new demand for freedom came with the rice riots in 1918. World War I had resulted in industrial growth and prosperity for Japan, but it also brought inflation. The price of rice rose to an intolerable level. Rioting began in the countryside, then spread to Tokyo, where mounted troops had to be called in to control the disturbances. In the aftermath the prime minister resigned. The new premier, Takashi Hara, was a commoner, the first ever to hold power, and a famous campaigner for party rule. His party, the Seiyukai (the Association of Political Friends), held a majority in the Diet, and he chose his cabinet exclusively from that party. For the first time Japan was under the rule of the elected representatives of the people. The Taisho era, it seemed, was to be the age of democracy.

To begin with, Yasujiro went knocking on the doors of his friends, and little by little everything began to fall into place, exactly

as he had promised. Businessmen, writers, artists and kabuki drama-
tists began to arrive at Kutsukake station and to move into the summer cottages above Hoshino Spa. Hoshino junior said, "What I
admire him most for—he carefully chose what kind of customer
would help his business. Not wealthy gamblers or estate agents—but
he chose men who could write books."

A new community began to take shape. The new arrivals needed
shops, they needed supplies. So Yasujiro constructed a primitive supermarket, a wooden shed the size of an aircraft hangar where the
Kutsukake villagers could set up stalls and bring their vegetables to
sell. He built a post office, he installed electricity, he set up telephone lines. And he widened the path that led up the hill above
Hoshino Spa into a road "wide enough for a Cessna to take off
from."

It was the talk of the village. At a time when everyone traveled by
ricksha, horse-drawn carriage or bicycle, why on earth make a road
the size of a baseball field? It was known as the *7-ken* road, one ken
being about six feet. In other words, it was more than forty feet
across. And it went, straight as a Roman road, through the village,
past the entrance to Hoshino Spa and up the hill to Yasujiro's cottage
development. It was Tsuchiya who had the unpleasant job of persuading people whose land lay in the way to part with it for the sake
of progress. Many of the conservative old villagers were against the
project, and there were protests and long meetings into the night by
the light of glimmering oil lamps.

But something was still needed, something that would symbolize
both to Yasujiro and to the villagers that the young man from Omi,
the boy who had arrived at Kutsukake station in his Waseda uniform
and cancan hat, had really done it. He had kept his promises, he had
done all he said he would, and more. The answer was a hotel—not a
homely inn, with tatami mats and sliding doors, but a real Western
hotel, every bit as grand and luxurious as the ones in rival Karuizawa.

When the Green Hotel was completed at the very top of the hill,
everyone had to go and have a look. It was a splendid edifice, several
storys high, painted brilliant green like young spring leaves and
roofed with lustrous copper. It stood on the common where the villagers had once pastured their cows and horses, looking out across
wooded hills to the blue hump of Mount Asama, plumed with

smoke. There were suites, there were dining rooms decked with tas-seled drapes and thick red carpets. There was outlandish Western fur-niture, such as the villagers had never seen in their lives before—tables, chairs, Art Deco lampstands, heavy wooden beds, cabinets, writing desks. Even the gardens were Western, with lawns, ornamental ponds and flower beds.

And it was open to everybody, not just the rich and privileged. Visitors from out of town stayed while they decided which cottage to buy. Hoshino drove up the long straight road in his Model T Ford to have dinner. The villagers walked; it took a long time, but that didn't matter: they went to drink, they went to dance.

Finally, with all this splendor, Tsuchiya decided that it was time for the village to have a new name. Kutsukake—"Hang up your shoes"—was no longer appropriate. It sounded too rustic and old-fashioned. Once again there were meetings deep into the night, while the villagers clung to this last vestige of the old life. In the end Tsuchiya won, and Kutsukake became Naka-karuizawa, Inner Karuizawa, taking on the name and luster of its glamorous neighbor.

It was 1923. Five years had passed and many things had changed. Sengataki Resorts Ltd., now renamed Hakone Resorts Ltd., sent out postcards to potential clients:

> After five years' hard work, we have built our cultural village in Karuizawa's Sengataki. Very convenient by train and horse carriage or ricksha. There is water, electricity, telephones, a market for every-day goods, a spa, concert hall, baseball field, tennis courts, drug-store, swimming pool, etc. Villas priced at ¥1,000 and ¥2,000, half to be paid on signing of contract, half on entry to property.[5]

Yasujiro too had changed. The pushy young upstart who had hus-tled the villagers out of their land had gone. At thirty-four, Yasujiro was juggling an empire of land and buildings that perpetually threat-ened to tumble around his feet.

Everyone called him Taisho—Boss, General. It was the perfect role for him. He would strut around the building sites, wielding his famous stick—he was never seen without it—exchanging banter with the builders and bellowing orders. If he found anyone slacking, he hit them. From time to time he lined up his staff and interrogated them about the business. "If you give me a stupid answer, this will happen," he would say, and pick up a china teacup and crush it in his bare hand.

The staff feared him; they respected him; and they loved him. Larger than life though he was, he was one of them, and they knew where they stood with him. When he barked orders in his rough Shiga accent or yelled, *"Baka!* Fool!" they trembled, but they understood him.

Michio Nagai, Nagai's son, was a child then. Now a distinguished man in his seventies, he remembers hearing the big voice of Yasujiro booming around the woods. A famous arm wrestler, Yasujiro, in his cotton *yukata* and straw sandals, would square up to a sinewy, sun-blackened builder with a handkerchief knotted around his sweaty head and the two would wrestle until one gave way. Usually it was the builder. Yasujiro was not a judo sixth dan for nothing. "If you want your workers to trust you, you have to have a strong arm," he used to comment with a guffaw.

At five in the morning, before the sun had risen, he would be hammering at the door of Nagai's cottage. Eventually Nagai refused even to get up and speak to him, so Yasujiro would call young Michio instead. "Come with Uncle," he would say, and the two would set off—the big man, whose stomach was beginning to protrude over the belt of his *yukata,* and the little boy.

They did the rounds: the shops, the post office, the office, the hotel. Everyone would be up; they knew that Taisho was going to arrive very early, but they were still half asleep, and he was wide awake. If anyone, from the hotel manager downward, yawned or looked sleepy, he hit him.

Yasujiro's empire had grown with dazzling speed. He used to keep maps in his office, where he marked the land he owned. Little by little the small pink patches spread like a cancer and joined to form networks.

Japanese like to look back on the men born in the Meiji era, between 1868 and 1912, as a different breed, a race of heroes, who engaged in epic struggles untrammeled by moral considerations. Born after the shackles of the shogunate had fallen away, they had the taste of freedom in their mouths. They thought they could do anything: the whole country lay at their feet, waiting to be conquered.

By the twenties, the jazz age, the long climb out of medieval darkness into the modern world was well under way. It was a great time for budding entrepreneurs. Men built railways and bridges, they carved out manufacturing empires, they imported and exported anything that would sell; they opened banks, they dealt in stocks and shares.

But no one was interested in land. Leave the sprawling smoky cities, step beyond the perimeters of the towns thrumming with manufacturing activity, and you were back in the Middle Ages. Outside the occasional village surrounded by rough-hewn paddy fields and vegetable patches, Japan was an undeveloped country. The highways, broad earthen tracks, cut through virgin territory of moorland, scrub and forest. The mountains rolled, range upon range of them, dark with forest, until they merged with the sky on the horizon.

As far as Yasujiro was concerned, it was all there for the taking. Some was government land, which was difficult to buy; but the rest was private, part of the estates of princes or lords, or owned by farmers or village communities. No one could fathom why he wanted it. It seemed eccentric, even crazy, to sink your last yen into a patch of land in the middle of nowhere. Yet the ink was scarcely dry on the contract with the Kutsukake villagers when he bought one hundred thousand *tsubo* (80 acres) in a new area, in Gora in the Hakone district. He also expanded his holdings in Karuizawa to encompass all the land he had coveted—the moorland strewn with black volcanic boulders, which stretched from the cottage development to the foot of Mount Asama, and the wetlands to the south of Karuizawa station where the villagers kept their cows.

A little more than two years after he had chased from bank to bank, desperately trying to raise that first ¥30,000, Hakone Resorts Ltd. had a capital value of ¥20 million (in the region of ¥100 billion or $1 billion by today's reckoning). It was a real business.

Then came an event so unutterably dreadful that it is etched into the memory of every Japanese. At one minute before noon on Saturday, September 1, 1923, as charcoal braziers were burning under the midday meal in almost every home throughout Tokyo, the first shock waves of the Great Kanto Earthquake struck. The shocks came, stronger and stronger, until the whole eastern plain around Tokyo was billowing like the sea. Within minutes the city was in ruins. The splendid brick-built Asakusa Twelve Stories, which had towered over the east end, toppled; temples collapsed under their heavy thatched roofs; flimsy wooden houses tumbled like packs of cards. Then came firestorms, lit by the still-burning braziers. The wooden city blazed uncontrollably for nearly two days. In the end more than 130,000 people died and 2.5 million lost their homes.

At the time, Yasujiro and Fumi were living in Mejiro, a long way from the center of Tokyo, near the burgeoning cultural village. They missed the full force of the quake, though Yasujiro was injured and damaged his leg.

He spent three days at home, stretched out on his futon, but eventually curiosity mingled with foreboding got the better of him. He called his staff and ordered them to make a platform of wooden planks on top of his car. They spread the futon on that, lifted him onto it, and he drove around the city, propped on his bedding, surveying the wreckage.

For Fumi, nothing could have been worse than the life she already had to endure. While Yasujiro was a strapping man in the prime of life, at thirty-six she looked like an old woman. Her shoulders were slumped, her face was worn. She had never been pretty, and now she had given up completely. She wore her hair wrenched back in a bun like a governess and the most dowdy and unbecoming of kimonos.

For years Yasujiro had made no secret of the fact that any love that he might once have felt for her had long since disappeared. He was cold and brusque. When they were in the house together, he hardly spoke to her. She stayed at home, bringing up two children who were not hers, while he was out nearly every night, sleeping with prostitutes.

Later he promised her that he would give up prostitutes, though not his nocturnal activities. Instead he took his pleasure with nonprofessional women. In the classic Japanese way, it was Fumi's job to run the house and rear the children while her husband's infidelities went unremarked. In this respect at least, she felt her position unthreatened. In Japan until extremely recently, few wives would dream of expecting or demanding sexual fidelity of their husbands. In exchange for turning a blind eye to endless escapades and sexual peccadilloes, they could be assured of a home and financial support throughout their lives.

But Fumi's suffering had only just begun. For Yasujiro had met his match. He had fallen in love—madly, obsessively, unlike ever before.

4

The Women
1923–1940

One day Father said, "Some people say I'm an incurable libertine, but I just don't have good luck with women. In order to revive the Tsumura family, which my grandfather entrusted to me, this is my method. To make children you need women. You could call it renting a womb."

TAKASHI TSUJII
In the Season of Roaming

The sight that greeted Yasujiro as he drove through the city, propped on his futon, was truly awesome. The great city of Tokyo, with its splendid buildings, its universities, its tram lines, its avenues lined with willows, was a plain of rubble. A few skeletal buildings remained, tottering above the ruins, and small fires still smoldered here and there.

For the first few days no one could think of anything but bare survival. There were corpses to be buried—the stench of putrefaction soon became unbearable. People searched frantically among the ruins for lost relatives. Many fled the city. Those who remained were reduced to standing in line for hours to receive a single rice ball. There was looting and rioting, and in some areas the government had to send in troops.

Some buildings survived fairly intact. Yasujiro had been engaged in a major building project in Koishikawa, in the northern part of the city. He was sure it would be in ruins. In fact it had survived, and in such fine condition that the Ministry of the Interior inspection team gave it a special mention. The public was impressed. Clearly this was a company to be trusted. The orders began to flood in.

For Yasujiro, and everyone engaged in the building trade, it was boom time. He started project after project, venturing into areas he had never tried before. In Shibuya, a thriving residential district to the west of the city, a whole shopping street had been destroyed. Yasujiro set to work to liven up the place. He made a grand plan for a huge shopping area, to be called the Hundred Shops. It was to be not merely shops but an entertainment district; and by the time it was finished there was a warren of bars, cinemas, geisha houses, mahjong parlors and gambling dens stretching behind the respectable shop fronts.

In all his projects there was one trusted lieutenant perpetually at his side. The sharp-eyed young cousin from Hokkaido, Kamibayashi, was now twenty. If his reports are to be trusted, he had been in on everything from the very start—after all, he was family; Yasujiro had almost no one else.

Kamibayashi was a clerk in the office of *New Japan* magazine when Yasujiro was still struggling to make ends meet. He worked on the development of Karuizawa and later joined a company called Chiyoda Rubber when Yasujiro took it over. He was there when the company nearly went bankrupt a year after the earthquake. And he was present on a famous occasion when Yasujiro acquired the nickname Pistol.

It all began when Yasujiro was busy buying up land in Hakone, the beautiful lakeland region to the south of Tokyo. Hakone is very close to the earthquake epicenter in Sagami Bay. Closer still is the Izu Peninsula, which sits like the lid of a pressure cooker almost on top of the bay. It is frequently rocked by tremors, and steam and hot mineral springs burst from its soil. One of the most spectacular regions in the country, Izu is full of precipitous crags that look as if they thrust only yesterday from the ground and small inns where invalids stayed to take the waters. It was here that Yasujiro had ambitions to extend his territory.

Unfortunately he was not the only developer with intentions on the region. There was a small railway there already, the Sunzu Line. So he began to buy up shares in the company, Sunzu Railway. Desperate to avoid a takeover, the president of the company too bought shares. Yasujiro bought still more, and the president took the time-honored course of hiring some thugs to go to Yasujiro's place and retrieve the shares by force.

Yasujiro was at home when there was a hubbub at his gate. His secretary rushed into his office gasping, "There's a fellow with a pistol—what shall we do?" Yasujiro strode past him into the garden and stood, arms folded, glaring at the intruders. There were twenty of them, no doubt thickset, broken-nosed and dressed in traditional jodhpur-type trousers and cloven-toed shoes; the days when Japanese gangsters dressed like Al Capone were still to come. They had already shoved open the wooden gate and were pushing into his garden, trampling the carefully raked gravel between the paving stones.

Yasujiro was no coward. He drew himself up to his full height and stood firmly in their path. Threats were exchanged, voices raised. The leader, one Tomio Iwata, a notorious nationalist fanatic and head of the right-wing Taika-kai group, was waving a pistol. Scowling, he stopped shouting and took aim.

"*Dozo,*" Yasujiro snorted contemptuously. "Go ahead!"

Iwata pulled the trigger. As a judo practitioner, Yasujiro could hold himself very, very still. He moved not a muscle. The bullet whizzed past his neck, practically grazing it, and embedded itself in a tree trunk behind him. He stood unmoved, like the guardian deity at a temple gate, staring disdainfully at his opponent.

Iwata was stunned by this display of sangfroid. He had expected Yasujiro to start begging for mercy. Instead he himself fell to his knees. Hands on the ground, he apologized for his presumption. "You're a brave man," he said.[1]

Thereafter Yasujiro was known by the nickname Pistol (*Pisutoru,* a Japanese word borrowed from English). Other versions of the story spread—that it was Yasujiro himself who had wielded the pistol, to force bankers to lend him money or to threaten a rival businessman. In any case, no one doubted that he deserved the name.

It was well before this incident that Yasujiro was asked to sort out the affairs of another concern that had gone bankrupt; and he took Kamibayashi along.

He had been approached by a man called Yoshizo Aoyama, a gentleman, a man of culture and cosmopolitan tastes. Aoyama spoke English, had traveled in the West, and was one of the few people in Tokyo to own a gramophone. He was never happier than when sitting at home listening to Western classical music surrounded by his children, and he also liked to sculpt. But he was no businessman. He came from one of the best samurai families and had grown up at a time when a gentleman was not expected to know how to make a living. In fact, he taught his nine children to believe that money was dirty.

For many years he had been the managing director of a bank and had a small company called Tokyo Land that imported furniture and building materials from the United States. He and his family had lived well, on inherited wealth and the proceeds of his businesses. They had a fine house in one of the best parts of town, full of treasures handed down through the generations: antique swords, priceless tea-ceremony ware wrapped in silk and stored in wooden boxes, scrolls of paintings and poems brushed by the masters.

But then he found himself in difficulties. A cousin of his was involved in politics and, like all politicians, needed money. During an election campaign he made use of funds from Aoyama's bank to such an extent that the bank went bankrupt. Scandal threatened; the depositors faced ruin. Aoyama, a man of honor, took full responsibility and vowed to repay the bank out of his own pocket. Overnight the family lost everything. The fine house with its treasures collected over generations, the land, the money, all disappeared.

When Yasujiro first visited them, they were living in a big ramshackle house that was practically empty, as grim and unwelcoming as a barracks. He stayed to dinner, and soon became a regular visitor.

In many ways their life was the exact reverse of his. They were gentlefolk down on their luck, cultured, rather unworldly people, whose education had not prepared them for the brutal new world they found themselves in, of which he was a part. What impressed him most was their family life. It was like the family he had never had. Once over dinner he said, rather wistfully, "I've never seen such a warm, close family before." Later the gentle Aoyama confided to his children, "Young Mr. Tsutsumi makes my heart ache. With a family like his . . ."[2]

Yasujiro agreed to help them out. He took over the bank and the company and he started spending more and more time at the house.

In particular he enjoyed the company of Aoyama's four beautiful daughters. All four were still at school and until recently they had lived like princesses; they were proud, haughty girls. Despite their poverty, they never forgot for a moment that they were of samurai stock.

Into this cloistered world, Yasujiro swaggered to rescue them. He was young, good-looking, humorous, and he was different: he was a peasant, tough and manly. He strutted around the house, telling everyone what to do in his rough Shiga accent. To complete his appeal, there was something of the lost little boy about him. He was touchingly careless about his clothes: sometimes there were holes in his socks. And there was never anything in his lunch box except rice balls and slabs of *konnyaku,* a sort of tasteless vegetable jelly. He needed mothering, in fact.

After a time the second sister yielded to his advances. To some extent she had no choice; the family was dependent on him. But he was not satisfied to let it rest at that. Some time later—it must have been a few years—he seduced the fourth sister; and after that he slept with both. "That was the kind of fellow he was," as Kamibayashi puts it.[3]

But it was the third, Misao, he really wanted. When they first met, on that memorable day when he came to dinner, she was fourteen. It was March 1922; he was thirty-three.

Kamibayashi remembers her as "sophisticated but very snobbish" even at that tender age. Of all the sisters, she was her father's favorite. She was everything that Yasujiro was not: refined, intellectual, sensitive. She would spend hours poring over *The Tale of Genji*—she could quote sections of that romantic classic by heart—or composing tanka, poignant thirty-one-syllable poems on loneliness or lost love. She could paint, she had an elegant brushstroke; in a word, she had all the traditional accomplishments expected of a samurai woman.

And, unlike poor Fumi, who had brains but no looks, she was beautiful. At fourteen she wore a plait and glasses and had the most delicate and aristocratic of features set in a perfect oval face. She was tiny, slender and carried herself with full knowledge of her noble origins. She was also a girl who knew her own mind.

Yasujiro was bowled over. She was everything he had ever wanted, and, in his rough Shiga fashion, he set his mind to seducing her. He tried everything he could think of—flattery, cajolery, gifts, arguments—everything short of force. But he had met his match: her will was even stronger than his. No matter what he tried, she spurned him; and the more she disdained him, the more obsessed he became.

So it went on for years. Yasujiro continued to sleep with two of her sisters, and with many other women too, according to the legends that have passed down within the company. He kept his promise to Fumi: no prostitutes, only nonprofessional women.

But still he wanted Misao, more and more; and still she spurned him.

Poor Aoyama watched all this helplessly. This man, he confided in Kamibayashi, this interloper that he himself had introduced into the house, had brought their happy family to ruin. Finally both sisters became pregnant, first the older, then the younger. Misao decided that she had to do something to save the family.

First she made herself unable to have children, according to Kamibayashi; though there are people within the company who claim that later she was seen pregnant. Then she made a bargain with Yasujiro. She would give herself to him, but it had to take place outside Tokyo. And, most important, he must stop seeing her sisters. She would bring up their children as her own.

Outside the town of Kamakura, where many years later Yasujiro would be installed in a grand tomb fit for a pharaoh, he had a small country house on a clifftop overlooking the sea. It was a wild, lonely place surrounded by woods. Here he waited. He sent a car for her. After she arrived the driver turned and drove away, leaving her alone with him. It was dark and there was no one nearby.

It was as she had asked. But for the young girl—she was still only twenty—it must have felt like rape. Yasujiro was a big man, and his methods of seduction were always rough. "All you have to do is sleep with them once and they'll follow you for the rest of your life," he used to say.[4]

He kept his side of the bargain. After keeping her for a few years in Osaki, a suburb of Tokyo, he bought a small house for her, surrounded by leek fields and cherry trees, in Mitaka, a distant suburb of Tokyo. She moved in and lived there with the two little children, Seiji, the son of her older sister, and Kuniko, the daughter of the younger, whom she brought up as her own. According to Kamibayashi, Aoyama killed himself. The disgrace to his family was more than he could bear.

Until Kamibayashi's article came out in 1987, the full details of this story were not known, though within the company it was common speculation that Misao was not Seiji's real mother. Seiji himself hinted at it in his novel *In the Season of Roaming,* where he gave a much more harrowing account of the encounter in Kamakura. In his fictionalized version of the story, the father of the main character forces himself on the mother against her will.

In a way Yasujiro's behavior reflected the decadence of the times. People spoke of "Taisho democracy," but it was more like an intoxication with everything that seemed to symbolize the new age. Girls— *moga,* "modern gals"—cut their hair so short that they looked like boys, and some even flaunted short flapper skirts, a far cry from the modest kimono. Boys—*mobo,* "modern boys"—wore their hair girlishly long and combed straight back in the "all-back" style, and sported horn-rimmed Harold Lloyd glasses. They listened to jazz, they danced the Charleston, they watched American movies, they ate ice cream, they made love in the back of taxis. Until the authorities clamped down, Marxism was all the rage and everyone was reading the latest revolutionary Russian novels, such as Aleksandra Kollontai's *A Great Love.*[5]

It was the age of speed, sport and sex, reported Kosei Ando, a historian of the time. Yet it was all hollow, just a façade of progress. There was no center, no reality. "They are dancing in a town that has no tomorrow."[6]

The emperor's illness was the most potent symbol of all this. Taisho had never been healthy. As a boy he had had meningitis, which was never treated. Over the years his behavior became more and more eccentric until people began to whisper that the emperor was mad. It came to a head one day on the occasion of the state opening of the Diet. The members were assembled, waiting for him to speak. Instead he stood silently staring at them for so long that they all began to fidget nervously. Then he started to laugh uncontrollably. He rolled up his speech, put it to his eye like a telescope and squinted around at the august assembly. After that memorable occasion he was relieved of his official duties and Hirohito, the crown prince, became regent.

The following year, 1924, Yasujiro was thirty-five. He was in the prime of life, with every reason to consider himself a successful man.

He had found a way to make money; he had laid the foundations of his business empire. The time had come, in fact, to go into politics.

It was a good moment to choose. Nagai had become a member of the Diet in 1920. He had campaigned as an independent, although as soon as he won he joined the Constitutional Association—the Progressive Party, which Okuma had founded, under another name. Once installed in the Diet, he used his famous powers of oratory to inveigh against Prime Minister Hara and the ruling party. Despite the high hopes that Nagai and other liberals had had of him, Japan's first commoner prime minister had proved a disappointment. Far from putting through democratic reforms, he had stood against universal suffrage. By the 1924 election the opposition parties were strong enough to make a serious bid for power.

As Nagai's trusted friend, Yasujiro had worked as head of his campaign staff. That year he too decided to stand as an independent.

Undoubtedly his reasons for entering politics were not as idealistic as Nagai's. Unlike his friend, he was not burning with crusading zeal to change Japan. The two were, however, partners in everything they did; each helped the other. Nagai had backed Yasujiro in building his business, and now, if he could, Yasujiro would provide an ally for him in the Diet. Besides, for an ambitious young man like him, it was an eminently sensible career move. He had promised his grandfather that he would do all he could to restore the name and honor of the Tsutsumi family. Simply making money would not achieve that end. As a farmer's son, how was he to rise in society? Perhaps politics might offer the path.

Yasujiro chose as his constituency a couple of small districts near his old home in Shiga. Under the slogan "Restore farmland," he campaigned for a fairer distribution of land so that the tenant farmers who actually worked the land could own it and profit from it. "Owning your own land makes you love your country," as he wrote.[7]

At the time it was not necessarily a popular platform. Universal suffrage had still not been achieved, and most of the people who would benefit from redistribution of land were not on the electoral register. To add to Yasujiro's problems, his opponent was a well-known local politician, the son of the mayor of Hikone (the town that Grandfather Kiyozaemon had once branded as a den of vice). For all his efforts at the Waseda Debating Society, Yasujiro was still not a powerful speaker; and until he decided to run for office, few people in the area had ever heard his name.

He must have built up support groups in the area among people who remembered him as the local boy who went to Tokyo and made his fortune and others whom he had helped in some way; and no doubt Nagai and other friends from his days at Waseda used their influence. He also found a characteristic way to make himself known. He arrived from Tokyo by car and rumbled around the countryside in his Model T Ford. Cars were still a rarity in those rustic parts. People came out to watch as he went by and soon everyone knew Tsutsumi: he was the one with the car. As he bumped along the earthen paths between the paddy fields his car often stalled and got stuck. In fact, it broke down surprisingly often. Whenever that happened, the local farmers would gather and push and shove or tinker with the engine until the car was back on the road. Then Yasujiro would thank them profusely and stuff banknotes into their hands. It was all perfectly aboveboard; and it certainly did no harm to his campaign. "I see, we'd all think," recalled one of the farmers, later to become the head of Yasujiro's support group. "What a smart way to buy votes. This fellow's doing the same thing wherever he goes!"[8]

When the votes were counted, Tsutsumi was in. In May 1924 he became one of the members for Shiga and shortly afterward joined Nagai as a member of the new ruling party, the reformist Constitutional Association. The following year all men over the age of twenty-five were given the vote. It was the pinnacle of Taisho democracy. Yet only a week afterward another bill was passed, the Peace Preservation Law, providing new powers to the police to clamp down on left-wing groups.

Among the new arrivals in the Diet was a man called Saburo Ishizuka, an acquaintance of Yasujiro's. Ishizuka too was a protégé of Marquis Okuma, although he was much older than Yasujiro. He had been one of the first students at Waseda, when it was still called Tokyo College. At forty-seven he was an earnest, rather dry man with a well-groomed mustache, given to frock coats and stand-up collars.

His constituency was Niigata, a large, breezy city on the Japan Sea coast, where he came from a wealthy family of oil merchants. Like many young men of his generation, he had taken advantage of the new freedoms that had come into being with the overthrow of the shogunate and had broken away from his family background to enter an entirely new field. He went into dentistry and was soon recognized as a pioneer. His clinic had the most advanced facilities and equipment in the country and he was one of the founders of Tokyo Dental University.

Yasujiro and Ishizuka renewed their acquaintance and became firm friends. Four years later, in 1928, both were reelected in the next general election.

Once he was well established as a member of the house, Ishizuka set up a home in Tokyo. In 1930, when his daughter Tsuneko reached the age of seventeen, he brought her down from Niigata to live with him and put her into one of the best finishing schools in Tokyo, Yamawaki Gakuen. He also insisted that she work in his office, serving tea to his guests. Later he arranged a secretarial job for her in the Ministry of Overseas Affairs. At the time the colonization minister was Ryutaro Nagai; the parliamentary vice minister was his and Ishizuka's friend Mr. Tsutsumi.

Yasujiro was in his early forties and beginning to take on the barrel shape appropriate for a man of means. Still perpetually strapped for cash, he was always on the brink of crisis, plunging more and more heavily into debt in order to expand his empire yet further. He could never sit back and be contented with what he had; he always wanted more.

It was the same with his women. He had several households now. Fumi was established in a big house in the Shimo Ochiai district of Tokyo, with Shukuko, the daughter of his first wife, now twenty-one, and Kiyoshi, who was sixteen, the son of the post-office clerk. As often as possible Yasujiro spent the night with his second family, the family in the shadows. Seiji was now three and Kuniko two.

He still incessantly searched out other women. It was becoming a problem, almost an addiction. No one knows how many unofficial children he fathered in these years; people in the company say that this was a particularly fecund period for him.

He especially liked women from Shiga, the home region where his mother had lived. It didn't matter how plain they were; in fact, the homelier the better. When the mood was upon him, anyone would do—he would ask employees for their wives, or seduce housemaids or clerks in the company, anyone.

The moment he saw Tsuneko, Yasujiro was smitten. She had a warmth about her that was irresistible. She was very beautiful in the classic Japanese way. At finishing school she was famous for the whiteness of her skin. Her face was elegantly rounded like the beauties painted by Utamaro. She had large liquid eyes, set wide apart, and the sweetest of smiles. She was no great intellect, but Yasujiro already had enough intellectual women. This one was born to be a lover, a mother and a homemaker.

It is not clear how Yasujiro seduced her. After graduating, she simply disappeared. Years later, when her friends from school heard what had become of her, they wondered why such a proud and beautiful girl would have chosen to become the mistress of a married man much older than herself. One asked her, and never forgot the answer: "I wanted extraordinary children. I didn't want to marry an average man."

In 1934, scarcely a year after she finished school, her first son, Yoshiaki, was born.

While these small domestic dramas were unfolding, the country was convulsed by the most bizarre and violent events. As Yasujiro went about his business—buying land, building roads, making housing developments—the news that came day by day was becoming more and more disturbing.

Mad Emperor Taisho had died in 1926 and been buried with great pomp and splendor in a distant suburb of Tokyo. The traditional coffin bearers came down from Kyoto by train, bringing the special imperial coffin with them, to perform their melancholy duties. The regent, Hirohito, then ascended the chrysanthemum throne.

Even before he became emperor, Hirohito's reign was bedeviled by violence. In 1923, the year of the earthquake, a fanatical youth had tried to assassinate him as he was passing Toranomon, Tiger Gate, on his way to the state opening of the Diet. Then in 1930 Prime Minister Hamaguchi, known as the Lion, was shot at point-blank range in Tokyo Station by a member of a right-wing group. He died the next year of his wounds.

Next came a succession of attempted coups d'état, some positively surreal in their extravagance. One, uncovered in 1931, involved launching an air strike on the cabinet and bombing them as they were sitting in session in the Diet, then bombing the headquarters of the two major political parties for good measure. Chaos would undoubtedly ensue and the army could with justification step in to restore order and establish a military junta.

Basically, the youthful right-wing officers who regarded it as their patriotic duty to protect their country had lost patience with the weak, vacillating elected politicians and decided to take matters into their own hands.

This became frighteningly obvious over the matter of the occupation of Manchuria. The government had got wind of a plot by the army to take over the whole territory and sent an urgent missive ordering them to stop. Unfortunately the chosen messenger, Major General Yoshitsugu Tatekawa, happened to be one of the plotters. He made a leisurely journey by boat and slow train to Mukden, then went to several geisha parties before finally delivering his message. By then it was far too late. There was a huge explosion on the Japanese-owned South Manchuria Railway, which, said the army, was clearly the work of Chinese saboteurs. Obviously, they said, there was no choice but to occupy the whole of Manchuria.

The next few years were dogged by madness. Japanese speak of the decade as the Dark Valley. Violence was becoming a fact of life. Early in 1932, a society of right-wing patriots called the League of Blood murdered a former finance minister and the head of the Mitsui zaibatsu. In May, uniformed naval cadets entered the residence of Prime Minister Inukai in broad daylight and shot him in the head. From then on, the army was effectively in control of the government. They chose the members of the cabinet, and nearly every prime minister was a general or an admiral. Although the façade of democracy continued and there were regular elections, the Diet members were expected to put aside party loyalties when they entered the government. Anyone who opposed the army risked assassination.

Throughout all these years Yasujiro was a member of the government. In election after election he was returned as one of the members for Shiga. For the two years, from 1932 to 1934, that Nagai was a member of the cabinet and minister for colonization, Yasujiro served as his parliamentary vice minister.[9] Nagai's position had shifted perceptibly. He was still opposed to Western imperialism. He felt that Asia needed to be led by a strong Japan and that colonization of parts of Asia was essential, in order both to strengthen Japan and to develop those colonies. He also still believed in reform; but he was beginning to think that the most effective way to effect reform might be to establish a single-party government, led by the military.[10]

While Nagai pondered the significance of the events that were transforming their lives, Yasujiro as far as possible simply got on with his job. He was a pragmatist and, even more, a survivor. He had entered politics in order to better himself, not in order to pursue some fervently held belief. Rather than wrestling with his conscience, he did his best to go on as if nothing were happening. He was genial, good-humored, he made friends wherever he needed to.

One of Nagai's responsibilities was to supervise the South Manchuria Railway in the newly formed Japanese colony of Manchukuo. As parliamentary vice secretary, Yasujiro went there on a tour of duty. The area, he wrote in his memoirs, was full of "bandits"—in other words, Manchurians, fighting their colonial masters. It was so dangerous that he had to ask the military to fly him in. "Well," they replied, "we've got an airplane. It's very old—but it can still fly. Will that do?"

The flight took ten hours in the old plane; it was impossible to set down even once because there were so many "bandits" on the ground. Yasujiro had barely arrived when a squadron of "bandits" one thousand strong attacked with heavy artillery and cannon. Somehow they had heard that a high official had arrived. The Japanese too were equipped with cannon and repelled the attack. "It was a dangerous time," wrote Yasujiro wryly, "to become a 'high official'!"[11]

Even though the military no longer needed to maintain even a semblance of consulting government officials, Yasujiro recalled, the army chief of staff in Manchuria, a Mr. Koiso, became a great friend of his and always treated him politely.

> One day the military had a completely impossible demand to make with regard to the railway. Young Koiso burst into my office. "You have to do this!" he bellowed, so loudly that his saber rattled violently. "Mr. Koiso, my friend," I said. "There's no need to get so excited, you'll damage your saber!" Koiso burst out laughing too. "I'm no match for you, vice minister!" he said.[12]

At home, the grip of repression was becoming tighter and tighter. From as early as 1925 the thought police had been in evidence, busily rounding up anyone who might be considered subversive or a threat to the established order. Communists were arrested, Communist sympathizers were arrested, people suspected of being Communist sympathizers were arrested. They were put in prison, mainly without trial, and some were tortured.

Little by little thought control spread—to books, newspapers, then to anything at all that smacked of the West. Jazz was suspect—finally the dancing had to come to an end. Cigarettes with names like Cherry or Golden Bat were given acceptable Japanese names. As for baseball, which was the great craze of the thirties, it had somehow to be turned into a Japanese game. It was renamed *yakyu* and every American term—"strike," "ball," "pitcher"—was replaced by a Japanese one.

It was not a time for selling second houses in the country; everyone had far more pressing things to think about. But by now Yasujiro had diversified into other lines of business more consonant with a nation moving deeper and deeper into crisis.

After the earthquake many people were desperate to move out of Tokyo. For developers it was a God-given opportunity. Along with many others, Yasujiro began to open up the wild country to the west of the city and turn it into suburbs. But by the time the first houses were ready to go on the market the situation had already begun to deteriorate. The economy was moving into recession, and not many people wanted to buy so far out of town.

The solution was to provide ease of access—a railway line, in fact. So Yasujiro decided to join the ranks of the railway barons. His first venture was fairly modest. He built a very short tramline with small red trams that trundled through the open country between the newly developed suburb of Kokubunji and Hagiyama, the nearest large town.

On the other side of Hagiyama was a very pretty area of open country surrounding a deep blue reservoir called Lake Tamako. There were green rounded hills, on one of which was a rather famous old temple with ornate carved pillars painted with dragons and two small pagodas with curving roofs. It was the perfect spot for picnics or Sunday outings. The only thing missing was visitors. Yasujiro extended his tramline out to the lake, named it the Tamako Line, and set to work to buy up land and transform the area into a suburban resort.

He had reckoned without the attentions of the other railways in the area. As far as land development was concerned, Yasujiro was an old hand, but in the railway business he was a rank beginner. And he had entered an arena crowded with ruthless competitors, all of whom were eager to muscle in and snatch his custom.

The two giants who dominated the area were the Musashino Line and the Seibu Line. Both were long-established railways with newly electrified trains shuttling between Tokyo and the towns in the western hills, skirting the Tamako area. Both were privately owned; in fact, the Musashino Line was owned by the townspeople themselves.

Compared with these, Yasujiro's little Tamako Line was a pygmy. As soon as he started developing the lake area, the two giants both built branch lines out to it. In the end there were three lines all going to this one small area, and the Tamako Line had hardly any passengers at all. Narrow-eyed, Yasujiro watched the antics of his two rivals and began to buy up stocks.

With the coming of the thirties and the Great Depression, all three found themselves in difficulties. The Musashino Line in particular had no holding company to support it and quickly went into the red. Things became so bad that at the close of business each day the debt collectors would arrive at every station on the line, push their way into the ticket office and remove all the day's takings in full view of the passengers. To make matters worse, one of the company's main creditors was the Tokyo Electricity Board, Tokyo Dento. Tokyo Dento didn't cut off the electricity supply to the line, but it decreased the voltage. As a result the trains limped along painfully slowly and the lighting inside was nothing but a dim flicker. Soon the *yure densha*, "ghost trains," were a standing joke. "The company had a truly terrible reputation," as Yasujiro writes.[13]

By now there were three main shareholders: two of the great zaibatsu conglomerates, owned by the Asano and the Yasuda families, respectively, and a certain Mr. Tsutsumi of Hakone Resorts Ltd.

Initially, writes Yasujiro, he wasn't interested in taking over the company. However, the first of his newly developed suburbs was on the Musashino Line, and he owned about one hundred *tsubo* (.08 acres) of land there. He had a meeting with Mr. Asano and Mr. Yasuda, both of whom begged him to put the company to rights. Reluctantly he agreed to do so.[14]

There followed seven years of negotiations. Eventually Yasujiro persuaded the creditors to write off 75 percent of their debts, and in 1938, the year after the Japanese army invaded China, the Musashino Line joined Hakone Resorts Ltd.

That left the Seibu Line. It was not until a few years later that Yasujiro was able to absorb that too. In fact, he spent most of the war years wrangling over it. He finally wrested it out of the hands of the Tobu group, one of the great railway corporations, in 1943, just as Japan's fortunes were beginning to turn sour. And, after the end of the war, he took the name Seibu for his entire conglomerate.

By 1937 no one could doubt any longer that Japan was at war. The crisis had begun one snowy morning in February 1936, when a group of over a thousand young right-wing army officers attempted a coup d'état. They seized the Diet buildings, the Ministry of War and the police headquarters and sent death squads to execute leading members of the government. Several they shot or slashed to death, including the prime minister's brother-in-law, whom the rebels mistook for the prime minister. Four days later they surrendered. Their leaders were given secret trials and summarily executed.

The following year the two main parties joined forces and campaigned for election on the platform of opposition to military rule. They won an overwhelming victory, but it was a worthless one. The army still controlled the cabinet. The elected representatives of the people were powerless. Prince Fumimaro Konoe, a compromise candidate who was acceptable to everyone—the army, the politicians, the bureaucracy and the business world—was installed as prime minister; and within a month Japan was engaged in full-scale war with China. By the end of that year most of the eastern edge of China, including Beijing, Shanghai and Nanjing, was under Japanese control.

In the only volume of his memoirs to be published in English, Yasujiro argued earnestly that he did all he could to oppose the military. Time and time again, he wrote, he stood up in the Diet to speak out against expanding the war and against the General Mobilization Law, which gave the government draconian powers to control industry, trade and finance. He even opposed Nagai, now minister of communications, who campaigned fiercely for the need to nationalize the electricity industry. He quotes the records of Diet proceedings in confirmation.[15]

After the war, of course, everyone took this line. The whole Diet, it seems, was composed of pacifists, all vehemently opposed in their hearts to the military buildup but powerless to stand in the way of the army. But people who knew Yasujiro in those days reiterate that he was always most concerned with economic matters. He was an opportunist. He had a business to build; he was not among those clamoring for war.

The invasion of China was always referred to euphemistically as the China Incident, but it was an incident that stubbornly refused to come to an end. For Japanese big business it was a bonanza. The zaibatsu, the huge family conglomerates that dominated the economy, swept into Shanghai and began snapping up Chinese-run industries there. But for the man in the street it was disaster. The whole economy was skewed to support the war effort. Rationing came into effect almost immediately and the goods available on the shelves of shops became pitifully few.

More than anything else it was the railways that saved Yasujiro. His land and building businesses floundered. But transport was the most essential service of all, and the railways thrived.

In 1940 he made one small venture that seemed insignificant at the time. The Tokyo terminus of the Musashino Line was in a rather rough neck of the woods called Ikebukuro, "Bag Pond." Just where the railway ended there was a shop that went under the name of Kikuya Department Store. It was big for the area, with about thirty full-time employees, and sold hardware, groceries and other everyday items.

Yasujiro bought Kikuya and renamed it Musashino Department Store. With the country on a war footing there was little he could do in the way of upgrading or refurbishing it. But he continued to buy land in the Ikebukuro area and waited for the situation to improve. After all, the war would surely end. And when it did, he would need land.

It was an optimistic view. The previous year Hitler had invaded Poland, plunging Europe into war. By the middle of 1940 half of Europe was in German hands. France was occupied and Britain seemed on the brink of surrender. The Japanese army had already negotiated an anti-Communist pact with Hitler's government. In September, exhilarated by the German successes, Japan signed the Tripartite Pact, forming a military alliance with Germany and Italy.

That year Yasujiro was busy setting his own life in order. For years he had led a very unsettled existence, moving from house to house and woman to woman. Part of the problem was money. Although he had plenty of property and even some railways, he never had any cash. He and Fumi would live in one house until it was ready to go on the market, then move on to another. The maids would hear him, from five o'clock in the morning, barking into the phone at his employees, then, after nine, when the banks opened, all bows and unctuousness, trying to keep his creditors at bay.

Partly it was inclination. In the summer in Karuizawa he had his women installed in different cottages around the town. In the evenings he would do the rounds. "He planted his seed all over," as Hoshino junior, the village squire, has it.

What shocked people was not his promiscuity—that was to be expected of such a successful and energetic man—but the fact that he slept with ordinary women. Respectable men restricted their activities to geisha.

As for the women, in those days they were very "service-minded," to quote Hoshino. It was their job to serve their man, to be quiet and obedient and not to complain. "He took very good care of all of them," adds Hoshino.

Yasujiro was now fifty-one; perhaps he felt it was time he had a home. For some time he had been preparing a house where he could settle down and live as a family with his children and the woman he thought of as his real wife—Misao.

Eighteen years had passed since Yasujiro first met the haughty schoolgirl with the long plait. Seiji was now thirteen, Kuniko twelve. As for Misao, at thirty-two she was at the height of her beauty—assured, graceful, always dressed in the most becoming of kimonos.

By now she was used to being the woman in the shadows, the "number two wife." She read, she wrote poetry, she raised her children, and she waited for the days when Yasujiro came to visit.

There was one wifely duty that she already performed. Every day she made a lunch and packed it into a lacquered wooden box. Yasujiro's driver would come to pick it up and take it to him at the office.

Fumi too made a packed lunch every day, and always put in salted salmon, which she knew Yasujiro loved. But Yasujiro always gave Fumi's lunch to his staff and ate the one that Misao had made.

By 1940 the house was ready, and by Japanese standards it was a palace. It occupied an enormous expanse of land in Hiroo, one of the most expensive residential districts of Tokyo. The building was a great barn of a place with a huge overhanging roof. At the back there were three storys, at the front two; the extra story at the back was at basement level, leading down into the garden. In design it was a traditional Japanese house, of wood and plaster with tatami-matted rooms. But the rooms were exceptionally large. There was an office for Yasujiro, private rooms for him, Misao and the two children, and enough small rooms upstairs to house maids, housekeepers and secretaries. Dotted around the garden were other houses where mistresses and their children could live.

The garden itself was spectacular. It plunged down a steep slope to a large pond shaped like Lake Biwa, the lake that borders Shiga, Yasujiro's home area. It was a magnificent wilderness of a garden, with stone bridges, lanterns, cherry trees and water lilies, even a peacock in a cage beside the house. Yasujiro moved in, taking the furniture from the house he had shared with Fumi, and Misao and the children moved from the little house in Mitaka.

Around the same time he also found a house for Tsuneko and her two children—Yoshiaki, who was six, and Yasuhiro, two—in Takagi-cho, ten minutes' walk or a few minutes' drive away.

For the women it must have been difficult. They had to practice that most Japanese of virtues, *gaman*—endurance, putting a brave face on it; for Yasujiro it was the fulfillment of all his unexpressed yearnings. He had never had a real family; now he had two, and a great extended family of mistresses, maids and secretaries. He had never had a home, he had mortgaged the family land; now at last he had one. He had finally fulfilled his promise to his grandfather to perpetuate the family line and ensure that the Tsutsumi name was a great one.

5

The War Years
1940–1945

Don't try to make money. If you really try to make money, money will
pass you by. Do what no one else wants to do, and money will come to
you.
YASUJIRO TSUTSUMI
My History

Less than a year after the signing of the Tripartite Pact, Japanese
troops were marching through the jungles of French Indochina. After
years of fighting in China, Japan's resources were becoming seriously
depleted. The military needed to ensure access to oil, rubber, tin and
other vital raw materials, all of which were in short supply.

The Western nations retaliated immediately. The United States,
followed by Britain and the Netherlands, imposed a total trade em-
bargo on Japan, cutting its lifeline to vital oil supplies. Next the
Americans demanded that the Japanese withdraw not only from Indochina but from China.

For Japan the choice was stark: either economic strangulation and
loss of its newly acquired empire or war. While Prince Konoe, the
prime minister, tried to negotiate with Washington, the generals prepared for war. There was little time to ponder. Oil was already running low. There was enough fuel to support the armed forces and the
domestic economy for only a few more weeks.

When negotiations with Washington broke down, Prince Konoe
resigned. His successor was the war minister, the rabidly militaristic
General Hideki Tojo.

With Tojo in power, war was inevitable. In December 1941 the Japanese launched a surprise attack on Pearl Harbor, quickly followed by attacks on Hong Kong and the Philippines. Within the first days of the war 90 percent of America's air and sea forces in the Pacific were destroyed or immobilized. Six months later the Japanese empire stretched from the Indo-Burmese border to the highlands of New Guinea. The whole country was galvanized to support the war effort. "Once the declaration of war had been issued, the war should be won," Yasujiro wrote.[1]

It soon became clear that the euphoria was premature. The first omens came in April 1942, when thirteen B-25s flew over Tokyo and demolished sections of the city. Gradually it became obvious that this was a war that Japan couldn't win.

For the people at home, life was becoming more and more intolerable. Even before Pearl Harbor there was rationing of rice, vegetables, fish and clothing. But in the big house in Hiroo lights still glowed and food and drink was plentiful.

For some reason the house conferred greater respectability on Yasujiro. Overnight he had found a new role: he became the genial host, rotund and affable, welcoming distinguished visitors into his home. Cabinet ministers, military men, members of the Diet and business leaders came to hobnob over dinner and enjoy the famous Tsutsumi hospitality. The house became an alternative meeting place for the cabinet. Finally the status of the house was recognized and it was declared the official guest house. Foreign allies stayed in the grand tatami rooms, ministers gathered to make decisions of state.

Of course, as a patriot, Yasujiro made no charge for the use of his house. What he had to gain was much more valuable. He was laying down a foundation of contacts and favors that would stand him in good stead no matter which way the war progressed.

In all this Misao was the perfect partner. Demurely clad in the most graceful of silk kimonos, she would greet the guests, all smiles and graciousness. She was cosmopolitan, sophisticated, charming, never at a loss for words, yet she never revealed her intelligence or her power. From the moment that she moved into the Hiroo house she was always at Yasujiro's side. Calm and competent, she helped him with his business; he consulted her in everything. She even bought his clothes for him, but, like a good Japanese wife, she made sure that he was always convinced that he was the boss.

Yasujiro had found what he was looking for: a strong woman. Of all the women in his life, Misao was the only one who had the measure of him. She alone could control him; she alone was stronger than he. She understood his powerful sexual appetite and she knew that this was the only way to bind him to her. She was perpetually seeking out new ways to seduce him, to stir his sexual passion.

According to the old cousin, Kamibayashi, from time to time Misao would allow her kimono skirts to open just a few centimeters, so that Yasujiro could glimpse what was beneath. Or she would run to greet him, pulling her kimono up to her knees. Or, most shocking of all in traditional Japan, she would press herself against him before leading him off to the bedroom.

And she understood his uncontrollable need to have new women—preferably coarse, primitive women, with rough hands and weather-reddened cheeks, from Shiga, his home country. It caused her great pain; many people speak of her suffering. But she turned a blind eye to it; and in fact there were usually maids from Shiga in the house. According to Kamibayashi it was she herself who ensured a regular supply; perhaps this was the only way in which she was able to retain control.[2]

To all intents and purposes, Misao was the official wife. She ran the house, she took care of the children's education, she organized the servants, she helped with the business. But when Yasujiro wanted to relax, he went to his second home in Takagi-cho, to the family in the shadows. The white-skinned, gentle Tsuneko now had three sons; the third was Yuji, born in 1942.

Around the time that Yasujiro established the house in Hiroo, he introduced the various members of his different families to one another. He began with the wives. Before he left Fumi, he asked her to *tsukiau*—to "get on"—with Misao. Fumi later commented on this, "To 'get on' would have meant that I recognized this woman as another 'wife,' so I absolutely refused. I always let Tsutsumi have his selfish way; but this I couldn't permit."[3]

Her friends tried to persuade her to divorce him, but she refused that too. Fumi wanted to avoid scandal; she also suspected that she would end up with no money at all.

Yasujiro had hoped to marry Misao, but instead all he could do was live with her, while Fumi remained his legal wife. When he moved to the big house in Hiroo, Fumi stayed in the house where they had lived with Shukuko, Yasujiro's first daughter, and Kiyoshi, his son by the post-office clerk Sono Iwasaki. Shukuko, now in her early thirties, had long since left home to get married, and Kiyoshi, who was in his late twenties, was soon called up and sent to join the army.

So Fumi, who was by now severely crippled with rheumatism and was developing cataracts, was left by herself. By all accounts her life was terrible. A woman from Shiga who had been their maid went to visit her shortly after war began with the United States. By then food was scarce in Tokyo, and she had brought vegetables and fruit from the country. She found her all alone, looking old and worn, wearing tattered clothes and socks with holes in them. When Fumi saw her, she began to weep. She'd been thrown out, she said, she had no money, not even enough for that day's rice.

Kamibayashi too reports that she had to move to Karuizawa during the war because she couldn't find enough food in Tokyo. There she used to visit him from time to time, complaining of the cold and of how little she had to eat.

Yasujiro was also busy introducing his children to one another. First Kiyoshi met Misao and the fourteen-year-old Seiji; later Seiji met Tsuneko and little Yoshiaki, who was seven.

For Yasujiro it was very simple. These were his children; this was his family. But for the children the shocking discovery that there were others led to dissonances that would be with them for the rest of their lives.

Kiyoshi was the first casualty. Of all the sons he was reputed to be the most brilliant and the most promising. He was a handsome young man, with a piercing intelligence that was almost painful. He had grown up quietly in the Shizuoka countryside with his mother, Sono Iwasaki. Then, when he was seventeen, Yasujiro recognized him as a member of the Tsutsumi family and brought him to Tokyo. He went to Tokyo University, the best university in the country, where he studied economics, and, until the war began, he worked as one of the directors of his father's company. It seemed obvious that he was being groomed to be Yasujiro's successor.

However, perhaps because of his intelligence, he could never forget for a moment that he was the product of a brutal, loveless encounter. His mother had never even had the recognition of a mistress. She had been discarded instantly. She was an embarrassment to Yasujiro, who had hastily paid her off and set up a marriage with a friend of his to give her belated respectability.

It was something he could never forgive, and it poisoned his relationship with his father. His bitterness was so pervasive that it was scarcely explicable by the sad circumstances of his childhood. Perhaps that was why Seiji invented the story of the Catholic nun who had been raped and committed suicide in a corner of the nunnery. Nothing less could explain such pain.

When the half brothers first met, Kiyoshi was already a grown man, polite, fastidious, soft-spoken. In *In the Season of Roaming*, the character of the elder brother seems to be modeled on him, and there are many tales of the endless clashes between the sensitive young man and the coarse, rough-spoken peasant of a father.

On one occasion, according to a story told in the novel, the family has gone to visit Magokyo in the army camp at Tsuruga, a bleak snowbound city on the Japan Sea coast. They take corned beef from Tokyo for a treat. Magojiro—closely modeled on Yasujiro—who is in a jocular mood, says cheerfully that he has heard that his son is to be sent to Botanko, on the border of Russia and China. For Magokyo this is terrible news. The chances of coming back alive from the front are getting slimmer by the day.

"I heard that if you get married you can come home in two years," he says nervously. He has already spoken to his father about a girl whom he is thinking of marrying.

The father, of course, is not interested in his fears, only in the sexual attractions of whatever woman he proposes to marry.

"Wouldn't do that if I were you," he grunts, taking a swig of tea. "I'd give up that woman. Looks like a fox if you ask me."

To try to cheer them all up he regales them with tales of his visit to China one summer.

"Summer's really hot there, because it's continental," he explains. "When I was there it was so hot that when a sparrow landed on the roof tiles it turned into *yakitori,* roast bird!"

But the Kiyoshi character seems to thrive on gloom. "If we go to war with Russia, we'll lose for sure," he persists in his soft voice. "I don't think I'll come back alive."

He goes on in this vein until finally the tough old father slams his cup down on the table in disgust.[4]

Two years later, after a stint in Manchuria, Kiyoshi was back. It was 1942, the year after Pearl Harbor, and Japan was on the brink of war with Russia. The soldiers were allowed to go home to say good-bye to their families before setting out on what was likely to be their last journey. Yasujiro decided it was time to use his position to save his son. One of his businesses was an ironworks supplying munitions to the army, and he gave Kiyoshi a job there as a manager; people in responsible positions contributing to the war effort were excused from military service.

The family had also decided that it was time Kiyoshi was married. According to Kamibayashi, it was Misao who arranged an introduction for him. The families met. The girl was from a good samurai family and both sets of parents were happy with the match. Everyone agreed that the future was so uncertain that they should have the wedding as soon as possible.

Yasujiro planned a splendid wedding for his eldest son and heir. In the traditional way the guests were to be friends of the parents, not of the happy couple, the function of marriage being basically a union of two families rather than two individuals. Everyone of any importance would be there. The most powerful men in the nation, from Prime Minister Tojo down, would attend. Despite the constraints of the war, it would be the most lavish of occasions. It would be a grand opportunity, in fact, to display his power and influence and reveal once and for all that he was an established figure, a leading member of society, equal to anyone.

Seiji tells the story in his novel. Magokyo, he writes, is less sanguine about the whole affair. The day before the wedding he goes to see his father. Whenever he speaks to him he always adopts a tone of icy politeness verging on insolence.

Bowing deeply, he says, "I am very grateful to you, sir, for your kindness."

"Tomorrow will be a great occasion," says the Yasujiro character in the novel, very pleased with himself. "I've invited more than six hundred guests. Mr. Tojo and the First Lord of the Admiralty are coming!"

"A great opportunity to promote yourself, isn't it?" mutters the son, curling his lip.

It is a moment before the father realizes what his son has said. "What?" he snaps incredulously.

"No, no," Magokyo insists. "I would be grateful if my wedding could be of some small help to you, sir."

The father reacts in the way he normally does on such occasions. *"Baka!"* he yells—"Fool!"—and, grabbing a wooden abacus, starts hitting him on the head with it.[5]

In his novel Seiji presents these stories under the guise of fiction. The names are different, but the characters are so close to the real actors in these dramas that it is hard not to believe that they are based on fact. Kuniko describes her brother Kiyoshi as a weak, sad character who couldn't stand up to Yasujiro, while Kamibayashi writes of his gentleness and brilliance.

In the end everything went ahead as planned. The wedding took place in Tokyo Kaikan, a magnificent domed hall resplendent with chandeliers, stained glass and lustrous gold screens. Kiyoshi was in traditional *hakama*, his bride in a succession of silken kimonos, and Yasujiro made the welcoming speeches. The guest list was a roll call of the great and powerful. As far as Yasujiro was concerned, he was doing the best that could possibly be done for his son. He was introducing him into society, recognizing him as his heir, making him known to the most influential men in the country.

For the first time, too, the various strands of Yasujiro's family were gathered together under one roof. Fumi attended as the official wife and Kiyoshi's "mother." Misao and her children and Tsuneko and hers were seated separately, not with the relatives but in the section reserved for "friends of the father."

By the middle of 1943, wartime conditions were becoming increasingly difficult. Many Tokyoites were fleeing the city and heading for the relative safety of the mountains. Yasujiro sent Tsuneko and her three boys to live in their cottage in Karuizawa for safety. As a member of the government, he had to stay in Tokyo. Business had to go on, he had to oversee his employees. And besides, even war offered opportunities for profit and advancement.

Many years later, Misao wrote of this period, "Tsutsumi believed that the country's fate was our fate, so we didn't run away even for a day. And of course the people in our company were all working really hard every day, so we couldn't even think of running away and leaving them."[6]

For those who opted to remain in Tokyo, life was being transformed at an alarming rate. People used to the basic amenities of civilized living—hot baths, good food, entertainment, efficient public transport—had to learn how to cope with hardship and deprivation. Soon even money began to lose its value; even if you had it there was nothing to spend it on.

One of the most devastating shortages was fuel. Without fuel there were no cars, no trucks, no buses; and the trains, which were still running, were overflowing. It became very difficult to transport food from the countryside to Tokyo, where it was needed. There were various ingenious solutions. Charcoal-fueled taxis sputtered around the streets, puffing out black smoke and fumes, and there was even an attempt to make fuel out of pine sap.

It was lack of fuel that led to one of the most absurd yet harrowing crises of all. It was exactly the kind of situation that Yasujiro relished. No doubt in later years he regaled dinner companions with the story of how he single-handedly solved one of wartime Tokyo's major crises; and he also wrote about it with gusto in one of his memoirs, *Thirty Years of Struggle*.

The problem was sewage: Tokyo was in danger of being buried under an avalanche of human waste. In those days there were no flush toilets in Tokyo; Japan has always been behind the West in this respect. And human excrement was a valuable commodity, not to be wasted. Before Tokyo expanded to unmanageable proportions, farmers would go from house to house, wheeling carts, clearing out the tank beneath the outside toilet and paying for the contents, which they took away to use as fertilizer. As the city spread, they came by horse and cart. And later still the government set up a system of local workers and trucks to drain the septic tanks. Some of the waste they sold to farmers and some was taken by ship and dumped in Tokyo Bay.

Once fuel became rationed, the trucks no longer ran. The young men who had driven them were called up, and in every house the septic tank was full to overflowing. This was no minor problem. It caused enormous ructions in everyone's lives. Yasujiro dwells on the situation with relish:

> Because the Tokyo government couldn't come and collect feces and urine, this sometimes led to domestic disputes. Wife: "You've used it again—we're in trouble! You have to keep our house toilet for me and the children!" Husband: "If you say so. But I can't do anything, it just comes out!" Wife: "So wake up early and use the company's toilet!" So the husband holds his stomach and rushes to the company's toilet—and when he gets there it's full.[7]

To make things worse, lack of fuel meant that ships had to dispose of their load of waste much closer to the city than they had before and ended up polluting areas where fishermen fished or harvested seaweed. The mayor of Tokyo, a Mr. Odachi, was bombarded with complaints. He confided to his friend Mr. Tsutsumi, "My head is full of feces. From morning to evening, whether I'm awake or whether I'm asleep—feces, feces, I'm always thinking about feces." As Yasujiro points out, despite the food shortage, Tokyo produced 38,000 *koku* (1.7 million gallons) of human waste a day. "Tokyo," he declaims, "was under feces attack!"

It was the perfect opportunity for him to demonstrate his devotion to his country, put himself in a situation where the government would be under a heavy obligation to him and maybe even make a profit. In fact, it could be considered "an order from heaven."

Understandably his staff was unenthusiastic. Sewage collection was traditionally the task of the lowest grade of society, the *burakumin*, the Japanese equivalent of untouchables. It was not a job that respectable people wanted to do. But Yasujiro was unmoved. He came up with a simple but inspired solution. Tokyo needed to get rid of its waste; farmers needed fertilizer. The solution was to transport fertilizer to the farmers and fresh vegetables back to Tokyo. Both the Musashino and the newly acquired Seibu Line linked Tokyo and the rural land to the west. So Yasujiro designed special freight cars made of wood (all rolling stock was made of wood in those days) with a mouth at the top and a tap at the bottom. At various stations along the two lines he built storage tanks, positioned under the tracks, so that the freight cars could pass directly above them. All the staff had to do was turn the tap and the waste would pour out.

A grand inaugural ceremony was held for the new service on November 21, 1944, at Iogi station on the Seibu Line. The minister of the interior, the minister of agriculture and forestry and several other dignitaries attended, and a curious crowd gathered. The first of the Gold Trains, as they were called, drew up over a large storage tank. Instead of breaking a bottle of champagne, the minister made a signal, the tap was turned and with a huge *zaaaa* the "gold" gushed out. The crowd roared. "It was a truly spectacular sight!"[8]

Yasujiro makes much of the difficulties that followed: the farmers turned out to prefer chemical fertilizer to human waste and the station storage tanks were overburdened with "gold." Still, the service continued for nearly ten years, until 1953. Mayor Odachi presented Yasujiro with an official letter of thanks and a copper sculpture of an ox, chosen, he thinks, because he was born in the year of the ox and was also famous for being as stubborn as one. As a more concrete reward, Seibu, as his company now was known, received the huge sum of ¥30 million. Yasujiro, of course, plowed it all into land.

The last year of the war, 1945, was a hellish time for everyone. Officially the line was that the war would be endless and Japan would win, but behind closed doors the business community, bureaucrats and many politicians had been counseling surrender for some time. General Tojo had been forced to resign as prime minister the previous July. Inexplicably, he was replaced by another general equally determined to fight on. By then Japan had almost no navy left. As a last, desperate measure, military planners came up with the idea of sending out a force of volunteer pilots as suicide bombers, *kamikaze,* named after the "divine wind" that drove off the last attempted invasion of Japan, by Kublai Khan, nearly seven hundred years before. Among other things, it would save on precious fuel; there would be no return trips.

Life in Tokyo was an unending nightmare. Nearly every night the air-raid sirens wailed. Nearly every night B-29s cruised the skies, raining down firebombs on the city. It was like a fox's wedding, people said, or a grand display of fireworks. The air was full of dancing lights and fiery shooting stars. In a single night, on March 9, more than one hundred thousand people were burned to death. The

whole of the old city, to the east of the Sumida River, was a wasteland of ashes.

Many people thought that Japan was bound to lose and that the
Americans would invade the country. They sold everything they
had—house, land, everything—and fled to the countryside. Money
and portable possessions were worth holding on to. But who could
think of land when life itself was at risk?

There was one person at least who was buying all this land. While
the sky was full of fire, Yasujiro sat in the underground shelter in his
garden, a telephone in each hand, negotiating prices.

"Michio-*san*," he said to Michio Nagai, the son of his friend Ryutaro Nagai. "The war will not continue forever. Now we have air
raids. Everyone sells their land and escapes from Tokyo. But when
peace comes again everyone will need land."[9]

Nagai explains:

> In spite of the fact that many people were leaving Tokyo because of
> the bombing, he strongly believed the war would be over anyway.
> And if that was the case it was wise to purchase cheap land at the
> time. So underground he had many telephones to find out what
> land would be available. I don't think he had a particularly good
> idea of what was going on on the military front. He knew that Japan
> was under bombing. From the standpoint of a person like Tsutsumi
> it was a chance to buy land.

And still the government refused to surrender.

Toward the end of May there was a final concerted blitz on central Tokyo—government buildings, the offices of the zaibatsu and big
business, the homes of the wealthy, the Imperial Palace itself. More
than five hundred B-29s appeared like a plague of giant black insects
in the sky above the city. The ground was shaking with the impact of
the bombs as if it were another earthquake. The noise, dust and
smoke were terrifying: buildings collapsed with a roar or broke into
flames, bombs exploded, guns went off, people screamed in panic as
they ran for shelter. The sky itself seemed to be on fire.

Yasujiro was lying in the underground shelter having his shoulders massaged by his favorite maid from Shiga when bombs began to
rain down on the big Hiroo house and its garden. Perhaps, he writes,
because it was a state guest house, more than ten bombs landed on it.

It was a wooden house and it went up in flames like a matchbox. Even the peacock was on fire. Misao and the children rushed around with water trying to put out the fire until they finally gave up and fled to the shelter.

As Seiji tells the story in his novel, Magojiro, the Yasujiro character, is still resting, oblivious to all this. Then one of his staff runs in to report that there are people at the gate, asking for refuge in the garden.

"Don't let any of them in," he yells. "If anyone tries to force their way in, hit them, it's trespass. . . . The house can burn down, but no one's going to put a foot on my land!"[10]

Then he rolls over and lies snoring as the house burns to the ground.

The devastation after that attack can hardly be imagined. The Ginza and the areas around it for many miles were a wasteland of blackened rubble. The main building of the Imperial Palace had burned down. The roads were pitted with holes, the tram tracks buckled and broken. The whole city was at a standstill.

It was like a reversion to an earlier, more primitive age. One of the small side houses in the garden at Hiroo had survived, and the family moved in there. The landscaped garden with its pond and stone bridges was turned into vegetable patches, where they planted potatoes, pumpkins and sweet corn. Survival was all that mattered.

In July the Allied leaders issued the Potsdam Declaration, demanding that Japan surrender unconditionally or face "prompt and utter destruction." In fact, secret negotiations had been going on for some time; the only stumbling block was the future position of the emperor, which was still not clear.

Then in August news began to filter through the censorship that some terrible catastrophe had happened in Hiroshima. At almost the same moment the Soviet Red Army was sweeping into Manchuria. The meaning of the words "utter destruction" was becoming clear. Two days later there was news of another extraordinary explosion, this time in Nagasaki.

The end came shortly afterward, on August 15. It was a sultry, windless day, heavy with heat. No one who was alive at that time has forgotten where they were and what they were doing when the emperor's high-pitched, rather unearthly voice came crackling out across the airwaves: "Despite the best that has been done by everyone—the gallant fighting of military and naval forces, the diligence and assiduity of our servants of the state, and the devoted service of our one hundred million people—the war situation has developed not necessarily to Japan's advantage. . . ."

According to Seiji's novel, the family sits around their radio listening in silence.

"We'll all be castrated," says the Kiyoshi character with a certain grim glee.

"Anyway, let's go to bed," says the father. "You can't do anything unless you're healthy."[11]

The Imperial Link
1945–1950

In those days, we had a great many servants, more than fifty in all. With such a big household the house was fairly large too. My memories are very faint now, but thinking back, if I count the number of rooms, there must have been about sixty, not including the ten toilets. For someone that has never lived in a big house, it's difficult to imagine, but living surrounded by all those empty rooms, I felt very lonely. . . . Nowadays we live in a small house, with my oldest boy and his family on the second floor above us. They are always coming to visit us; it's much more lively and fun. TSUNEYOSHI TAKEDA (FORMER PRINCE TAKEDA)
In Inose, *Portrait of the Emperor*

The war had ended—but no one dared imagine what the future might bring.

For the first days after the emperor's momentous announcement the country was numbed. People stumbled around the shattered streets as if sleepwalking. The August heat was unbearable. Flies buzzed and mosquitoes gathered in swarms. Everything they had fought for had been lost, all their sacrifices had been in vain. The whole world they had known had been destroyed. Everything had completely fallen apart. A haze of dust hung over the broken rubble of Tokyo. The buildings that still stood were crumbling and blackened, burned-out skeletons of trams and buses lay abandoned along the roads, wires and telegraph poles and electric cables were fused and melted. The desolation was so complete that no one could even begin to think of rebuilding.

The most pressing need—the one thing that shook people out of their apathy—was the need for food. Throughout the war the country had relied on imports of rice from the occupied territories of Korea and Taiwan, but now that Japan no longer had an empire, these sources of food had dried up. For days at a time in Tokyo there was little but yams to eat.

The Tsutsumis were better off than most. They had land, they had their garden, they had shelter, but like everyone else they were overcome with a numbing helplessness. Yasujiro, the strong, self-reliant man who had built an enormous business out of nothing, had at a stroke lost control of his own destiny.

In this strange limbo people awaited the arrival of their conquerors. No one could imagine what they would do. Some feared dreadful retribution, and there were several plots among the military in the days after the announcement to make a last suicidal stand against the invaders. There was such fear of rape and pillage that when the first American troops landed at Yokohama they found themselves in a ghost town. Every house that still stood was locked and shuttered and all the young girls from the local girls' high schools had been evacuated to the most distant countryside.

It was two weeks to the day after the emperor's announcement, on August 28, 1945, that the supreme commander for the Allied Powers, General Douglas MacArthur, stepped out of his plane onto the tarmac at Atsugi air base. He paused at the top of the steps to look around before he descended. He was in uniform but he wore no tie and he had a corncob pipe in his mouth. There was no bodyguard and he was unarmed; his only attendants were his private staff. It was a grand moment of theater. This was no avenging conqueror. A new act was about to begin.

MacArthur seemed a man that the Japanese could talk to. He carried himself like a shogun—big, imposing, brimming with charisma and confidence—and in Japan he had practically the powers of a god. His brief was staggering in its simplicity. It was to reshape the Japanese mind, to take the pieces of this shattered country and put them together in a brand-new way—to form a democratic society, a country that would never again go to war.

In concrete terms, as a first move, he was to disarm and demilitarize the country, to have all military equipment destroyed, to dismantle the last vestiges of the Japanese empire in Asia, to instigate free elections and to encourage the development of a free economy in every way possible. It was an enormously ambitious program, rendered all the more difficult by two handicaps. Firstly, MacArthur and his fellow officers within the occupation forces had a very limited understanding of Japan, the Japanese language and the complexities of its political and business structures. As the postwar prime minister

Shigeru Yoshida later commented, "The occupation was hampered by its lack of knowledge, and even more so perhaps by its generally happy ignorance of the amount of requisite knowledge it lacked." And secondly the only way in which they could make any long-term impact on the country was by working through its existing institutions—those very people who had the most to lose by any changes or reforms in society. The government, in other words, remained the same as before the war.

Those at the very top, however, who had led the country into war had to go. Soon after the surrender documents were formally signed, the former prime minister General Tojo—who had been such an honored guest at Kiyoshi's wedding—together with many of the leading members of the government, was arrested to be put on trial for war crimes. Of the remaining members of the government, all those who were deemed to have cooperated with the war effort were removed from their positions for an unspecified period of time.

Yasujiro was among those purged. He was at home when he got the news. All that day and for many days thereafter he sat, slumped in his chair on the veranda, staring at the garden.

For the old order, those who had got fat on the war, they were fearful times. No one knew whose assets would be seized, or who would be the next to be purged.

For the younger generation and all those who had been opposed to the war even if they had not dared to speak out, it was a time of exhilaration. They were helping to build a new society, shaping a new Japan out of the ashes of the old. Early on in the occupation the thought police were swept away. All the Communists, Communist sympathizers and suspected Communist sympathizers who had been imprisoned under the old regime were freed. Sanzo Nosaka, almost a Che Guevara figure, a hero of the revolutionary left, set off on his triumphal return after nearly fifteen years' exile. He had lived in Moscow and spent the last years of the war in China, with the Chinese Communist party, making converts out of captured Japanese soldiers. The stifling censorship of the war years was lifted and Marxist tracts and revolutionary literature circulated freely. Anything that might further the democratic spirit—revolutionary gatherings, fiery speeches, calls for strikes—was encouraged in those early, idealistic days.

While Yasujiro slumped gloomily in his chair, the younger members of the family were afire with all the change that was in the air. They marched, they chanted, they read every issue of *Red Flag* avidly, they attended the huge Communist rally in December and like everyone else they stamped and shouted and cheered themselves hoarse when the emperor himself was denounced and his name added to the long list of war criminals.

Yasujiro, never one to be brought down for long, was busy hatching plans to install Kiyoshi in his place as a member for Shiga, when he began to hear rumors that Kiyoshi's wife, more than anyone else in the family, was associating with the Communists.

The relationship between father and son was already intolerably strained. Immediately after the wedding, the young wife, as the bride of the Tsutsumis, had moved into the big family house in Hiroo. At first she tried to keep herself aloof from the suffocating atmosphere of the place, but it was difficult to ignore the nightly comings and goings, the maids sliding open the door to the master's room, the mistress storming out, the endless quarrels and recriminations, and the icy hatred of son for father. Then Yasujiro began to take notice of this proud and beautiful samurai girl who had joined his household. Already gossip and rumors had begun to circulate. The maids and housekeepers whispered that Kiyoshi was infertile or, even worse, that he had not even been able to consummate his marriage.

It was an irresistible opportunity. Yasujiro was now in his midfifties and nearly as big as a sumo wrestler. Still, he had no doubts about his powers over women. In Seiji's novel, the father, Magojiro, accosts his son's wife one day and, in his usual blunt way, says, "Have a child with me, or two—make it two! If you do it now no one will ever know if they're mine or his!"[1]

After that the young woman refused to have anything further to do with him. Kiyoshi himself was at breaking point. His hatred and resentment of his father poisoned every minute of his waking day.

Yasujiro couldn't bear to have any woman reject him. It was like the pain of his mother's departure all over again, as if his manhood itself were under attack. Worse, his country was defeated, his life's work in ruins, and he himself disgraced. Then, to cap it all, someone informed him that Kiyoshi's wife had been seen with a young man who was a member of the Communist party. His household was full of spies and counterspies, alliances and factions. Presumably it was someone with a grudge against the haughty young bride who betrayed her.

To Yasujiro, the doughty old capitalist, this was a shocking and intolerable betrayal. There was nothing he hated more than Communism. Seiji, in his socialist phase, once described him as not just bourgeois but extremely right-wing. In his novel, Seiji tells the story in dramatic terms. The father summons the young couple to his study and makes them kneel before him while he sits cross-legged in his formal *hakama*, glaring at them.

"This is a serious matter!" he bellows. "This woman is a bride of the Tsumura house!"

Magokyo keeps his head humbly lowered. But his wife has been contaminated by the newfangled egalitarian ideas springing up around them. She refuses to behave like a modest Japanese maiden. Instead she stares the old tyrant straight in the eye.

This is rank insolence. The Yasujiro character jerks his chin at her and snaps, "You! Divorce her!"

Magokyo, on his knees, buries his head in his hands and presses it against the tatami. He can't move.

"Oi! You! What's it to be, then?" the father yells. "You want me to throw you out too?"

He heaves himself to his feet and raises his hand to hit him. Then Magokyo's voice emerges from the tatami. "Actually . . . actually . . ." he blurts, "we just bought an American washing machine."

"What?" the father snarls incredulously.

Magokyo's words come tumbling out. "Even though we live in the country, we managed to get a washing machine from the American military, so we're starting to lead really quite a cultured life. So please be merciful, please overlook this one occasion, in two or three years we'll be able to get a fridge. . . ."

In the novel, the Yasujiro character can't bear to be treated like a fool. His son always behaves like this, with exaggerated deference, ignoring whatever his father has to say and coming out with some absurd, completely irrelevant remark. It drives him to a frenzy.

"Boss . . ." comes the voice of the young wife, calling the old man by the name that everyone in the company uses.

Reduced to impotent fury, the father can do no more than splutter, "Damn you, you bitch!"[2]

It was the end of spring 1946. The first grim winter had passed, in many ways more terrible an ordeal than the war and all the bombing had been. Life had been reduced to the barest of essentials—how to keep warm, how to find food. Sixty percent of all the housing in the city had been destroyed. The buildings that were still intact were unheated, and the miserable makeshift shelters where many had to live, cobbled together out of broken bits of wood and rubble, were no protection at all against the icy winds and snow. People died of exposure or pneumonia, or they died of the plagues that overran the stricken city—typhus, smallpox, cholera.

Some died of starvation; others pushed and fought their way onto the overcrowded trains that went out to the countryside in order to buy precious rice to smuggle back to their families in the city. The trains were so packed that the glass in the windows cracked from the pressure. People traveled hanging on the outside of the carriages, and when they got back to Tokyo they were liable to have their rice confiscated by the police if they were caught. Women sold their kimonos, peeling them off layer by layer like the layers of a bamboo shoot; they called it "bamboo-shoot living." One kimono, preferably one of the brightly colored ones that young girls wore, would buy enough rice and sweet potatoes to feed a whole family for three or four days. Everyone got thinner and thinner.

Black markets sprang up around every station in the city, selling smuggled rice and foreign goods to supplement the meager rations. One of the biggest was in Ikebukuro, where Yasujiro had bought his small department store.

The Tsutsumis were better off than most. They were rebuilding their big house and there was always plenty to eat. But they couldn't avoid being affected by the grim struggle for survival outside the walls of the house. They too felt as if their lives were teetering on the edge of some unspeakable abyss. And it threw into relief all the divisions between them.

One day—according to Seiji's fictionalized account—Magokyo's wife goes too far. The family is all together at the time. The father and son have been quarreling again.

"No matter how much Magokyo's mother hated you, that doesn't stop his being your son!" she spits at the burly old father.

The room goes silent. The old man never discusses his son's

mother. It is the most taboo subject of all. Even worse, the girl has brought it up in front of the other children. He grabs her by the hair, shouting, "I'll kill you, you bitch!"

The next day the family is summoned to the study. Magojiro, the Yasujiro character, is kneeling very formally in his starched *hakama*, knees apart and hands on his knees, as the family members file in and take their allotted places. Grim-faced, he brings out a document brushed in Magokyo's hand. Holding it out in front of him stiffly with both hands, the father intones the measured formal sentence: " 'I hereby separate myself from the Tsumura family and renounce completely all rights as the eldest son to any assets or other inheritance thereafter.' "

He pauses.

"You agree?" he snaps.

Magokyo, on his knees, stares at the tatami and says nothing. His wife answers for him. "We agree," she says, as clear and cold as ice.[3]

The old cousin, Kamibayashi, too, told the tale.

Kiyoshi, as Kamibayashi recounts, nicked the little finger of his left hand with a razor blade, squeezed out a few drops of blood into a teacup, dipped the forefinger of his right hand into the cup, then slowly pressed it on the document to make a blood-red fingerprint. Together he and his wife rose to their feet and left the room and the house forever.

After this Kiyoshi virtually disappears. He is by far the saddest figure in the Tsutsumi saga. His life was permanently blighted by the bitterness that surrounded his birth and by his father's bullying. For a time he and his wife lived in their small house in the Tokyo suburbs. In his novel, Seiji describes how Hajime, the Seiji character, goes to visit them. He finds them in a grim house, which they have barely tried to make comfortable. Water seeps through holes in the roof and the tables and chairs are still encased in plastic. They haven't bothered to unpack them. Here in this miserable environment, Magokyo sits, eaten up by his own unhappiness.

Yasujiro made sure that Kiyoshi always had work and an income; after all, he was still family. But he was demoted again and again. Before the quarrel he had been one of the directors of the whole group. First he was made president of Omi Railways, one small company within the group, and later, humiliatingly, became a mere section chief in a company that Yasujiro had taken over after the war, Asahi Chemical Fertilizers.

He left Tokyo and moved to Omi, where the family had sprung from. Many years passed, but his bitterness never decreased. Finally, as an old man, he retired to Tokyo, to a small flat provided by his brothers. He and his wife live there still, on the seventh floor of a block of flats in a quiet, rather run-down neighborhood twenty minutes' walk from the big house in Hiroo, where Seiji now lives in splendor. He turned eighty in 1994; the couple never had children. He is fiercely reclusive and jealous of his privacy. While the family has become wealthier and wealthier, none of their wealth, fame or notoriety has cast any shadow on him. While they are dogged by the tabloid press, he refuses even to speak to any journalists. He seldom goes out; he is seldom seen. Most people, in fact, do not even know that there ever was an eldest son: they believe that the family line passed straight from Yasujiro to Seiji. His brothers take care of his material needs, and once a year he emerges to attend the New Year's observances and pay his respects at the tomb of the father who treated him so badly.

The convulsions within the big Hiroo house were like a mirror image of the anarchy outside its walls. All over the country, sons, fired by the new spirit of radicalism, were turning against their fathers, criticizing them for their conservative views and their support for the war. Families were falling apart; the whole structure of society seemed to be under threat. And everyone was hungry. Rations were meager, prices shooting up at a frightening rate and wages fixed at pitifully low levels.

Then, in May 1946, the distribution system seized up completely. For nearly three weeks no rice at all arrived in Tokyo. It was the final blow. People had had enough. Emboldened by the occupation's encouragement of democracy, strikes and demonstrations, they took to the streets. There were marches and mass meetings. Carrying placards proclaiming GIVE US RICE, a stream of demonstrators paraded up and down outside the Diet and the prime minister's residence.

Finally on May 1 nearly half a million people massed, not outside the Diet but in the sacrosanct grounds of the Imperial Palace itself.

Led by the Communist leader Sanzo Nosaka, they demanded to know what the emperor had to eat. A delegation went into the palace and scoured the imperial larder. While the people were starving, they reported, the emperor received daily supplies of milk, chicken, pork, eggs and butter.

"This is what the emperor and his officials eat," they shouted. "Do you think they understand the meaning of the word 'hunger'?"[4]

One man brandished a placard reading WE HAVE PLENTY TO EAT, YOU PEOPLE CAN STARVE, using the word *chin* for the royal "we," a word only the emperor can use. Written with another character, *chin* also means "penis." The crowd roared with derision.[5]

Before the occupation no one had ever dared to criticize the sacred person of the emperor, let alone poke fun at him. Now in the new liberal climate, with all the heady talk of democracy, the young and the left wing could voice their resentment at the unimaginable wealth and privilege in which he lived.

As MacArthur and his colleagues among the occupation forces struggled to draw up a blueprint for the new democratic Japan, they were much exercised about the question of the emperor. Was he a war criminal? Should he be tried for war crimes? Or was he an innocent bystander, a token ruler who had had no choice but to rubber-stamp the decisions of the military? In the mass of the people he still inspired the utmost devotion and respect, and to have laid hands on him would have been to provoke an uncontrollable rebellion.

In the end, the best course by far seemed to be compromise. As a first step, the emperor had already renounced his divinity. "The ties between us and our people . . . are not predicated upon the false conception that the emperor is divine and that the Japanese people are superior to other races and fated to rule the world," he declared in the Imperial Rescript of January 1, 1946; though, given the difference between the concept of "god" in Japan and the concept of "god" in the West, whether that meant what MacArthur thought it meant was another matter. Still, at least it was no longer an offense to look upon the face of the emperor, nor would people suffer punishment if they failed to close their shutters when he passed down the street.

The new constitution of March that year defined his position more sharply. The emperor, it stated, was no more than a constitutional monarch, "the symbol of the state and of the unity of the people," whose role was purely ceremonial. As if to prove that he was a mere human, the emperor set out on a tour of the country, to give everyone the chance to look upon the imperial visage.

As a final blow, MacArthur's officers were determined to remove as much of the emperor's vast private wealth as possible. And, almost incidentally, they decided to strike out at a small group of people whose riches and decadence appalled the democratic-minded Americans. With a few strokes of the pen, their lives were to be cruelly transformed, with enormous repercussions on the fortunes of the Tsutsumi family.

Emperor Hirohito headed a large extended family of aunts, uncles, cousins, nephews and nieces. All were descended from Emperor Meiji and all enjoyed lives of unimaginable luxury. They lived in splendid palaces on vast estates of rolling country practically in the center of Tokyo. If one looks at a modern-day map of Tokyo, all the green patches, denoting parkland, were once the estates of imperial princes; and besides this these relatives also owned vast tracts of land in rural Japan, particularly in the north. None, of course, was required to work. All were supported by generous stipends paid from the public purse. Naturally they paid no taxes on any of this wealth, and the government was also committed to furnishing their households with servants.

All in all there were fourteen families. Three were the families of the emperor's brothers; the other eleven were his uncles and cousins. Two of the families in particular became inextricably intertwined with the Tsutsumis: the Asaka family and the Kitashirakawa family.

In the 1910s and early 1920s, the golden years of Taisho democracy before the Great Earthquake, two of the most dashing young men around town were Prince Yasahiko Asaka and Prince Naruhisa Kitashirakawa. Both sprang from the noble house of Fushimi, which also furnished the wife of Emperor Hirohito, Empress Nagako, and both were married to the beautiful daughters of Emperor Meiji. Prince Kitashirakawa married Meiji's seventh daughter, Princess Fusako, and Prince Asaka married Princess Nobuko, the eighth. (All Meiji's fifteen children were the offspring of concubines; the empress had no children.) After the nuptials each princess received, as a sort of dowry, a parcel of land—estates in Tokyo, tracts of land in the northern countryside.

Initially Prince Asaka and Prince Kitashirakawa were neighbors, along with a cousin of theirs, Prince Tsunehisa Takeda, who was married to Princess Masako, the sixth daughter of Meiji. The three princes had adjoining estates in Takanawa, the southernmost section of Tokyo, overlooking Tokyo Bay, with acres of well-kept lawns, elegant flower beds, woodland and ponds. High on the hill, overlooking the panorama of the bay and the Tokaido highway, lined with inns and teahouses, winding away along the coast, were the three magnificent palaces.

Prince Takeda's palace still stands. It was designed by the Japanese architect Tokuma Katayama in 1911 in the style of a French château with Italianate flourishes. It is a grandiose two-story building of pale-gray stone, with a front porch big enough for carriages to draw in, ornately carved balustrades and a steep mansard roof edged with iridescent copper. From the colonnade outside the second-floor drawing room you can look across the spacious wooded tracts of land with their beautiful gardens that were once the estates of the three princes.

In 1922, the year before the Great Earthquake, the two princes, Asaka and Kitashirakawa, set out for what was intended to be a two-year stay in France. Prince Kitashirakawa's wife, Princess Fusako, went with them. In Paris the handsome young Japanese princes and their glamorous princess were welcomed into the highest levels of society. They settled into a grand residence beside the Bois de Boulogne, and attended all the balls and parties of the season.

While Princess Fusako filled her wardrobe with the latest Paris fashions, Prince Kitashirakawa was eager to indulge his passion for fast cars. Soon after they arrived he took possession of a soft-top Bugatti.

It was the car that was to lead to disaster. One fine spring day—it was April 1, 1923—the three set out for a spin in the country. Prince Kitashirakawa was at the wheel, with the French chauffeur in the passenger seat beside him.

At four-thirty in the afternoon they were in Normandy, hurtling through a village called Perriers-la-Campagne, near the town of Bernay, about ninety miles west of Paris. On a sharp curve—to this day known as "Kita's curve"—the prince swerved to avoid an oncoming car, lost control of his own car and smashed at full speed into an acacia tree. Both he and the French chauffeur were killed instantly. Prince Asaka was thrown clear but suffered multiple fractures of his left leg, while Princess Fusako, in the backseat, was severely injured with both legs broken.

Prince Kitashirakawa lay in state at the Japanese embassy in Paris for three weeks before being shipped home to Japan for cremation. Princess Fusako and Prince Asaka were taken to a hospital in Paris, where they stayed for more than a year. Asaka's wife, the gentle Princess Nobuko, set sail from Japan to take care of her husband.

Two years later, in December 1925, Asaka and Nobuko sailed for home, determined to take something of that Paris world, which they now felt so much a part of, back with them.

Their first project was to design a summer house. They owned some land in the Sengataki area of Karuizawa, directly opposite Hoshino Spa and just below the hillside on which the brash young speculator Mr. Tsutsumi was busy building cheap country cottages. By now Yasujiro was a member of the Diet and a pillar of the community.

The imperial couple called in an architect who had studied in England and was *au fait* with exotic Western styles. He designed a rather grand two-story house akin to an Edwardian vicarage, of wood and stone with chimneys and tiled chalet roofs.

Prince Asaka's next project was far more ambitious. His palace in Takanawa had been damaged in the earthquake, providing him with the perfect opportunity to build the palace he had always dreamed of. Instead of the Takanawa land, the couple decided to build their new palace in the nearby area of Shirogane, on the estate that Nobuko had received as her dowry.

In 1933 it was all completed. Prince Asaka threw a housewarming party in celebration. For six months the great halls and dining rooms of the palace were filled with some of the most splendid parties in Tokyo. As the guests arrived—military men, foreign diplomats, statesmen and leading business figures—they would gasp at the glass angels and mosaic floors, the sumptuous ornamentation, the marble fireplaces and etched mirrored doors, the sheer mannered opulence of the elegant rooms. Princess Nobuko would greet them, dressed, as always, in the latest evening gown from Paris; she never wore kimonos. As they entered the great hall, their senses would be assailed by the subtle lighting, the textured walls and the musky scent of perfume, wafting from the huge white "perfume tower," an urn of Sèvres porcelain, taller than a man. Then after dinner the servants would turn on the gramophone and, led by the prince and princess, the guests would dance—the waltz, the foxtrot, the tango.

Then—a mere six months after the dream palace was completed—the gentle Princess Nobuko suddenly fell ill and died, at the age of forty-four. Prince Asaka never recovered from the blow. The parties stopped. Alone with his children, his servants and his ruined leg, he grew morose and became a stickler for punctuality. Sometimes, when he had been drinking, he would reminisce about his wife and the happy days in Paris.

Toward the end of 1937 the fifty-year-old prince—thinner now, sterner, more punctilious than ever—was ordered to the front. He was to set out for China forthwith, to take command of the Japanese forces fighting their way past Shanghai; and he was to ensure the capture and subjugation of Chiang Kai-shek's capital, Nanking.

The events that followed were the most dreadful of the entire war. Nanking was captured on December 13. Japanese troops rampaged through the city, massacring over one hundred thousand Chinese prisoners of war and civilians.

How much Prince Asaka can be held responsible for the behavior of his troops is a moot point. In any case, his imperial status ensured that he was never tried for war crimes. After the war he walked free, a respected member of society.

In any event, MacArthur found another way to punish the imperial princes. In October 1946, MacArthur's officers pushed through an ordinance to cut the imperial family down to size. It was too big, it was a drain on the public purse, and besides, the existence of such a grossly privileged class went against all the vital notions of democracy and egalitarianism that the Americans were eager to instill.

The Imperial House Law was signed by the emperor on January 16, 1947. In convoluted legal prose it defined the role, the duties and, almost incidentally, the limits of the imperial family. All but those descended directly from an emperor through the male line were to "leave the status of imperial family members." They would receive a sum of money "for the maintenance of dignity as persons who have been members of the imperial family, in one-time payment to be made at the time when they leave their status." And they were to be subject to the constitution and to the same laws as everyone else.

On October 13, 1947, the details of the settlement were announced. Of the fourteen imperial households, only three, those of the emperor's three brothers, would remain within the imperial family. The rest, eleven families in all, a total of fifty-one persons, were to leave the imperial family and become commoners forthwith. Automatically they would lose all the privileges accorded to them as members of the imperial family: the right to have land and servants provided by the state, the right to receive a stipend, the right of freedom from taxation.

All but one of the families were allocated a sum of money as a last and final settlement from the government. The exception was the family of Prince Yamashina, which was given nothing because the prince had been in the military. How the other princes escaped being stigmatized as ex-members of the military remains one of the many mysteries of the chaotic postwar days in Japan.

At first sight the settlements were more than generous, and an enormous drain on the impoverished public purse. But out of these settlements each family was required to pay a crippling tax bill, levied on their lands and fortune. And they were to pay immediately. The deadline was the day after, October 14, 1947.

Prince Asaka and his family were allotted almost ¥4 million, about ¥400 million or $4 million by modern reckoning. For comparison, in 1946 the prime minister's monthly income was ¥3,000 and the average wage about ¥300. (By 1948, in those days of raging inflation, the prime minister was collecting ¥25,000 a month.) But the prince's tax bill, levied the very same day, amounted to ¥8.5 million, more than twice as much as his allowance.[6]

For the princes—now commoners—it was a terrible blow. Like the British royal family, none had ever had to dirty their fingers with money before. They were innocents, who had no idea how to function in the world of commerce or business.

Before the fateful day the settlement was announced they had been casting around helplessly for ways to make money. Some tried selling their belongings. Prince Higashikuni put his antique inkstones and priceless silks on the market; but in those grim postwar days, no

one wanted useless stones or silks, they wanted food. Prince Asaka—
now plain Mr. Asaka—put his luxury imported car up for sale.

But much more drastic measures were needed if they were ever to
raise the cash to pay these gigantic tax bills. And October 14 was
looming. At this point Yasujiro steps into the picture.

Yasujiro and Asaka had been neighbors in the Sengataki area of
Naka-karuizawa, where Yasujiro first built his country cottages and
Asaka had his summer house, for more than twenty years; it is impossible that they would not have been acquainted with each other. Anyway, the princes' plight was common knowledge. Even the
leathery-faced farmers of Naka-karuizawa, passing one another on the
village street, would shake their heads and suck their teeth and mutter, "So the prince has come to this!" And there were plenty of voracious entrepreneurs, waiting to snatch at a fragment of the princes'
fortunes.

Still, many things remain unclear about the transactions that followed. The Japanese journalist Naoki Inose has done detailed research on the subject, which he published in his best-selling book
Mikado no shozo (Portrait of the Emperor). The outlines of the story
are as follows.

Whether or not Asaka knew Yasujiro, the steward of his household, a certain Toraichi Nakada, certainly did. It was probably
Nakada who made the first approach. Yasujiro was legendary in the
Sengataki area. He had transformed it, he had turned the impoverished farming village into a minor holiday resort. Clearly he was a
canny businessman, who could seize an opportunity and would not
be afraid to take a risk. Above all, he was a man with access to capital.

We can imagine that Nakada went to visit him, either in the big
Hiroo house or in his offices in Karuizawa. The two—Yasujiro, big
and imposing in his bulky suit and beginning to bald a little; Nakada,
a thin, rather desiccated man, slightly younger than his host—put
their heads together. Here was a situation that from the ex-prince's
point of view was desperate. Yasujiro was no philanthropist, but if he
could be persuaded there was a profit in it, nothing would hold him
back. Even Nakada might be able to make a yen or two out of the
transaction.

The steward's key card was the prince's lands, and in particular
the prime piece of land in Sengataki, where the prince had his

Edwardian-style country house. To Yasujiro, land was irresistible. He was convinced that it was the only sure investment. For years this had been the most eccentric of views. In the years leading up to the war, the value of land had hardly risen; from 1937 to 1945 it rose by barely a percentage point, while retail prices tripled. Now at last it was beginning to seem that his obsession with land had not been so foolish after all. With the war over, the country was in the grip of uncontrollable inflation; and the value of land was shooting up at a dizzying pace. In the five years between 1945 and 1950 it was to multiply more than two-hundredfold.

Over several meetings the two arrived at a deal. It was the steward Nakada who conducted all the negotiations on behalf of the prince, who was far too grand to sully himself with such mundane matters. Before the business was concluded, Yasujiro paid a courtesy call on the Asaka family and offered to buy their country residence in Sengataki. He appreciated that they were in financial difficulties and hoped that he could be of assistance.[7]

Here the story becomes a little murky. Did the stiff old aristocrat—inexperienced in practical matters—realize that Yasujiro was actually buying his property? Or was he led to believe that Seibu was simply taking over the management of the estate in exchange for an immediate cash settlement? Or—to follow a trail which leads deep into conspiracy theory—was the whole deal part of something far more devious?

According to one school of thought, within Japan's rigid social structures a rough peasant from Shiga would never have been allowed to buy imperial land. Could it be that Yasujiro, the old prince and Nakada between them pulled the wool over everyone's eyes, and that the Tsutsumis were—and still are—mere retainers of the princes, who in reality still own the land and pay the family a salary to manage it? In other words, could it be that it was yet another of the complex maneuvers by which the Japanese tried to foil the occupation's plans to change the established social structure? When MacArthur's officers broke up the zaibatsu, they ordered them to sell their assets to the public. In fact many of the assets were bought by loyal retainers, with the intention of later returning them to the family that had run the conglomerate. Could this have been a similar ploy, to leave the imperial estates intact?

The retainer theory is more than a little far-fetched, but it indicates the amount of speculation surrounding the Tsutsumis and their activities. In any case, the deal that Nakada and Yasujiro finally arrived at was a very Japanese one. It was far from just a cold matter of buying and selling or the signing of a contract. It was the building of an enduring connection.

Curiously—fuel, perhaps, for the conspiracy theorists—Nakada proved loath to talk about the arrangement he had reached with Yasujiro all those years before. In 1985 the investigative journalist Naoki Inose tracked him down to his home in Ogikubo in the suburbs of Tokyo and found a ninety-year-old man, dressed, as old men do, in the traditional navy-blue kimono, suspicious and taciturn. It was a cold winter day, Inose recalls, but whenever Nakada's son started to turn on the gas heater, the old man stopped him, hoping to drive away the unwanted visitor.

Inose pressed Nakada to admit that the prince's property now belonged to Seibu and that it was Nakada who had sold it to the company.

After much probing, Nakada snapped, "We didn't sell!"

Inose, who had researched the land registry, insisted there was full documentation that the right of ownership had passed from the Asaka family to Tsutsumi and the Seibu company.

Finally Nakada's son responded, "My father doesn't like words like 'buying and selling.' It wasn't 'buying and selling.' We entrusted the management of the estate to Mr. Tsutsumi, that was all."

"If he was just a manager, doesn't that mean that he couldn't sell the land?" Inose asked.

"It wasn't a business relationship with Mr. Tsutsumi," Nakada insisted, "it was a spiritual bond . . . almost a request from the prince."

"So afterward he'd take care of them completely. . . ." added the son.[8]

In fact, according to the land registry, the Asaka family sold the Sengataki estates to Kokudo Keikaku, National Land Planning Corporation, part of the Seibu group, on August 12, 1947. Kokudo Keikaku were recorded as the owners on August 14, 1947, exactly two months before the prince's deadline for paying his tax bill.

One can assume that the price was extremely low. Land was still not worth much at the time. In fact, the price was fairly irrelevant.

The prince did not want to receive a large lump sum that would be taxable. Instead, Yasujiro agreed to "take care" of him and his family—to provide a monthly salary, the equivalent of the interest on the capital, in exchange for the property. He also took care of Nakada: in 1950 he offered him a job as an auditor in Seibu, and Nakada remained there for the next thirty-two years.

In hindsight Asaka's children regretted that they had lost the property. Japanese journalists, led by Inose, insist that the ex-prince was cheated, that Yasujiro took advantage of his gullibility and effectively stole the land. But when Inose interviewed Asaka's son, a saddened, rather eccentric old man in a black cardigan and sandals, he refused to make any such statement. No matter how much Inose insisted, he would commit himself no further than to say, with typical Japanese hesitancy, "If we hadn't sold our land to Seibu it would have been a bit different. . . ."

Asaka, however, was satisfied with the deal. His financial embarrassment was over, at least for the time being. He and Yasujiro became firm friends, and he suggested to his imperial cousins that they too should let Mr. Tsutsumi help them with their tax bills. Yasujiro too must have been happy. In exchange for paying out a monthly stipend, he had made himself master of one of the most desirable and exclusive pieces of property in the Karuizawa area. And he had expanded his social network into a higher dimension. The decline in the princes' fortunes was a technical matter; they were still the imperial family. To be linked with them was bound to give immense kudos and respectability to Yasujiro and his growing empire.

The connection with Asaka opened up broad new avenues for Yasujiro's growing ambition. The Sengataki palace was only a beginning: there were the other princes' lands—spectacular lands, some of the best in the country, which the aristocracy had always jealously guarded for themselves. Within the rigid structure of Tokugawa society, it would have been inconceivable for a member of the lower classes to acquire such land, even if it were for sale. Now, in the chaos and confusion after the war, anything was possible. The princes' discomfiture was unprecedented. Anyone, even a peasant from Shiga, who had the presence of mind and the cash, could lay his hands on the imperial land. This was democracy with a vengeance.

Then there was the imperial family, for all the fluctuations in their fortunes still the pinnacle of society. The more he grappled onto them, the closer he became to them, the more Yasujiro would prosper. That was how the zaibatsu had risen: not merely by the accumulation of wealth but by making links with the aristocracy and the imperial family. It would be a long, slow process, but it was a new goal for Yasujiro's ambition.

Even as he negotiated for the Sengataki estates, Yasujiro already had his eye on Asaka's main house, the glorious Art Deco palace in Shirogane. He expressed an interest to Nakada. Then he waited.

Asaka's financial problems were far from over. All his life he had lived lavishly on the munificence of the government's bottomless purse; now he was reduced to counting every yen. He was reluctant to let go of the grand house, which he and his princess, Nobuko, had planned with such love and care, and which embodied so much of their past life together. However, it was beginning to seem as if there was no alternative.

First he let the house. The prime minister, Shigeru Yoshida, took it as his official residence, and was determined to buy it. He had long admired it; it was one of the most famous and beautiful buildings in Tokyo, and a perfect example of Art Deco.

By 1950 Asaka's fortunes were once again at a low ebb. He summoned his children and announced brusquely, *"Urimasu!* I'm selling!"* Nakada was put in charge of the sale. Despite Yoshida's bid, the magnificent palace with its spreading lawns and tennis courts went to Mr. Tsutsumi of the Seibu company. Only a few corners of the grounds, which had already been bought by the Ministry of Finance, were not included in the sale. Ownership of the property passed to Seibu on October 7, 1950, for the price of a mere ¥700 per *tsubo* (3.95 square yards).

The old prince had no cause to be dissatisfied. Yasujiro agreed to preserve the house exactly as it was; he also said that for the rest of his life Asaka should continue to live in his beloved palace and treat it as his home; and he provided him with a car, driver, secretary and all the servants he needed. In later years, whenever Yasujiro went to visit, Asaka was every inch the princely host. Everyone chose to forget that the property actually belonged not to him but to Mr. Tsutsumi, the guest.

Yasujiro kept his promise. Seibu took care of Asaka until he died in 1981, at the age of ninety-four. And the two—the rough-spoken thickset businessman and the taciturn old prince—remained friends and golfing companions. Asaka, with a handicap of four, became famous as one of the best golfers in Tokyo; and he designed the O-Hakone golf course for the Seibu development in the Hakone area.

As for the Kitashirakawas, neither the daredevil prince nor his son lived to see the ignominy of the postwar years. After the dreadful car crash in France, people sometimes murmured that the family was jinxed. In 1940 young Prince Nagahisa Kitashirakawa, then aged thirty, was posted to Inner Mongolia; all the imperial princes were required to engage in active service during the period of hostilities. There he was in a plane crash in which he was killed instantly.

His bereft family was left without an adult head of the household. His successor, Prince Michihisa Kitashirakawa, was three years old. At the end of the war he was still only eight, and the responsibility for settling the family's tax affairs fell to the household steward, one Makoto Mitobe.

Initially the huge and splendid palace, complete with sentry boxes and storehouses, was sold to the government to be used as the official residence of the Speaker of the Lower House.[9] The young ex-prince, his sister and his widowed mother, reduced to the rank of commoners, moved to a small residence in the Shibuya area of Tokyo; though, as the pictorial *Asahigraph* magazine observed dryly, "they still have two butlers, a driver and four maids, so compared to the ordinary citizen their life is really not so tough."[10]

Meanwhile, as the princes' fortunes fell, Yasujiro's rose. In 1951, after a long campaign in which he asserted that he had been vehemently opposed to the military buildup and to the war, he finally succeeded in being depurged. He immediately reentered politics and was once again voted into the House as the member for Shiga. On May 18, 1953, he was selected to be Speaker.

As a result he found himself installed in the Kitashirakawa palace. From its grand Palladian windows he could look over the Takeda estate, which he had already bought, and the Kitashirakawa estate, which was even larger. Naturally he began to covet both the land and the palace. The difficulty was that the government already owned the palace and had also rented more than half the land. The Kitashirakawas were not entitled to sell either. So Seibu engaged in some complicated and rather underhand maneuvers. The first thing was to court the steward, who was in charge of the family finances. Accordingly, the directors of Seibu sedulously engaged him in games of golf, built up a relationship with him and suggested that Seibu might be able to take care of the Kitashirakawa family and their staff just as they had the Asaka and Takeda families.

On August 24 that same year, 1953, Seibu Railways, a member of the Seibu group of companies, purchased the Kitashirakawa land, twelve thousand *tsubo* (9.8 acres) at ¥8,000 per *tsubo*. They agreed to pay a deposit followed by the interest but not the capital, thus ensuring that the family's taxable income remained low. Over the following twenty-five years, the value of the Kitashirakawa land was to rise to ¥3 million per *tsubo*. But Seibu continued to pay nothing but the interest on the original purchase price. Whether by luck, foresight or, as Japanese journalists would have it, fraudulence, Seibu had got an outstanding bargain.

In fact, the whole purchase had to remain secret during the entire period of time in which the government rented the land. It was not until 1979 that Seibu officially took over the right of ownership from the Kitashirakawa family, the nominal owners. As for the palace, Yasujiro never succeeded in buying that. Had he done so, it might be standing to this day. It was demolished to make way for an undistinguished eleven-story building that provides accommodation for members of the House.

Thus it was that Yasujiro and his Seibu group of companies became the owners of some of the most spectacular buildings and the most beautiful tracts of land in Tokyo. They were far from being the only company buying imperial lands at the time. The rival Keihin Kyuko Railway, for one, bought the land in Takanawa, where the Asaka family had had their first home, by that time occupied by Prince Higashikuni. The beautiful estates of Prince Fushimi in Akasaka, one of the most expensive parts of Tokyo, were purchased by the wealthy Otani family.

But Seibu bought the most. Besides the Asaka, Takeda and Kitashirakawa lands, the company also acquired the elegant Art Deco palace of Prince Higashi Fushimi outside Yokohama, the spectacular palace of King Li of Korea in Akasaka, designed by the British architect Josiah Conder in 1930, and other palaces around Tokyo and outside it.

And they bought land. As well as their estates in Tokyo, the ex-princes also owned vast tracts of wilderness—moorland, mountain and forest, land covered in wildflowers, land where foxes and badgers roamed, mainly to the north of the country, in the Tohoku and Hokkaido regions. While land prices in Tokyo were already beginning to soar, land in the countryside was still worthless. No one lived there, nothing could be done with it, no one wanted it.

No one, that is, except Yasujiro. Steadily he and Seibu (by now their fortunes were so closely entwined that they were largely indistinguishable) increased their land holdings. They owned, by now, far more than any individual prince had ever owned, far more than the richest tycoon had ever dreamed of owning. And this was the land that Yasujiro was to use as the foundation for his Seibu empire.

For Yasujiro it was enough simply to own the land. Another generation could decide how to use it. As for the splendid palaces with their many bedrooms and bathrooms, he turned them into hotels. Merchants, businessmen, farmers, anyone who could afford it could spend a night in the luxurious bedrooms that had once been the private quarters of princes. The public came to dine in the grand halls and hushed chambers where the princes had entertained counts, lords and foreign potentates, and clattered about the high-ceilinged corridors where once only soft-shod servants had crept. It was another small step toward democracy.

The first palace that Yasujiro bought, Asaka's Edwardian villa in Karuizawa, had a different fate.

It all began with the crown prince's American tutor, Mrs. Elizabeth Vining. In the ferment of reform after the war, it was decided that Prince Akihito, then a solemn little boy of eleven, needed to know about English, democracy and Christianity. Mrs. Vining, a Quaker, was invited to Japan to teach him and arrived in October 1946. A sweet-natured, gentle woman, who writes about all her experiences in nothing but the most glowing of terms in her book *Windows for the Crown Prince,* she quickly became not only a teacher but a friend and confidante to him. She named him "Jimmy" so that, in her class at least, he would feel no different from the other boys, and for him her presence provided a welcome relief from the rigid life within the palace walls.[11]

When the heavy heat of summer descended on Tokyo it was natural that the imperial household should arrange a cottage for Mrs. Vining in Karuizawa. She was given a large, comfortable house, no doubt far grander than Yasujiro's simple cottage developments in neighboring Naka-karuizawa, where Asaka also had had his palace.

In the summer of 1949 Akihito went to visit her. He had never before been to Karuizawa and spent several happy days climbing the hills, playing bridge and tennis, going on excursions and receiving guests. He liked the place so much that the following year the imperial household decided to look for a house for him there.

At the time Asaka's summer villa had been requisitioned, as were many of the hotels in Japan's hill resorts, and was being used as a rest hotel for the occupation troops, under the management of Seibu. For the crown prince it was the perfect retreat. It was a few miles from the bustle of central Karuizawa, secluded and easy to guard, deep within larch forests at the end of a long curving drive. It was grand, with eight bedrooms, enough to sleep Akihito and his retinue in the Western style he had come to prefer. And it even had tennis courts so that he could enjoy his favorite sport.

Yasujiro, no doubt, was more than pleased to accede to the imperial request. And hence developed a curious relationship. While the villa remained the property of Seibu, it was given over every summer to the exclusive use of the imperial family, who became nonpaying guests of the company. In the winter it was thrown open to the public, though after some years this practice ceased; it is now well guarded throughout the year.

The villa was named the Karuizawa Prince Hotel. And though whenever they were in other parts of the country the imperial family stayed in their own private property, in Karuizawa they always stayed at the Prince Hotel. Later Yasujiro took the name Prince for many of his hotels: Prince Takeda's French-Italianate château was to become the Takanawa Prince Hotel, King Li's splendid Art Deco palace the Akasaka Prince Hotel and Prince Higashi Fushimi's palace the Yokohama Prince Hotel. Undoubtedly the imperial presence added cachet to the name.

To underline the imperial link, the Prince hotels also took the chrysanthemum as their emblem. In fact, this was the Takeda family crest: when Takeda sold his French-Italianate château to Seibu he gave them permission to use it. But by chance it is very similar to the imperial chrysanthemum, the symbol of the emperor.

Thus, through quirks of fate and clever planning, Yasujiro was spinning a web of connections, binding him and his Seibu group ever closer to the imperial family. He even became entangled in the fringes of the great imperial love story that brightened the postwar years.

Some years after Akihito first visited Mrs. Vining in Karuizawa, he spent his summer vacation, as usual, in the Prince Hotel there. It was 1957, and he was a solemn, rather chubby-faced young man of twenty-three. One fine day he went to play tennis on the Seibu-managed public courts in the town center. There he found himself matched against a young girl of startlingly radiant beauty.

Her name was Michiko Shoda. Akihito fell in love, and the Japanese people with him. It was a perfect fairy tale. Never before had a member of the imperial family, let alone a future emperor, even considered marrying a commoner. Until the end of the war such a match would never have been permitted. Their love was like a symbol of the new Japan, the decline of the old rigid order and the coming of a new democratic world in which the crown prince could fall in love with a miller's daughter.

She was not, of course, really a miller's daughter, although the press liked to refer to her as such. Her father was a wealthy industrialist who owned a flour-manufacturing company; the family lived in one of the most exclusive parts of Tokyo (in an area, as it happened, developed by Seibu); and she had attended one of the country's best universities. Their meeting was not even really chance. It was orchestrated by a man who had been the prince's mentor since he was a boy, his adviser and director of his education, Shinzo Koizumi, who felt that the imperial family needed both a new image and new blood.

Still, for the Japanese people it remained the great romance of the postwar years. Everyone began to play tennis. And Karuizawa, where the two had met, became the most fashionable resort in Japan.

The War of Hakone Mountain
1950–1961

A traveler who visited Japan from abroad once remarked: "I was impressed by the beauty of Mount Fuji and by the roads that run through the Hakone Mountain." God created the Mount Fuji; Seibu built the Hakone highways.   Seibu PR booklet, 1961

In the stillness of the Hakone mountains on a bitter December day in 1942, it was as if nothing had changed for a thousand years. The hills around Lake Ashi were in shadow, though the sky behind was still pale and translucent; and the waves that lashed the shore were the color of ink.

High on the hill above the lake, at the top of a long flight of rough stone steps, was a complex of small squat buildings—Hakone Gongen Shrine, dedicated to Ryujin, the dragon god of Hakone. The last rays of sunlight glinted on the copper roofs and bloodred pillars, on the carved dragons, gold ornamentation and intense green fretwork on the gates. It was a powerful, mysterious place, set deep in forests of cedar and cryptomeria.

The shrine was deserted, a bitter wind whipped across the stone courtyards and rustled the thick straw ropes hanging across the archways; but at the bottom of the steps, standing beside the lake and beside the huge red *torii* gateway that rose out of the water, were two figures. One was rotund like a bear or a *tanuki*, the Japanese badger legendary for its sexual prowess, and wearing a baggy, rather ill-fitting suit. The other was a younger, slighter man, square-jawed, with glasses.

Turning to the younger man, the older one yelled, "Look here, young Ogawa, I'm the dragon god incarnate! Okay? Anyone who gets in my way in Hakone is in for trouble—got it?"[1]

Then he swung around, opened his fly and pissed into the lake in a great steaming arc. The younger man looked on, impressed despite himself at this display of hubris. Surely even Yasujiro Tsutsumi could never get away with such presumption.

Although it was the elegant hill resort of Karuizawa that raised his social standing, it was Hakone that Yasujiro truly loved. Ryujin, the dragon god, was his chosen deity, and he would sweep down to Hakone in his car from Tokyo to pray for success in his business or help against his enemies.

In the centuries before the shoguns, when warlords battled to carve up the country, people used to say, "He who controls Hakone controls the world." It was the highest point along the great Tokaido highway between Kyoto and Tokyo, a place where enemy troops were liable to swoop down from the mountaintops or lurk in the deep passes. It was also the most beautiful place in Japan—few disputed that. Soaring over its corrugated hills and mist-filled ravines, rising behind the jewel-like blue of Lake Ashi, was the ethereal shape of Mount Fuji. Wherever you were in Hakone, it dominated the landscape.

People compared Hakone to a beautiful woman. The warlords had tussled over who should have it; and Yasujiro too wanted Hakone for himself.

That day when he brought young Eiichi Ogawa down to Hakone to pay his respects at the shrine of his patron deity, he was engaged in another struggle. He was trying to take over Toshimaen, a pleasure park just outside Tokyo. Ogawa, an employee of Yasuda Trust Bank, had the job of defending it. Ogawa had had the temerity to buy up Seibu stocks; he had bought all the stocks in Musashino Railway held by financial institutions, 50 percent in all. Clearly he needed to be shown what kind of a man he was dealing with.

Yasujiro won that battle. Shortly after the episode at Lake Ashi, Ogawa sold him back all the stocks and also sold him Toshimaen. But he still had to pay the price for his presumption. Ryujin was not going to take such insulting behavior lightly.

What happened next was so memorable that it forms the first section of Yasujiro's memoirs, *Thirty Years of Struggle*. Part I is entitled "How I didn't die of a serious illness," and Chapter One, "My urine stops." He begins his first page with the dramatic words: "It was March 20, 1943. That afternoon, even though I hadn't had any problems until then, suddenly my urine stopped. No matter how hard I pushed, nothing would come out. Something was strange!"

Wryly he dwells on his appalling predicament. No matter how hard he tried, he couldn't urinate. He took a hot bath, but still nothing happened. As the hours passed, the pressure and the pain became unbearable. Finally he yelled to have an ambulance called and was rushed to a hospital. There were yet more delays, until at last, at 4 A.M., a tube was inserted into his urethra and nearly a quart of urine emptied out.

There was worse to come. The doctor diagnosed hypertrophy of the prostate and stones in the bladder. The disease, he said, was incurable, added to which, little by little it was likely to bring about inflammation of the urethra, bladder and kidneys, a condition known as uremia. "Once you have uremia," he warned, "you won't live a day."

"Suddenly," writes Yasujiro, "everything went dark in front of my eyes. This was a death sentence! Until yesterday I was healthy, I worked hard with no problems—but suddenly, this death sentence!"

What was he to do? He could indulge all the extravagant whims he had ever had—but that would pall after a few days, and he would be left with this death sentence hanging over his head. Finally he concluded, "If I have to die, I will work until the last minute. Work, work, work. I want to use my short life for the people, the world, the country. And at the end I'll make a dazzling farewell to the world!"

His enemies all observed maliciously that he had suffered a fitting retribution from the gods. Every day, as if in punishment for all his past misdeeds, he had to suffer the pain and humiliation of having a rubber tube inserted into his penis to draw out the urine. And every day, for every second of the day, he was haunted by the fear of death.

As he had vowed, he used this sudden discovery of his own frailty to concentrate his mind on his work. The harder he worked, the less he remembered his physical condition. Bombs fell over Tokyo. He organized the Gold Train, to take human waste to the countryside and vegetables to the city; he lay in his underground shelter, making land deals over the telephone; and after the war was over he negotiated with the princes to buy their land. And all this time he was in pain.

Through his illness, Yasujiro was becoming more and more dependent on Misao. As he said later, she was more like a mother than a wife to him. It was her nimble fingers that fed the tube gently into his urethra to draw out the urine, the most intimate of tasks; no one else could make him relax in the same way. Wherever he went, she had to go too, to perform this vital task. She planned his menu, varying it every day to make sure he was properly nourished. And she even chose his clothes. He was obstinately careless about his appearance, and unless she checked, would go out with his shirttails hanging or his clothes inside out. Their daughter Kuniko said that when she walked down the street with him, she always tried to keep her distance so that no one would know that this slovenly fellow was her father.

Nine years passed like this. Yasujiro grew weaker and weaker until finally he had to stop for breath several times when he climbed the stairs. By now it took two hours to extract just a few drops of urine. The doctor warned him that he had little time left to live. "Sometimes I thought, let me just urinate once to my heart's content and I'll die happy," he wrote.

There was one last chance. There was an operation to remove the hardened flesh from the urethra; but it had a very low success rate, and if it failed he would undoubtedly die. But he was so near death anyway that it seemed worth taking the risk.

It was Misao who made the decision to persuade him to go into the hospital. Every day she nagged him to have the operation. She found fellow sufferers who had had it and were now healthy, and brought them to talk to him. Finally he agreed. It was June 1952; he was sixty-three. He paid a last visit to each of his companies, and even engaged in some gentle bouts of judo so that they would remember him looking healthy.

The operation was surrounded by ill omens. For a start it was scheduled for Friday 13. That day, in the morning, one of the big orange carp in the pond of the Hiroo house died and was found floating on the surface, and an *udonge* flower, a flower of bad luck, blossomed in the toilet. Despite all this, the operation was a success. Yasujiro, never one to miss an opportunity for bombast, boasted that the hardened flesh removed from his urethra was the biggest and heaviest ever recorded in Japan. He was the *yokozuna,* the grand champion of prostate sufferers.

Finally he had paid the penalty for his hubris. He was no longer under sentence of death. He returned to perfect health and shortly afterward, in May 1953, became Speaker of the House.

Although the dragon god had exacted his revenge, Yasujiro's involvement with the mountains and lake of Hakone was far from over. By now, despite his illness, he was deeply embroiled in a fierce conflict that was to dominate the rest of his career. The battle over Hakone became one of the most celebrated sagas of the fifties; and everyone who lived through that era still chuckles over tales of the enmity between Pistol Tsutsumi and Goto the Thief.

It began in 1920, when Yasujiro was a young man, just setting out on his career as a land developer. In those days Hakone was the preserve of the privileged few, the Baden-Baden of Japan. The rich and leisured came to take the waters and pamper themselves at its luxurious spas.

Here, not long after he built his first cottages at Karuizawa, Yasujiro began to buy land. He bought tracts of wild undeveloped country—the mountains covered in rough forest that rose around Lake Ashi, the moorlands spreading toward the foot of Mount Fuji. It was unwanted, unused land. The price was low, and Yasujiro would pay only the smallest of deposits. By the time he finally came to pay the capital, the value of the land had risen, and all the farmers grumbled about his sharp practices.

By the end of the war, Yasujiro and his Seibu company owned, or held in permanent leasehold from the government, more than half of the whole expanse of Hakone. In terms of figures, they owned about 2 million *tsubo* (1,600 acres) and held two thirds of all the government land in the area.

Yasujiro had long before started building the facilities that would turn the area into the country's prime resort. One project of which he was particularly proud was the road that he had started building in 1930. He liked to boast that it was the best private motor road in Japan. It stretched seventeen miles from the coastal resort of Atami through the mountains to the heart of Hakone, it took thirteen years to build, and it was always in perfect repair—there was never a single pothole along its entire length. Buses owned by Yasujiro's Izu Hakone Railway Company ran up and down the road.

Yasujiro was indisputably the king of Hakone. What he lacked was the ability to transport visitors from Tokyo out to his newly developing resort. As a start he decided to run a bus from Odawara, where the trains from Tokyo terminated, to Kowakudani, in the heart of the Hakone mountains, where his territory began. In September 1947, two years after the war ended, he applied to the Ministry of Transport for a license to extend his bus line along this route.

However, there was another company that until now had monopolized transportation from Tokyo through Odawara into Hakone. This company was called Odakyu (short for *Oda*wara *Kyuko*—Odawara Express). It was affiliated with the Tokyu Group (*Tokyo Kyuko*—Tokyo Express), a huge conglomerate that owned much of the land between Tokyo and Odawara, and it ran a transport company called Hakone Mountain Railways that already ran buses precisely along the road where Yasujiro wanted to run his.

Odakyu protested to the Ministry of Transport; this was their territory, their lifeline, they had developed it, they wanted to keep the monopoly on it. Japan, however, was desperately trying to rebuild its transportation network after the war. There was a shortage of staff and a shortage of buses and railway carriages; and the ministry was eager to encourage any improvements to the network. In December 1949 Yasujiro got his license, on two conditions: his buses had to travel nonstop between the two termini of Odawara and Kowakudani, they could not stop along the road to pick up passengers; and they were to run only at specified times.

It was a suspiciously easy victory. This was far from the first occasion that Yasujiro and his Seibu Group had collided with the Tokyu Group. Yasujiro must have guessed that it would only be a matter of time before Tokyu struck back.

At the head of Tokyu was a formidable character called Keita Goto. He and Yasujiro had known each other for years; their paths had crossed many times before. Like Yasujiro, Goto was a man of the Meiji era, who had carved out a vast empire for himself with precious little concern for all the people he trampled underfoot. (As his son Noboru Goto once said, "For a man to be successful a lot of people have to be sacrificed.")[2] His Tokyu empire encompassed railways, land developments, department stores and the Toei movie studios. Most of the plush suburban developments to the west of Tokyo, out toward Yokohama, were Tokyu's, while Shibuya, the section of Tokyo where Tokyu's railway networks terminated, was effectively Tokyu city; most of the land there was owned by Tokyu. Goto had built Tokyo's first station department store there, right above the railway terminus, so that shoppers could spend their money without even leaving the station.

People often compared Goto and Yasujiro. Seibu and Tokyu were the two new zaibatsu of the postwar era; and they were the two moguls. Of the two, Goto was the older. He was sixty-seven in 1949, when Yasujiro was sixty. He was a slighter man, with a bullet head, bristly gray hair, thick neck and a stubborn downturn to his mouth; in old age he was never seen without his stick and his wire-rimmed glasses. Like Yasujiro, he was a terror to his employees and to those with whom he did business. He would wake up in the middle of the night, call one of his secretaries and shout, "Take over that company!" or "Buy those stocks!" or "Buy that factory!" He never offered any praise, but if the secretary failed in the takeover bid, he would yell, "Go hang yourself!" One of his secretaries actually did.

He was an arrogant, aggressive man, but at least you knew where you stood with him. As a businessman, Yasujiro had the reputation of being a two-faced schemer, whereas Goto was like a bulldozer, flattening businesses, gobbling up land and laying down railways almost at random.

As for his private life, that was irreproachable. At twenty-nine he had married a gentle and beautiful girl called Machiyo, who bore him one child, but died when she was only thirty-one. For the rest of his life he mourned her. He never married again. Instead, like any well-behaved Japanese man, he restricted his sexual activities to the geisha houses. In his time he was a famous charmer and to the end of his life always slept with a geisha on either side, one older and one younger.

Goto was a rough player. In one of his first encounters with Yasujiro his men hired thugs to kidnap two Seibu executives. They threatened them and kept them locked up until they wrote a letter advising Yasujiro to sell all the shares in his Musashino Railway to Goto. In the end the executives were sacked and Yasujiro kept his railway company; but he realized that Goto was a serious threat. Takeovers were Goto's specialty. Rather than building up his own businesses, he would wait until a business was well developed, then move in and buy up all the shares. In fact, he was so notorious that he was dubbed Goto the Thief; the syllables *go-tō*, lengthened to *gō-tō* and written with different characters, mean a thief or a mugger, a thug who attacks you in the night and steals your money.

As far as Yasujiro was concerned, Goto was a dangerous man. His business interests overlapped to an uncomfortable degree with Seibu's. Both were involved in the service industry, in land, railways, stores and tourism. And he was an immensely powerful figure. His power base was different from Yasujiro's. Whereas Yasujiro was a politician and knew politicians, Goto was a bureaucrat. He had worked in the Railways Ministry and the Ministry of Transport; and whenever a leading bureaucrat retired, he would always be assured of a directorship within the Tokyu Group, particularly if he had favored Tokyu while in office. This ensured that there were close bonds between Tokyu and the Ministry of Transport. As a result, whenever Tokyu needed a license for a new bus route or railway line, it was likely to be successful.

By applying to run buses along the route of Tokyu's subsidiary, Odakyu, Yasujiro had inadvertently opened a chink in his own armor. He had provided Goto with the perfect opportunity to fulfill one of his longest-held ambitions: to invade Hakone, to extend his transport network deep into Yasujiro's territory.

Precisely a week before Yasujiro's buses were due to start running between Kowakudani and Odawara, on March 13, 1950, Goto's Hakone Mountain Railways applied to the Ministry of Transport for a license to run buses along Yasujiro's private motor road, the road he had spent thirteen years building and of which he was so proud. The ministry predictably favored Goto's request and ordered Yasujiro to agree to it.

Yasujiro was outraged. Oblivious to the fact that it was his buses that had started the quarrel, he was filled with self-righteous fury. "I developed Hakone, I developed Karuizawa, for our country, for the world," he splutters in his memoirs.

> Not just for business. Come rain or shine I struggled. We were perpetually in the red, it was really tough for me. Then, just as we were little by little going into the black, I had to face the terrible blow that half my rights over my road were to be taken away by just one approval from the ministry. It's intolerable when this kind of thing is done openly! It's daylight robbery![3]

It was, he wrote, the worst time of his life. He was racked by illness, his prostate problem was growing steadily worse, he was still purged and could not engage in public affairs—and now he was to be forced to allow his worst enemy to invade his territory and run buses along his road. In May that year there was a public hearing. Yasujiro argued fiercely that what Goto was proposing was an illegal invasion of private property, but it was to no avail. The ministry and the public disagreed with him and Goto got his license.

There was one condition. The license was to be for one year only, renewable annually. Goto assumed that this was a mere formality, but he reckoned without Yasujiro's determination. So for several years Yasujiro's Izu Hakone Railway Company and Goto's Hakone Mountain Railways ran buses together from Odawara, the gateway of Hakone, to Kowakudani, where Yasujiro's territory began, and from Kowakudani along Yasujiro's toll road deep into his territory.

Gradually the nightmare of the war years faded and the terrible privations of the early days of the occupation abated. After a decade people were able to say that their standard of living was at least back at the prewar level. In 1955 the country looked as it had in 1940. The next step was to move forward.

The first five years had been the worst. For the first four years, inflation was terrifyingly out of control. Prices rose in all by 1,200 percent, so fast that people could barely afford to feed and clothe themselves, let alone repair the buildings that had been so badly damaged during the war. Savings were worthless. Everyone was reduced to survival level; and the only way in which the economy could be revived was through large injections of American aid.

Then, in 1949, the conservative banker Joseph Dodge was appointed economic commissar for Japan. His brief was to put a brake on inflation and to strengthen the economy; he succeeded in both these aims. He stabilized the currency, balanced the budget and focused the economy on exports rather than domestic consumption. But in order to do so he imposed such draconian measures that for most people life became harder than ever.

There were large-scale layoffs to improve productivity levels in industry. Public spending was pared sharply, with the result that businesses which had relied on government subsidies went bankrupt. A quarter of a million government officials lost their jobs. There were fewer and fewer goods on the shelves. As Dodge declared sternly to the press, "Nothing should have been expected as a result of the war but a long term of hardship and self-denial."

It was a harsh time for the Japanese. Many felt great despair. It truly seemed as if there were nothing more than hardship and self-denial to look forward to. In the end it was events in the world outside that were the catalyst for change.

On Monday, June 26, 1950, news broke that the North Koreans had pushed across the border into South Korea and taken Seoul. The Korean peninsula was in a state of war. Overnight Japan's relationship to the United States was utterly changed. There was heavy pressure on the Japanese to rearm. Japanese factories were needed to provide munitions for American troops fighting in Korea under the United Nations banner, and factories which had been forced under the occupation to produce peaceful items such as lightbulbs and nails now returned to the far more lucrative business of arms production.

For Japan itself, the fear of Japanese militarism had been completely eclipsed by the bogey of world Communism. Now America needed a strong Japan as its ally in Asia. The United States opened its doors to Japanese exports; American foods, raw materials and fuels were supplied under generous terms; and American investment helped to fund the rebuilding of the economy and the country. By the time the war ended in 1953 the economy had strengthened to such an extent that Japan no longer needed any direct American aid. The period of recovery was nearly over.

Just as in the Meiji era, Japan had been brought face-to-face with the affluence of the West. Once again the West, with its more advanced material culture, had proved stronger than Japan. Throughout the occupation the Japanese had been brought into daily contact with well-fed, energetic young American soldiers and had watched their huge cars careering down the narrow Japanese streets. It was like a symbol of the gap between the two countries—a gap that the Japanese were determined to close.

No one doubted what was needed: higher incomes, better housing, a lifestyle closer to what they saw on their imported American television programs. To achieve it, everyone would have to work. Development was all, no matter what the cost. And the two giants in the forefront, battling against each other to develop further and faster, were Pistol Tsutsumi and Goto the Thief.

For five years the two maintained an uneasy peace. The two bus companies used the roads in tandem, and as the buses swung round the last hairpin bend of the mountain road, Lake Ashi would come into view, brilliantly blue, glittering like a jewel, cut into the wooded hills, Mount Fuji soaring behind. And there, where the buses terminated, moored at the pier was Yasujiro's pleasure steamer, waiting to take passengers on a cruise around the lake.

Finally Goto and his Odakyu colleagues began to suspect that their victory was worthless. Everything they did simply served Yasujiro's interests. Their buses provided him with extra customers to travel in his pleasure steamer. In fact, they were doing him a favor.

In order to run his buses along Yasujiro's road, Goto had agreed not to interfere with Yasujiro's business in Hakone in any other way; but he was not a man famous for keeping his word. In those days there was no need for a license to run a ship of less than twenty tons. So in April 1956, just before the annual contract was due to be renewed, Goto launched a pleasure steamer of his own: the *Otohime-maru*, a vessel of just 19.96 tons. It berthed in the next inlet up from Yasujiro's steamer and plied almost exactly the same route, down to the little town of Hakone, where the dragon god's shrine was, and back again.

Once again Yasujiro was consumed with rage. On June 30, when the license came up for renewal, he refused it outright. To make doubly sure, he ordered his men to erect a barrier that very night at the junction where the toll road began.

The morning of July 1 dawned gray and wet. It was nearing the end of the rainy season and the clouds were so low that the mountains rising to each side of the junction were barely visible. Overnight a barrier had appeared across the road, a simple bamboo pole manned by a group of bedraggled men, each hunched under an umbrella. The first bus to appear that day, looming out of the mist, was a white Izu Hakone bus. The barrier snapped up, the men stood back, and the bus swept through.

Immediately behind it was a blue Hakone Mountain bus. Down came the barrier with a thump and the men, oblivious to the puddles and the drenching rain, raced out and threw themselves in the road in the path of the bus. The driver, taken by surprise, jammed on the brakes. He leaped out of his cab, cursing. "Get out of the way!" he yelled. "Get your bus out of here! Turn back!" bawled the men in the road. The passengers were on their feet, shouting angrily. But the men would not budge and the bus had to turn back.

Minutes passed. A group of Goto's men came into sight, marching down the road through the teeming rain. Yasujiro's men lined up, fists clenched, ready to confront them. At the barrier the two sides began to tussle. Goto's men tried to break the bamboo pole while Yasujiro's men forced them back. They heaved and shoved with much cursing and shouting and a few blows were exchanged before anxious onlookers arrived and persuaded the two sides to cool down.

This was the first skirmish in what came to be known as "the war of Hakone mountain." At the time it seemed as if the whole of Hakone were up in arms. Most of the drivers and bus conductors were local men. In the evening they still went drinking together but in the daytime, loyal to the death to their respective companies, they fought.

The fighting began at Odawara, where the trains from Tokyo pulled in. Both white and blue buses would be lined up, waiting in front of the station. As the passengers straggled out the drivers would start bellowing through microphones, "Hakone—this way!"; "Hakone—*this* way!" Sometimes they grabbed the bewildered passengers and dragged them bodily into their buses. And as often as not they turned on one another, shouting and swinging punches.

All the drivers were determined to be the first to leave. As a result, two buses invariably left at once, a white one and a blue one, and raced each other along the mountain roads, swinging out to overtake on the most precarious of hairpin bends. Deep in the Hakone mountain country, people would be waiting, growing more and more impatient, at the bus stop. Finally, after a good half hour, not one but two buses would appear, dust churning from their wheels, racing side by side down the narrow road.

The critical moment was when the buses arrived at the barrier. If the white bus got there first, the guard would raise the barrier and salute. Usually there was a blue bus hot on its tail. The guard had to bring the barrier down with a smack; if the bus driver was skillful enough he sometimes managed to swerve through. There were fights everywhere—at the barrier, at bus stops, at roadside stalls, at the piers where the rival steamers docked on Lake Ashi.

Finally the rivalry reached such a pitch that there seemed to be nothing for it but to call on Ryujin, the dragon god, for help. One fine August evening the entire staff of Yasujiro's Izu Hakone Railway Company, 1,167 people in all, marched down to the small bloodred shrine above the placid waters of Lake Ashi. They crowded along its stone courtyards, they pressed below the red arches, they stood shoulder to shoulder all the way down the rough-hewn steps to the huge red gateway on the lake. At a signal, solemnly they all bowed together toward the shrine, clapped their hands twice, then intoned, "Goto and his evil associates are invading our Hakone toll road with their buses. These villains misuse their political powers to achieve their evil ends. Lord, use your divine powers to give us victory over these evil men as quickly as possible. From our hearts, we—more than a thousand of us—pray to you with tears!"[4]

The dispute was now well beyond the level of fistfights. The contenders had long since resorted to the courts, issuing writs for every imaginable tiny violation of the transport regulations. Yasujiro accused Goto's Odakyu subsidiary of running fewer than the statutory number of buses, as stipulated in their contract, while Odakyu retaliated by accusing Yasujiro's buses of not following the prescribed route.

The confrontation reached a new level of intensity when Yasujiro refused to renew the license to let Goto's buses use his road. Odakyu filed a civil case against him in the Odawara district court, arguing that ample public transport was to the benefit of the general public and therefore even though the license had expired, the contract remained valid. The litigation dragged on for years. When Odakyu lost, they appealed to the Tokyo High Court, which sent the case back to the Odawara district court. Then, when the judgment seemed to be about to go against Yasujiro, he threatened to take the case up to the Supreme Court, where, as the ex-Speaker of the House, he wielded considerable influence.

For Yasujiro it had become a crusade. While Goto stayed in the background, letting his subsidiary, Odakyu, fight on his behalf, Yasujiro was perpetually at the forefront of the battle, blazing with righteous fury. At one point he was so overcome with anger that he summoned his staff in batches of six hundred to the roof of Seibu department store in Tokyo. There, he declaimed against the perfidy of Goto, who, he stormed, was another Hitler—he would stoop to anything, no matter how despicable, to achieve his evil ends. He also attacked Odakyu in more conventional ways. Takeovers were Goto's speciality; Goto, as far as he was concerned, had tried to take over his road. It was only justice that his own weapon should be used against him. So Yasujiro ordered his staff to start buying Odakyu stocks, no matter what the price. Within a few days they had acquired 1.3 million shares—though this was still much less than 10 percent of the total. At this point the minister of transport intervened. Odakyu, he ruled, should retract their lawsuit and Yasujiro should sell back the stocks.

The two parties agreed and held a banquet to celebrate, in a grand geisha house in Tokyo. The president of Odakyu, Nararoku Ando, flushed with the joy of reconciliation, burbled "Let's go for it!" and kissed Yasujiro's son Seiji full on the lips, an event that was duly recorded by the assembled press with great merriment. But despite all the demonstrations of affection, Odakyu in fact made no move to retract their lawsuit and the litigation continued.

By now Yasujiro had taken to stomping around the Ministry of Transport with his shirttails hanging out and his wrapped lunch—rice balls—swinging from a string around his waist, like some weather-beaten old peasant on his way to the rice fields. He would pop his head into people's offices, yelling, "You buggers, what the hell do you think you're up to?" Everyone there came to hate him thoroughly.[5]

Finally, in 1960, eleven years after Yasujiro had first applied to run his buses along Goto's route, the minister gave in and agreed to hold an exceptional hearing.

At last, it seemed, the endgame was to be played out. That day more than a hundred members of the press squeezed into the stuffy eighth-floor room. Several Diet members too came along to watch the sport. Sadly, only one of the main contenders was there to give battle. Goto had already fought his last fight. He had died the previous year, at the age of seventy-seven, in the arms of his favorite geisha. With his dying breath he instructed her to become a nun. "Don't let another man touch this flesh," he whispered. "I've already bought a temple for you."

When Yasujiro heard the news, instead of expressing the conventional respect, he gleefully summoned the press and announced, "In all the world there's never been anything more cheering than the death of this evil man!" Then, despite the fact he had been a teetotaler for his entire life, he filled a glass, raised it in the air and shouted *"Kampai!*—Three cheers!" for the death of his rival.[6]

So that hot July day in the Ministry of Transport's meeting hall, the main protagonist was Yasujiro. He heaved himself to his feet, leaning on his stick, and took the microphone. He was seventy-one, but as big and brawny as ever. His features had mellowed; but that day his mouth was set in a stubborn scowl.

He held the floor for more than an hour. The matter at issue, he said, was not a question of opening a road; it was a question of a hostile takeover bid. He spoke of forty years ago, when he had first started developing Hakone, of all the pain and effort and money that had been poured into it. And then, when the project was half completed, here was Odakyu, elbowing in, trying to take advantage of all his hard work.

"Mr. Ando here," he shouted, "even grabbed my son Seiji and kissed him on the mouth!" The reporters, jammed together in the hot sweaty room, roared with laughter.

"Stand up, you two!" yelled Yasujiro peremptorily, swinging round to point out Odakyu's president, Ando, and the president of Hakone Mountain Railways. Sheepishly, the two rose to their feet, wondering what was coming next.

"You can see, they're not the kind of handsome young men you'd want to kiss! They appreciated that all right—and then to forget their obligations straightaway, to commit theft [*goto*]!"[7]

A few days later, before the minister could reach a decision, the entire cabinet resigned and the whole matter had to be put aside. It was not until nine months later, on Thursday, March 16, 1961, that the affair finally came to an end. That day many Seibu employees took time off work to sit in the public galleries of the Tokyo High Court, while the judges deliberated their verdict.

It took a day of argument, with both sides presenting their cases yet again. But the verdict when it came was straightforward. Odakyu was banned from using Seibu's private road without permission.

"Seibu Line Wins Battle for Road," trumpeted the papers the following day. "The Seibu Railway Co. yesterday won its five-year-old lawsuit with the Odakyu Electric Railway Co. over the use of a Seibu-owned highway in the sight-seeing resort of Hakone, Shizuoka Prefecture. . . ."[8]

Seibu had won. Yasujiro had defeated his lifelong enemy. Ryujin, the dragon god, had forgiven his wayward devotee and answered the prayers of his staff. Hakone was at peace.

But Odakyu no longer had much interest in running buses on Seibu's road. The judgment when it came was no great blow to them. The previous year they had finished constructing a cable car, which swung from the top of Mount Sounzan, out across a spectacular barren landscape where steam and hot sulfur springs spurted from the ground, down to Lake Ashi. There, like a fairy-tale vessel, with banners streaming, was a steamer—owned by Odakyu—waiting to ferry passengers across the lake.

It was a brilliant move. From the heights of the cable car, passengers could admire Yasujiro's kingdom sprawling almost as far as Mount Fuji, but they put their fares into Odakyu's pocket. Shortly after the cable car opened, Yasujiro's buses were practically empty. He had lost more than 90 percent of his customers. A few months later Yasujiro sold his toll road to the prefecture for a considerable fee and it became a public highway.

Despite Seibu's victory in the courts, the battle of Hakone ended in a draw. Today most people take Odakyu's Hakone Mountain Railway to climb to the top of Mount Sounzan and from there swing by cable car down to Lake Ashi. But the land they see from the cable car belongs to Seibu and they probably stay in one of Seibu's Prince hotels. The roads are still crowded with buses—white Izu Hakone Railway Company buses and blue ones run by Hakone Mountain Railways.

Elder Statesman
1953–1964

People generally think we had an easy life; but there is no harder task than to follow someone whom people call a hero or a great man. Both family and staff had little choice but to advance along the path laid out by the great man, pursuing the same goal single-mindedly, burning with passion and utterly absorbed. Once you passed through the Tsutsumi gate, everyone was consumed in the circle of fire. However, the other side of his strictness was his very deep love for people; he was brimming over with it.
MISAO TSUTSUMI
"Thirty-nine Years with the
Demon of Business"

When Yasujiro accepted the post of Speaker in May 1953, he could not have been prepared for all the trouble it would bring him.

At the time the prime minister was Shigeru Yoshida. Yoshida was a formidable figure, the leading statesman of the postwar era and more responsible than anyone else for laying the foundations of the new Japan. Never seen without his wire-rimmed pince-nez balanced on his nose, he was a short, broad man of quite literally Churchillian proportions, with a square-jowled bulldog face. He had spent years in England as ambassador, where he mixed with the aristocracy and became a confirmed Anglophile and lover of good living and fat cigars. At the end of the war, when he stepped out of retirement to take up the post of foreign minister, MacArthur and his fellow officers identified this urbane and cosmopolitan man as someone they could talk to. He quickly became recognized as the main liaison between the occupying forces and the Japanese government.

Then, in 1946, after the first postwar election, he became leader of the victorious Liberal Party (which, despite the name, was conservative) and was called upon to form a government. As prime minister his powers were frustratingly limited. His role was simply to implement the reforms that MacArthur and the occupying army insisted on; he had no alternative but to obey their instructions. Most ran counter to all his strongest convictions about what was best for the future of Japan: the new constitution, in particular, with its clauses renouncing war and declaring the emperor to be simply a constitutional monarch; and the stern measures to break up the family-run zaibatsu conglomerates and to give more rights to the workers. He did his best to limit their impact. The occupation would have to end; and when it did a strong Japan could reemerge.

Yoshida's first government lasted a year. For two years he was out of power. In 1949 he became prime minister again, following a couple of coalition governments.

By now many things had changed. The Americans were becoming embroiled in the Cold War, Mao Tse-tung had brought Communism as close as neighboring China, and in 1950 the Korean War broke out. As a result, the Americans now wanted exactly what Yoshida wanted: an economically strong Japan to act as the United States' chief ally in Asia.

It soon became apparent that there was no need to continue the military occupation of Japan. Yoshida threw all his energies into negotiating the treaties that would bring it to an end: the San Francisco Treaty and a parallel defense treaty. After months of negotiations he emerged happy that he had won terms very favorable to his country. As an American ally Japan was to receive preferential economic treatment and the United States would be responsible for its defense. The treaties were signed in September 1951 and ratified in April 1952; and, amid great rejoicing, Japan regained its independence.

The signing of the San Francisco Treaty was the pinnacle of Yoshida's career. Months later his popularity was already crumbling. Power had gone to his head; he was beginning to behave like a dictator. He took to making autocratic decisions and insisted that Diet members should approach him only through his favorites; he would listen to no one else.

Finally his high-handedness became intolerable. On February 28, 1953, he was presiding over a budget committee meeting in the Lower House. A member of the opposition insisted on asking difficult questions. Like a headmaster addressing some errant schoolboy,

Yoshida barked, *"Bakayaro!* Fool!" The members were outraged. It was an unforgivable breach of propriety and etiquette, which seemed to epitomize the complete contempt in which Yoshida held the Diet and its members and, by implication, the people who had elected them. The opposition moved for him to be disciplined, the House passed a vote of no confidence, and Yoshida was forced to dissolve the Diet.

In the election that followed, the Liberals regained power, but with a much reduced majority. Two months later, in a critical vote, the members were called upon to choose a new Speaker and Vice Speaker. The ruling Liberal Party was in such disarray that there was a chance that the opposition might be able to snatch up these key positions.

On the day of the vote the various opposition parties argued and horsetraded over the choice of candidates for more than eight hours. Finally at 6 P.M. the candidates were announced: for Speaker, Yasujiro Tsutsumi of the Democratic Party; for Vice Speaker, Hyo Hara of the left-wing Socialist Party.[1] The vote was taken, and the opposition won the day.

It was a surprise result, and no one was more surprised than Yasujiro. He had had no idea that he would be nominated; as he records in his memoirs, he had not even brought a formal dress suit in which to make his inaugural speech. His aides rushed around in a panic looking for a suit for him. Finally another Diet member volunteered his pinstriped trousers.

Yasujiro's first duty as Speaker was to preside over the election of the next prime minister. The vote was taken the following day and Yoshida was chosen again, but he no longer had a working majority; and everyone was certain that the next Diet session would be a turbulent one.

For Yasujiro it was a personal triumph. He had finally achieved the recognition he craved in his political career. Everyone knew him as a business magnate, a land developer and property speculator, one of the wealthiest and most successful in the country. Shortly after his appointment the *Nippon Times* listed his assets: "a department store, three railways, two golf courses, two recreation parks, hundreds of acres of land and a dozen hotels."[2]

But he had always said that politics was his first and real love. He had embarked on a business career simply to make the necessary funds to enter the world of politics, which offered a path to respectability and status that mere wealth did not.

As a politician Yasujiro tended toward the middle of the road. To quote the *Tokyo Evening News* of the day of his election, "He is considered a conservative, being a quiet speaker and always treading the safe road. He is neither intensely liked nor vigorously disliked."[3] He was neither a great intellect nor an inspiring orator. Instead he preferred to deal in human relationships—networking, making connections, operating behind the scenes. As Speaker he held one of the most prestigious positions in the country. It put him on a par with the prime minister and with those who had been peers and princes. He was a leading member, in fact, of the new postwar aristocracy that had risen to fill the gap created by the abolition of the old aristocracy: one based on power and wealth. The boy from Yagiso village in the rice fields of Omi had come a long way.

But his triumph was to be short-lived. In his new position he was thrust into the public eye; and sooner or later the irregularities of his private life were bound to be noticed.

Yasujiro's first engagement as Speaker was to attend a reception at the Imperial Palace, along with Yoshida and the members of the new government, to be formally presented to the emperor. Misao, too, was present, wearing an elegant silk kimono. As Speaker Yasujiro would be expected to entertain many dignitaries and the position of Speaker's wife was an important one.

At forty-five, Misao had aged hardly at all. She was slender and girlish still, with a perfect oval face and radiant smile. For years she had been the hostess at the many parties at the big Hiroo house, and she was very much at ease with the wealthy and powerful of the nation, ready with charm and witty conversation. She was the perfect foil for Yasujiro, who tended to be rather gruff, and the ideal Speaker's wife—brilliant, gracious, assured, more like a Western woman than the traditional Japanese wife.

But, almost without thinking, Yasujiro had committed an outrageous breach of propriety. Even though they had lived together for years as man and wife, Misao was not his wife. She was his mistress. Not only had he taken her into the sacred grounds of the Imperial Palace, he had introduced her to the emperor, the empress and the empress-mother as his wife. The next day the newspapers were full of the scandal. The empress-mother in particular, it was said, was deeply offended.

Yasujiro's offense was a matter of propriety, not of morals. A wealthy and powerful man was expected to support several mistresses; his wife, on the other hand, would be a woman from a highly respectable family. The important thing was to maintain the distinction. Wives appeared at public functions, mistresses remained in the shadows; they were for pleasure and private life.

Yasujiro always confused the two. Misao behaved in every way like his wife, while Tsuneko, the quiet, gentle mother of Yoshiaki and his two brothers, was the mistress in the shadows. He had almost forgotten that Misao was not formally his wife, and he had done everything he could to put out of his mind his real wife—the miserable, downtrodden Fumi, living in solitude somewhere in an obscure corner of Tokyo. Clearly it was time to put his affairs in order.

The last fifteen years had been very hard for Fumi. She was sixty-six now and in poor health, crippled with rheumatism, half blind with cataracts and suffering from high blood pressure. Yasujiro had made sure that she always had enough money to get by on and a roof over her head, but for years she had been forced to move from place to place, from one of his housing developments to another. For a while she lived in Karuizawa, then settled in Tokyo in a small house in a quiet part of town. The Japanese press made much of the fact that there was no nameplate on the gate; it was as if Yasujiro was trying to deny her very existence.

From time to time he asked for a divorce, but she always refused. She was, she said, a traditional Japanese woman, brought up to believe that a wife should never divorce, no matter what the provocation. As for husbands, they had no need to divorce. They could do anything they wanted just so long as they observed the proprieties. When divorce did occur, the wife seldom received alimony, and when she did, it was very small. In 1952 the most common alimony awarded was between ¥10,000 and ¥50,000.[4]

Fumi was determined that, if nothing else, Yasujiro should have to pay for all her years of suffering. When he asked her once again for divorce, she demanded ¥15 million. It was an outrageous sum— though still very small compared to his assumed wealth. For a month the two wrangled over the figure. Finally Fumi accepted ¥8 million: ¥1 million in cash and ¥7 million in land and property. The couple were divorced in July 1954, forty years after they had first married. A few days later, very quietly, Yasujiro and Misao completed the paper formalities to become man and wife.[5]

The public quickly forgot about Yasujiro's private affairs. There were matters of far greater moment happening in the public domain.

As Speaker, Yasujiro presided over a time of the utmost upheaval. Japan had just regained its independence. It was barely a year since the San Francisco Treaty had come into effect. Freed from the restraining presence of American troops on the streets, the city erupted into rioting. There were marches, demonstrations and strikes, partly in protest against the American bases that remained on Japanese soil, and partly against the government itself. As far as Prime Minister Yoshida and his right-wing Liberals were concerned, the country was in a serious state of instability. And, like the West, the Japanese were obsessed with the fear of Communism. To Japan, it was uncomfortably close. It had engulfed neighboring China and it was threatening to overwhelm the entire Korean peninsula, little farther away from Japan than France is from England. A Communist revolution in Japan itself seemed a real threat.

Yoshida was convinced that it was the democratizing reforms initiated in the early days of the occupation that had laid Japan open to the threat of Communism. As soon as the American mood changed he set about revoking them. Even before the occupation had ended he initiated a "red purge" that removed twenty-two thousand suspected leftists from their jobs in the civil service and industry; and he began to force through a variety of bills to restrain the left. As far as he was concerned these were urgent measures to prevent the country from crumbling into disorder. But to the opposition he was threatening the individual freedoms that had been won after the war; he seemed to be doing his best to reestablish the police state of the prewar years. The stage was set for violent confrontation.

The first battle broke out over the strike-control bill. Under the occupation workers had been guaranteed basic rights, including the right to strike for an unlimited period of time. Yoshida perceived this

as potentially very dangerous. Coal miners, power workers or others
working in essential industries could cripple the country if they decided to go on strike. It could even lead to a Communist revolution.
He was determined to pass legislation to curb the right to strike, but
the Socialists were equally determined to obstruct him.

Trying to arbitrate between the two sides was Yasujiro. He was
officially neutral; he had left the Progressive Party in order to take up
the position of Speaker. On this issue, however, he supported the
government. He was naturally a conservative. He hated Communism,
and he was afraid that if the legislation was not passed, the country
would erupt in chaos.

On the last day of that Diet session the legislation had still not
passed. The government instructed Speaker Tsutsumi to extend the
session by another week, but as he shouted out the words, the opposition began to hurl papers and ashtrays at him, and clambered up on
to the podium to try to pull him down. He was forced to exit at what
he describes in his memoirs as "a dignified trot."[6] While he sneaked
out a back door of the Diet, the opposition members were smashing
down the door of his office, searching for him. Some secretaries were
trampled in the melee and one of the directors of his office was quite
badly beaten. Yasujiro, meanwhile, was on his way to the Hakone
shrine to commune with the dragon god.

But he had already succeeded in extending the Diet session, and
the bill became law.

Then, in 1954, Prime Minister Yoshida proposed a revision of the
police law. Under the occupation the police force had been broken
up into regional forces with no unifying central authority. Whenever
there were riots or strikes overstepping local boundaries, the police
were unable to control them. Yoshida was eager to strengthen and
unify the police force and thereby bolster law and order. To the opposition Yoshida was treading on extremely slippery ground: they
feared that his real aim was to clamp down on individual liberties and
to increase his own powers—to move closer to a dictatorship or a police state.

That Diet session was a particularly stormy one. After three ex-
tensions the police-law revision had still not gone through. The opposition was determined to block any further extension, so that the
bill would have to be thrown out. There was only one man who had

the authority to extend the Diet session further, and to do so he had to take a vote by midnight of June 3.

At nine o'clock that evening Speaker Tsutsumi was resting in a private room in the Diet when he heard footsteps and shouting in the corridor outside. He rushed for the door—he knew that the Socialists would try to barricade him inside—but before he could escape he was shoved roughly back and the door slammed shut. There were some Liberals trapped inside with him. Together they put their shoulders against the door and tried to thrust it open, but the Socialists had wedged a bench up against it with ten hefty men standing on it to weight it down.

Meanwhile in the chamber itself the whole podium was bristling with Socialists, filling every available inch of floor. The public gallery was crowded with spectators, watching eagerly, and television cameras were installed, ready to record the event. By 10:35 P.M. Yasujiro and his supporters had managed to break out of the room. The bell rang for the opening of the plenary session. But when Yasujiro tried to reach the chamber, he found the corridors completely jammed with people. The Socialists, their secretaries and their muscular, crew-cut young staff were blocking every entrance.

Yasujiro ran full tilt for the podium, with supporters clinging to his belt, shoving him from behind and pulling him from in front. For such a big man, he moved extremely fast. Keeping his weight low, dodging and ducking like a boxer, thrusting interceptors aside with his shoulders, he got as far as the steps.

There the women were shrieking and screaming and lashing out with their handbags, the men tried to throttle one another with their ties, and several were picked up bodily and thrown over the railing onto the floor below. Yasujiro plunged into the melee, beating and wrestling his way through. He managed to get one knee onto the steps but could push no farther. Finally he was shoved back out into the corridor and retired to the Speaker's room to recover. His watch had disappeared, his clothes were ripped, his underwear was hanging out and he was covered in bruises.

Midnight was approaching, and he still hadn't managed to extend the session. In desperation, Yasujiro decided to invoke his emergency powers. He took the unprecedented measure of calling in the police. Three hundred massed outside while two hundred, all in uniform, marched into the corridors of the Diet building, rank upon rank of them, and joined in the battle.

Finally they managed to clear the corridors and escorted Yasujiro to the entrance to the chamber. He looked at the clock. It was 11:50. The chamber was still jammed with people. It was impossible to get to the Speaker's seat, so Yasujiro decided to extend the session from where he stood. He made sure both feet were firmly inside the chamber. There was so much noise that he could hardly be heard. Raising his voice as high as he could, he yelled, "I declare the plenary session open. I propose that this Diet session be extended by two days. Please show your agreement by standing!"

All the members, of course, were already on their feet, stomping, shouting and fighting.

"I see that the majority is standing," shouted Yasujiro. "I declare this motion passed!"[7]

While the opposition stood by sullenly, the Liberals threw both hands in the air and yelled, "*Banzai!* Hurray!"

The public, however, was outraged. They read about the brawling in their newspapers. The *Nippon Times* wrote of "the unprecedented police-quelled riot" and added, "More than fifty persons received minor injuries as results of the disturbance in which excited Socialists fiercely battled Liberals, guards and even police."[8] The *Japan News* discussed the "well-publicized parliamentary 'mystery' " of why Yasujiro had not used his vaunted judo skills to quell the riot, and recorded his answer: "For anyone well versed in the art of judo, it would have been the easiest thing to administer *atemi* [a deadly judo punch]. But it would necessarily have caused murder and for me as Speaker to indulge in such violence was out of the question."[9]

Those who had television, which had started broadcasting only a few months before, watched their elected representatives behaving like thugs. As the representative of the House, Yasujiro had to make a formal apology to the nation from the Speaker's seat; and he also visited the Imperial Palace to proffer his apologies to the emperor.

It was not only the public that was outraged. More important, the leaders of big business too had concluded that Prime Minister Yoshida was a liability. Besides his personal unpopularity and the chaotic political situation, his party had also been tainted by a serious corruption scandal. It was time to bring his administration to an end.

At that time, as in Japan throughout the modern era, the real power was in the hands not of the electorate, nor even the politicians, but of two formidable and largely faceless groups: the government bureaucracy and the barons of big business. The business leaders formed clubs that met for ostensibly social purposes in teahouses, restaurants or the private dining rooms of hotels. Here they discussed the running of the country and key matters of government policy. Through their financial power, they selected and installed prime ministers, and also acted as an advisory committee to their chosen man. Behind Yoshida were four very powerful men known as the Four Emperors: the president of the Japan Development Bank; the presidents of a steel and a textile company; and a close friend of Yasujiro, Shigeo Mizuno, the owner of the Sankei Newspaper Group.

Behind the scenes these men put pressure on Yoshida to retire. In the Diet too there were moves to try to force him out. Finally, on December 6, 1954, the House passed a vote of no confidence in the government and the next day the entire cabinet resigned. As Speaker, it was Yasujiro's job to accept the formal letters of resignation from the cabinet members. Then he too tendered his resignation. He had been Speaker for a year and seven months.

Yasujiro's period as Speaker coincided with a period of intense political debate in Japan. For the powers that really ran the country, the situation was far too volatile. What Japan needed was rapid economic growth, and to achieve that it had to have stable government.

In the election of 1955, a year after the Yoshida cabinet had fallen, the two main Socialist parties, the right and the left-wing Socialists, won a large share of the vote. There was consternation in the business community. Clearly the conservatives needed to be strengthened, to such an extent that the left would never again be a threat. Under considerable pressure from business, the two main conservative parties, the Liberals and the Democrats (of which Yasujiro was a member), merged to form the Liberal Democratic Party, the LDP.

Ultimately the ploy was successful. The Socialists had had their fangs drawn. For the next four decades, with enormous support from the business community, the LDP was to rule the country. Eventually politics was reduced to factional infighting. The most important question became not which party one was in—most members of the Diet were in the LDP—but which faction within the party; and the differences between the factions had more to do with power struggles between the leaders than with any differences in policy. For a few years there was turbulence and occasionally violent demonstrations, but the period of political debate and instability was coming to an end. The period of unstoppable economic growth was about to begin.

Yasujiro returned to the back benches. "When I look at the Speaker's seat now," he wrote in his memoirs, "I feel truly sorry for the person sitting there!"[10]

Like his fellow business leaders, Yasujiro preferred to remain in the background, to operate out of the shadows through his extensive network of powerful connections. He was famous for his parties, which were reputed to veer toward the uproarious; it was through these that he built up his web of contacts. Once he was relieved of his duties as Speaker he was free to concentrate on entertaining. Whenever a foreign dignitary visited Japan he was likely to be entertained by ex-Speaker Tsutsumi. There were parties for everyone, from President Sukarno of Indonesia to the mayor of Los Angeles. When Edwin Reischauer became American ambassador in 1961, Yasujiro held an exuberant reception for him, to which, despite the Cold War tensions of the time, he invited the Soviet ambassador. In his memoirs Reischauer describes the evening as "particularly boisterous" and adds that "normal protocol procedures were disregarded, with the result that the whole occasion was completely unpredictable, a little chaotic, but very amusing."[11]

Thus Yasujiro built up a formidable web of contacts, at the very highest levels of society and on an international scale—a network of relationships that formed an intangible foundation for his business empire and that was to stand both him and his sons in good stead.

Many people remember Yasujiro in old age. While he was busy sending up shoots to the powerful people above him, acting the bluff and genial host at his parties, to his employees he remained an absolute terror. Everyone was afraid of him. Some, who are now at the highest levels of the company, remember quaking for half an hour before they had to go and report to him.

There was no relaxing in his presence. Before the fresh young employees went in to see him, his secretaries would check that their ties were correctly knotted and would show them the proper way to sit, head bowed, hands on thighs, elbows turned out. Once in his presence, they would sit, rigid with fear, not daring to move an inch for the duration of the interview. No matter what they said, he always got angry.

"Which division do you work in?" he would bellow.

"The food division, sir," or "the railway division, sir," would come the trembling reply.

"You're working here thanks to me!"

One, a Mr. Nishibei, now retired, first met Yasujiro in March 1953, shortly before he took up the post of Speaker. He was a bright and sensitive young man, who had just finished university and was looking for a job. The Japanese economy was still weak and jobs were difficult to find. Many of his contemporaries were entering securities companies or the fledgling television industry.

As for Nishibei, he had an asset that it would have been foolish to ignore. As it happened, one of his closest friends worked for Seibu, and offered to introduce him and to be his guarantor. Thus it was that one day young Nishibei found himself in the living room of the big house in Hiroo, sitting opposite the formidable figure of Yasujiro Tsutsumi. He was, he remembers, very nervous. He sat stiffly, looking the great man square in the eye, nodding and saying, *"Hai, hai. Yes, yes."*

Scowling, Yasujiro barked a few questions. Then he took a sharp look at the quaking young man, broke into a guffaw and roared, "Come tomorrow!"

Joining Seibu was like becoming part of a big family. As in most Japanese companies, once you had joined you never left. And, for all their fear, most of the staff were utterly devoted to the gruff old patriarch. People compared him to the Japanese hero Takamori Saigo, a charismatic rebel leader of the last century. Like him, they said, he was a man of strong emotions, larger than life.

Once, one of Yasujiro's employees was killed while trying to save an old woman. Deeply moved by his courage, Yasujiro had him promoted posthumously and arranged a splendid funeral, paid for by the company. He himself led the mourners, walking with measured pace, carrying the traditional prayer stick to the cemetery with tears running down his face. All his staff, it was said, impressed at the strength of his emotion, said to one another, "I would happily die for this chairman!"

While Yasujiro was the ogre, Misao was the gentle presence constantly in the background. She was the only person who could calm him. If she saw his temper rising, she would quickly clear away ashtrays, ink blocks, scales, paperweights, anything he might throw, and put them well out of his reach.

As he grew older he came to rely on her more and more. In a radio interview he gave in February 1964, he said she was not so much his wife as his mother. "When it gets cold, she puts out warm clothing for me and I wear it. When it's hot, she gives me the right clothing. And when I'm hungry she gives me something to eat." She even checked his stool every day and adjusted his menu depending on what she found, ordering the cook to include more vegetables or more protein.[12]

By now she also played an important part in his business. More and more he was delegating responsibility for sections of the company to her. In an article that she published after his death, she wrote of the demands that her dual roles, of wife and business partner, put on her:

> Tsutsumi hated tears; no matter how hard life became, he never allowed me to cry and complain. As a result, no matter what difficulties I was confronted with, it was as if I had drummed into me the idea that you should maintain an unflinching attitude at all times. There were times when I thought life was tough and harsh, when I had used up all my strength; but fortunately I still had poetry to support me. . . .
>
> Tsutsumi was always tough both on his family and his staff, but I think that was natural for a man who did such an important job. My daily schedule was completely full from morning to night; unlike ordinary housewives, I didn't have even one hour's spare time. I felt as if I were going round and round like a cog in a huge machine. The pressure of daily business was so intense that I never had the space to express my own feelings. I feel as if our lives were about giving up our own desires and throwing ourselves into the greater purpose of work. Even at night I felt as if I were being watched in my sleep.[13]

In fact, she was completely indispensable to Yasujiro. She wielded enormous power—not directly but, like the traditional Japanese wife, because she was the real power behind her husband. Wherever he went on any of his official duties, even on occasions when other wives were not present, she was always there at his shoulder, ready with a charming word and radiant smile. And every Tuesday she attended the Seibu board meeting, sitting in the place of honor next to Yasujiro, higher in position than any of the company presidents. The Seibu executives knew better than to ignore what this dainty but immensely strong-willed woman had to say.

But when Yasujiro wanted to relax, when his work was over for the week, he left her behind. Then he turned to the gentle, white-skinned Tsuneko. Sometimes all three went out together. Misao would walk three paces behind Yasujiro, as was proper for a wife. And three paces behind Misao came Tsuneko.

Tsuneko had begun life with the same advantages as Misao. She too was of a good family. She had been one of the few women of her generation to go on to higher education. Yet once she became Yasujiro's mistress, she was thrust into the shadows. And while Misao had managed to break out, Tsuneko seemed destined to live out her life there.

By nature she was very much the traditional Japanese woman—quiet, passive, resigned to whatever fate had to offer her. She spent her life perpetually hidden from the public gaze, in her small wooden house with its garden full of flowers. There, deprived of the company of her man like many Japanese women, she devoted herself to her children.

Yasujiro was getting old. In 1959 he was seventy, and it was time to set his affairs in order. There was one issue that preoccupied him more than any other: what would become of his empire when he died? He had seen what had happened to his old enemy, Goto the Thief. Goto had insisted on holding on to the reins until he was well into his dotage; and he had made some very bad decisions. Before he died, his son Noboru had had to step in, to stop him from one last rash takeover bid. And after his death, little by little his Tokyu empire began to break up.

As Noboru Goto put it, Yasujiro and his own father were part of a race of giants. They had happily trampled over a mountain of sacrificial victims in order to get what they wanted. But the world had changed. The generation that would replace them would be a different breed.

Yasujiro had always had a long-term vision. But who was to be his successor? Which of his sons had the stature to continue the business that he had begun? For years he had assumed that his business would pass, in the usual way, to the eldest son. He had brought up Kiyoshi to be his successor; he had used his son's wedding as an opportunity to introduce him into the highest levels of society. But Kiyoshi had failed him. Because he was dominated not by the lust for money and power but by his own emotions, Kiyoshi was disinherited. Yasujiro turned to the next in line, Seiji.

When Yasujiro became Speaker, Seiji was one of his political secretaries. Then, when Yasujiro stepped down, he entrusted Seiji with the running of the department store, one small corner of the Seibu empire that had been neglected. Seiji set to work to make it a department store equal to the most prestigious in Japan. Installed as president, he began to take on university graduates and to upgrade the image of the store. The business community watched with approval. Here was a young man with talent and foresight, a fit person to take over his father's kingdom. He was described as the crown prince of Seibu.

By now Yasujiro had delegated the day-to-day running of the company almost entirely to the presidents of its different branches, though as chairman he retained the final say on any matter. The company was as impenetrable as a fortress. At the head of it was Yasujiro, while the inner circle consisted almost entirely of family members: Shojiro Kojima, his eldest daughter Shukuko's husband, the president of Seibu Railways; Juro Morita, Kuniko's husband, president of Seibu Chemicals; and Misao, who was responsible for the Tokyo Prince Hotel.

In his second family, Yasujiro made sure that the eldest of Tsuneko's three boys, Yoshiaki, was always by his side. Yoshiaki was very young still. When his father was seventy, he was only twenty-five. But Yasujiro got on best with him of all his children. He began to train him in the land-development business; and at the family's business meetings every Tuesday, Yoshiaki always sat near the head of the table, at his father's right hand.

With the younger members of the family running the business, Yasujiro was free to take on the role of patriarch and elder statesman. He devoted some time to writing. He contributed an article on his life story to the *Nihon Keizai Shimbun* (Japan Economic Journal), and he wrote several volumes of memoirs. No doubt one of his aims was to ensure that posterity remembered him as he chose to be remembered, but another was simply to indulge his mischievous sense of humor. The core of the story is a fairly idealized version of his own life, spiced with plenty of earthy, self-deprecating humor. He portrays himself as a young wide-eyed country boy, doing his best to make money and failing at every turn. Finally he learns the great lesson: if you try to make money you will fail. The only way to succeed is by developing the "heart of contribution" by serving your fellowman. Thus he develops his philosophy of "gratitude and service," which, he says, has governed his life ever since. He records many occasions when he was praised—for his fine work, for his courage, for his service to his country.

Nevertheless he cannot repress his own nature. In the middle of these pious homilies the malevolent old man breaks in: in a chapter devoted to a long tirade against the much hated Goto the Thief. And Yasujiro can never resist including a funny story—usually raunchy and usually to do with bodily functions. He dwells at length on the Gold Train and on how he tipped a bucket of feces over his head while running across an icy field, and he writes in excruciating detail about those terrible nine years when his urine stopped.

At the same time Yasujiro was also operating within the inner circles of political power. Not only was he close to the Japanese leaders, from the prime minister down, but he was also a personal friend of some of the leading representatives of the United States government in Japan. He was involved in many of the complex diplomatic maneuvers of the day—restoring good relations with the United States after Japan had established rapprochement with the Soviet Union, as well as renegotiating the Mutual Security Pact with the United States, in the face of enormous public opposition.

These were great years for Yasujiro. He was old, he was successful, he was rich; people estimated that he was one of the five wealthiest men in Japan. His business ran itself, and as Japan became more and more prosperous, so the value of his landholdings rose ever higher. In his political career he had reached the highest position of eminence. He had achieved everything he could ever have dreamed of achieving, and more.

Yasujiro—as elder statesman—was very firmly on the side of the United States, and he was opposed to rapprochement with the Soviet Union, which had badly soured Japan's relationship with Washington. As if to underline his position, he became a close friend of General Lyman L. Lemnitzer, who in the mid-fifties was commander of the U.S. forces in Japan. It was Yasujiro who engineered an informal meeting between the general, as representative of the United States, and Nobusuke Kishi, then foreign minister, under the pretext of a judo demonstration. Lemnitzer was outraged that the Japanese government had established rapprochement with the Soviet Union. "Have the Japanese become pro-Soviet?" he demanded of Yasujiro, who had himself proffered his resignation as a Diet member over the issue. Yasujiro, determined to make peace, assured the general that although Kishi had supported rapprochement, "this was an action he was forced to take as secretary general of the party; but actually he positively supported close relations between the United States and Japan." After three hours of persuasion, the general agreed to meet Kishi.

> I thought it better to let them meet each other in an informal atmosphere, and said to the general, "Let me invite you to a judo match. I will show you the exquisite skill of Mr. Mifune." . . .
>
> I held a reception at the Geihin-kan [the state guest house] in Shiba, Tokyo, on February 13, 1957, and the general and his staff and their families, over 300 people in all, enjoyed the judo matches. The general seemed relaxed and talked to Kishi, then foreign minister, for a long period of time, listening to the explanation of the play and watching the contests and exhibitions.[14]

It was effectively thanks to Yasujiro's diplomacy that Kishi, by then prime minister, finally went to the United States to meet Eisenhower and sign the revised U.S.-Japan Security Treaty.

Shortly before this historic visit, in January 1959, Yasujiro received an invitation. By now General Lemnitzer was back in Washington, and he wanted his old friends Mr. and Mrs. Tsutsumi to attend his daughter's wedding. Yasujiro wrote in his memoirs, "Just to travel to a wedding in Tokyo from Osaka is troublesome. I had never heard of anyone flying from Tokyo to Washington for a wedding, and thought that the man in charge must have failed to examine the general's mailing list closely." He consulted with the prime minister. The wily Kishi was convinced that there was some hidden diplomatic significance and urged him to accept.

So, at the age of seventy, Yasujiro set foot in the United States for the first time. When he and Misao arrived, as Kishi had guessed, they were given a welcome worthy of guests of state and representatives of their country. They attended the wedding as planned, but Yasujiro was also invited to visit Arlington Cemetery and to pay his respects at the Tomb of the Unknown Soldier, "a privilege," he wrote, "ordinarily offered only to a sovereign or a chief of state." In Washington Vice President Richard Nixon held a grand reception in their honor, attended by high-society figures, politicians and the diplomatic corps.[15]

The greatest honor was still to come, however. It began with the cancellation of President Eisenhower's proposed visit to Japan in June 1960.

At the time the country was in a state of enormous upheaval. Prime Minister Kishi was busy forcing through the ratification of the Security Treaty, and Eisenhower's visit was intended to strengthen the ties between the two countries, but many Japanese were violently opposed to the continuing presence of American troops on Japanese soil. For months huge demonstrations raged in the streets of Tokyo—against the treaty, against the Americans, against the presidential visit. Often the demonstrations turned into violent confrontation with the police. More than six million workers went on strike. There were many injuries, and one student was killed.

Finally, four days before the president was due to arrive, the government conceded that it was too dangerous. The rioting was out of control. They could not be responsible for his safety, and the invitation was withdrawn.

The treaty was ratified, rammed through in another violent Diet session by the infamously right-wing Kishi, but public anger was so great that he himself was forced to resign. Hayato Ikeda, the brilliant minister of international trade and industry who was the protégé and accepted successor of Shigeru Yoshida, took his place as prime minister. According to a distinguished Japanese journalist, it was Yasujiro who, "working behind the scenes, arranged Ikeda's selection as prime minister."[16]

To old establishment figures like Yasujiro, the episode was a disgraceful blot on Japan's international image. Their country had been shamed, their reputation for courtesy and hospitality tarnished. As soon as order had been restored, it was imperative that a spokesman should be dispatched to deliver apologies to President Eisenhower and ask him to revive his plans to visit Japan.

It was an important and delicate task; and to do it Prime Minister Ikeda chose the man who had shored up the bridge between Japan and the United States by introducing Kishi to General Lemnitzer—ex-Speaker Tsutsumi. Yasujiro later wrote:

> I said I was not qualified for that mission, for I could not speak English and I was already old. Ikeda said that he would prefer a man with a little antique look and an absent-minded atmosphere rather than one who spoke English too fluently and looked too bright. He thought I was the most suitable man for the mission.[17]

Despite Yasujiro's becoming modesty, it was a very great honor for the old man, a recognition of all he had achieved in a lifetime of work, dedicated, he always liked to think, to the service of the nation.

So one crisp January morning just a few days into 1961, Yasujiro set off on what was to be a six-week grand tour, in which, as goodwill ambassador, he would visit Europe and India as well as America. His job was to do exactly what he was best at—making friendships, building bridges, smoothing the relationships between Japan and its allies. This time Misao and Seiji went along too. As both spoke some English, both could serve as interpreters, and for the young heir apparent to the Seibu empire, it was an unrepeatable opportunity to shake the hands of the world's most powerful leaders and to lay the foundations of a dizzying network of connections.

After stopovers in Los Angeles, San Francisco and New York, the three arrived in Washington. According to the *Japan Times*, "the Eisenhower administration arranged an unusually elaborate welcome" for them.[18] Yasujiro had assumed that he would see Eisenhower alone, but the president invited Misao and Seiji into the Oval Office also. Photographs show Yasujiro, bluff and jovial—with, indeed, "an absent-minded atmosphere"—at ease in the role of official emissary; while Misao, glamorous in a dark Yves Saint-Laurent suit and elegant hat, exchanges smiles with the president.

Yasujiro's task was to rebuild Japan's relationship with its most important ally, the United States, and to restore confidence in his country abroad. The first step was to make amends for the insult that had been perpetrated on the United States in the person of its president. As emissary, Yasujiro had brought with him sixty-eight volumes of signatures, sixty-eight thousand in all, of Japanese citizens, begging the president to visit Japan. He discussed the trade issue, already a thorny problem, and explained the politics of the new Ikeda administration, laying the groundwork for a visit by Ikeda later on in the same year. Eisenhower in his turn promised to do all he could to visit Japan after he left office.

Yasujiro had also hoped to meet President-elect Kennedy, who declined on grounds of protocol. So Yasujiro left a letter for him at the Japanese embassy, promising friendship to the new administration and inviting Kennedy too to visit Japan.

From Washington the three set off on a whirlwind tour of the European capitals. In London Yasujiro invited Prime Minister Macmillan to visit Japan—September, he said, was the best season—and discussed trade with Foreign Secretary Lord Home. In Paris he met Premier Michel Debré. He shook hands with Chancellor Adenauer in Bonn and with President Adolf Schaerf in Vienna. He was guest of honor at a lunch in Rome. And in Delhi he renewed his acquaintance with Nehru, while Misao, glamorous in a kimono and stole, stood by smiling. Finally, after a marathon forty-five days the three arrived back in Tokyo. A crowd of Diet members were there to greet Yasujiro as he stepped off the plane.

His last years, it seemed, were to be an unending success story—honored at home, feted abroad. He was one of the country's grand old men, celebrated in radio and television documentaries. He wanted to put the questionable acts of his past behind him, to be remembered only as a benefactor of the nation, a humble practitioner of the philosophy of "gratitude and service." Not that anyone believed him for a moment, but that was not the point. Japan is not a society that demands naked honesty. Far more important is to preserve the harmony of the whole. Businessmen and politicians are expected to mouth pious platitudes in the same way that philanderers are expected to get married.

But, as the saying goes in Japan, a sparrow never forgets its path nor a three-year-old child its soul, though a hundred years may pass. Yasujiro had not changed. And there were many who were determined not to let him forget it.

One of his most persistent critics was the distinguished journalist Yonosuke Miki, Goto's biographer and founder of the influential *Zaikai* (Financial World) magazine. Miki had followed Yasujiro's career during the Hakone conflict, and he often compared Tsutsumi and Goto the Thief. Goto, he wrote, was transparent. He was ruthless, in many ways he was a bad man. But he concealed nothing. Pistol Tsutsumi, however, was an enigma. The more Miki dug, the less he could find out about him. When he interviewed him, he said, "I found his answers full of fiction. . . . To be frank, my impression was of a person you could never trust." There was a huge discrepancy between the saintly image that Yasujiro worked so hard to project and the murky reality.

When Miki asked the two enemies, "Which have you done more of, taking over companies or relationships with women?" Goto answered quite accurately, "Companies, of course." But Yasujiro said piously, "I never go out with geisha. I only eat lunch made by my wife." "Young people might be impressed with that," writes Miki, "but to men of my generation it was a bit . . ."[19]

Two areas in Yasujiro's life remained impenetrable. One was his relationships with women, which he carried on, endlessly and obsessively, even as he projected the image of being a happily married man. And the other was the strange discrepancy in his financial affairs. Even though his business continued to expand at an amazing rate, his tax bill remained inexplicably small. In fact, although everyone knew he was a billionaire, it was very difficult to discover any record of his income. It was only after 1958 that he first started declaring any income at all, and that was suspiciously low.

Miki tackled him on the question at a meeting in 1955. No one could mention Japanese big business without talking about Tsutsumi; yet officially he held no more than thirty thousand or forty thousand shares in Seibu, which was surely a tiny fraction of the total. The company was family-owned and unlisted. Its financial affairs remained unknown. Surely he must have billions or tens of billions of yen worth of hidden assets . . .

The audience began to mutter, but Yasujiro was unmoved. "You call me a billionaire, but you are mistaken," he said icily. "I've never seen my money. Please ask my staff how much property I have. It's true that I have only thirty thousand or forty thousand Seibu stocks."

Miki snorted with laughter. "Mr. Tsutsumi, you talk like the emperor himself!"

Yasujiro said, stony-faced, "The tax office has been investigating my property for the last year and a half. But they found nothing—because I have nothing."

Miki was looking hard at his face as he said this, but there was not a flicker of emotion. It was as if he was so practiced in lying that he believed himself.[20]

In fact, as far as the tax office was concerned, Yasujiro really did have nothing. The company owned everything, even the big house in Hiroo. Yasujiro received only a salary. The real question was, who owned the company? But Yasujiro was powerful enough to ensure that his financial affairs were never investigated with unseemly thoroughness.

Then in 1963 a scandal broke that threatened to besmirch the saintly image that Yasujiro had cultivated so carefully. Japan was now more prosperous than anyone had ever imagined, and more than anyone else the architect of the new prosperity was the soft-spoken, bespectacled prime minister, Hayato Ikeda. He had come into power in the aftermath of the riots that unseated Kishi, and he was convinced that the best way to curb political dissent was not by force or confrontation but by conciliation. Put people to work, put money into their pockets, give them spending power, and they would lose interest in protest; they would cease to pay attention to what the government was doing.

In 1960, when he took power, he promised to put the economy first. Within ten years, he said, he would double the national income. Almost immediately it was obvious that his policies were working. Standards of living shot up, and, as he had hoped, material aspirations replaced the old idealistic political ones.

Nineteen sixty-three was an election year; no one doubted that the Liberal Democrats and Ikeda would be returned to power. As always, Yasujiro stood as the candidate for Shiga. In election after election he had never failed to be returned, but recently his majority had become worryingly small.

He went the rounds of the hustings. At seventy-four he was big, bearlike and dignified, and he liked to play the role of the bumbling old man. "I'm a bit absent-minded these days," he would start off in his surprisingly reedy, quavering voice, one hand deep in his trouser pocket. "I know I don't look all that bright . . ." Then he would launch into a recital of all his past achievements, making sure to insert plenty of "Eeh"s and "Aah"s into his speech so as not to appear overly brash or confident. From time to time the mask would slip and he would drop in a remark like "There has to be someone in the Diet to act as proxy for the prime minister. So please vote for me. . . ."[21]

The election passed without incident. Ikeda was returned to power, and Yasujiro was once more returned as member for Shiga, with an increased majority. The trouble started a few days later. Down in Shiga there was a sudden flurry of arrests. Day by day the number increased until ninety men in all had been taken into custody. Strangely, all were highly respectable members of the community and all were in their fifties—the mayor of Hikone, where Yasujiro had gone to school; local politicians; local government officials; the chairman of the education board; and the head of the local election organizing committee. They were charged with giving or receiving bribes.

It turned out that well before campaigning had even begun, officials of Omi Railways, one of Yasujiro's companies, had visited the local elders and given them large "gifts" of money. They had asked them to use their influence to ensure that ex-Speaker Tsutsumi got a respectable majority of votes. The amount of money in question was staggering; more than ¥10 million had changed hands. Many of the city elders also went on luxurious excursions, courtesy of Omi Railways, and accepted travel passes.[22]

Nothing in this was unusual, except the scale of the corruption. Every election threw up many cases of bribery; on this particular occasion nearly three thousand people were arrested nationwide. But there were many more arrests among the Tsutsumi faction than in any other. It was also strange that such a powerful man had allowed himself to be put into such an embarrassing position. For, although Yasujiro himself was not directly implicated in any of this, his dignity and his reputation as ex-Speaker and elder statesman were badly sullied.

The journalist Yonosuke Miki, who records the story, comments that the most irritating aspect to the affair was the way the Tsutsumi faction tried to cover up the whole thing. It was a supreme example of the hypocrisy that, he felt, surrounded Yasujiro Tsutsumi. All they had to do was acknowledge that bribery had occurred—after all, it was a normal part of any election campaign. Had they added something like "the great man himself was very worried by the whole business—in fact, it may have hastened his death," then, writes Miki, "I'd go to his wake."[23]

In fact it was not long after this that Yasujiro became ill; and many people whispered that it was indeed the shame that hastened his death. Throughout his life he had been a survivor. No matter what happened—the excesses of the jazz age, the rise of militarism, the outbreak of World War II, the rebuilding of the country after the war—he had always found a way to turn it to his advantage. He was the last of the men of Meiji, the giants who had built fortunes out of nothing with scant concern for ethics, morality or the people they sacrificed. That age had passed. It was time for a new generation to take over.

II

The Sons

The Rebel

Seiji's Story 1927–1955

Father's despotic temperament did not change and Mother's heart swung back and forth between love and hate for him. Kumiko and I grew up scraping our young skins against the naked discord between this adult man and woman.   TAKASHI TSUJII
A Spring Like Any Other

Long after Yasujiro's death, it seemed that no one in the family would ever be able to escape his monstrous shadow. His children were the products of his outrageous behavior, and it cast a blight on all their lives.

All but one of his children grew up in the shadows. That one was Shukuko, his first daughter and the only child to be born more or less in wedlock. All the rest were the children of mistresses, and all spent their childhoods far removed from the brilliant world of money and power that Yasujiro was moving deeper and deeper into.

When Seiji was born, on March 30, 1927, Yasujiro was already a rising young politician and in his first term as a member of the Diet. He was thirty-eight and expanding his business at such a rate that he was perpetually teetering on the edge of bankruptcy. Only a few years had passed since the Great Earthquake of 1923.

As the son of the mistress, Seiji lived hidden away in the small cottage surrounded by leek fields and cherry trees that Yasujiro had bought for Misao. It was in Mitaka, in those days a country village of small wooden shops and houses scattered among wheat fields with woods just behind, several miles to the west of Tokyo. Here he lived a quiet, isolated existence, cloistered with three women: Misao, whom he knew as his mother; Kuniko, his small sister; and the maid, who came from Shiga.

He was a thin, rather shy and sickly boy, perpetually ill with one malaise or another. At school he had few friends, and he spent much time alone, reading, playing in the garden, watching the insects or sitting with his mother. It was a strange claustrophobic world.

From time to time, from his earliest childhood, something would happen to jar the uneventful peace of his existence. He became aware that his family was different in some inexplicable way from those of the rude country boys around him. There were no grandparents, no aunts, no uncles, no cousins. Above all, there was no father. In his autobiographical novel *In the Season of Roaming,* he tells the story of Hajime, who seems a mirror image of himself. Sometimes, he writes, Hajime's schoolfriends taunt him. One day, when he is just six or seven, the school bully, a big muscular boy, jeers at him, "Bastard, bastard—mistress's kid!" Hajime is so incensed that despite the difference in size he leaps on the boy and beats him until he bleeds.

A few days later Hajime's sister, Mia—modeled, apparently, on Kuniko—comes crying home from school, complaining that everyone taunts her too as "little bastard—mistress's kid." Their mother, Takayo, turns away so that they can't see her face. "You are the descendants of samurai. You are my children. No one can point a finger at you!" she says sternly.[1]

Seiji adored Misao. He would sit for hours at her side while she sewed or read poetry to him or talked about *The Tale of Genji,* the overpoweringly romantic eleventh-century classic about Prince Genji and his many loves. Later Seiji wrote that she lived in a world of poetry in order to escape the disappointments and sadness of her everyday life. To her, Yasujiro was a modern-day Genji, the Shining Prince who turned up from time to time to bestow his favors on his lovers, then disappeared again as mysteriously as he had come.

In the novel the boy, Hajime, is proud of his mother. She is beautiful, like a geisha, unlike all the other mothers in the village, but she is also somehow distant. She doesn't treat him as his friends' mothers treat their children; she never hugs him or cuddles him or lets him sleep pressed up close against her; she doesn't spoil him or indulge his whims. And sometimes, when he does something that makes her angry, she ties him to a pole and hits him with a ruler and screams again and again, "If I let you go on like this you'll turn out like your father!" If this is what it means to be the descendant of a samurai, he thinks he doesn't want to be one.

All these tales Seiji recorded later in his novels *In the Season of Roaming* and *A Spring Like Any Other*. No doubt he altered details, just as he changed the names of the characters to give a semblance of fiction. But the stories are told with such passion that no one doubts that they are close to the truth; and Seiji himself has acknowledged in interviews that this is the case.

Kuniko too has spoken about her childhood. She and Seiji were nearly the same age; and growing up together in the hothouse atmosphere of the cottage in Mitaka they were always very close. While Seiji was the poetic, sensitive soul who took after his mother, she was the tomboy. More than any of the other children she had her father's spirit in her; she was tough and fearless. When Seiji came home crying because he had been bullied, she would go out and beat up the boys who had tormented him.

Once a week something happened that utterly disrupted the peace of the little household. Yasujiro—big, burly, noisy, fierce— burst in like a typhoon, blowing their frail world apart. He would stomp around issuing orders, scolding, shouting, teasing the maid from Shiga or lying for hours in one of the rooms while she massaged him. They would all have to creep around quietly so as not to disturb him. In his novel Seiji writes that the fictional mother, Takayo, is always happy at those times, which makes Hajime jealous. To him this big aggressive man is a stranger and a hateful intruder. From time to time the Yasujiro character tries to play the father. "Come and watch me bathe," he says genially to the little boy. Hajime, writes Seiji, would stand awkwardly beside the bath, feeling faintly repelled, looking at the big white stomach and the penis floating underneath it.

Then the intrusion would come to an end. The father would drive away in his big car early in the morning. "The world outside disappeared as if a curtain had fallen across it. Once again my gentle-hearted mother and my sister and I were left in our suburban house. Nature began to breathe and talk to me again. Under the sink a cricket was singing."[2]

The years passed. Gradually the world outside began to impinge on the peaceful rural existence of the little household. Japan invaded

China; the economy was put on a war footing; and around the same time Yasujiro became ill with typhoid fever. For some weeks the family had nothing to live on but the few yen that Misao could scrape together by sewing kimonos and selling them.

In 1940, when he was thirteen, Seiji's life changed dramatically. The first he knew of it was when Misao told him that he was to have a new name. From now on he would no longer be known by her surname, Aoyama, but by his father's, Tsutsumi.

At the same time they left their quiet home in Mitaka and moved to the palatial residence in Hiroo. From now on they were to live together with Yasujiro. Misao became his helper. She began to work with him on his business; and she had less and less time to spend with her children.

Seiji was no longer the child in the shadows but the young prince, the son of a rich family. He went to the prefectural middle school, one of the best in Tokyo. Instead of the black school uniform with gold buttons that everyone else wore, he had an expensive navy-blue one with red lines down the sides of the trousers. People who knew him then remember that he seemed ashamed of his background: he didn't want his schoolmates to know that he was the son of a rich man. He never talked about his family; and only his closest friends were ever invited back to the enormous house in Hiroo.

Yasujiro made sure that he learned judo, and he also began to train him in the family business. When he visited construction sites or houses that he was thinking of buying, he often took him along. But no matter how hard he tried to ingratiate himself with his son, the boy remained distrustful. He was beginning to catch glimpses of the true nature of the man who had sired him. Sometimes inadvertently he found himself witness to events which he barely understood but which frightened and revolted him. From time to time he would disturb one of the maids leaving his parents' room with her clothes disheveled. Yasujiro saw no need to conceal the fact that he slept with the maids. Sometimes one of them would go into the bedroom when Misao was there and she would have to turn away and put her bedclothes over her head so as not to hear the woman's moans.

These fragile teenage years were dogged by unwelcome revelations. Seiji was, he discovered, part of a large, strange family. He was introduced to family members who he had never imagined existed—

to Shukuko, his half sister, to Kiyoshi, the embittered elder brother who was perpetually at loggerheads with his father, and to a new younger brother, Yoshiaki, who was only seven at the time. There were more and more puzzles, more and more complications that were hard to fathom. Often the boy yearned for the simple days in Mitaka, when he had lived happily with just his mother and sister.

The war intensified. Seiji started Seijo high school, one of the most exclusive schools in Tokyo, attended by youthful aristocrats and the sons of the wealthy. Every day he went along in his black uniform with his dirty satchel full of books. But there was very little time for studying. While Kuniko and the other children were evacuated to the countryside, Seiji was in Tokyo working, helping with the war effort—tearing down houses to make way for canals to stop fires from spreading, building an airport runway, manning the fire station. He was there when his father lay in the underground shelter, a telephone in each hand, making land deals. And he was there, helplessly running with buckets of water, when the big house went up in flames and even the peacock was consumed in the conflagration.

When the war ended in 1945, Seiji was just eighteen. He was slight still, rather withdrawn, a thoughtful boy with a round gentle face and large inquiring eyes set wide apart. For him and his generation, the occupation forces opened a door to an entirely new world. He had grown up in a country ruled by the iron hand of the military, with its tight controls over thought, speech and reading matter. With the coming of the Americans everything was let loose. In the early days of the occupation, MacArthur's aim was to do everything to encourage freedom of thought, to instill the concept of democracy into the Japanese mind. And the idealistic young people of those days, who had participated unwillingly in the war—Seiji and his contemporaries—were more than ready to absorb such ideas.

Suddenly everyone was talking about democracy, staying up all night discussing socialism and capitalism and how society should develop. The country was flooded with books that none of the younger generation had ever known existed before—the works of Marx, Lenin, Keynes. It was heady stuff.

In December, just four montins after the end of the war, he was one of the thousands who pressed into the huge public hall for the first postwar rally of the Communist Party. The speaker, Yoshio Shiga, a thin, intense figure in an overcoat and a handmade sweater, had recently been released from prison, along with 150 other Communist leaders. Standing on the rostrum, gripping the sides of the desk with both hands, he denounced the men who had led Japan into war. "The time has come," he shouted, "to name those guilty; to list the men who brought Japan to ruin, who made her a place of terror and oppression. Our list is long. It has 1,300 names. There are 357 members of the Lower House, who voted as their taskmaster ruled. . . ."[3] The audience roared and cheered. Seiji cheered too, he writes in his novel, and bawled "Hear, hear!" That means my father is a war criminal too, he thought.

The last on the list was Emperor Hirohito. There was a shock of silence in the hall. Then everyone began to cheer and shout and stamp their feet, until the whole hall was in an uproar of noise.

Everyone, in fact, seemed to have turned democrat. The bristly old politicians too were busy declaring that in their hearts they had always been democrats. Although they hadn't dared say so, they had opposed the war from the very start. And the proper way for the country to be governed was of course as a democracy—which meant that they, as the representatives of the people, would continue to rule, under the authority of the emperor.

To the younger generation this was the most scurrilous insolence. In an interview, when Seiji was asked why he became a Communist, he replied:

> During the war the prevailing opinion was that the Americans and British were devils, not even human, and that the Japanese were superior. Then the very next day, after the war, those same people became democrats. Those cheating tricky adults could not be forgiven, I felt. Even now that incredible volte-face on the part of the leadership incenses me. I thought that the only thing to be done was to drive them out—so I did all I could.[4]

In his young mind his revolutionary fervor fused with his distrust and hatred of his father. "My father appeared to me to be a symbol of those dishonest figures of authority. I felt if I didn't overthrow my father I couldn't overthrow authority."[5]

The ferment outside the house infected the atmosphere within.

Yasujiro, the famous capitalist and leading member of the Diet, had been purged. The younger members of the family felt freer than ever before to speak out against him and everything he stood for.

Seiji had witnessed the endless confrontations between Kiyoshi and his father. It was a dreadful atmosphere in which to grow up. It blackened Seiji's youth and made the house, this palatial mansion in Hiroo, feel less of a home than ever.

Finally the tension between the father and the eldest son became intolerable. The family was summoned into Yasujiro's study and in front of all of them Kiyoshi formally gave up all rights to the inheritance. After Kiyoshi had fingerprinted the document of renunciation in blood, Yasujiro announced grimly, "Seiji will succeed to the Tsutsumi family." Seiji was taken aback. As he tells it in his novel, he hadn't realized that he was the next in line. He felt profoundly ambivalent about this sudden access of responsibility, for he too wanted to shake himself free from this oppressive family. But in some way he was inextricably tied to them. "I felt the bellflower—the family crest—imprinted on my forehead."[6]

Kuniko was the next to leave.

Whereas Kiyoshi was driven out because he was too weak to withstand his father's bullying, Kuniko left from choice. It was she more than any of the other children who had inherited her father's stubborn fearlessness. She was a fiercely independent girl: of all the children, she was the only one who could say no to the rough old patriarch. It was only she who dared confront him about his behavior toward women. And when he fondled the maids in front of them all, it was she who told him to stop.

She had grown into a striking young woman, "beautiful in the Aoyama way," say people in the company, with her mother's delicate features and a soft whispering voice that belied the strength of her will. Like Seiji, she couldn't bear to live in this oppressive house with their despotic old father, but unlike her brother, she felt no constraint to stay. One day, when the parents were out, she packed her bags and left. No one but Seiji knew where she had gone. It was an extraordinarily brave and desperate move. Even today most Japanese girls do not leave home until they are ready to marry, and then they move straight from their parents' home to their husband's. In the late 1940s, it was unthinkable for a young girl to leave home and live on her own.

In the end her parents found her. She had moved in with a young man whom Seiji in his novels describes as a dance teacher. Despite Yasujiro's opposition to this scruffy, rather nondescript young man, he wanted to make his daughter respectable. He arranged for the two to marry and gave the young man a job in his company. Later the pair went to live with the young man's family in the country, but Kuniko had already confided to Seiji that she suspected that her marriage would not last. In this respect too she seemed to be taking after her father.

Seiji's rebellion took a different form. In 1948, by the time he started university, he was already deeply involved in the student movement. In those days militant Communist leaders were doing the rounds of the schools, giving speeches larded with Marxist phrases, criticizing the old imperialist system. At Seijo high school, that bastion of privilege for the children of the wealthy, Seiji had been one of the leaders of a campaign to expel the principal, who had supported the war and had encouraged a militaristic line in classes. He had attended conferences of radical high school students where he met fellow revolutionaries who were to become lifelong friends. Like Kiyoshi, the other intellectual among the children, he easily got a place at Tokyo University, the best and most prestigious university in the country and the most difficult to enter. There, like Kiyoshi, he officially studied economics. But in practice, in those heady days, only the most timid and unimaginative students ever attended classes.

In those days, as now, Tokyo University occupied a grand and spacious campus to the northeast of the city, on the other side of town from the big house in Hiroo. Miraculously, most of the Victorian-era neo-Gothic brick buildings had escaped damage during the war, and the famous pond surrounded by woods, in the center of the campus, where many of the country's greatest thinkers had found inspiration for their ideas, was still intact. Unlike Waseda, Yasujiro's alma mater, Tokyo was, and is, a public non-fee-paying institution. Like Oxbridge, it took only the very best students in the country; and it was a cradle for the nation's elite. The civil service and the country's best companies all recruited their staff almost entirely from Tokyo University.

It was, in other words, a great honor and a great opportunity to be offered a place at Tokyo University. But from the very start, Seiji never attended a lecture, nor did he go skating or to the cinema; he never engaged in any of the normal student activities. Instead he spent all day in the offices of the Tokyo University cell of Zengakuren, the revolutionary student body, earnestly discussing tactics or reading Marx and Engels and underlining important sections in red pencil.

Zengakuren—the All-Japan Federation of Student Self-Governing Associations—had been formed in September that year as a union of the radical student bodies of all the universities in the country. It had a membership of three hundred thousand and was closely tied to the Japan Communist Party. For the first months the students were engaged mainly in militant protests against some of the occupation's educational reforms and against a proposed rise in university fees; but gradually as the occupation changed its policies and began to clamp down on the left, their activities became more political.

Seiji was not simply a member of the rank and file. He was one of the core members of the Tokyo University chapter, a small elite within the radical student body. Here he bumped into a young man whom he had first met as a high school student, a fiery, outspoken youth called Jinbei Ando, with a dramatic bony face with high cheekbones, eyes set wide apart and a tiny flat nose. The two were diametrically opposed in personality—the quiet, pensive, rich boy and the noisy, bumptious youth. Perhaps because of this they liked each other immediately and became firm friends.

As a reserved young man, Seiji preferred to remain in the background. While the other members of the group argued and shouted and made inflammatory speeches, Seiji was working. He took on the essential, unglamorous tasks—doing the group's accounting, collecting subscriptions, writing leaflets, working in the print shop turning out pamphlets and posters. Whenever anyone asked where he was, the answer was always, "He's printing."

Seiji had an added reason for remaining in the shadows. In Communist circles the name of Tsutsumi was one of the most hated of all. Yasujiro had a reputation as a ruthlessly aggressive capitalist, greedy and unprincipled, and at the time he was very much in the public eye. He was busy buying up the ex-princes' lands and his battle with Goto the Thief over Hakone was already causing much merriment as it was broadcast across the press. Seiji's family background was therefore not just an embarrassment to him but a danger. As a member of the core group, he went by an assumed name, Yokosei. Only his closest friends, such as Ando, knew that he was really the son of the notorious capitalist Yasujiro Tsutsumi.

His friends from those days remember him as a *botchan,* a rich kid, a pretty boy with soft white skin who had never worked in his life, a quiet young man who listened very carefully to everything that everyone said. He was completely committed to the cause. While other students were struggling to support their studies with part-time jobs, Seiji never had to work. In fact, he subsidized the movement from his own pocket, topping up the group's purse when there were not enough funds and using his own money to print the newsletter.

A couple of times he invited the inner circle, the members of the core group, back to his room in the big Hiroo house for a meeting. All but he lived in tiny rabbit-hutch houses, and all remember sneaking through the vast carpeted rooms of the splendid residence, with its high ceilings and exotic Western furniture, to Seiji's quarters upstairs.

At first the student movement seemed to be the answer to everything he had been looking for. It was as if he had finally found a way to break out of the dark confines of his family life and had found something worth fighting for. He had even found a new family; his soulmates in the core group were like brothers and sisters to him. Seiji, an intense and serious young man, was no camp follower; he was one of the most committed, willing to jeopardize his university career and his future for the cause.

Day after day the friends gathered in the Tokyo cell's little office, lit by a single lightbulb, with posters and placards piled against the wall and empty bottles rolling on the floor. The passionate discussions went on sometimes until the small hours of the morning—the nature of the Japanese revolution and which way it should go; what tactics to use to further the next stage in the struggle.

One night a group of the students straggled out to a street stall to have noodles. Among them was a girl called Yoshiko Nakao.

Nakao-*kun*—Comrade Nakao—was one of the leading members of the core group. She was a small pretty girl, rather plump, with long hair and big round eyes, perpetually bubbling with words, ideas and laughter. Like all the girl students at that time, she dressed conservatively in a blouse, knee-length skirt and ankle socks. All her youthful energy she directed to the revolutionary cause. She was "very active and brilliant," say her contemporaries, "a hero of the student move-ment." As a student of music, every day at lunchtime she organized a chorus group to gather at the university gates and sing Russian folk songs and revolutionary anthems like the "Internationale"; and she played the organ for the music circle. Where Seiji was dark, she was bright; where he was quiet, she was noisy.

That night over noodles she was chatting. "If my mother saw me here she'd weep," she exclaimed. She had a loud, raucous laugh, like a boy's.

"Own up, Nakao-*kun*," teased the irrepressible Ando. "You're an *ojōsan*, a spoiled little rich kid!"

"That's right," she said archly. "I'm a dropout from the bour-geoisie! All my family are!"

Everyone laughed, happy careless laughter. Seiji watched, sitting a little apart from the group. He could never laugh about his family in the same way, he wrote in his novel. It was a dark secret he could never share. "It was a time when I felt that even though I was a part of the student movement I could never be the same as the others."[7]

Over the weeks and months he felt more and more drawn to this confident, lively girl with her boyish laugh, but she repelled all his bashful attempts to woo her. They worked together, pasting up posters, planning poetry meetings or musical gatherings for the stu-dent radicals, or discussing the next phase in the revolutionary strug-gle. Whenever he tried to turn the conversation to personal matters, she always changed the subject or told him, in her direct way, that he was fine as a friend but nothing else.

By now the mood of the country and, more significantly, of the authorities, had swung alarmingly to the right. General MacArthur and the occupation forces had largely reversed their policy toward Japan. Where to begin with they had encouraged left-wing gatherings and inflammatory speeches as signs of the development of freedom of thought, now they clamped down hard on the left. With their en-couragement, Prime Minister Yoshida instituted a red purge, removing Communist Party members and sympathizers from the government, media and the important coal and steel industries. For Seiji and his fellow radicals it was time to stop talking. They now had a real struggle to engage in, and a real enemy: America and American imperialism.

To the authorities the student radicals had become a nuisance and a threat. Once the Korean War broke out in June 1950, they banned all meetings and demonstrations in Tokyo. No more than three people were to meet together at any one time. In December that year, contemptuous of the ban, the militants at Tokyo University organized a political strike. Eight hundred students gathered. In the lecture hall one of the leaders clambered onto the platform to make a speech. To everyone's surprise, it was not one of the usual rabble-rousers like Ando but the earnest, soft-spoken Yokosei (Seiji's assumed name).

Raising his voice above the hubbub, he pointed out the professors standing along the edge of the room and condemned them for not being brave enough to stand up for what they believed in, against the authorities. "We have to present a united front against this threat to peace and freedom," he yelled. "Imperialists out of Korea! We will not be Truman's mercenaries!"[8]

The students all cheered and stamped their feet.

Meanwhile a mob of students from Waseda, several hundred strong, had marched through the streets to the gates of Tokyo University, carrying placards and chanting. They planned to link up with the Tokyo students to make one huge demonstration, but when they reached the gates they found that the authorities had barred and locked them. Police were guarding them to make sure that no one broke through.

While the Waseda students were milling about in the street outside, the Tokyo students inside the campus rushed the gates and began to batter and shake them, beating off the policemen who tried to stop them. They were hefty wooden gates with a thick bolt drawn across and no one could budge them. Seiji was at the front of the crowd, madly pounding the gates and pushing away the police.

Suddenly he remembered the hammer that he had been using to nail placards onto poles. He shoved his way through the battling students and ran back to the militants' headquarters. He grabbed the hammer, stuffed it into his belt and pushed his way back into the fray. Just as he reached the gate and was raising his arm to smash through the iron grille, a policeman thrust his way toward him, brandishing a club. Seiji spat in his face. The policeman stopped in his tracks; and Seiji brought down the hammer on the padlock holding the bolt in place. It broke. With a roar the gates swung open and the Waseda students flooded in.

Joining together in a huge mob, the Waseda and Tokyo students all linked arms and began to sing, "Friends, let's yoke shoulder to shoulder and fight! Mountain and river are different—but we are the world's youth!"

Seiji, crushed in the middle, sang at the top of his voice, nearly in tears with the emotion of it. At that moment, he writes, he (or, rather, Hajime, the Seiji character) had no father, no mother, no sister. They all disappeared. For that moment at least he felt free of them.[9]

Over the next few days he became aware that Nakao-*kun*'s attitude to him had changed. A year after that day when he had first sat and watched her eating noodles, they began to go out together. After all the years of being forced to watch his father's outrageous behavior, he wanted to do no more than hold her hand.

But those intoxicating days of freedom and solidarity, when everyone linked arms against the oppressors, were rapidly coming to an end. Seiji and his friends were in their final year at university and most of them had begun the grim search for work. Seiji alone had no idea what he would do. His comrades looked askance at him. Of course—he was a rich kid, he had no need to look for a job.

In the harsh repressive atmosphere of the early fifties, the left was beginning to split apart. Many Communist Party members had lost their jobs in the red purge and their leaders—like the flamboyant Sanzo Nosaka—had been driven underground or hounded back into exile. Under pressure from the government and the occupation forces, the old men of the Communist Party hierarchy insisted on a policy of compromise with the authorities. Seiji and his comrades in the Tokyo University cell—effectively the leaders of Zengakuren, the nationwide student movement—were outraged. This was a rank betrayal of everything that they and the movement stood for. With the single-mindedness of youth, they were convinced that nothing short of violent revolution was acceptable. Taking with them a section of Zengakuren, they broke away and formed a faction within the Communist Party committed to militant action. They called themselves the Internationalists, to indicate that they followed the line of international Communism as laid down by the Cominform in Moscow.

The Communist Party bureaucracy was determined to crush the rebel faction. The best way was to break it up, and to do so, they needed scapegoats. What had begun as youthful idealism was rapidly becoming mired in the dirty adult world of politics.

Part of the strategy was to set the members of the core group against one another. Early in 1951 Seiji was summoned to appear before the central committee of the Communist Party. The fiery Ando, as the leader of the militants, was ordered to interrogate him.

Seiji was an easy target. By now the Communist leaders had discovered that he was the son of the rapacious and much hated Yasujiro Tsutsumi. It was unimaginable that the child of such a man could really be a committed revolutionary.

Seiji himself was painfully aware of the dichotomy between his father's activities and his own. As he wrote pamphlets and pasted up posters, he became more and more aware that it was not enough simply to struggle against capitalism in the abstract or against the ogre of American imperialism. His own father was the supreme capitalist, a man famous for making his fortune by trampling others into the dust. His father, in fact, was the real enemy. Unless he confronted him or at least did his best to liberate the workers in his companies, all his revolutionary activities would be pure hypocrisy.

As a first step, sometime before he was pulled up in front of the central committee, he had located and made contact with members of the Communist cell within Seibu Railways. He started trying to organize a union in the company. But his idealistic plans backfired.

When Ando and Seiji arrived at Communist Party headquarters, they were marched into a small dingy room like a prison cell, with tiny barred windows set high up in the walls. A row of Communist Party officials were sitting there as a court of inquiry, grim middle-aged men with shaved heads and droopy, sallow cheeks. With them was their principal witness, a man in the uniform of Seibu Railways.

Yasujiro, it transpired, had discovered that there were Communists within Seibu Railways and had effectively foiled their plans to go on strike. Someone had been leaking information to him. It was all too obvious that the guilty party must be this son of his, who had suddenly begun taking such an interest in the Communist cell there. Surely he must be working as an underground agent for his father.

For hours the Communist officials and Ando bombarded Seiji with questions until he was utterly exhausted and confused. They had

had him followed, they said, they had searched his desk at the university. In fact, they had found no evidence against him. But in the end it was his transparent honesty that convinced them. He answered each of their accusations quietly and thoughtfully, insisting again and again, "I'm not a spy." Finally they lifted the charges against him. After all, he was only a *botchan,* a rich kid. He was not dangerous.

Ando, who had been forced to betray his friend, was furious. He made a fierce speech, bitterly denouncing the Communist Party leaders, but Seiji's standing among his comrades had been permanently damaged. Many of them shunned him; and even Nakao-*kun,* with her long hair and boyish laughter, confessed that as a dedicated party loyalist she had doubts. "Well," she said. "If the party says he's a spy . . ."[10]

For Seiji it was the most bitter of experiences. As he commented in an interview, "It hurt that I had not been recognized as an individual, independent from my father."[11] Once again he had been betrayed; once again he had lost a family. He could never escape his heritage.

In March 1951 Seiji graduated from the university. Over the following months he immersed himself in revolutionary activities. There were local elections for the governor of Tokyo, in which the Communist Party and the international faction fielded separate candidates. Seiji traveled around the area, canvassing on behalf of the internationalist candidates, visiting grim little housing projects, standing on beer crates in the rain making passionate speeches. He threw himself into the movement as if to ensure that he had no time left to think. He was busy all the time—reading, organizing meetings, visiting factories, editing the newsletter, planning a magazine. He was permanently exhausted and developed a persistent cough.

He was fully committed to the internationalist cause, convinced that this alone represented the pure Communist path. Then something happened that at the time seemed to be the ultimate betrayal.

In September 1951 Prime Minister Yoshida flew to San Francisco to sign the San Francisco Treaty and the parallel defense treaty, to end the American occupation of Japan and give the country back its independence. Taking its lead from the Soviet Union, the Japanese left was strongly opposed to the treaty. It made Japan into a satellite of the United States. American troops would continue to be stationed on Japanese soil; but they were under no obligation to defend the country in the case of an outside attack. As far as the left was concerned, it was a treaty highly disadvantageous to Japan.

For the left it was a time of crisis. The Communist Party put out a call to end factionalism. It needed strength and unity to fight the threat of "the American military and American imperialism." But to the idealistic members of the international faction compromise was unthinkable. The Communist Party had betrayed the revolution, and they could never join forces with it. As Seiji and Ando and their comrades listened to the radio broadcast exhorting them to unify, they looked at one another in despair. "We've lost," muttered one of them grimly. "The international faction has lost completely."

The end came a few days later. Seiji was busy working, pasting up posters, collecting signatures, when he heard the news. The international faction had merged back into the Communist Party. There was no longer an international faction. Its members could choose, if they wished, to rejoin the main party.

For Seiji it was a bitter moment: everything he had fought for in the purity of his beliefs had been betrayed. He had devoted his youth and his energy to fighting for this cause; but the cause itself—or at least those who represented it—had proved worthless. The San Francisco Treaty, the future of Japan, hardly mattered anymore. It had all been devalued.

In later years he spoke about his disappointment. In an interview he said that his worst memory from those early days was the student movement. In the end it was an utter failure—it taught him nothing but the pain of isolation and defeat.

The day after he heard the news he coughed up blood. His exhaustion and cough had been the first symptoms of tuberculosis, and he was rushed to the hospital. For weeks he lay in a dream, burning with fever, not knowing whether he would live or die. He was vaguely aware of his family tending him—his sister Kuniko gently lifting his head to change the ice pack, Misao pattering in with chicken soup and orange juice. She seemed more beautiful than ever. Later, when he was stronger, Yasujiro too came in to visit. He always barreled into the room radiating energy, shouting out orders as if he were in his own home. "Open the curtains, Mother, the boy needs more light! How are you getting on, boy?" he would ask, then settle down with Misao to argue about business and company matters.

For a long time Seiji was so weak that he could do nothing for himself. He could barely turn over, and received no visitors except his family; and the doctors forbade him to read. Instead he lay day after day in his hospital bed and thought. All through his student life he had thrown himself madly into the revolutionary struggle, almost as if he were trying to avoid having to think. Now he had nothing to do but muse and reflect.

Along with almost everyone in his generation, he had fought wholeheartedly to build a new society. When, one by one, his comrades dropped out, driven by the need to look for work, he had stayed on, grimly sticking by his beliefs. But the movement itself had betrayed him. Left alone with himself, he began for the first time to question his own motives. He began to suspect that the same passion that drove his father was the passion that had burned in him during his days as a militant. The dreadful truth, at least as the Seiji character phrased it in his novel, was that "we are father and son, we resemble each other as closely as a reflection in a mirror. To escape this fate I joined the revolutionary struggle; but they wouldn't accept me. In the end I couldn't resist the blood connection."[12]

Little by little he was beginning to come to terms with the fact that he was his father's son; and he wondered whether much of his revolutionary fervor had been fired solely by the urge to rebel against Yasujiro and everything he stood for. He also discovered that his parents had known all along that he was involved in the student movement. It turned out that people at Seibu Railways had informed Yasujiro that his son was a member of the Communist Party. His reply was unequivocal. "I trust Seiji," he said. "It's a lie."

By now he was allowed to read again—but only poems, which the doctors considered to be less exhausting, because they were shorter than books or newspapers. It was like his childhood, when Misao used to read poems to him. He began to write poetry, something he had not done since his teens.

From his hospital bed, the frenetic days of the student movement seemed unimaginably distant. Once he was allowed to receive visitors, Nakao-*kun* and Ando came from time to time, bursting with news of the struggle. Nakao-*kun* had joined the Communist Party while Ando remained independent. But to Seiji all this talk, which had once seemed so important to him, had lost its meaning, and the further he drifted from the students and their struggle and the intricacies of the revolutionary dialectic, the more he lost interest in Nakao-*kun*.

All in all it was three years before Seiji was fully recovered. By then the revolutionary ideals and political aspirations of his youth had gone forever. In the summer he convalesced in the splendid Green Hotel, which Yasujiro had built in Karuizawa, walking in the larch forests or sitting quietly in his room reading and writing. The staff all commented on his modesty and politeness; he didn't behave at all like a son of the arrogant Yasujiro Tsutsumi.

He had still not solved the great problem of what he would do with his life. He felt more and more isolated. His university friends had disappeared; they all had jobs. He was the only one still undecided, using his illness as an excuse to avoid committing himself to one path or another. He toyed with the idea of going back to the university and studying Japanese literature. Perhaps he should become a writer like his mother. Then, toward the end of his convalescence, an opportunity arose from an unexpected quarter.

Recently Yasujiro's political duties had doubled. He had been voted in as Speaker of the House, at a time when the country and the Diet were in a state of great ferment. The responsibilities were great; he needed many helpers. Perhaps this son of his, who had taken such an interest in politics, should have a taste of the real political world.

Yasujiro had never shown any sign that he held his son's political activities against him. He feared and hated Communism, yet even when Seiji tried to subvert Yasujiro's own company and set up a union in Seibu Railways, the old father remained silent. Now, as if to show that he had full confidence in his son, he took him along to the Diet and made him one of his political secretaries.

Seiji's period of rebellion against his father had long since fizzled out. In some ways he felt utterly defeated. His illness had weakened him, and he no longer felt inclined to battle the wrongs of the entire world. He was aware, too, that throughout his period of youthful revolt, his father had never ceased to stand by him. Although the party, which he had fought for, had betrayed him, his father had not. And though he still felt deep misgivings about the old man's life and everything that he stood for, he was ready to compromise.

Established at his father's office in the Diet, he found himself deeply immersed in the very world of politics and intrigue that as a student he had rejected so violently. Because of his father, politicians of all persuasions were eager to woo him. But he had not forgotten his left-wing sympathies. While as his father's secretary he was expected to associate with the conservatives of the Liberal Party, he also sought out the more progressive members of the House. One, one of the first women to be voted into the House, remembers him well as "an intellectual sort of man."

It was around this time that Seiji met a woman named Motoko Yamaguchi, who was to become his first wife. Seiji's first marriage is surrounded with mystery. He himself never speaks about Motoko, and those of his colleagues who know her refuse to reveal much. It seems that she too was working in Yasujiro's office at the Diet, as a so-called office lady, making tea and answering the telephone. Yasujiro strongly suggested to Seiji that it was time he had a wife and that Yamaguchi-*san* would be a good person to marry. The marriage, in other words, was arranged by Yasujiro; Seiji must have been at the lowest ebb of his confidence, to allow his father to dictate to him whom to marry.

There are only the smallest, most unsatisfactory snippets of information available about Motoko. One source within the company, who knew her well, revealed only that she was thin-faced and very much liked going out at night. "I don't know what she's doing now," he added, "anyway, I can't tell you."

It is not clear when the two finally married. According to one source it was as late as 1957. In any case, the marriage did not go well. Yasujiro provided the young couple with a house in Higashi Kurume, just outside Tokyo. But friends from his student days recall that when they met Seiji at the time, he looked depressed and lonely. When they boasted to him of their own romances, he would mutter gloomily, "I'm jealous."

Seiji's role as his father's political secretary came to an abrupt end when Yasujiro resigned as Speaker along with the whole of the Yoshida cabinet in December 1954. At twenty-seven he was cast back into the position of having to make a decision about what to do with his life. He started studying Japanese literature at Tokyo University but soon gave that up too. He was writing poetry and essays, but he still felt very uncertain about his life's direction. He was still living in the big house at Hiroo, and for the first time he began to pay attention to his father's businesses.

Taking Flight
Seiji's Story 1955–1964

In those days, when I started out, [Seibu department store] was just a little alley shop in front of the station. All I could do was to think how to keep my head above water in the face of all the competition from the big companies. But, come to think of it, perhaps it was more fun in those days!   SEIJI TSUTSUMI
                                                                    TV interview

At the time Yasujiro's businesses were flourishing—all, that is, except one. The small department store out in Ikebukuro was a neglected corner of the empire. It had to be subsidized by the other companies in the Seibu group and was perpetually struggling on the brink of collapse.

When Yasujiro bought Kikuya department store back in 1940 it was almost as an afterthought. His newly acquired railway, the Musashino Line, terminated in Ikebukuro, one of the rougher out-skirts on the very edge of Tokyo, an area of mud streets and corrugated-iron roofs where gangsters and laborers congregated along with bohemian artist types. Land was cheap there and Yasujiro bought plenty of it. And when the small hardware and grocery store came on the market, it seemed sensible to buy it. Most of the railway lines in Tokyo had terminal department stores connected with them where commuters could shop. When the commuters on the Musashino line arrived in Ikebukuro from their farms to the west of Tokyo, in their muddy clogs and homespun kimonos, they bought their watering cans and pots and pans at Kikuya, now renamed Musashino department store. Then, in the carpet bombing at the end of the war, the wooden store was reduced to ash and rubble along with the rest of Ikebukuro and most of Tokyo.

With the end of the war people began to set up stalls, often no more than straw mats spread on the ground. Food was so scarce that customers would squabble over anything—long-dead fish, apples, rice. Ikebukuro, where the trains came in from the farming districts, quickly became a thriving black-market center. Where the Musashino department store had been, the Seibu staff set up shop in a tent, which was surplus from the Japanese army. They sold anything they could get—river fish, the only food that was not controlled by the government rationing system; secondhand clothes, gramophone records, chipped china, toys and sweets. After a year they graduated to a wooden building, then to a larger reinforced concrete one. The name of the store changed from Musashino to Seibu, and they were able to acquire a license to sell American goods imported for the military. Customers would queue for hours to buy shirts and trousers, chewing gum, Lipton's tea (sold by the ounce) and Gillette razors.

Yasujiro took little interest in the fate of the store. As far as he was concerned, its only function was to generate capital to be invested in land and land development, the main focus of his business. Just so long as it turned a profit he was satisfied.

By 1955 the shop had run into difficulties. Yasujiro had put the management of it into the hands of one of Misao's brothers, Jiro Aoyama. Aoyama was a bighearted, kind man, and he was more of a gentleman than a businessman. He helped people out, he did favors, he let debts slide, and soon the little store was badly in the red.

Irritated with this problem, Yasujiro decided to set his feckless son to work. He had sown his wild oats, he had had his period of youthful rebellion. Now, as de facto eldest son, it was time to take on some of the burden, at least, of the family business. To quote Seiji, he had begun to "hang around my father's company. I noticed that the top executives there weren't very smart, so I told my father I thought there was a better way to do certain things. He said, 'Okay, try things your way.' "[1] Yasujiro had tolerated Seiji's flirtation with Communism with uncharacteristic restraint. Still, despite his silence, perhaps his faith in his son had been shaken. Certainly, he was taking no great risk in putting the department store into Seiji's hands; of the whole vast empire that he had built, it was the smallest, least significant part.

At the beginning of 1955 Seiji joined the store as an ordinary clerk in the book department; in October he was promoted to director. Within a few months the store was showing a profit.

In many ways it was the store that saved him. He put aside his personal troubles and worries and flung himself into his work with all the enthusiasm and energy with which he had fought the revolutionary struggle. He studied the company finances with the same rigor with which he had organized the finances of the student militants; he applied proper accounting procedures; and very quickly he balanced the books.

The material was unpromising. Ikebukuro was still one of the roughest ends of town, a warren of dingy alleyways jammed with "pink cabarets" (sex shows) and raucous smoke-filled bars. And Seibu's customers still stomped into the shop in muddy clogs and homespun kimonos. But Seiji had rediscovered the ardor that he had felt as a student. He would take this miserable store and make it the best department store in the country—better still, in the world. And perhaps he could use the power it gave him to achieve something greater. Perhaps his youthful egalitarian ideals would not have to be totally cast aside after all.

To start with he needed money—to invest, to build up stocks, to expand the variety of goods. But he quickly discovered he would have no help or cooperation from his father. Yasujiro was adamant: Seibu was a real estate company and there was no spare cash whatsoever to waste on the department store.

So Seiji set off in search of loans. In each bank he was welcomed as the son of the famous Mr. Tsutsumi, but once the staff realized that he did not have his father's backing, they began to make excuses. He found himself sitting in a side room, sipping tea, waiting for an answer, and usually he was told, "We'll think about it." Finally, after much humiliation and many rejections, he managed to borrow enough money to begin putting his plans into action. He also visited other department stores to see how things were done.

Yasujiro's utter indifference to the department store meant that Seiji could get away with anything he wanted. He began to instigate changes that went against everything his gruff old father believed in.

Yasujiro, old peasant that he was, was very much a man of his time—
a pioneer, out to grab as much money and as much power as possible, with little concern for the niceties. Seiji was of a new generation,
a softer breed with a different, gentler upbringing. As far as he was
concerned, making money was fine, but he was also driven by notions
of quality, style, class, glamour. He wanted to upgrade his department store, to overtake not merely Tokyu—Seibu's traditional rival,
owned by Noboru Goto, the son of Goto the Thief—but even Mitsukoshi, the grandest oldest department store of them all.

He planned a two-pronged attack: to raise the quality of the staff
and the quality of the merchandise. For the staff, he decided to take
on university graduates and organize a union. Yasujiro had always
been suspicious of graduates. He was suspicious of anyone, in fact,
who he thought was too smart and might undermine his position.
"Shopkeepers don't need a fancy education," he would snort.

A few months after Seiji joined Seibu, in 1956, he took on his
first batch of graduates. There was a stiff entrance examination with
papers in English and economics, followed by interviews. Of the six
hundred applicants, twenty-one were accepted. Those twenty-one became Seiji's comrades-in-arms, the spearhead of his battle to transform the department store. As in his student days, Seiji was doing
what he most enjoyed—fighting for change, for what he believed in,
against the powers of reaction. This time the enemy was the in-
tractable old men who ran the store. They were Yasujiro's men, and
they were very suspicious of the newfangled ideas that his upstart
young son was introducing.

For the twenty-one graduates, their first years at Seibu were an
ordeal. None of them has forgotten that time. The work itself was
hard enough. All day long, from 10 A.M. till 7 P.M., they were on their
feet behind the counters, selling pickles, bread, sake, or imported
foods—Hershey's chocolate, Hennessy cognac. In the evening they
had to stay behind to sweep up and prepare for the next day. The
store was open seven days a week, and the staff too worked a seven-
day week, without a break.

The old-timers made sure that the twenty-one new boys worked
harder than anyone else. They were nicely brought-up young men
who had been to good schools and universities, and they were merci-
lessly bullied. They were the ones who had to be in at seven in the

morning to sweep the floors. When there was a heavy crate to carry, it was always one of them who carried it. And in the office they had to put up with perpetual ragging and horseplay.

Only one person was on their side: Seiji. In the evenings they would gather at his house and, over beer, dried squid and rice crackers, engage in long earnest discussions about the department-store business and where it was headed, and how to solve the problems at their store.

Even more than to the taking-on of graduates, the old men at the department store were opposed to unionization. Yasujiro had never for a second considered tolerating such socialistic nonsense. The staff at Seibu were all one big happy family; they had no need for a union. In fact, Seibu was famous as the company that never had strikes. Yasujiro put this down to the fact that everyone was happy; others suggested that perhaps it was because Yasujiro himself was such a tyrant that no one dared.

In the end Seiji wheedled his father into agreeing to institute a union in the store. He called a general staff meeting so that everyone could have a voice in drawing up the contract. Only the old men at the top of the company refused to participate, cracking jokes like "Can't have a union with women in it—they'll just go wherever any fellow leads!"

The young graduates from 1955 recall that in those days their department store was like a symbol of hope. While Yasujiro held the rest of the Seibu companies firmly in his grip, only in the department store was there the possibility of progress. Every time Seiji wanted to make a change, he had to ask his father's permission; and on almost every issue the son and the old man clashed. If he wanted to expand the floor space, take on a new line of goods, make an investment, insert a single advertisement in the paper, he had to go to his father and beg his permission. Yasujiro was particularly opposed to advertising and insisted on scrutinizing every ad before it could be published.

Yet, against all the odds, the store was changing and growing. It expanded upward and outward. It got longer and longer, until it stretched like a wall along the side of the railway tracks at Ikebukuro. One by one the old-timers disappeared, to be replaced by new graduates and talented staff headhunted from other companies—another newfangled procedure of which Yasujiro disapproved intensely.

So here was Seiji, the one-time revolutionary socialist, cheerfully engaged in making money, just as his much despised father had done before him. He was no less sensitive than he had been as a boy; he could see the irony in his situation, and the greatest irony of all was that he had finally found his niche. The department store had provided him with exactly what he needed—a challenge worth taking up.

As he said in an interview, "I tried things my way and found out that a person like me could accomplish something. My way worked. I could see the results. . . . Even small successes encouraged me enormously. I decided business wasn't so bad. It was a game and I could be useful at it. So I became more and more deeply involved in business."[2]

In his work Seiji had found satisfaction and a degree of reconciliation with his father. They were both part of the same world now, though all too often he was forced up against the old man's stubborn conservatism. But at home life remained irredeemably dismal. Trapped in a loveless marriage that, he could never forget, had been foisted upon him by his father, Seiji devoted all his waking hours to work. Whenever he found himself at home he shut himself away in his study and wrote. In some ways he still felt beaten. He lacked the strength of will to oppose his father by breaking out of the marriage. Instead, like many Japanese men, he treated it as a formality. He did what was necessary to produce an heir; that was, after all, the function of the marriage.

His sister Kuniko was not so long-suffering. Of the two it was she who was the wayward rebel. Yasujiro used to say that she should have been a boy and Seiji a girl. She too was locked into a miserable marriage of her father's making.

As she had predicted, her marriage did not last long. In his different autobiographical novels, Seiji puts forward various reasons for this. It may have been because the headstrong young woman couldn't bear the traditional role of daughter-in-law, forced to live with her husband's parents and obey her mother-in-law's every whim. Or it may just have been that, like Yasujiro, whom she resembled so much, she quickly began to see the inadequacies of her mate and started wanting something new.

Not long after she married, when Seiji was just beginning his life as a student, she turned up one day back at the big house in Hiroo. She had left her husband. It was 1948. She was just twenty and in the full bloom of her beauty, still childishly plump with large, penetrating eyes. She radiated zest, gaiety and willfulness.

For women in those days divorce meant ruin. Once divorced they had little chance of ever marrying again. Usually the unfortunate woman spent the rest of her life taking care of her aging parents. Oblivious of the number of women whom he himself had ruined, Yasujiro was determined that his daughter should not suffer the same fate. Quickly, before the fact was known, he arranged another marriage for her.

The man he chose was one of the most promising Seibu executives, a protégé of his called Juro Morita. On the surface of it Morita was the archetypal company man. He had a bland, even-featured face and was never seen in anything other than the most conservative of mouse-gray suits and inconspicuous ties. He wore glasses and his hair was always immaculately oiled into place. He was twenty-six—young enough to be a prospective bridegroom for Kuniko—and reasonably good-looking.

He was also, beneath the bland exterior, a clever and ambitious man. A rough country boy himself, he had found ways to ingratiate himself with Yasujiro. Like the old man, he came from a poor rural family and had fought his way up with the help of nothing but his own relentless ambition and a certain oleaginous charm. He was now one of the leading executives in the company.

Morita leaped at the chance to marry into the Tsutsumi family. After all, besides being his employer, it was one of the richest and most powerful families in the country. With such a marriage behind him, his rise was bound to be meteoric.

As for poor Kuniko, she didn't like Morita at all. But Yasujiro brushed aside her objections. "Father said I had to marry him," she later recalled in her mouselike whisper. "He said, 'You can't say you don't like him.' "

No doubt her father was sure that he was doing the best for her. Once she had been to bed with Morita a few times, she would surely start to love him; this was Yasujiro's primitive theory of human relationships. In any case, there was no question about it: she had to marry. In the usual way, he hired private detectives to check Morita's family and background. It was impeccably respectable and satisfyingly poor; this man would always be dependent on him and therefore a loyal subordinate. And, without indecent haste, the two were married.

Kuniko tolerated the marriage for six years. She bore two children, a girl and a boy, and she did her best to become fond of this unctuous, self-seeking man. But the two were utterly unsuited. Gradually her repulsion and dislike of him grew until she could bear it no longer.

It was Seiji who had to break the news to his father. Once again his wayward daughter had left her husband. She had also left her children and taken a job as a bar hostess in the Ginza. She insisted on another divorce.

For Yasujiro she was becoming an embarrassment. It was 1956. He was a weighty figure in the political world, hosting parties for international leaders. He didn't want rumors and scandal to blacken the family name. As it happened, a relative of Misao's, an art collector called Shigetaro Fukushima, was planning a trip to Paris. He would be gone for a couple of weeks. It was the perfect opportunity to bundle Kuniko off out of the public eye until this latest scandal had been forgotten.

No one, it seems, consulted Kuniko. Like her marriage, her banishment was a family decision, not hers. She had no say in the matter. According to her she didn't want to go abroad and didn't care where she was sent. It was out of her hands.

Seiji went to the airport to see her off. In *A Spring Like Any Other,* he writes about her departure as if it were the final escape from the prison of living in the Tsutsumi household.

After two weeks her uncle the art collector returned to Japan. But Kuniko had tasted the air of another world, altogether different from the claustrophobic atmosphere of Tokyo. Paris, she says, seemed very cold. It was a city of stone. She wondered what was behind those stones. She wanted to find out, so she stayed behind in Paris, and took a room in the Hôtel d'Orsay. Every morning she had coffee and croissants in the hotel and in the evening she went to a language school to study French. She sat alone in cafés, reading and watching people. No one spoke to her and she spoke to no one.

The world outside the cozy confines of Japan, where everyone took care of everyone else, was a terrifying place. For a young woman to go abroad alone was almost unthinkable. Nowadays many Japanese girls flee abroad for the very reasons that drove Kuniko: to escape the stifling atmosphere of Japan in which there is nothing for a girl to do but marry. In Kuniko's day it was an extraordinary act.

Her first months in Paris were unbearably lonely. It was November when she arrived and for months every day was gray and dreary. From time to time it snowed but only enough to leave a gray sludge on the stone streets. From the Hôtel d'Orsay Kuniko moved to a room on the eighth floor of a small boardinghouse near St.-Michel, with eight flights of stone steps that she trudged up and down day after day. Sometimes she spoke to no one from morning till night, and she thought of her two children whom she had left with the wretched Morita back in Japan.

She did some writing. Like Seiji and Misao, she had a talent with words, and she had been asked by various Japanese magazines to send them dispatches. Then, when her money began to run out, she set to work on a novel. Finally she had found the freedom she had been looking for, with all its attendant pain and loneliness. She was far from Japan where she had been pampered and cared for. Now every day she was faced with decisions to make. She was learning, she said, what it was to be human; she was learning to make choices, to have likes and dislikes; and she also—here she giggled girlishly—discovered passion.

Slowly the young Japanese girl was drawn into the world of fifties Paris. She hung around Montparnasse with its international community of artists. She became friends with the sculptor Alberto Giacometti and the novelist Françoise Sagan. She had breakfast with Jean-Paul Sartre at the Coupole in Montparnasse or the Café de Flore. It was an exciting time to be in Paris. There were very few Japanese there, let alone beautiful young women. Everyone was curious to meet her, everyone was charmed by her.

Her novel *Rootless* came out in November 1957, a year after she arrived in Paris, and even before it was published Japanese film companies were squabbling over the rights. In fifties Japan it caused a small scandal. It was the story of a young Japanese girl, alone in Paris, having an affair with a French drug addict. Finally she realizes that

West and East will never understand each other; white and yellow will never get on. Beneath their skins their experiences are too different. Wanting to hold on to the memory of this love before it is sullied, she flees, leaving Paris on Bastille night as fireworks explode overhead. Once again she is a rolling stone, setting off on an aimless journey.

The book sold eighty thousand copies. It was a minor best-seller, though in the end it was never made into a film. Kuniko opposed the idea. She had written it for herself; filming it would take it out of her hands. But it had given her her independence. With the money she made, she bought a flat and a car.

The years passed. She plunged deeper and deeper into Paris and Paris life. She studied French literature at the Sorbonne, she fraternized with intellectuals, artists and the bohemian left. And from time to time she sent articles back to Japanese magazines, on life in Paris and on fashion. Having fought against her father for so long, she was finally free of him, free to shape her own life as she pleased.

Meanwhile, the Japan she had left behind was entering a period of extraordinary change. The years after Kuniko's departure for Paris were the beginning of the boom in Japan. Industrial production doubled, then trebled, then quadrupled. Finally the war and the occupation were over, a dark memory quickly receding into the distant past. The black marketeers, the rice dealers who hung around the stations, disappeared. There was no longer any need for them. Instead penniless young men took on jobs as pushers, dressed in uniforms and white gloves, shoving Japan's growing army of commuters onto the packed urban trains.

Everyone was earning, everyone had money—yet they still felt poor. It was a struggle just to get back to the level of material prosperity they had enjoyed before the war. Housing was a terrible problem. Tokyo in particular was hopelessly overcrowded, full of refugees from the countryside who had fled there in search of work. Most people lived in tiny spartan apartments or rickety wooden houses.

After a time things began to improve. The first sign was the goods on the shelves of the shops. Once gloomy, empty shops were now crammed with alluring items—not just pots and pans and the mundane necessities of daily life, but goods that held out the promise of a new age. The first to arrive were the "three treasures": television, washing machine and refrigerator. Everyone desperately wanted to possess these luxury items that proved that they were no longer poor. People took to window-shopping: even if they couldn't afford the glamorous new appliances, they could at least go and look at them.

When he first took on his department store in the backwater of Ikebukuro, Seiji had anticipated the time when people would no longer be restricted to the bare necessities. He began to stock luxury goods, he displayed the latest electrical appliances. He stocked cameras, he stocked televisions, and when they first came out in 1958, he stocked the newfangled transistor radios made by an unknown little company called Sony. While the grand traditional department stores like Mitsukoshi were slow to respond to changes in demand, Seiji was just building his business; he could take it in any direction he liked.

By 1960 Seibu was a vast emporium with a heliport on the roof. It was a cathedral of materialism, with a food hall many times the size of Harrods, and seven floors where people could buy everything from clothes and books to yachts and prefab houses. To lure customers there were fashion shows, art exhibitions and a culture hall where plays were performed. Like a cathedral, Seibu dominated Ikebukuro; it had grown to absorb the station and was the hub of the whole area. It was an enormous monolith, offering everything one could ever want, big enough to spend all day there, roaming from floor to floor, admiring the displays.

Seiji had achieved a miracle. Where Seibu had been an inconsequential little store in 1955, it now had the fourth largest sales of all the department stores in Tokyo. Seiji himself had changed; he had gained in confidence and taken on the veneer of the brash, dynamic young businessman. In an interview with the *Japan Times* in 1960 he is quoted as saying, with careless assurance, "Our store has only just caught up with such established competitors as Mitsukoshi and Takashimaya. We are now trying to get ahead of them—which should not be very difficult."[3]

The interview in fact took place on June 17, just two days after Tokyo was racked by violent demonstrations against the ratification of the renewed Security Treaty and Eisenhower's visit; one young girl student had been trampled to death. Seiji's comment on this was uncharacteristically acerbic: "I don't understand today's Zengakuren students. They are fanatics. One thing I can say is that many of these fanatic young men return to normalcy after they have passed a certain phase, as I did. But something must be done to them if they behave as they are doing today."[4]

It was quite an about-turn for the young man who had smashed the bolt on the gate at Tokyo University. Perhaps Seiji was simply covering his tracks. Or perhaps he had discovered in the world of work the satisfaction that had eluded him as a revolutionary student. Certainly he had managed to iron out many of his early difficulties. It was around this time that he managed to extricate himself from his marriage. He had done his duty: the couple had finally produced a son and heir. Young Koji was born in 1958. Shortly afterward, as discreetly as possible so as not to embarrass old Yasujiro, the two divorced. Motoko stayed in the house that Yasujiro had given the young couple, in Higashi Kurume, while Seiji moved back to the big house in Hiroo, taking little Koji with him.

Marriage had been a grim experience for him, and he was in no hurry to look for a new partner. Instead he focused all his energies on business. Living under the same roof as his father, he had ample opportunity to discuss every phase and every new development in the store with him.

For Seiji everything he had achieved so far was only a beginning. Like his father, he was never satisfied. In spite of its grandiose expansion, in spite of its spectacular sales figures, Seibu was still just a large emporium in the rather rough, downmarket backwater of Ikebukuro. Sales figures were not enough. Somehow Seiji wanted to create a store that would have an impact on society. There was no need any longer to follow in the footsteps of such moribund old stores as the dowagers Mitsukoshi and Takashimaya, nor to be judged by their standards. Seibu could move off in another direction. It could be a new store for a new age. Now that it was firmly established as a viable part of the Seibu empire, Seiji felt freer to imprint it with his own personality. After all, he was no mere businessman; he was also a poet. His friends were poets, artists and members of the revolutionary left. Surely some of this creative ardor could burn into the way in which he shaped his store.

As a first step he decided to open a buying office in Paris. It was time that Seibu established links with the world outside Japan, and Paris above all epitomized glamour, luxury and high fashion. Besides, Seibu already had someone there, perfectly placed to open a buying office: Kuniko.

Kuniko was by now almost more Parisian than Japanese, *au fait* with fashions, styles, moods and trends, with an ever-widening circle of friends and contacts throughout fashionable French society. As early as 1957 she had come across a young designer called Louis Feraud. His designs, she thought, would be right for Japan, and she had arranged for samples to be sent to Seibu.

Kuniko was no businesswoman. She had no idea how to deal with employees or draw up a contract. She needed a French partner to help her function in this alien environment. So Seiji found a young French journalist who had been working in Tokyo and sent him to Paris to help her. Kuniko found an office to rent in the Champs-Élysées, and in 1961 Seibu opened its Paris office.

For Kuniko it was an opportunity to reconcile with the family while retaining her independence. And it opened many doors for her. As the Paris representative of Seibu she had a seat at all the collections, though, she recalled, at the beginning she was always right at the back. In those days a Japanese department store was a mere curiosity. There was no kudos to be had or money to be made by selling in Japan. It was a poor country, struggling to recover after the devastation of the war, branded in everyone's memories by the horrors of that war. There were no more than three hundred Japanese in Paris, and Parisians invariably confused Chinese and Japanese.

To begin with, Kuniko sent samples of French designs to Seibu, to be copied and sold much more cheaply than the originals. A team of seamstresses was sent out to Paris to learn French design and methods. Then she began to meet young designers whose work excited her and who she felt would be right for Japan. One was a young man called Yves Saint-Laurent; another was the ready-to-wear designer Daniel Hechter. From 1963 Seibu took the sole rights to represent them in Japan.

Six months after the Paris office opened, Kuniko was married again—to the young Frenchman whom Seiji had sent from Tokyo to help her with her work. "It was just business," she later said dismissively. "I didn't like him." Like Yasujiro, she seemed doomed to be perpetually seeking and never finding the perfect partner.

So the big brash department store out in the Ikebukuro outback suddenly began to stock French fashions. In 1961 it seemed the most eccentric of ideas. People put their money into homes, into household gadgets, into savings. But no one had any spare cash for luxurious French fashions, nor the taste for them.

It was, as Kuniko later said, rather early to start a buying office in Paris. In sales terms it was a mistake, and the old-timers in Seibu muttered about the money wasted on such an absurd and extravagant project. But the brother and sister were convinced that Japan would become richer. Tastes and aspirations would change and become more sophisticated. And when that happened, Seibu would be ready.

While Seiji and Kuniko plotted the future of fashion and taste in Japan, another member of the family had come up with a far more daring plan—a project so wildly ambitious that even Seiji had doubts. Even before he went to the United States in 1959 as the guest of General Lemnitzer, Yasujiro had been toying with the idea of opening a department store there. He had never done things on a small scale. If Seibu was to expand abroad, it should do so grandly and boldly. The buying office in Paris was just a beginning. What he wanted to see was a full-fledged department store in Los Angeles.

His visit to America strengthened his determination. He was ashamed, he wrote, to see the poor quality of the Japanese goods on display there. What was needed was a showcase, a store that would display and sell the very best in Japanese goods.[5]

Yasujiro was in his seventies, near the end of his life and the end of his career. Perhaps he was looking for some last grand project that would pull together the twin strands of his career: politician and businessman. A store in Los Angeles would be a symbol of everything he had been trying to achieve in his last years. It would be a bridge across the Pacific, a bond of friendship between the United States and Japan. Now that he was an old man, Yasujiro wanted to put behind him the ruffianly ways in which he had made his money. He wanted to be remembered as a benefactor, to leave behind some monument to the good he had done for humanity.

Having concocted the idea, Yasujiro put it into Seiji's hands to work out the details. Seiji was taken aback. The idea was not just ahead of its time; it was too early. It was more of a political gesture than a business proposition. Seibu had expanded: there were seven branches, located in and around Tokyo, but it still didn't have the financial base to support such a grandiose project. Besides, Japan was still a poor country. Its export drive was only just beginning. "Made in Japan" was synonymous with cheap and shoddy. It seemed unlikely that a store devoted to Japanese goods could be a success.

Yasujiro was adamant: no other Japanese department store had opened a full-sized branch abroad, and Seibu would be the first. By the time Yasujiro, accompanied by Misao and Seiji, set out on his grand tour of the United States in 1961 as Prime Minister Ikeda's special envoy, the plans were all in place. In Los Angeles Mayor Yorty welcomed them and gave them the freedom of the city. And on March 14, 1962, at a cost of $10 million, the Seibu department store opened with much fanfare. Seibu published a booklet in English to celebrate its opening, introducing the Seibu empire to the American public in lavish terms: "Seibu has conquered wildernesses, leveled mountains, reclaimed inland waterways, built railroads. . . . If the total expanse of the land developed by Seibu was made into a road of one meter in width, the length will amount to 78,422 km or twice the circumference of the earth."[6]

Seibu Los Angeles occupied a large building in the center of the city, with curving roofs reminiscent of a Japanese castle shading the main entrance and a staff of 330, mainly local. The four floors were lavishly decorated with Japanese artifacts: exquisite gold screens, lacquerwork, mirrors, ceramics, kimonos and models of kabuki actors. Half the goods on display were American, half Japanese, chosen to represent the best that Japan had to offer: the finest Japanese silk, gifts, traditional handicrafts and the latest electronic goods—cameras, transistor radios. The message was clear: the Japanese were now making high-quality competitive goods. The label "Made in Japan" was no longer something to be ashamed of.

It was an admirable project, but almost from the beginning it foundered. The costs were simply too high and, according to one company insider, there were problems with planning and distribution. Shipping goods from Japan was expensive, and many of the goods were sent by air, which raised the costs enormously. As a result, prices had to be jacked up and sales fell. The modest profits were never enough to recoup the vast expenditure. By 1963, less than a year after it had opened, it was clear that the project was a disaster. Seiji begged his father to let him close the store, and finally even the old man had to concede that this last grand project had been misconceived. Toward the end of 1963 the Los Angeles store closed, leaving Seibu department store burdened with a frightening debt of close to ¥5 billion, equivalent in 1995 terms to ¥500 billion.

Worse was to come. That same year, on August 22, Seiji was having dinner with one of the most powerful men in Japan, Shigeo Mizuno. Mizuno was the owner of the Sankei Newspaper group and one of the Four Emperors who financed and dictated the rise and fall of prime ministers. He was a longtime friend of Yasujiro's and particularly liked young Seiji, whom he thought of as a protégé.

They were eating when the telephone rang. It was for Seiji. He took the call, then returned to the table, apologized for his absence and carried on talking as if nothing had happened. It was only after all the guests had left that he confided in Mizuno: there had been a fire; the top three floors of the store had burned down and there was millions of yen's worth of damage.

It turned out that the fire had started during cleaning time. The cleaners had been using oil to clean the floors. Up on the seventh, in the furniture department, a young boy was killing cockroaches with matches and accidentally set the oil on fire. Fortunately it was a holiday; otherwise the shop would have been crowded with customers. But there were still deaths; some members of staff were killed and there were several injuries.

Yasujiro was in Karuizawa at the time, resting, in company with Michio Nagai, the son of his old friend and mentor Ryutaro Nagai. When the news came Nagai assumed that Yasujiro would want to pack his bags and rush straight back to Tokyo. "No," said the old man. "Seiji's there. He can take care of it. I trust him. It will be a good experience for him." Nagai remembered those words. It showed, he says, that Yasujiro had confidence in his son, and that he was training him for leadership. "There was expectation by Tsutsumi that Seiji would be leader."

In the press the fire sparked criticism of Seiji and his methods. Seibu department store, it was said, was expanding far too rapidly. There was not enough concern for safety, and fire precautions were not adequate. The sharpest criticism came two days later.

Seiji had thought of a way to turn even the fire to profit. He rushed to Karuizawa to talk to his father. The best way to provide service for his customers, he said, was to open immediately, to carry on with business as usual. In fact, he would hold a sale of fire- and water-damaged goods, with huge discounts.

Yasujiro called in Yoshiaki. In those days the two—the father and his younger son—were always together. Yasujiro always consulted Yoshiaki before making any decision.

Yoshiaki was strongly opposed to the plan. It was outrageous, he declared. People had died. It was quite improper, most disrespectful, to open the store. Seiji was not prepared to be bossed around by his younger brother. "I'm doing it!" he insisted.

In the end Yasujiro mediated. "I see," he grunted. "Let Seiji do as he wants."

The store duly opened on the twenty-fourth after the staff had spent the previous day frantically cleaning the surviving floors. That morning there were announcements in the press and on the radio, advertising the grand discount sale. Customers stampeded the shop. Some fifty thousand shoved through the blackened doors and jammed against the counters. People fainted in the crush, and an hour after opening the shop had to close again.

This time there was severe censure in the press. People were outraged at the lack of respect for the dead. After that the store remained closed for several days. Yoshiaki had seen all this coming. According to the journalist Eiji Oshita, in his book *My Youthful Waseda,* after Seiji left the room, Yasujiro explained why he had allowed his elder son to follow such a rash course of action.

"His way of doing business is not good," he told Yoshiaki. "To come like that with his ideas already set—if he comes to see me and his plan gets turned down, his staff will stop listening to him. I let him do what he wants, even if he's wrong. But as for you, don't imitate him.

"If he fails," he went on, "he'll learn a lot. He always has to have his own way. So let him fail. It won't do him any harm just so long as I'm alive."

In fact, the old man did not have much longer to live. Sooner than anyone expected, Seiji was to find himself on his own—saddled with an overwhelming burden of debt and with a department store to rebuild.

A Very Ordinary Boy
Yoshiaki's Story 1934–1964

My business concepts almost all come from the fun I had when I was
young. YOSHIAKI TSUTSUMI
In Akimoto's "Yasushi Akimoto and the
'Boy' Who Became 'Chairman' "

Of all his women, it was Tsuneko whom Yasujiro loved the most. She
had all the traditional womanly virtues: she was gentle, yielding, passive, and she was very pretty, with a fresh, open beauty and warm
smile. She was a sweet, simple girl.

When Yasujiro met her, according to his sharp-eyed cousin
Kamibayashi, he wanted to settle down with her and discard Misao as
he had Fumi. But Misao, in many ways the forerunner of the modern
liberated woman, was too strong for him. She was tough, intellectual,
assertive and determined to get her own way. So Misao became the
wife and business partner, while Tsuneko remained in the background. As Yasujiro's business grew and flourished, Misao was the
partner always at his side. But when he wanted to relax, he went to
Tsuneko. He fussed about her appearance. He shouted at her when
she had a perm. He grumbled when she used too much makeup, and
he insisted that she wear only the plainest and simplest of kimonos.

Tsuneko was only twenty when she became Yasujiro's mistress.
While Yasujiro's affairs with Misao and her two sisters had destroyed
the Aoyama family and brought Misao's father to suicide, Tsuneko's
father, Saburo Ishizuka, was apparently unperturbed by the liaison.

At the time Yasujiro was forty-four. He was a man of substance, a property magnate and a member of the House of Representatives of ten years' standing. He was also one of Ishizuka's closest friends. So perhaps the canny dentist from Niigata decided that this was an advantageous alliance to make, despite the loss of his daughter's honor.

Even after she became Yasujiro's mistress, Tsuneko continued to live with her father. As a dentist, Ishizuka was a man of means. He had a sizable two-story house down a quiet back lane in a prosperous residential section of Tokyo, backing on to Shinjuku Gyoen, a beautiful old park famous for its cherry blossoms and ornamental gardens. In Ishizuka's garden too there were cherry trees and a little stream meandering between the park and the garden. Here Tsuneko lived with her dry old father, perpetually busy with his dentistry or developing new medicines, his number two wife—Tsuneko's mother, the number one wife, kept the house in Niigata—and her baby daughter Matsuko, Tsuneko's half sister. It was a happy, peaceful little household.

A year after she met Yasujiro, Tsuneko had her first child—Yoshiaki. He was born on May 29, 1934, in the Japanese year of the dog. Until he was six he lived in the house in Shinjuku with his mother, his grandparents and little Matsuko, just two years older than he, who became his playmate. He was a tough little boy, with a pugnacious square-jawed face like a boxer. Matsuko, as a lively birdlike woman of sixty-one, remembered how the two used to fight. "I'm the year of the monkey, he's the year of the dog," she said, "so we fought all the time." When she was seven and he was five, the two went together to the local shrine, hand in hand, she in a red kimono with flowers in her hair, he in a dark-blue child's kimono, for the traditional ceremony performed on the third, fifth and seventh birthdays.

Yoshiaki was Yasujiro's third son and the child of the number three wife, so he had none of the pressure that Seiji and Kiyoshi suffered. There was almost no chance that he would succeed to his father's business. He was an ordinary little boy, left to lead an ordinary childhood. And Yasujiro had mellowed with age. His business was well established, he had more time to spend with his young children; and he was not as much of a bully as he had been when he was younger.

The first change in Yoshiaki's young life happened when he was six. By then he had a brother, Yasuhiro, born in 1938. That year—1940—Tsuneko and her two boys moved to the wooden house in Takagi-cho, ten minutes' walk from the big house in Hiroo. Little Yoshiaki was taken to meet his half brothers, Seiji, who was fourteen, and Kiyoshi, a grown man of twenty-six.

At six it was no great trauma to discover that he was part of a much larger family than he had realized. Besides, his own life changed very little. While Seiji was thrown into the middle of his father's world, living with the irascible old man and being forced to watch his escapades with the maids, Yoshiaki grew up very quietly with his mother and brothers (Yuji, the third son, was born in 1942). He went on picnics with his grandparents and Matsuko and at New Year's the whole family spent the day together in Tsuneko's house in Takagi-cho. From time to time Yasujiro came to visit; by then he was over fifty, hefty and barrel-shaped, more like a grandfather than a father. And sometimes Yoshiaki was taken to the big house in Hiroo.

The war disrupted everyone's life. When the bombing made Tokyo too dangerous, Yasujiro sent the little family to the mountains, to Naka-karuizawa. They already had a summer house there, which Yasujiro had provided for Tsuneko, in one of his cottage developments in the larch woods in the Sengataki area, near Prince Asaka's splendid Edwardian-style villa.

In the end they spent several years there. Yoshiaki went to the local kindergarten and made friends with the village boys. His best friend was a boy called Akira Hoshino.

The two were naturally drawn to each other. Their fathers had been friends ever since the days when Yasujiro arrived in Kutsukake (as Naka-karuizawa was called then) in his Waseda uniform to make his first land purchases. Young Hoshino's father was the owner of Hoshino Spa, at the bottom of the hill where Yasujiro had built his first cottage developments.

Hoshino's mother was the village doctor, and a kind and formidable woman. As the doctor, she knew everyone's secrets. And, as the villagers paid her in meat and vegetables, the family always had plenty to eat, even during the leanest of the war years.

One of her patients was Mr. Tsutsumi's number three wife, Tsuneko. Mrs. Hoshino felt sorry for this pretty woman. Tsuneko was beginning to lose her fresh, girlish beauty, and looked rather thin and careworn. She hardly ever saw Yasujiro; during the war years he could barely afford to send her enough money to feed her children. Besides, despite the freedom with which Japanese men ran their affairs, the mistresses and their children always suffered. People frowned on them, there was prejudice against them. As Yoshiaki grew older, he too began to discover, as Seiji had done, that he was a bastard, a mistress's kid. The other children would taunt him with it. He grew quiet and reserved.

Mrs. Hoshino took the little family under her wing. She told Akira, who was a year older than Yoshiaki, to help him. At dinnertime Yoshiaki often came to eat, and every day she made two packed lunches for her son to take to school—one for him and one for Yoshiaki.

The two boys became close friends. Young Hoshino—when I met him, a mischievous balding man of sixty, who had taken on his father's mantle as owner of Hoshino Spa—remembered that of all the evacuees, the toffee-nosed white-skinned city boys forced to spend the war years in the mountains, Yoshiaki was the only one who took an interest in the local village lads. In the dark days when there was no fuel, the schoolchildren had to go foraging for wood in the hills. For Yoshiaki this was a terrible job. Hoshino helped him out, carrying the heaviest branches for him. In exchange Yoshiaki gave him some of the treasures he had brought from the city—pencils with erasers on the end, notebooks of filmy white paper finer than any young Hoshino had ever seen before.

While bombs rained down on Tokyo, the two boys were pedaling up and down the hills of Karuizawa on their big black bicycles, through the larch forests, around the cottages, looking for adventure.

Their two hotelier fathers both had warehouses stocked to the beams with blocks of ice as big as tables, packed between thick layers of sawdust. In the winter they cut it out from the frozen ponds and in the summer used it to make primitive iceboxes to store milk and fresh food. On hot summer days the two boys used to sneak into one of the warehouses and burrow through the sawdust until it was sticking to their clothes and ears and hair. When they came upon a huge wall of ice, they would chip away at it, then gobble down the shavings, mixed with sugar. Or they would open the door of one of their fathers' warehouses, stacked with cans of salmon and beef for wartime rations, steal a tin and devour the forbidden delicacy.

Sometimes they went cycling to the lava beds at the top of the hill. Their big primitive bicycles had no gears. So they would circle in the road in front of the gates of the spa until a truck trundled by, laden sky-high with goods. They would pedal madly to catch up with it, then grab hold of the back with one hand and let it tow them up the hill.

Sometimes they explored the forest. There were logging trucks there that ran along iron tracks for 10 miles through the woods, from the top of the mountain down to the station, piled with huge logs for firewood. On holidays when no one was there, the two boys would go and steal one of the trucks. They would drag it up to the top of the mountain, then the two of them would leap onto it and toboggan at breakneck speed down the track. The trucks had no brakes. The only way to stop them was to stick a piece of wood in the wheels. When this failed the boys had to jump off the hurtling truck and roll over and over down the mountainside until they landed up against a tree trunk or plunged into the bushes.

Those were wild, carefree years. At school there was very little studying. The children had to collect firewood and sometimes they caught fish by hand; and on weekends they worked on making airplane seats, their contribution to the war effort. Once two B-29s flew overhead, on their way to bomb Niigata, Grandfather Ishizuka's home city. But apart from that the war was nothing but a distant rumor that saved the children from their books.

When the war ended, life slowly returned to normal. While, over in the big house in Hiroo, Kiyoshi was arguing endlessly with his father and Seiji was sneaking out to attend Communist meetings, in Takagi-cho everything was very quiet. Yoshiaki, who was eleven by then, went back to Hiroo primary school. Tsuneko taught tea ceremony to young ladies of marriageable age. And once or twice a week Yasujiro came to visit. He had had a judo dojo, a training hall, built onto the house. Whenever he visited he would get up in the morning, sometimes as early as four, to teach his three boys judo. Long before the sun rose the neighbors used to hear thumps and bangs and cries of "Usss!"

Early in 1946 Kiyoshi was disinherited, and Seiji became the next in line. It was around then that Yasujiro told Yoshiaki that he should start paying attention to business. The villagers in Naka-karuizawa, however, remember that years before, when Yoshiaki was small, Yasujiro would take him along to business meetings. "Sit there!" he would say to the little boy. "Listen!" And the child would sit obediently, listening while the adults discussed development plans for the area.

No doubt Yasujiro was deeply disappointed. He had assumed that his eldest son, Kiyoshi, the cleverest of all the boys, would succeed him in the traditional way. But Kiyoshi had failed him. Yasujiro could not afford to make the same mistake again. It would be foolish to put all his trust in one son—particularly when that one son, Seiji, was going against everything his father believed in.

As for Yoshiaki, he was growing into the kind of boy that Yasujiro could get on with. Like his mother, he was no intellectual. Kiyoshi and Seiji were too sharp, too quick to see their father's weaknesses and to criticize. Yoshiaki was more straightforward. He was a quiet, polite boy, rather old-fashioned. When the other boys spoke street slang, he always used proper, rather formal Japanese. He was his mother's son, in fact; and it was always Tsuneko whom Yasujiro loved best.

In 1947, when he was thirteen, Yoshiaki started middle school. He went to Azabu Gakuen, one of the best schools in Tokyo, for the sons of rich families. His schoolfriends there remember that he never spoke about his background or his family. When they visited his home, it was a modest wooden house without even a proper entrance hall. They all assumed he was not well off. No one suspected that he was a son of the famous property magnate Yasujiro Tsutsumi.

He was in fact a very ordinary boy. He was rather taciturn, he hated speaking in public, and he was not particularly interested in his studies. But from time to time he surprised everyone. Once one of his friends, a boy called Takashi Yokota, invited him home. Yokota's mother was a teacher of Urasenke, the same school of tea ceremony as Tsuneko's. She took the boys into her tea-ceremony room, knelt them down on the cushions and whisked up a cup of foaming green tea for them. Like any teenage boy, Yokota had no idea of the proper way to behave in a tea ceremony. It was something that old ladies did, and young girls preparing to be married—not tough young teenage boys. He shuffled around on his cushion and slurped his tea carelessly.

When the bowl was passed to Yoshiaki, he received it in the proper formal way, bowing and turning it with his hands. He knew exactly what to do, right down to tidying up the icing sugar that fell from the small ceremonial cake. He performed the whole ritual to perfection, with great punctiliousness. Yokota's mother was impressed. "You should be like young Tsutsumi!" she scolded her son.

And at school he followed the rules to the letter. While the other boys didn't bother to take their sports shoes home in the evening, Yoshiaki always did.

Everyone remembers that he was a good runner. He was tall for his age and very fast. He took sports very seriously. In 1948, when the Tokyo city government held its first sports meet since the war, he competed in the 400-meter relay race and he and his teammates won. The following year they did the 800-meter relay, running 200 meters each, and won again. Then he gave up running. He gave up all extracurricular activities. In the evening after school, when the other boys went off to have fun, Yoshiaki always rushed straight home. His schoolfriends never saw him anymore. Later he confided to friends that it was at this time that his father said to him, "You will be my successor. Prepare your spirit!"

Seiji's activities were becoming more and more unacceptable. Every night he was out until late, attending revolutionary meetings. Sometimes he even sneaked his radical student friends into the family house in Hiroo to hold a meeting in his room. It was more than Yasujiro could tolerate. He said nothing to his elder son and heir apparent. But while Seiji was out marching, demonstrating and plotting the overthrow of the capitalist system, Yasujiro was walking with Yoshiaki in Arisugawa Park, the grand old park behind the Hiroo house, teaching him about business and leadership.

The punctilious boy absorbed everything that his father told him, and began to grow to fill the mold his father had chosen for him. As a friend of his said many years later, it was as if a small man took on the mantle of emperor.

The years passed. In 1953, the year that Yasujiro became Speaker, Yoshiaki was nineteen. He had grown into a strong, fit young man with a lean, clean-cut face, a sullen set to his mouth and the rugged, rather brutish good looks of a sportsman.

In April that year he started university. While Kiyoshi and Seiji had gone to Tokyo, the university for intellectuals and highfliers, Yoshiaki consulted with his father and went to the same university as he had: Waseda; and like his father, he entered the school of commerce.

Waseda was still a training ground for budding politicians. A lot of the students were talented boys from outside Tokyo, country lads who had got there on the strength of their wits rather than their parents' riches. They drank and smoked and caroused until late, and clattered around the concrete corridors in their wooden *geta* sandals, or strolled the avenues lined with plane trees and Himalayan cedars, passionately discussing the proper way for society to go.

Yoshiaki had no interest in left-wing politics. Instead he mixed with the youthful businessmen of the commerce department and the sporting fraternity. Unlike his father, he drank, although, like Yasujiro, he was strictly against smoking. College mates remember that he held his drink well. In an interview he recalled that he had a bar in his room at home, where he made cocktails, with a pump primed with carbon dioxide. He could shake his cocktails in a figure eight like a true professional, he claimed.[1]

Three or four days a week he went in to Waseda, by train and bus. On his way home to Takagi-cho, where he lived still with his mother and two brothers, he had to pass through the dark streets of an area that was to grow into the wildest, most lively nightlife district of Tokyo—Roppongi. At the time it was home to a barracks used by the American military. He would saunter up the main street, passing groups of brawny GIs out for a night on the town, or drop into Sicilia, one of Roppongi's two exotic Italian restaurants, for a plate of spaghetti. Until then he had never had anything but his mother's cooking. And it was in Roppongi, in its back alleys and tiny crowded bars, that he had his first encounters with girls.

Like Yasujiro, Yoshiaki wasted little time attending classes. In fact, some of his classmates remember him primarily as the boy who used to copy other students' notes. Two days a week—on Fridays and Saturdays—he was invariably absent. He spent those two days at his father's side, from well before dawn until late at night, following him around the building sites, checking new land acquisitions, inspecting building projects, learning all the details of his business. "I had to be with him all the time," he said in an interview. "If I was away for thirty minutes he beat me."[2]

He was no longer the quiet, polite little boy. He had had to grow up fast. There was a weight of responsibility on his shoulders, growing ever heavier. He was a marked man. While the other students flaunted their Waseda uniforms, black, buttoned to the neck, with a square mortarboard and a towel carelessly knotted to their belts, he wore a sober gray suit. They were children still, but he was an adult. He was part of his father's world, a fledgling businessman already. And he was impatient to work on some projects of his own.

Yasujiro too had spent his student years doing business, but besides business he had also been involved in politics. He had been close to the fiery demagogue Nagai, he had been fired by his idealistic plans to democratize Japan. Yoshiaki had known his father only as a conservative old man. He had no vision, no yearning to transform society. It was enough to follow in his father's footsteps. His father had made money; he would make more money. He would take his father's empire if it was offered to him, and make it grow. And if there were some casualties along the way, that was part of the course.

Yoshiaki's classmate at Waseda was a boy called Hiroshi Tsuruoka, an outgoing young man with an open smile and easy laugh. The two sat side by side; the desks were arranged alphabetically and Tsuruoka came next to Tsutsumi. They became close friends. They had the same interests: Tsuruoka too was a sportsman and his family was in the tourism business.

All the students at Waseda joined clubs. That was where they pursued their real interests and developed the friendships that would stay with them for the rest of their lives. Yoshiaki naturally joined the judo club. He also joined the photography club; he had been a keen photographer ever since middle school. But for his main activity he and his friend Tsuruoka chose the tourism study group.

It was 1953. The occupation had ended barely a year before and people were struggling to survive, living in ramshackle houses, working long hours day and night. The Korean War had given a boost to the economy, but that year it ended. The American military no longer needed Japanese armaments and the country was hit by recession. Tourism was the last thing anyone was interested in—except, that is, for a handful of dilettante students.

At the time there were thirty or forty students in the tourism group. They met at lunchtime in the club room on the fourth floor of the commercial-studies department and talked and studied to-gether—how to develop tourism, how to advertise, how to attract foreign tourists, and from time to time they organized small excursions. But Yoshiaki and Tsuruoka had far more ambitious plans in mind.

Tsuruoka, now a member of the Diet for Komeito, the Clean Government Party, remembers his friend as a dark, closed personality, a bit of a mystery. "His father was Speaker," he explained, "so I knew he would do great things." But he was giving nothing away. He was the exact opposite of the easygoing, flamboyant Tsuruoka. "He had a closed heart," Tsuruoka remembered. "He was always looking out for a challenge."

So it was the outgoing Tsuruoka, the future politician, who ran for president of the group. He won, although everyone knew that Tsutsumi was behind him. Between them, the two of them took over the group.

Yasujiro was keeping a watchful eye on his son's progress. He had built his empire by accumulating vast landholdings, and he expected his son to do the same. "First, number one, borrow money; and next, buy land," he told Yoshiaki; that was 99 percent of the business.[3] But times had changed. Investing in land had been a stroke of genius in the prewar years. Now, however, land was multiplying in value a hundredfold; everyone wanted to buy it. If Yoshiaki was to be a worthy successor, he would need to find a new stratagem for the new age. He would need to keep ahead of the times; so Yasujiro decided to set him a test. He gave him a problem to solve. The old man had bought half of Karuizawa. He had spent millions of yen on developing it, building cottages, shops and hotels, yet for half the year his facilities went unused. People went to the mountains in the summer, to escape the Tokyo heat, but in the winter Karuizawa was far too cold. Everything was buried under deep snow. Cottages, shops, hotels—everything shut down.

The challenge that the old man set his son was this: to bring customers to Karuizawa in the winter. Seibu would provide the land, the builders and the money. It was Yoshiaki's job to come up with the idea and to work it through in every detail.

Yoshiaki was ready. He knew his market: students and young people, who were not yet as burdened with work as their parents. He was sure that they would pay money to have fun, and he knew that in the gray workaholic Japan of the 1950s, fun was hard to come by. Soccer and rugby had not yet arrived, there were no discos. There was nothing, in fact, except baseball, which everyone played and watched with fanatic enthusiasm.

No one was putting money into leisure. The government was pouring money into heavy industry, manufacturing steel, ships, cars. New housing, roads and sewerage were all forgotten; those would have to wait until later. And as for leisure—no one had even a moment to think about it.

Yoshiaki was a sportsman and a serious student of fun. He worked by instinct, not intellect. His answer to his father's challenge was simple: skating. In Karuizawa people skated on lakes, ponds and frozen rice paddies, but there was no indoor rink. He would build a 400-meter rink, the first indoor rink in Japan, where people could skate in warmth and comfort, right in the heart of Yasujiro's cottage developments.

The first job was to persuade his father that the project was feasible. He did his research, he drew up a budget, and one morning at four o'clock, Yasujiro's chosen hour, Yoshiaki went into his office in the big house in Hiroo to see him. One of the younger members of the tourism group, Ryuichi Ishida, went with him. While Ishida stood trembling in the presence of the formidable Speaker of the House, Yoshiaki presented his plan to him. Ishida later remembered how formal the two were with each other—like a soldier and his general or an executive and his managing director, not like father and son.

"You got the confidence to do it?" Yasujiro growled.

"Let me have a go." Yoshiaki rapped out the words with a deep bow.

A few weeks later, a bevy of Waseda students descended on Naka-karuizawa. For the next six months they would be traveling up and down between Tokyo and Karuizawa, working on the project. They would miss classes, but there was plenty to learn here. They were engaged in real business, they would even be paid a wage.

The entire project was Yoshiaki's to plan in every detail. Everyone became familiar with the sound of his voice—high-pitched, like his father's, imperious, issuing orders. He was like an emperor. Some of the students began to call him "*Tenno*—Emperor." According to

Tsuruoka, they were together twenty-four hours a day. It was like one large family, with Yoshiaki at the center.

The rink was constructed inside an old airplane hangar a little way up the hill above Hoshino Spa. By the end of the year everything was completed. The opening was planned for January 7, 1956. Ishida had bought the tape and had the gold scissors ready for Yasujiro to perform the opening ceremony. But as the day approached, everyone began to worry. Yoshiaki had promised his father that the rink would attract one hundred busloads—five thousand customers—a day. But supposing he failed? Skating was not a popular sport in Japan. Tsuruoka and Ishida were more worried about the weather. It was too warm. There was no ice.

By January 6 the rink had still not frozen over. Everyone was in a panic. Then someone—maybe it was Yoshiaki—remembered the storehouses full of ice where he had played with Hoshino in those carefree years during the war. Seibu trucks were loaded with huge blocks of ice and the students laid them in place by hand, then shoveled dry ice and snow from nearby Mount Asama into the cracks to level them out. The surface was just smooth enough to skate on.

The opening ceremony the following day went without a hitch. Prince Takamatsu, the emperor's brother, attended and so did the press. Japan's Olympic figure skaters gave a display. A country-and-western band played, and Yasujiro cut the tape with the golden scissors.

No one in Naka-karuizawa has forgotten what happened next. Yoshiaki had promised his father five thousand customers a day. The first day after the opening five thousand came; the next day, more; the day after that, more still, until there were six hundred buses a day leaving Tokyo, carrying thirty thousand enthusiastic skaters to Naka-karuizawa. The buses left from different parts of Tokyo, around eleven at night, and wound up the long mountain road to arrive in Naka-karuizawa at six in the morning. The skaters skated all day, then left in the late afternoon for the journey back to Tokyo. It created a minor boom. Skating rinks began to open all over Japan.

"Boy, it was popular," said the mischievous Hoshino. He had been away in America studying. When he met up with Yoshiaki again he was struck by the change in his boyhood friend. The lad who had followed him on their escapades around the hills had turned into a leader, an emperor. "He used to be very quiet, very modest, not out-going," recalled Hoshino. "I was more aggressive. I didn't know he had such Napoleon-type power."

The buses jammed the road to Naka-karuizawa. What with the noise of traffic and people, no one could get any sleep. But they didn't mind, said Hoshino. Winter had been a moribund season, but now Naka-karuizawa was bustling with customers. Others were less sanguine. Some of the villagers grumbled that all the money went to Seibu. The skaters hired skates and ate at the restaurants at the rink. All the village got was inconvenience.

Still, Yoshiaki had undoubtedly proved himself. Yasujiro was more and more convinced that this son had not only the will but the ability to rule the empire.

Yoshiaki's last project as a student was one that even Tsuruoka had doubts about. Yasujiro had long had his eye on the luxurious and exclusive resort of Oiso. It was a beautiful wooded area on Sagami Bay, along the coast from Tokyo on the way to Hakone. For the last hundred years, ever since the beginning of the Meiji period, aristo-crats and wealthy and powerful families had had villas there. Hi-robumi Ito, the preeminent Meiji statesman and father of the first Japanese constitution, had had a splendid seaside villa built in the Western style, with gables and a steep tiled roof and Tiffany-style stained-glass insets in the windows. Shigeru Yoshida too, the grand old man of the postwar period, had a mansion there, hidden within thick woods, with the sea in front and a river behind, like a natural fortress. Little by little, as it became available, Yasujiro began to buy land. As it happened, one of the pieces of land that he acquired was a grand sweep of coast, right next to the grounds of former prime min-ister Yoshida's mansion. There was a small hotel there, but customers were few. The beach was gray and shingly and the ocean rough and forbidding.

Yoshiaki was on the lookout for a topic for his graduation thesis. At the time sea-bathing was in its infancy in Japan. Traditionally peo-ple went to the mountains, to spas and hot springs to relax, not to the coast. There were almost no seaside resorts. Here was a challenge for Yoshiaki to ponder. How could one make money out of the seaside? There must be a way in which one could draw crowds of customers to the coast, and charge them money.

He did his research, he studied the data. Most people, he concluded, went to the sea to relax. Mostly they stayed on the beach. Only a few swam in the ocean. So he proposed a luxurious seaside resort, with a huge freshwater pool 328 feet long and 164 feet across, right beside the ocean. There would be a variety of smaller pools, with umbrellas and awnings and groves of palm trees to provide shade, rock gardens, piped music and fairy lights at night.

The Seibu staff members shook their heads. Who would pay money to swim in a pool when they could swim in the sea for nothing? But Yasujiro by now had full confidence in his son's instincts. When the pool at Oiso Long Beach opened on July 1, 1957, even the former prime minister Yoshida came to have a look and declared that it was as vast as a sea. Customers came down the coast by the busload. And other developers began to build pools beside the ocean.

Despite their neglect of their studies, all the students passed their final examinations. Yoshiaki and Tsuruoka graduated in 1957, Ishida in 1958. After a brief period with his family firm, Tsuruoka joined Seibu and worked there for four years. When he left to go into politics, Yoshiaki shook his hand and said, "If you ever want to come back, you'll be welcome." The two have remained friends ever since. Ishida too was eager to work for Seibu, but he was obliged to join his family firm.

As for Yoshiaki, Yasujiro made him the head of the tourism division of Kokudo Keikaku, the central company within the Seibu Group, responsible for land acquisition and planning; and later in the same year, in October 1957, he became a director of the company at the youthful age of twenty-four. Yasujiro himself was nearly seventy.

Over the next years, Yasujiro was training his son full-time in business and leadership. He often said to him, "Yoshiaki, I'm going to teach you what I learned from my father and what I worked out for myself—two generations' worth of knowledge."[4]

The two were seldom seen apart. Whenever there was a decision to be made, Yasujiro always demanded his son's opinion. At first Yoshiaki would have to go away and ponder. When he finally returned with his conclusion, Yasujiro would shout at him and tell him where he was wrong. He would never put his stamp to a document until the two were in complete agreement.

Later the Kokudo Keikaku executives worked out a way to

shorten the process. They would approach Yoshiaki first, put their proposals to him, discuss them, make changes, then, when they had his approval, go to Yasujiro.

As the years passed the father and son became closer and closer. Finally, it is said, their opinions coincided 99 percent of the time. It had been a tough apprenticeship, but Yoshiaki had proved a worthy student.

Of all the boys, surely this one was made in his father's image. He had the same unerring business instinct, the same unswerving determination to make money, the same ability to be out in front, ahead of the times. And he could manage people. If he was to rule an empire, he would have to be an emperor.

Death of the Last Giant
1964

Anyway he was certainly audacious when it came to business. He'd go
to any lengths to get what he wanted, even use force. But now that he's
dead, it feels like we've lost a man that had guts. Look around you.
Most company owners are like top-grade students now. There's plenty
of smart guys in Keidanren and Doyukai [economic management asso-
ciations]. But Goto and Tsutsumi were on a different scale. Scholars
and businessmen are completely different.   HIROSHI OKAWA
                              In Miki, "Death of the Last Monster"

It was Thursday, April 23, 1964. In Tokyo the cherry-blossom season
had just finished. The last of the fragile pink blossoms still clung to
the trees or wafted to the pavements. People strolled the streets in
their bright spring clothes.

In the garden of the big house at Hiroo the irises were just coming into bloom. That morning Yasujiro rose at five, as he did every
morning, and took a turn around the grounds. Leaning on his stick—
he was never without his stick now—he shuffled down the steep slope
behind the house to the large pond shaped like Lake Biwa. Halfway
across the red stone bridge he paused to sniff the morning air and
watch the doves flocking overhead. "Look at the doves," he called to
Misao. He loved to watch them fluttering.

He was seventy-five. He had become a little slower, his skin was
developing the thinness and transparency of age, his hair was gray and
thinning. But he was still big and barrel-shaped and full of irrepressible roguishness. Every morning without fail he practiced judo, he did
a little gentle exercise. He prided himself on his good health.

By now he had largely set his affairs in order. The younger
members of the family were running the different sections of the

empire. Seiji was the president of the department store. Yoshiaki, under his father's guidance, was the president of Kokudo Keikaku, in charge of land acquisition and development. Shojiro Kojima, the husband of Shukuko, Yasujiro's eldest daughter, was the president of Seibu Railways. And the oily, bespectacled Juro Morita, whom Kuniko had fled to Paris to escape, was ensconced as the president of Seibu Chemicals, the company that Kiyoshi had joined after being disinherited.[1]

The old ex-Speaker was now free to concentrate on politics—though his image had been tarnished recently by the allegations of corruption among his supporters in Shiga. He had also become quite a celebrity. On February 24, 1964, just three months earlier, he had been the guest on the radio show *Talking About My Wife*. He declared fondly that Misao was not so much a wife as a mother to him. "She treats me as if she's bringing up her own child," he said with a chuckle. And he declared that on a scale of 1 to 100, he would give Misao a rating of 120. "I'm the *yokozuna*, the grand champion, of wife-praisers," he boasted.[2]

Only a few days before, the national broadcasting corporation, NHK, had invited him to their studios to film an hour-long interview with him for a program celebrating his long and distinguished career, entitled "This Man, This Road." In the company of friends and admirers like Michio Nagai, his old friend Nagai's son, he mused on his life's experiences and the lessons he had learned.

Asked about his plans for the future, he replied:

I still want to carry on [with politics], but naturally man has his limits. So I want to find someone really good to take over from me. Taking my age into account, I want to carry on, that's what I think. As for business, other people are doing it for me and I'm watching. That's how I want to do it.[3]

There was just one decision he had still to make. He had not yet named his successor. Outside the company, everyone assumed that Seiji was the one. The financial community, the barons of big business, had watched and admired the way he had transformed the department store. He had proved himself a formidable and imaginative businessman, a fit successor to his father's crown. But the Seibu executives, the old men who had been there nearly as long as Yasujiro, knew that he was closest to Yoshiaki. However, Yoshiaki was young still, and far too inexperienced to head a huge concern like Seibu. His achievements were small compared with Seiji's, but he had enormous promise. As if to underline the trust he had in him Yasujiro had already installed him as president of the core company of the entire group, Kokudo Keikaku.

That sunny April morning, as usual, Yasujiro went to inspect some of the new construction work. He ordered his driver to take him to the Tokyo Prince Hotel, in the Shiba section of Tokyo.

This was to be Seibu's first modern, purpose-built, multistory hotel, to join the ranks of the Imperial, the Okura, the Hilton and the Palace, the only first-class hotels in Tokyo at the time. It would be a hotel equal to any in the world, with every conceivable modern luxury: an arcade of shops stocking glossy European goods, elegant banqueting halls, a rooftop restaurant with views across Tokyo and a landscaped swimming pool.

Yasujiro had plenty of choice land available for such a project. The plot he chose was one he had bought years before when he had been busy snatching up imperial lands—the old graveyard of the Tokugawa shoguns. Many towering cedars that had shaded the shoguns' tombs for centuries had had to be cut down to make way for the new hotel. To run the project he chose the person whom he trusted more than any other: Misao. He made her the president of the hotel and left the details of the planning entirely to her. It was an extraordinarily powerful position for a Japanese woman to hold. In an interview in the *Mainichi Daily News* a few days before, Misao had spoken of "my debut, as I step from the wings, from behind the screen, on stage for the first time." Yasujiro added that he "addressed the greatest importance to her new hotel. . . . This is why I put my better half in charge of such a significant development."[4]

Everyone was working at breakneck speed. The hotel had to be completed and perfect and ready to open by the beginning of October, to house the hordes of foreign visitors who would be descending on Tokyo for the Olympic Games. It was to be Tokyo's greatest moment—the first Olympics ever to be held in Asia and Japan's chance to show off to the world just how much had been achieved since the war.

All over the city everyone was in a frenzy of activity. Everywhere there was building work under way. In the Harajuku area, where the games would take place, the soaring curves of Kenzo Tange's spectacular Olympic stadium were beginning to take shape. Long straight roads, broader than ever before, were flung down to take the Olympic traffic from the airport to the stadium. Three raised expressways, the first in Tokyo, and two ring roads were built. There was a new monorail serving the airport, new subway lines, splendid new high-rise buildings; and the first Shinkansen, the "bullet train," the fastest train in the world, linking Tokyo and Osaka, was scheduled to open in time for the Olympics.

Yasujiro, of course, was keen to take part in this national celebration and to take advantage of the governmental largess that was being offered for projects connected with the Olympics.

That fine April day he stomped around the building, shouting an instruction here, bellowing reproof there, then suddenly barked, "This hotel needs an extra wing—build an extension!"

For Misao this was too much to demand. She was already overwhelmed with work. "This is one more burden added to my load," she sighed.

She waited for Yasujiro to yell his usual response, *"Baka!* Idiot!" But instead he quoted a poem:

"In this life, still piling up so many things to do.
Our time is short—but let us do what we can."

She was astounded. He had never before shown the slightest interest in poetry, let alone quote a poem. He had always sniffed at her writing; and he once said to Seiji, who had inherited his mother's poetic leanings, "Up till midnight writing poetry—that's no way for a manager to behave!"

With a qualm, she wondered if it was a premonition.[5]

The next day he rose at five as usual. In the morning he paid a call on Prime Minister Ikeda. When he came back to the Hiroo house, he sat down heavily in a chair in the living room, complaining that he had felt numb when he was out. He sat silently for a while as if he was thinking.

By chance Kuniko was home at the time. It was her first visit since she had left for Paris eight years before. She was thirty-six, a sophisticated Parisian who outlined her eyes in black, painted her lips pale pink and wore her hair combed into a beehive with a deep fringe and a curl in front of each ear. She still spoke in the same mouselike whispery voice; and she had still not found the right man to settle down with. She had come back to make peace with her father. She had planned to come earlier, but had been delayed.

Kuniko, her father and Misao went to have lunch. The old man ordered simmered bream and, uncharacteristically, insisted on complimenting Misao on her kimono and the hostess of the restaurant on her soup. Then they parted company. One of Yasujiro's young male secretaries and his favorite maid from Shiga were waiting to go with him to Atami, to spend the weekend at his country house on the coast.

At Tokyo station, just as they passed through the ticket barrier, Yasujiro collapsed. The secretary rushed to call Misao. She was at his side in minutes, holding his hand. His face was gray and his pulse was weak, but when he spoke his voice was clear and his mind seemed clear too.

"This is not it," she kept saying to him reassuringly. "This is not the stroke you were afraid of." For years he had been afraid of suffering a cerebral hemorrhage, as his grandfather had.

In fact he had suffered a very light case of cerebral anemia.

Seiji arrived a few minutes later. As the old man was rushed to hospital, he kept muttering, "Let's go home. I want to go home."

For a day and a half the family kept constant vigil at his bedside. Misao had not left his side for a moment. She and Seiji went to rest, and it was his errant, strong-willed daughter Kuniko who was left to sit with him. Even though they had quarreled, the father and daughter had always loved each other. It was she more than any of the other children who took after him. Later Kuniko often said that the reason why she could never settle down with one man was that she could never find a man to match her father.

By then he could no longer speak. For a moment their eyes met, and with a gesture he communicated that he was sorry. And, she said later, she told him that she forgave him.

It was Kuniko who closed his eyes, at 8:10 A.M. on Sunday, April 26. The grand old man, the last of the giants, was dead.

That evening the obituaries came out. One, in the *Asahi* newspaper, was by Hyo Hara, who had been Vice Speaker when Yasujiro was Speaker. Ex-Speaker Tsutsumi was, he wrote, a man with a good sense of humor, very fit and healthy; "as a public figure, he was serious and polite." He recalled the tumultuous events in the Diet ten years before, when Yasujiro had had nearly all his clothes torn off.

Several of the obituaries mentioned Seiji as if he were the appointed successor. Hyo Hara wrote:

> His son, young Seiji, is a rising young businessman, president of Seibu department store. Recently Seiji has been doing a lot of business. Tsutsumi used to control everything himself; but that has changed. Recently there has been much talk about expanding Seibu department store into Shibuya, the territory of their rival, Tokyu. It seems that Tsutsumi accepted Seiji's new approach to business.[6]

But actually nothing had been decided. Yasujiro had died too soon. It was after his death that the trouble began.

An hour after Yasujiro had breathed his last, the most powerful people in the Seibu empire met in a back room in the Hiroo house, in the boardroom where they had always held the Tuesday meeting. They took their allotted seats around the long table. The place at the head, Yasujiro's seat, was empty. A large photograph of the old man stood on a shelf behind, watching over the group.

Yoshiaki sat to the right of his father's seat, Misao to the left. Next to her came Seiji. Seated around the table were Yoshiaki's two brothers, Yasuhiro and Yuji; the two sons-in-law, Shojiro Kojima and Juro Morita; and the three most powerful Seibu executives outside the family.

The question they had to decide was the most urgent of all: Who should be the successor? Who should rule the empire now that the old man was gone? It was the gravest crisis that the company had ever faced. If they couldn't reach an amicable settlement, the empire would split. That would be the end of everything that the old man had built and fought for. The choice of successor was the final test. Posterity would judge Yasujiro by how well he had chosen.

As far as the outside world was concerned, the matter was already settled. Seiji was the eldest son now that Kiyoshi had been disinherited. He was effectively the legitimate son, regarded as the son of Misao, Yasujiro's legal wife. The succession was his by right. It was obvious that Misao, who was enormously powerful, would support him.

Besides, he had already proved himself. He had made a great success of Seibu department store. He was intelligent, personable, good-looking, gentle and well liked, and he had built up a formidable network of contacts in the political and business worlds. The only point against him was his past, the fact that he had been an agitator, a member of the Communist Party. But he had long since been reconciled with his father and become a worthy scion of the Tsutsumi family.

Only Seiji and his father knew just how deep the antagonism had been between them. When Seiji rejected the capitalist system, he was rejecting his father and everything he stood for. By the very fact of joining the Communist Party he gave up his right to the succession. And all the time that he was developing the department store, he had had to suffer opposition and hostility from his father. Yasujiro feared Seiji. He was too smart, too critical, too different. His management methods were those of a new age. Instead of yelling at people, he listened to them. Yasujiro was afraid that if Seiji inherited, he might undo everything that he himself had done.

The old men of Seibu knew that Yasujiro wanted Yoshiaki to inherit. He had molded him in his own image. He knew that he would follow the path that his father had laid out; but Yoshiaki had no reputation, he had no network, and if he inherited, Misao and Seiji might oppose him and the empire would split.

There are various stories about how the final decision was reached. At the time people assumed that Yasujiro had chosen Yoshiaki with his dying breath, though the journalist Yonosuke Miki, writing soon after the old man's death, suggested that it was the old men of Seibu who had outmaneuvered Seiji, fearing for their jobs if a new regime came in.[7]

The journalist Toshiaki Kaminogo, researching his book *Seibu okoku* (Seibu Empire) in 1983, interviewed a man called Kunio Fukumoto, who gave a different account.

Fukumoto is a mysterious, rather sinister figure, who has since become one of the most powerful and feared backstage operators in Japanese politics. Like many people, he rarely agrees to talk about his links with the Tsutsumi family. It seems that he had been close to Seiji since their days together at Tokyo University. He was privy to the dispute that was splitting the family. At the time he was in the influential position of secretary to one of the cabinet ministers. He decided that it was time for an outsider to intervene.

Shortly before Yasujiro died, Fukumoto took Seiji to a secluded restaurant called Komatsu. There in a private room the two sat down to talk.

Fukumoto came straight to the point. "What's happening about the succession?" he asked.

Seiji's face changed.

"Your father still wants to choose your brother?" persisted Fukumoto.

"Certainly," said Seiji reluctantly, "as far as his feelings go as a father, he wants Yoshiaki to succeed. But he can't decide. Yoshiaki is still young, he has no network. My father must be worried about whether he can do the job or not. He may decide to alternate so that I have power one year, Yoshiaki the next. But that could lead to trouble. . . ."

Fukumoto was ready with his opinion. "The crucial thing," he said firmly, "is not to divide the empire. There has to be close cooperation within the Seibu empire."

"You're right," said Seiji.

"You have to think it over. In this situation it doesn't matter which of you has more experience or ability. You'll have to compromise, you'll have to face up to reality."

"I trained myself like that," said Seiji. "I don't want to make a mistake either at such an important time."

"I'm relieved to hear that. Here is my opinion as an outsider. Maybe you should step down and let Yoshiaki succeed. You should be his guardian, his helper, to make sure that everything in the Seibu empire runs smoothly. You brothers should cooperate. It's a hard thing to have to do. But sometimes you have to take a step back to show your real strength."

"I understand what you're saying," said Seiji, looking brighter.

"Even if I left the company, I know I can take care of myself. To-morrow I'll tell my father that I will support Yoshiaki. So I can do my duty by him while he's alive."

"Do it," said Fukumoto.

"Okay," said Seiji.[8]

Fukumoto's intervention must have helped Seiji to clarify his thoughts. He has always said that it was his own choice to give up the inheritance. "I said that I was not going to take anything from [my father]," he said in an interview on Belgian television in 1990. "My consciousness was like the students in the May revolution in the Quartier Latin—no looking back! I would never accept anything from him. I decided I would do whatever it takes—I'd do it all by myself."[9] And in *In the Season of Roaming*, which was published five years after Yasujiro's death, in 1969, he says that he wrote a letter to the old man, formally announcing his intention to leave the family and asking him to remove his name from the family register.

Seiji was a highly intelligent, sensitive young man; he must have been well aware of his father's wishes. He was far too proud to assert his own right to the inheritance; and perhaps he really did want to prove that he could make his way entirely by himself. Yet, even though the decision was his, that did not make it any easier to bear.

At the time he showed no sign of rancor. Before his death his father had said to him, "Don't make things complicated in the family." He was determined to stand by his last promise to the old man. The matter was irrevocably decided. The empire was to go to Yoshiaki.

That day in the meeting room at Hiroo, under the portrait of the dead Yasujiro, the family hammered out the details of the agreement. The empire would be run by a committee of five: the two sons, Seiji and Yoshiaki; the sons-in-law, Kojima and Morita; and the most venerable of the top Seibu executives, a man called Iwao Miyauchi. Each would continue to run the companies of which they were already presidents. As for Yoshiaki's younger brothers, Yasuhiro, a quiet, withdrawn young man of twenty-six, would become president of Toshimaen amusement park. And Yuji, who was twenty-two, would take over the management of the hotels—all but two, Misao's pet project, the glamorous new Tokyo Prince, and the new Prince Hotel at Haneda International Airport. Those, together with the Asahi Koyo helicopter corporation, would go to Seiji. That, plus the department stores, made up his portion. It was Yoshiaki, however, who took overall control. From now on he would be in his father's place.

Yasujiro's funeral four days later, on April 30, was a splendid affair. It was held in the roller-skating rink at Toshimaen amusement park. Vast though it was, all the people who wanted to pay their last respects to the great man could not fit inside. Altogether fifty thousand people came to attend the last rites.

The first hour was a private ceremony for the family and the staff of Seibu. Nishibei, who had once trembled in front of Yasujiro, remembers how sad everyone felt. "After all," he said, "I'd been in to say good morning to him all those years. . . ." Other employees, though, declare that they were not sad at all. The old man had been a tyrant. They were more apprehensive, wondering what was to become of their company and themselves now that he was dead.

The whole family was there, the women in formal black kimonos, the men in black suits. Yoshiaki led the procession, holding the urn containing his father's ashes. Then came Misao, carrying the traditional mortuary tablet, followed by Seiji bearing offerings received from the emperor, then Kuniko carrying a large order of honor that Yasujiro had received, resting on a velvet cushion. The youngest son, Yuji, came last, holding a photograph of the old man as everyone remembered him. Kiyoshi and his wife too attended, though Yasujiro's many mistresses, including Tsuneko, were absent.

The public ceremony followed. Among the mourners were Prime Minister Hayato Ikeda, the Speaker of the House and the leader of the opposition Socialist Party. The emperor, Crown Prince Akihito, Princess Michiko and many members of the imperial family and the cabinet sent condolences, garlands of flowers and offerings. Yasujiro's portrait was placed ceremoniously on the altar and framed with the traditional white chrysanthemums. The whole hall was awash with bank upon bank of the flowers.

But what set everyone talking was that the chief mourner was not the eldest son, as was customary, but the younger, Yoshiaki. It was he who led the funeral procession and who made a dignified speech. The observers were aghast. This was the first public indication that the son who would inherit the vast Seibu empire was not Seiji, as everyone had expected, but the unknown young Yoshiaki. It was like a public slight to poor Seiji.

• • •

Exactly a year after his death, on April 26, 1965, the old man's ashes were finally laid to rest with great ceremony in a tomb that he had planned himself, on a hill just outside the city of Kamakura.

Yasujiro's tomb had been many years in the making. Years before, when he was a young man, he used to drive to this ancient city of temples, just a few miles outside Tokyo. Kamakura was also where he took the beautiful young Misao when she first yielded to his advances.

There was a small family temple there of which he grew particularly fond. It was in a clearing on the very top of a hill. He would stand on the temple veranda, gazing out across a spectacular landscape. There was Mount Fuji, immaculately outlined on the horizon with the sun setting behind it. In front of it he could make out the corrugated hills of Hakone, the place he loved most in the world. He would daydream or chat to his companions about how someday he would buy Hakone and transform it into a holiday land, a place that everyone could enjoy.

Later he bought the temple and the hill that went with it. From time to time he wondered what to do with it; he thought of building cottages among the trees. Then in 1959 he was invited to the United States. While he was there he visited Arlington Cemetery. He was impressed by its grandeur, by the lawns and serried ranks of tombs, and above all by its brightness. Traditional Japanese graveyards are dark, gloomy places, where towering cedars and cryptomerias cast deep shadows and the tombs are overgrown with moss.

Yasujiro was inspired. In Tokyo the cemeteries were all full and there was less and less land available to make new ones. He decided to turn his hill in Kamakura into a cemetery. It would be bright and cheerful, with lawns where children could fly kites and play football and people could picnic. There would be a temple, a rest house, a music hall and ten thousand tombs, each with its own plot of land surrounding a granite tombstone twenty-six inches cubed. The tombs, of course, would be for sale. At the top of the hill he planned his own.

Although in the end the old man didn't live to see the work completed, it was all exactly as he had planned. The whole top of the hill was sculpted into a sort of amphitheater. Flights of steps led up past a temple and a huge bronze bell to a broad expanse of lawns and paving stones, guarded by two stone lions. At the end of the paved promenade, elevated a few steps above the level of the lawns, with beds full of flowers in front and clipped hedges behind, was the tomb itself.

In the middle of a spacious expanse of gleaming white pebbles, raked perfectly flat, was the tombstone. Of black granite, inscribed with the words "Yasujiro Tsutsumi's tomb," it was awesome, majestic, fit for a pharaoh or an emperor.

Once Yasujiro's ashes were installed in state, the custom of the nightly watch began. At first it was the top executives of the company, men who had spent their lives with Yasujiro. "The old chairman must be lonely up there," they said, "all by himself. Let's go and keep him company." In groups of three or five they went to the cemetery to spend the night there and tend the grave.

Later the whole procedure was formalized. The number was set at two and a manual was drawn up, laying out the proper way to behave. It became a duty that all the staff in the various companies of the group vied to perform. There was always a long waiting list of applicants.

The chosen two would arrive around 5:30 P.M., just as the sky was turning a shade of deep apricot behind Mount Fuji. They went first to the tomb, where they stood, hands together and heads bowed, to pay their respects to the old chairman.

Then they prepared for the first of their duties. Just before six, with the sky now a dark violet, they stood ready by the bronze bell, far taller than either of them. While one counted, the other drew back the tree trunk used to strike the bell, then swung it with all his might. The first boom rang out at six on the dot and echoed across the hills of Kamakura. Then came nine more, deep booming reverberations, exactly thirty seconds between each. At nine-thirty the two did the rounds of the grounds, checking that everything was in order, then retired to the small austere rest house to chat, study Yasujiro's books and sleep. In the morning, at six precisely, they repeated the ritual of the bell. Winter or summer, in pouring rain or driving snow, their duties were always the same.

For many of the young men it was almost a religious experience. Most of them as schoolboys had studied a martial art or spent half a day in a Zen monastery. The ethic of hardship and asceticism, the small unheated rest house, shivering in the winter, sweating in the summer, struggling from their futons before dawn to perform some ritual—these were all familiar experiences for them. It was like a purification.

In the rest house there was an album where everyone was required to record his impressions. Most of the entries ran like this one:

> This is the first time that I have been granted the opportunity to perform service at the late chairman's grave. Studying the album and the books I felt the expanse of the late chairman's human network and the breadth of his greatness. Once again I was amazed at the strength of the unifying power of the group and I myself feel proud to be one member of it. From now on I want to devote myself to the company. Thank you.

Not all the participants were so reverential. On one famous occasion, not long after the practice had begun, a group of them were tending the tomb one steamy summer evening. Up there on the top of the hill with its velvety lawns and spectacular views they felt as if they were at a picnic. They took their shirts off, brought out bottles of beer and began to relax, laugh and tell stories. Unfortunately they had timed their picnic badly. That day Yoshiaki had been playing golf and decided to stop by to pay his respects at his father's grave. He heard the shouts and guffaws before he even saw the group.

In consternation they began to pull on their shirts and hide their bottles. But it was too late. He stormed down upon them. "You impudent scoundrels!" he exploded.[10]

It was a black day for all of them. Under the lifetime employment system none of them lost their jobs, but they were all demoted and remained in the lowest ranks of the company for the rest of their careers.

Yasujiro had become a god. His photograph hung in every office of every company of the group, and the morning meeting every day was held under the watchful eye of the old chairman.

III

New Beginnings

The Midas Years

Seiji's Story 1964–1973

Disorder was the order of the age
Ideas a precious food
With humor always dressed in tears
Crunching a red apple
Disorder flashed vivid as a fire in a far-off village
A wan wind blew in the crumbling castle

TAKASHI TSUJII
Age of Disorder

In January 1968 a memo arrived in the menswear department on the fourth floor of Seibu department store in Ikebukuro. It came from the personal secretary of the president of the store, Mr. Tsutsumi. Nishibei received it. He had lost a little hair by now, but was still the same nervous bubbly Nishibei who had trembled in front of Yasujiro many years before. He was in his fifteenth year with the store and was the head of menswear.

The memo read: "We have an order for clothes from Mr. Yukio Mishima."

Shortly afterward Seiji himself passed by. "You heard about the order," he said. "Make sure you do it well."

A few days later a short, rather boyish man in a suit appeared. His face was familiar—a square, fine-boned face, eyes set wide apart, hair cropped close to his head like a soldier's. In 1968 Mishima was at the height of his fame. He had published several highly acclaimed novels and had even been nominated as a candidate for the Nobel Prize, but his actions were becoming more and more controversial and extremist. Among his coterie of friends—whose politics were mainly as virulently right-wing as his own—was a man whom he often described as "the only interesting businessman in Japan": Seiji Tsutsumi.

Mishima was just two years older than Seiji. Both were recognized literary figures. Seiji some years before had won the prestigious Seisei Muro Prize for his poetry. Although people who were close to Mishima say that he didn't take him seriously as a writer, in public at least he lavished praise upon him. And both had a passionate interest in politics. Mishima too had flirted with Communism in his youth, although his politics since then had veered violently in the opposite direction, and he enjoyed this quirky, energetic young man who had flown in the face of everything his powerful father believed in. The two dined together from time to time, argued about politics and discussed aesthetics.

"He was a man with a lot of talent," said Seiji in an interview. "We had very different opinions, but that made our friendship stronger. He was a great influence on me aesthetically. I learned from him."[1]

For all his fame, he seemed quite ordinary, Nishibei remembered. He was a body builder and he had thick black hair bursting out of his cuffs.

Very politely Mishima explained his order. He wanted uniforms, he said, twenty-five uniforms; winter and summer, twenty-five of each.

For a moment Nishibei wondered why; but his job was to serve, not to ask questions. He was a little worried about the order. After all, Seibu was not a specialist uniform shop. Other shops specialized in formal wear—morning dress, the emperor's clothes, that sort of thing. Seibu was a general store. As it happened, one of Seibu's top tailors was a man who had worked in France. He had the distinction of being the only tailor in Japan to have made uniforms for General de Gaulle. Mishima laughed with delight at the news—he had a noisy, raucous laugh. The tailor, Tsukumo Igarashii, was summoned.

While the two made notes, Mishima explained in elaborate detail precisely what he wanted. He had thought long and hard about it. He had studied uniforms in the big *Heibonsha Encyclopedia,* which he had brought along with him. He described the fabric he wanted, the exact color, the styling, everything down to the buttons and the studs on the collar. For the crest on the cap, he had done a drawing, carefully annotated in his neat characters. It was a stylized version of a samurai helmet with rays radiating behind it like the rising sun, and it was to be shiny, like a mirror.

Nishibei soon found out what the uniforms were for. Mishima was in the process of forming a private army. He had gathered around him a group of right-wing students, mainly Waseda boys, whom he called the Shield Society. Like a shield, they were to "protect His Imperial Majesty against the corruption of the Japanese spirit on the right and on the left." He had arranged for them to train with the Self-Defense Forces, the Japanese army, but the first thing an army had to have was uniforms.

Nishibei's first job was to find the fabric. Mishima wanted a particular shade of burnished gold. After much searching Nishibei found some attractive woolen material, but there was only enough for thirty uniforms. By now the order had increased. The Shield Society was growing. Mishima needed fifty uniforms. After combing the shops of Tokyo, Nishibei finally found enough fabric. Next he had to measure Mishima's men. He visited the headquarters of the Shield Society and met, among others, Masakatsu Morita, the young man who was the leader among the students of the Shield Society and Mishima's close companion.

The finished uniforms were stunning. Made of the finest dark gold fabric, they were uniforms for the designer age. The jackets tapered to the waist to accentuate the chest and shoulders, just as Mishima liked, with a double row of brass buttons, epaulettes, a black stand-up collar and matching panel on the sleeves. On the front of the smart peaked cap gleamed the badge that Mishima had designed. Mishima was inordinately proud of the uniforms. He showed them off to his friend Henry Scott Stokes, roaring with laughter and boasting that they had been designed by de Gaulle's tailor. Stokes was less impressed. "Mishima's kitsch taste, that's about all," he wrote in his biography of Mishima. "Color is sort of yellow-brown and rows of brass buttons down front which give wasp waists to Mishima's young men. Is this a homosexual club?"[2]

Mishima himself wrote gleefully, "The uniform, especially designed for the SS [Shield Society], is so striking that passers-by stop on the street in amazement."[3]

The cost, remembered Nishibei, was extremely reasonable—a mere ¥25,000 per uniform.

A little less than three years later, on November 25, 1970, Mishima made his last public appearance, on the balcony of the Eastern Army Headquarters, wearing the uniform he had ordered from Seibu. For a few minutes he harangued the soldiers, their scruffy khaki uniforms contrasting with his splendid double-breasted gold. The army must rise up, he yelled. Japan had become decadent. They must overthrow the constitution, protect the emperor, their heritage, their country. The soldiers, all well-fed lads born long after the war, had no idea what he was talking about. They jeered and heckled. Mishima retired into an inner room where he carried out the act that he had been planning for many years. Drawing his antique sword, made by a famous swordsmith in 1620, he committed *seppuku* (harakiri). His favorite, Morita, died with him.

It was the most barbaric and unexpected of events, as horrifying as the death of Kennedy had been; no one in Japan has forgotten what he or she was doing at the moment when the news came. "I was shocked for a week," recalled Seiji. "He never told me his plan. If I had known I would have stopped him."

Seiji was in his early forties at the time and seldom out of the public eye himself. He was utterly unlike any other member of the stolid Japanese business community. He was a maverick, an outsider. His friends ranged from artists, composers, writers and fashion designers to people on the most outrageous fringes of the Japanese underground. Instead of the regulation gray suit he wore smartly tailored suits by young designers, and even on the most sober of occasions often appeared sporting an unsuitably exuberant tie. Rather than attending management conferences, he was more likely to be found at high-society parties, openings of art exhibitions or concerts.

He was an attractive figure, slight, boyish, with a soft voice and self-effacing manner, bubbling with energy and enthusiasm. His round young face was everywhere—in the press, on television, pontificating about the state of the Japanese economy or the latest developments in the retail trade. In his private life he did all he could to shun publicity, but the gossip weeklies trailed him relentlessly and occasionally were rewarded with a glimpse of him slipping out of the side gate of an exclusive restaurant with an actress on his arm or climbing hurriedly into a waiting limousine.

In the first six years after Yasujiro's death Seiji had somehow managed to swing the balance. He had kept his promise: the empire was still intact, and he had not made things complicated in the family. He was still involved in all the companies that made up the empire. He was a vice president of Seibu Railways, and the railways held half the stocks of the department store. But when people heard the name Seibu, they no longer thought of the railway or the vast tracts of land or the hotels or the chemical company. They thought of the department store. To young people graduating in the late sixties, it was retailing, not manufacturing, that was the frontier: the most coveted prize of all was a job at Seibu department store.

Despite all the agonies over the succession, Seiji was still the public face of Seibu. Where he had been the young crown prince, he was now the regent. Yoshiaki was far too young to take over the command of such a vast concern. He remained in the background, watching and learning. The committee of five—the two sons, the sons-in-law and chief executive Miyauchi—were the nominal rulers of the empire and took final responsibility. The real day-to-day decisions, at least in the railway and real estate sides of the empire, were in the hands of the managers, old men who had been with Yasujiro for most of his life and were devoted to his memory. They ensured that everything continued as he would have wished, and every Tuesday the family and the top executives of the group gathered under Yasujiro's portrait, just as they had before his death.

Seiji was under no illusions. He knew that the empire was Yoshiaki's, not his. He could do no more than help and support his brother, who would, when he was ready, step out from the shadows to take control. So, although he was involved in every part of the business, he focused his energy on the section he had taken as his own: the department store.

As soon as the obsequies for his father had been decently completed, he turned his attention to the legacy the old man had left him: the disastrous ¥5 billion debt incurred by the demise of the Los Angeles store. At the exchange rate of the time, this was equivalent to about $15 million, in 1995 terms closer to $1.5 billion. It was a crippling liability. Even with careful economies it would still take twenty years before the store was in the black again. The railways and property side of the empire needed all their money to invest in land; there was no help there. He confided in some of the top executives of the department store. Their advice was predictable: retrench and pay back the debt little by little—that was the only safe course. Seiji listened very carefully to what they had to say. Finally, when they had finished, he said very politely in his gentle voice, "Please indulge me. Let me have my way."

Ever since he had taken over the department store, Seiji had been hobbled by his father. The old man had opposed his ideas, stood in the way of his innovations and insisted that all the profits from the store should go to the property-development side of the group. He had had to fight for every expansion and every extension. Now the stores were his, and he could do as he pleased. He was no longer tied to the real estate side nor required to pour his profits into their coffers.

He had his own ideas about how to clear the debt. In fact, as he later said, the debt was an enormous impetus. It forced him to take action. Rather than harboring his resources, like his father he intended to expand. "In retrospect [the debt] turned out to be a great piece of luck."[4]

He plunged into action straightaway. The two hotels he had received as part of his portion—the Tokyo Prince and the Prince at Haneda Airport—would have to be sold. They were absorbed back into the empire—Yoshiaki's Kokudo Keikaku bought them—though the department store retained the management.

Ever since his father had shunted him off to the retail side of the business, Seiji, on the lookout for new ideas, had followed the latest developments in the business. In retail as in everything, America was the role model. In 1955 he had gone to Los Angeles to attend a course on a unique American institution: the supermarket.

One supermarket had already opened in Tokyo, in the most exclusive section of town, where the maids of foreign diplomats and moneyed Japanese prowled the gleaming aisles, filling their baskets with imported goods. To the Japanese, who habitually bought their rice and vegetables at markets or small corner shops, supermarkets symbolized prosperity, Westernization and the future.

With his father in control of the purse strings, Seiji could do little more than experiment. When he returned from Los Angeles, he opened four small self-service stores called Seibu Stores, selling food and basic household goods. All were in cities outside Tokyo; and any profits they made were plowed back into the property and railways side of the empire. By 1963 he was sure Japan was ready for supermarkets to be introduced on a far larger scale. Moreover, the Los Angeles store was visibly on the verge of collapse. Seiji needed desperately to find some new business to bolster his failing resources. That year he renamed the Seibu Stores, calling them Seiyu Stores, and opened five new branches of what was now a supermarket chain, all this time in Tokyo, in the prosperous western suburbs.

At the same time another young man, named Isao Nakauchi, whose base was in the southern island of Kyushu, had had the same idea. While Seiji was struggling with the old men of Seibu, insisting that the only way to make the new venture a success was to open more and more branches as quickly as possible, several branches of the rival Daiei chain sprang up in the western city of Osaka.

Seiji had found a moneymaker. The Seiyu Stores began to boom. By 1966 the original four had grown to thirty, by 1967 to thirty-six and by 1968 to fifty. Daiei meanwhile was opening ten to twenty new stores a year. It became obvious that supermarkets were destined to outdo department stores, both in popularity and profits. Young men with an eye to the future raced to enter one of the two great rivals, Seiyu and Daiei. In 1968 there were more than a thousand applicants for the forty or fifty jobs available for university graduates in Seiyu. In the end the company took on one hundred new staff and one thousand high school leavers, and continued to expand at the same rate every year.[5]

Supermarkets transformed people's shopping habits. But Seiji could see far more dramatic and profound changes happening at every level of society, and he wanted to be sure that he and his Seibu department store were at the forefront.

Ikebukuro, the rough backwater full of seedy little bars and pink cabarets up in the southwest corner of Tokyo, was the Seibu heartland. While Yasujiro was alive he had opposed all Seiji's attempts to expand the store outside Ikebukuro, but now that the young man was free to do as he pleased, he intended to indulge a long-cherished dream.

He began by approaching Dai-ichi Kangyo Bank, the largest bank in the world. What he was looking for was not just a loan of millions of yen; he wanted to establish a working relationship. He wanted the bank to support him and provide the necessary funding and backup for his projects. Unlike the days when he had first gone the rounds of the banks, trying to secure loans without his father's blessing, he was now the most visible figure in the mighty Seibu empire. In Japan the only acceptable surety is land. Seibu, possibly the largest landholder in the country, provided ample security. With Yoshiaki, the true landowner, as his guarantor, Seiji was assured of funds; and he had proved once again with his Seiyu Stores that as a businessman he had the magic touch.

It was the bank that came up with the site. One of their customers was the owner of the Toei cinema in the Shibuya area of Tokyo. The cinema was doing badly, and the owner wanted to close it and lease the land. This was exactly the area where Seiji wanted to open a store. With help from the railways side he invested in the land and work began on a new department store.

In April 1968—the same year that Mishima was ordering his uniforms in the Ikebukuro store—the last of the scaffolding and dust sheets came down. Everyone went to look at the glossy new store. But the real talking point was the location. Shibuya was Tokyu country! Seibu had invaded Goto's fortress!

Like Ikebukuro, Shibuya had started out as frontier country. It was right on the western edge of Tokyo. In the time of the shoguns, the river Shibuya marked the point where the daimyo residences and artisan cottages straggled to an end and open country began. Slowly the city pushed westward and Shibuya grew. After the Great Earthquake of 1923, many people left the devastated east end and fled west. Yasujiro, always ready when there was profit to be made, bought land there and built the Hundred Shops. By then Shibuya was already a lively suburban center with a busy railway station.

It was Goto the Thief, however, who really transformed it. He arrived almost by accident in the course of one of his notorious takeovers. He snapped up broad tracts of land to the west of Shibuya, then had the brainstorm of building a railway to link the area with the great port city of Yokohama. Overnight Shibuya became one of the main gateways to Tokyo. By the time that Seiji, as a young man, was wandering the streets there, it had become a place where students congregated and well-heeled matrons from the western suburbs shopped. There was one department store, right on top of the station—Goto's Tokyu store, selling everything that a middle-aged housewife could possibly require, floor upon floor of kimono fabric, underwear, refrigerators, Japanese cakes and pots and pans. Then came the Olympics and the place began to wake up.

The games were a dazzling success for Japan. The whole nation was gripped with Olympic fever. There was despair when at the last minute a Dutchman made off with the judo gold medal and national rejoicing when the women's volleyball team won their gold. In all, Japan took sixteen gold medals, to come fourth in the world stakes, and Avery Brundage, the chairman of the International Olympic Committee, declared them "the greatest Olympics ever held."

More than anything they marked a turning point, the end of the old postwar era of hardship and poverty. At last all the hard work had paid off. For the first time, people were beginning to feel positively prosperous. In 1960 Prime Minister Ikeda had promised that he would double the national income in ten years; in fact, it took four. By the time of the Olympics the economy was booming. The city of Tokyo was changing. It had grown smarter and glossier as a result of all the building work leading up to the games. Little by little— though it was a long, slow process—the squalid jerry-built houses that had formed the environment of the postwar years were replaced by sweeping boulevards and high-rise buildings.

And with money in their pockets, people were beginning to look round for new ways to spend it. It was no longer a question of equipping their homes with electronic gadgets or washing machines. Even after they had bought the latest, most up-to-date model, the people of Tokyo still had plenty of money left to spend.

Just as Seiji had anticipated, tastes were beginning to change. People wanted quality and glamour. They wanted a lifestyle that reflected their newly acquired wealth.

Seibu Shibuya opened in May 1968, in Golden Week, when everyone traditionally has a holiday. It was unlike anything Shibuya had ever seen before.

At the time it seemed a foolhardy venture. Seiji had taken on an enormous burden of debt in order to open this store, but Shibuya was simply not the kind of place where a store like this could possibly succeed. It was a quiet, prosperous suburb, perfectly well served by the Tokyu store. The old men running the Seibu empire shook their heads. Had the old chairman still been alive, he would surely have opposed such a risky plan. This was a supreme example of Seiji's rashness. But Seiji had no intention of competing with Tokyu. Seibu was aimed not at Tokyu's middle-aged matrons, but at their children. It was the baby-boomers who flocked to Seibu, the new generation who had never known the war years, who had their parents' money in their pocket and were not afraid to spend it.

Every element of the store, from the building itself to the tiniest detail of display, had been carefully put together with one overriding concept in mind. This was a shop devoted to design, style, fashion—everything that young Japanese of the sixties were hungry for. Instead of Tokyu's refrigerators and underwear, there were clothes, hats and handbags. The styles were youthful and modern, created by Kuniko's French designers, established Japanese names and many young unknowns. People no one had ever heard of—such as Kansai Yamamoto, busily making up his designs and delivering them by hand, and Takeo Kikuchi, both now luminaries of the fashion world—were featured in the opening show.

And two years later, in 1970, when a young designer named Issey Miyake returned to Tokyo after having made his name in New York and Paris, it was obvious that the only place where he could possibly debut was Seibu Shibuya. The show was wildly successful. It was held in the car park, with models wearing Issey's spiky, irregular designs and magical fabrics prowling between the cars and jeeps and motorcycles.

Seibu had become a gateway through which everything young and modern—the youth culture of the West as well as the wilder extremes of the Japanese avant-garde—flowed into Japanese life. It was an expression of Seiji's interests and idiosyncrasies. While other department stores showed exhibitions of Impressionist art and other safe choices that drew customers and sold well, Seibu provided a forum for contemporary artists, Western and Japanese, to display their work.

For Seiji it was an intoxicating time. Whatever he touched turned to gold. Even when he played—indulging his whims, sponsoring his artist friends, creating a shop selling dreams—his ideas seemed to correspond to a need, to fulfill some demand that no one else had even realized existed. He was building an empire of his own, with as much determination as his father ever had, but for the time being it was an empire of intangibles, of ideas and influence, rather than of land and money. The economy was on his side. From 1965 to 1970 Japan enjoyed an unprecedented boom. No matter what Seiji did, he was bound to make money; he didn't even need to think about it. With an average annual growth rate of 11.8 percent, no matter how much he borrowed the value of the interest simply shriveled to nothing. In effect, borrowing was free. And the country seemed to be awash with money. After the long years of belt-tightening, people could hardly believe their good fortune. The government encouraged consumption, keen to create a strong domestic market. Spending was in fashion. Everyone wanted a new television, a new car, the latest clothes. It was a retailer's dream come true.

Seiji continued to expand his empire with reckless exuberance. He borrowed and expanded, borrowed and expanded. He took over department stores in towns outside Tokyo and transformed them into branches of Seibu. Bright college graduates competed to work for this aggressive young president. By 1970 the original Seibu department store had mushroomed into a chain of eight stores, mainly in the Tokyo area, and three more opened the following year, stretching as far as Osaka.

The expansion was not without setbacks. There were miscalculations, disasters—and too many accidents. A few years after the fire of 1963 there was another fire at the Ikebukuro store, and during the opening week of Seibu Shibuya, a window-cleaning gondola plummeted from the top of the building to the street below. Some schoolchildren were walking underneath at the time and were killed.

Seiji did the proper thing. He visited the parents, wept, paid compensation, but the incident cast a shadow on Seibu's reputation. People began to speak of it as the company that had accidents. There were suggestions that it was expanding too fast, without enough care for details.

As for Seiji himself, the eager young graduates who jostled to join the company soon discovered that he was a man of many faces. When he was interviewed by the press or appeared on television, he was boyish, charming, gentle, soft-spoken, still the nervous young man who had so surprised his comrades when he had stood up many years before at Tokyo University to harangue them. When he greeted the new entrants at the welcoming ceremony every April in the public hall, in Hibiya Park, he was aggressive, sophisticated, arrogant in his beautifully cut suit and flamboyant tie. Everyone congratulated himself on having joined a company led by such a charismatic president. But within the company they saw an entirely different face.

A few years after the opening of Seibu Shibuya, the issue of overtime pay arose. A member of the Socialist opposition had revealed that the Seiyu Stores supermarket chain had paid its workers no overtime at all for the last three years. The Ministry of Labor investigated and ordered Seiyu to cover all the back pay. At that time there was no union at Seiyu. Seiji began to suspect that the Communists were planning to start one, which would naturally be hostile to the management. To forestall them he set one up himself and appointed a friendly president. At the time this was standard procedure in most Japanese companies. As a result, labor disputes and strikes were almost unknown. Considering his revolutionary past, it was all rather ironic.

Shortly afterward, there was a meeting of union and management. One of the union leaders had written in the union paper that Mr. Tsutsumi was interested in nothing but his crazy expansion plans; he didn't care about the work conditions of his staff. Seiji leaped to his feet and thumped the table, yelling, "You talk about crazy expansion, you say I'm too aggressive. . . . This is cheap tabloid talk! I can't respect talk like this!"

"In interviews," a longtime member of the company remembered, "he used very soft language. But at meetings he was an animal. He said *baka*, fool. He threw things—ashtrays—at you."

However, as the same ex-employee recalled, once the union members had left the room to discuss their next move, Seiji turned to the leader of the negotiations on the management side and said, very meekly, "Was that okay, Mr. Y?"

And when the union members returned, they were ready to agree to all the management conditions.

Whether Seiji was simply emulating his father's dictatorial style or whether it was the Tsutsumi blood flowing in his veins, it was clear that he was driven by very contradictory impulses. One of the most powerful contradictions, which he himself frequently speaks about, was between his literary life and his life as a businessman—the poetic, sensitive side to his personality, inherited from his mother, and the relentless drive to build an empire. As a poet, he wrote under the pen name Takashi Tsujii, perhaps as a way of distinguishing the two facets of his personality. In an interview he was once asked, "As the rich entrepreneur Seiji Tsutsumi, have you ever wanted to destroy the penniless poet Takashi Tsujii?" His reply was "I've thought he's a pretty awkward bugger and a troublesome sod and I wanted to fight with him but I never wanted to exterminate him. In fact it's the entrepreneurial self that I've sometimes wanted to get rid of."[6]

The year after the new Seibu opened in Shibuya, Seiji made his debut as a novelist. *In the Season of Roaming* came out in September 1969. All the characters in the novel had fictitious names, but, as everyone says, they were very easy to recognize. On the whole the literary world acclaimed it. It was clearly an example of the "I" novel, the confessional, autobiographical style of writing that has dominated modern Japanese literature. The genre requires utter honesty, in which literary style is pushed aside and the novelist "lays himself out naked on the table," telling the story of *watakushi* (I) in painful detail and baring his soul to the reader's scrutiny.

While the literary critics were lavishing praise on it, the public was devouring it avidly. And the Seibu staff were asking, "Why?" Why did he write it? Why did he have to reveal all this? People who had known Yasujiro well and worked at Seibu for years were stunned by some of the revelations. Even Seiji's most devoted supporters had to agree that although for a literary figure it might have been a good move, for a company president it was definitely a minus.

Of the family, only Misao and Kuniko supported Seiji. Yoshiaki and Kojima, Shukuko's husband, were particularly angry. In interviews Yoshiaki always declares that he has never read the book. It's fiction, he says, so he has nothing to say about it. But he certainly knew the contents. "I don't look at those [Seiji's novels] because they make me angry," he said on one occasion, with a laugh. "So many things in them are far from the truth. But if I get angry, that means I admit it's fact. He too says they are novels. When I tell him they're not interesting, he says, 'That's because it's the world of the novel.' "[7]

Seiji's editor was a man called Tadao Sakamoto, chief editor at the Shinchosha publishing house. In an interview recorded by the journalist Toshiaki Kaminogo in his book *Seibu Empire,* he described how Seiji wrote every night from eleven o'clock until the small hours of the morning. The busier he became with his department stores, the more feverishly he wrote; and as the deadline for the manuscript approached, he was sleeping only one or two hours a night.

Whenever the two had a meeting, it was always at eleven at night. Sakamoto would visit Seiji's home in the grounds of the big house at Hiroo, and the two would sit together in his spacious study, its walls lined with books and records and decorated with two or three contemporary paintings. "Why did Mr. Tsutsumi write a novel like that at that time?" Sakamoto pondered. "He seemed possessed, as if he had to dig up the roots of everything that had happened in his life, to clear out his unconscious mind; he wanted to find some conclusion. . . . The busier Seibu got, the more he wanted to find a conclusion. I felt he really had to write it."[8]

It was almost like an exorcism, as if he were trying to free himself from his father and the shadow he had cast over his life. He wanted to pour out everything, all the suffering of his childhood, his entire history, once and for all. Then perhaps he would be able to cut off the past and make a new life, start afresh.

In one respect he had already freed himself from his father's dead hand. After he separated from Motoko Yamaguchi, Seiji found himself one of Tokyo's most eligible bachelors. Many powerful figures in the business and political worlds, keen to make an alliance with the Tsutsumis, came up with candidates for marriage. Time and time again Seiji attended the traditional first meeting, usually held in a tea salon in the Ginza. The go-between would make the introductions and expound on the young woman's qualities, then the putative couple, each accompanied by a friend, would make stiff conversation.

Seiji often took along Kunio Fukumoto, the old friend who had helped to persuade him to give up his claims to the empire before Yasujiro's death. After the meeting, Seiji was always impeccably polite. When asked for his decision, he would reply gravely, "I've only just divorced. It's really too early for me to say . . ." It usually fell to Fukumoto to interpret this ambiguous response to the young lady in question and inform her that sadly the answer was no.[9]

From time to time, as was the custom among Japanese men, old and young, the two friends made a foray to the geisha houses. At that time one of the most elegant geisha districts was Yanagibashi (Willow Bridge), a cluster of traditional wooden tile-roofed restaurants and geisha houses on each side of Kanda River. At dusk one of the most inviting sights in the city was the brightly lit rooms of the geisha houses reflected in the water. Many of Japan's most powerful men went there to relax. Fukumoto and Seiji would spend the evening there in the company of ladies trained in the arts of singing and dancing, full of charming pleasantries, risqué tales and silvery laughter.

The very powerful Shigeo Mizuno, Seiji's friend and one of the Four Emperors of the postwar years, also frequented the geisha houses of Yanagibashi. It may have been he who introduced Seiji to his favorite, a geisha who worked under the name of Katsuko. Katsuko's real name was Asako. She was tiny and, beneath the stylized makeup, very pretty, with large candid eyes set in an oval face, a straight nose and a wide generous mouth. When the two first met she was little more than twenty, and still had the sweet bashfulness expected of a young Japanese woman. She spoke little, but she had an underlying serenity that was very appealing. She was also a graceful performer of traditional Japanese dance.

For five years the two young men continued to visit the geisha quarters. In private Seiji was still as quiet and secretive as when he was a boy. He was always the listener, never the talker. He concealed his feelings so well that Fukumoto never guessed his partiality for Mizuno's favorite. Seiji was desperate to marry her. But he knew that in practical terms there were serious obstacles. Geisha were very different from prostitutes, but they were still far from respectable. It was a little like marrying a barmaid. It was fine to visit them and have affairs with them, but it would certainly not do for a man in Seiji's position to marry one.

In the end Mizuno helped him. He adopted Asako and made her his stepdaughter. She left Yanagibashi and went to Paris for three years to study French and cooking. There Kuniko befriended her and introduced her into the high-society circles in which she moved. Asako was transformed. Freed from the geisha world in which she had always had to please, her natural candor and strength of character emerged. She was still sweet and coquettish, but she also acquired Parisian gloss. She wore her hair cut fashionably short and geometric, which set off her large eyes and wide smile, wore miniskirts, and became an accomplished cook. In 1968 Seiji could wait no longer. He joined her in Paris, and the two were married very quietly in a room at the Japanese embassy. Asako was thirty and Seiji forty-one.

The real celebrations took place later, when the couple returned to Tokyo. Asako, of course, was introduced as Mizuno's daughter who had been living in France, though it was not long before the truth leaked out. There was a grand reception at the Tokyo Prince Hotel. The country's political and business leaders made congratulatory speeches and a famous concert pianist provided music. All the staff of every branch of the empire were invited. And the whole family—Yoshiaki, Kojima, everyone—attended.

In 1970, the sixth anniversary of their father's death, Seiji and Yoshiaki agreed that the time had come to separate. It was obvious that instead of one empire there were now two. Perhaps it was Seiji's unsuitable marriage; perhaps it was the publication of *In the Season of Roaming;* or perhaps it was the crazy expansion, the plethora of new stores springing up, all on borrowed money and all with Yoshiaki as the guarantor.

The initiative was Yoshiaki's. At the time Seibu Railways and Kokudo Keikaku, the property side of the empire, still owned more than half the stocks of Seibu department stores. Yoshiaki offered to give Seiji a money settlement of several billion yen and enough stocks to give him a controlling interest in the department stores. He would also add to his portion the Seibu Chemical Company, with its assets of 5 million *tsubo* (4,000 acres) of land. But hereafter the two empires—the Seibu Retail group and the Seibu Railway group—would be completely separate, autonomous groups. Yoshiaki would no longer stand surety for Seiji's loans.

Seiji, however, would still retain a toehold in the empire, in a private capacity. Like Yoshiaki, he remained a vice president of Seibu Railways.

It is said that Yoshiaki gave Seiji a short lecture on the occasion of the separation. "Seiji-*san*," he said. "To be honest, I would like you to show more respect to our late father. No matter how successful you've become, it's a fact that it was Dad who set up the department store you've built your retail group on!"[10]

Seiji had lost the security of being a part of the Seibu empire. But he had gained his freedom. To use his own imagery, the department store had been a colony, a neglected outpost of the great Seibu empire. Now it was an independent state, with Seiji as its ruler. And he had already begun to expand into new and uncharted territory.

Up in Ikebukuro, there was a small department-store war going on. Besides the monolithic Seibu, cutting through the town along the east side of the railway tracks, Mitsukoshi, the dowager of department stores, had also opened a branch there. Meanwhile, to the west of the station, where the Tobu private railway line terminated, there was a Tobu store, owned by one of the great railway families, the Nezu family. Right in the middle of these three giants, occupying the plum position on top of the main station building, was a small department store called Marubutsu.

Marubutsu was on the verge of bankruptcy. It was an old-fashioned little store and it couldn't compete with its powerful neighbors. To Seiji, the great danger was that a rival, such as Daiei, the great supermarket chain stretching its tentacles all over the west of Japan, might take it over. Daiei was heading closer and closer to Tokyo. If it opened a discount store in the heart of Ikebukuro, it would be disastrous for Seibu's trade. So Seiji decided to take over Marubutsu himself.

The question was what to do with it. He didn't need two department stores in Ikebukuro. Marubutsu was a liability. It was swamped with debts, ¥800 million ($2 million) worth.

Seiji had an old school friend called Tsuji Masuda. Their fathers were friends; Yasujiro sponsored Masuda's father, who was an artist. Masuda was a wild, irresponsible boy, who read Baudelaire and *Lady Chatterley's Lover* and regaled the bashful Seiji with tales of his nightly adventures around the town. While he was a student Yasujiro gave him a job as one of his secretaries at Hiroo. The old man liked this noisy irreverent friend of his son's and let him get away with all sorts of unthinkable offenses, such as smoking when the two were in the car together.

Years passed. Masuda dabbled in different jobs. Then in 1961 Seiji, as president of Seibu department store, invited him to join the company again.

By 1968 Masuda was getting bored. Selling things was not his métier. He was interested in large-scale projects, in design and architecture. He had been involved in the planning of the new store in Shibuya, the concept of a "feminine" building was his. But now the store was open and he was back in the office.

He went to see Seiji. "I'm leaving," he said. "I have something else to do."

"This is the second time you've handed in your notice," said Seiji. "You won't get a third chance. You understand that?"

"That's okay," said Masuda.

"What are you going to do?" asked Seiji.

"I don't have definite plans yet."

Seiji thought for a while, then told him to go and wait in a coffee shop around the corner. He joined him a little while later. "I'll make you a proposal," he said. "If you don't like it, you can leave." He paused.

"What is it?" asked Masuda.

"I want you to run Tokyo Marubutsu."

Masuda didn't hesitate. "I'll do it," he said.[11]

Masuda thrived on challenge. He was the archetypal "nail that sticks up," who, in traditional Japanese parlance, needs to be hammered down. In most Japanese companies he would never have risen very far. He was much too irreverent and anarchic. Someone as young and untried as he would certainly never have been given the chance to reconstruct an entire department store. It was far too great a risk. But Seibu was different. Seiji ran it in his own idiosyncratic way, following whims, plucking people from nowhere when he felt that they could do the job. At Marubutsu, Masuda would be free to be as wild and unconventional as he pleased.

The first thing he did was to walk around Ikebukuro. He walked and walked, and pondered what kind of store would do well there. Ikebukuro, he concluded, had an image problem. In commercial terms it was viable, with its three department stores. But it was still the outback, the sort of place where the *yakuza*, the Japanese mafia, ran extortion rackets and there were brawls on the street at night. It had not caught up with the rest of the city. There was nothing there to attract young people—and they were the people spending money.

Instead of calling in the accountants, he decided to start afresh. He gathered architects, designers, art directors and television directors and set them to work to plan a brand-new store, different from anything that Tokyo had ever seen before. The name Marubutsu would have to go. It was too nondescript, too old-fashioned. Instead, Masuda decided to call the new store Parco. In those days everything to do with fashion had to have a French name, but Masuda wanted to evoke a younger, more lively image. Italian was better for his purpose. And a park—that was where people gathered.

Parco opened in November 1969, the year that the miniskirt hit Tokyo; and straightaway people began to gather there. It was a multistory shopping mall, the first of its kind, floor after floor packed with small boutiques, nearly two hundred in all. The shops targeted a very specific market: young women in their twenties. The clothes they sold were modern, all ready-made, no *haute couture,* and their stock changed as rapidly as the fluxes of fashion. But Parco was more than simply the clothes it sold. Somehow the new store caught the mood of the times. Even Seibu Shibuya was still a department store, but Parco was something new. The baby boomers had come into their own and Parco was their shop.

Parco itself sold nothing but air. It was simply a shell, a tenant building. All the boutiques were tenants who paid 10 percent of their takings to the Parco management. It was up to the boutiques to sell their clothes. Parco's job was to lure the right type of customers. What it was selling was an image. Part of the image was created by the store itself—the way it looked, the type of goods that was sold. Traditionally Japanese shops prided themselves on their continuity, their long history; Mitsukoshi was a prime example. Parco was the very opposite. It was like a bazaar, ever changing, in tune with the vagaries of fashion. It was a celebration of shopping—shopping as a lifestyle.

In June 1973 the second Parco opened, in Shibuya. By now the era of the miniskirt had passed; the maxi was in. The baby boomers had grown up and turned into career women. It was time for a more sophisticated store to suit a more sophisticated age.

It was Shibuya that really made Parco and Parco that made Shibuya. After Parco opened, boutiques grew up all along Park Road and in the alleys that led off it to wind around the hummocky hills of Shibuya. In the years to follow, Shibuya was to become one of the most sophisticated and fashionable areas of Tokyo. Parco itself became an icon, synonymous with Japan's brave new world of fashion.

It was as if Tokyo had been waiting for Parco. Here was a company with the professed aim of selling image and inspiration. For youthful artists, graphic designers, copywriters, photographers, it was a heaven-sent opportunity. Masuda surrounded himself with talented young people, as iconoclastic and bursting with ideas as he was.

The first television commercial for the new Parco lasted just fifteen seconds. Parco didn't have the budget to pay for anything longer. It consisted of a tall, thin black woman, dressed in a black bikini, dancing with a very small man in a Santa Claus outfit. At the end came the words "Shibuya Parco—open June 14."

The commercial was the inspiration of a young designer named Eiko Ishioka. Masuda had spotted her when she was working for the Shiseido makeup house. She was the only female art director in Japan and an extraordinarily dynamic woman. For ten years she and Masuda worked together, and Eiko's startling, unforgettable advertisements and commercials had an immense impact on the evolving image of Parco.

Eiko recalls how on the opening day of the new Parco, she and Masuda sat together in the coffee shop on the ground floor, watching the crowds of people. "Can you believe it?" he said. "The men and women coming into my Parco are very neat, very trendy, very fashionable, very good-looking—can you believe it?"

Eiko's most famous campaign and the last she did for Parco featured the actress Faye Dunaway, who had just won an Oscar for *Network*. For a year she was "the face of Parco." One commercial—which became a legend—showed the beautiful, mysterious Faye Dunaway in a black Chinese dress, sitting on a black chair at a black table in front of a black wall. On the table was a white boiled egg. She picks it up, peels it, eats it, all in one minute, then, in her husky tones, says, "This . . . is a film for Parco." It was the epitome of the Parco style.

The Oil Shock and Its Aftermath
Seiji's Story 1973–1984

I am what I am
So I joined no club
Even with those I love I spoke only inside my heart
And so I built my streets one by one

TAKASHI TSUJII
Quiet Town

Nineteen seventy-three, the year that the new Parco opened in Shibuya, marked the ninth anniversary of Yasujiro's death. In those nine years Seiji had taken his miserable inheritance, the one department store out in the Ikebukuro backwoods, and had transmuted it into a formidable empire. There were now eleven elegant Seibu department stores; two Parcos, immensely popular and influential; and a network of 157 Seiyu Store supermarkets, located mainly at stations along Yoshiaki's Seibu railway lines. All had transformed, if not society, at least the nation's shopping habits. And all were making money. As for the dreadful legacy of debt that Seiji had inherited, it had been subsumed into a far greater debt. Like Yasujiro, Seiji had built his empire on a foundation of debt, but while the economy continued to boom he was in no danger. His businesses were thriving and he had the support of the banks behind him.

In his private life too he had found happiness. He was no longer the tormented youth desperately searching for the family he had never had. He was settling into middle age now. In public he was still as gentle and modest as ever, a shy unassuming man, but always bubbling with curiosity and eager for new ideas. Often when he had fin-

ished work for the day he would go to a bar or a coffee shop to mix
with students and young people. He liked to keep his ideas young.
And from time to time he confessed to dancing in the discos of Roppongi or Akasaka. "Go-go dancing is something you should try, not
merely see," he said in an interview. "The darkness of the place hides
my age from the young people around me!"[1]

Asako had grown into the perfect wife. She had the gaiety,
warmth and strength of spirit to counteract his reserve and black
moods. As was proper for a Japanese wife, she kept well in the background, and took no part in his business life. Instead she stayed in
their spacious home in the grounds of the big house in Hiroo and
took care of their son, little Tadao, born in 1970.

Freed from all the shadows that had troubled him, Seiji threw
himself unreservedly into his work. Like his father, he was always impatient. He always had to be out in front, taking impossible chances,
pushing against some new frontier. When he first joined his father's
department store he had felt conscious of an uncomfortable contra-
diction between the revolutionary ideals of his youth and his new position in this huge capitalist corporation. But now he had found a way
to express his creativity fully through his work. It was everything for
Seibu. The company was his. It was not listed, it was not public, he
had no responsibility to shareholders, no need to worry about quarterly returns. He was no employee manager, he was the owner, and
he could do anything he wanted. He could experiment, and he could
afford to plan for the long term and diversify into untried areas of
business.

As a start he had recently completed negotiations for a partnership with Sears, Roebuck and Company, the venerable American
mail-order giant.

Seiji recognized that in many ways Japan still lagged behind the
developed countries of the West. In the fields of retail and distribution there was much to learn. He needed to update his knowledge of
the latest techniques and technologies. Sears was the ideal model. In
their years of experience they had perfected a system of homing in on
consumer needs, then applying this knowledge to product planning
so that they could satisfy customer demands immediately and with
great precision.

The negotiations were not straightforward. Other Japanese companies too wanted to make a link with the American firm. But finally, after two years, everything was agreed and in 1972 Seiji went to Chicago to sign the contract.

To begin with, the plan was that Seibu would be Sears's agent in Japan. The colorful Sears catalog, as big as a telephone directory, was available in a catalog corner in every Seibu store, where customers could buy it and take it home. As it turned out, mail-order shopping never really caught on in Japan. It was a far smaller country than the United States and everyone was used to shopping in the local corner stores. Seibu acquired cachet by stocking American household goods—barbecues, mailboxes, bedsheets—but sales were never good. Most American domestic appliances were far too big for tiny Japanese kitchens. The only item that ever really became popular was the splendid and capacious Sears refrigerator.

From Seibu's point of view the main benefit was in know-how and access to the latest technology. Seiji had regular meetings with Sears executives, from whom he learned much about American retailing and international business. He also had a chance to examine the workings of some areas of business that were new to him. Besides retail, Sears was also involved in insurance, real estate and credit cards, all areas in which Seiji was interested.

For the time being the most urgent priority was land. Land was the basis of the Japanese economy; it underpinned all transactions. Land provided the collateral on the basis of which Yoshiaki could borrow as much money as he wanted. It gave him credibility and strength. Seiji's landholdings, however, were very small. Without land to support his debts, his empire was frighteningly vulnerable. While the economy was buoyant, he had no need to fear, but if ever there was to be a slump, he would be in danger of losing everything.

Whenever he could, he invested in land. And in 1972 an irresistible opportunity had arisen. The charismatic new prime minister, Kakuei Tanaka, had just swept into power. He was soon to be disgraced for his "money politics" and involvement in the Lockheed corruption scandal, but at the time he was the most popular prime minister the country had seen for years.

He had come to power promising to tackle the many problems that beset the country. Japan's economic miracle had been achieved at the expense of living standards. People had flocked to the cities in search of work. Many lived in intolerably cramped conditions while the countryside was becoming depopulated. Roads, railways and sewerage had been neglected in the rush for industrial development. The environment was being devastated and the level of pollution in the industrial belt along the Pacific coast was truly appalling. This was the time when the notorious Minamata case was going through the courts (industrial waste had polluted Minamata Bay with mercury, causing horrific disease and death). In the industrial city of Kawasaki you could see and smell the pollution in the air, and when it rained the rain was black.

Tanaka's proposal, published under the title "Building a new Japan: a plan for remodeling the Japanese archipelago," was a grand and sweeping plan to remake the entire country. The idea was to pour money into the neglected regional areas and to relocate industries there. There would be eleven bullet-train lines (there was only one at the time) and a network of motorways to link every part of Japan. These were farsighted and necessary reforms. The immediate—and unplanned—result, however, was a fever of land speculation. Construction and real estate companies rushed to buy land designated for future development, and the price of land soared.

Within Seiji's group of companies, it was Seibu Chemicals, under the presidency of Morita, Kuniko's ex-husband, that had the largest landholdings. Morita parceled off the section of the company that dealt with land, renamed it Seibu Urban Development, and began to take out huge bank loans at high rates of interest to invest.

Then, in October 1973, something happened that no one could ever have anticipated. More than four thousand miles away in the Middle East, the Arab states had gone to war to try to eject Israel from the occupied territories. In the aftermath OPEC (the Organization of Petroleum-Exporting Countries) demanded that the Western powers offer them full support. Unless they did so, they would be obliged to use the most potent weapon at their disposal. In November that year they carried out their threat. There had already been severe cuts to the oil supply and prices had risen by as much as 70 percent. Now the Arab states announced a 25 percent production cut.

For Japan it was a sudden and cruel end to the euphoria of the last few years. The spectacular economic boom of 1965 to 1970 had been fueled by cheap oil. Japan was dependent on imported oil for 75 percent of its energy needs. To compound the injury, the Western oil companies responsible for distributing the oil announced that they would favor the United States. Japan was to be left out in the cold.

Throughout the country there was panic. Overnight, prices of everything doubled, trebled, then quadrupled. The shelves of the shops emptied as shoppers snatched up precious goods—salt, soy sauce, sugar—which were rapidly disappearing. There were long queues at petrol stations and stampedes for the last deliveries of toilet paper. Then the government stepped in. Most of the bright neon lights of the Ginza that had gleamed through the night, symbolizing the economic miracle, were turned off. Heating had to be turned down to a regulation 68 degrees Fahrenheit, lights were dimmed, cinemas and theaters closed early. The boom years were over. Belt-tightening was back.

Businesses began to go to the wall, and employees were laid off in the thousands. Prime Minister Tanaka's grand schemes to rebuild Japan had to be shelved indefinitely. All the speculators who had invested in land, expecting to get rich, suddenly found themselves the owners of acre upon acre of useless land and burdened with debts they could not possibly repay. Seibu Urban Development had debts to the order of ¥70 billion.

The situation was desperate. If Seibu Urban Development collapsed, there was a danger that it would bring the whole of Seiji's empire tumbling with it. Within the company rumors circulated that Yoshiaki was about to take them over. It was a prospect that no one relished. No one wanted to be the undernourished retail section of Yoshiaki's vast railway empire.

Seiji approached his bankers, Dai-ichi Kangyo. He needed yet another loan to cover the interest payments on the company's loans to date. The bank refused. In the end he had no choice but to turn to Yoshiaki. Yoshiaki did no more than call the bank. He would, he said, stand surety for his brother, and the bank agreed to top up Seiji's loan.

Seiji's empire was saved, but the crisis was far from over. The first priority was to get the business back on its feet again. All the companies had to pull together. The empire was slimmed down, and the stronger sections were called upon to prop up the weaker.

It was not in Seiji's nature to be on the defensive for long. As soon as he could he was determined to return to the attack.

Japan recovered more quickly and more thoroughly from the oil crisis than anyone could ever have expected. It was another economic miracle, achieved this time against all odds. The first year after the crisis was particularly tough, and brought the worst recession the country had suffered since the war. Prices were impossibly high and business was barely ticking over, but the nation pulled together. Managers took voluntary pay cuts and people soldiered on. People did all they could to save energy, while the government encouraged the development of new energy sources—nuclear, solar and hydroelectric. By the end of 1975, two years after the crisis began, the worst was over, and the country was back on its feet. The economy was growing again, and continued to grow far more rapidly than the economies of the Western nations for the rest of the decade.

But the mood of the country had changed: people were no longer so intoxicated with their newfound wealth that they would buy anything—electrical goods, the latest fashion—just because it was new, just for the joy of spending. The golden age of retail was over.

Seiji responded to the new situation as aggressively as ever. What was amazing was not that he had been on the brink of disaster but how quickly he bounced back. He had dealt with the last great crisis—the huge debt incurred by the collapse of the Los Angeles store—by expanding. In the face of the oil crisis and the deep recession that followed it, there was only one course: to go for broke.

Even before the oil crisis, he had begun to look beyond traditional retailing. From the very start he had used his department stores to promote the arts, and he had always let his own preferences rule his choice. When the new Parco opened, gathered under the same roof as the boutiques were art galleries, restaurants, a coffee shop and, up on the ninth floor with a view across the streets of Shibuya, the Seibu Theater.

From the beginning the theater was an absurdly uncommercial venture. It was designed specifically to provide a venue for two of Seiji's friends, both creative people whom he greatly admired. One was the writer Kobo Abe, the author of *Woman in the Dunes* and one of Japan's leading modern novelists. The other was the composer

Toru Takemitsu. Neither was likely to be a crowd-pleaser; both produced work that was often of impenetrable difficulty.

The first play in the new theater, *Tomodachi* (Friend), was written and directed by Abe, with stage designs by his wife, Machi. It was followed by concerts of Takemitsu's incandescent music and performances by some of the wildest and most outrageous of Tokyo's street performers. The butoh dancer Tatsumi Hijikata and the most famous of all the underground theater troupes, Tenjo Sajiki, under its leader Shuji Terayama, were among the first to appear on the stage—or rampage among the audience—at Parco.

The Seibu Theater never made a profit. The audiences gazing raptly at the antics on the stage consisted largely of students and young girls in spotless white blouses, who were unlikely to spend large amounts of money in Parco's boutiques. But in the cultural desert that was Japan in the seventies, it was an oasis. And it quickly became recognized as the leading theater for avant-garde work.

Somehow in the last hundred years Japan's rich and vibrant culture had disappeared. Beginning in the late 1930s everything had been focused on the war effort. And in the postwar years, the Japanese devoted themselves with the same single-mindedness to reviving the country's economy. Japan had become a nation of economic animals, interested in little but making and spending money.

One result was that Japan's many great and idiosyncratic creative figures were given very little recognition or help at home. There was—and is—no arts council, no system of governmental patronage of the arts. Only 0.03 percent of the government's budget was devoted to culture. Although there were theaters for the traditional dramatic forms—Noh, kabuki, bunraku—there was a striking lack of venues for the work of contemporary or experimental writers.

Seiji was very conscious of this poverty in the national life and aware that he was now in a position to do something to rectify it. Both his supporters and his critics agree that he has never been much interested in profits. Perhaps because of his complicated relationship with his father, perhaps because of his mother's influence, perhaps simply because he was born into a new generation, he never felt the same urge to make money as the old man did. He was just as driven, but his ambition lay in other directions. He had, after all, fallen into the retail business almost by accident. For a long time he had been looking for ways to use his creativity to transform his business, and to use the wealth and power his business gave him toward some more creative end. Rather than using culture to draw customers, as other stores did, Seiji wanted to use his stores to spread culture.

Surely, now that the first wave of hedonistic consumerism had passed, now that people had realized that the struggle to survive was really over, they would begin to consider the quality of their lives. They could not live forever simply on material wealth. To quote Seiji, "From now on spirit will predominate over material things. We are entering an age that will emphasize feelings."

In 1975, well before the oil crisis had run its course, he opened an art museum occupying most of the top floor of Seibu Ikebukuro. Following Seiji's own inclinations, the Seibu Art Museum was devoted to the contemporary arts, including photography, design, crafts, fashion, architecture and anything else the curators chose to feature. The first exhibitions included contemporary Japanese art, Kandinsky, Max Ernst, Issey Miyake's "clothing art" and the work of Charles Rennie Mackintosh. In Western terms it was not particularly revolutionary, but in Japan very few galleries and museums at the time showed contemporary work. Many of Seibu's exhibitions brought works to the country that art lovers had only been able to see in books. In economic terms Japan was rapidly catching up with the West, but culturally it was still way behind. Seiji had embarked on a one-person crusade to make a dent in Japan's increasingly materialistic culture.

In the art community the new museum was welcomed. From the start it was financially independent of the department store, on a par with any other major museum. The staff, in fact, was specifically instructed not to consider making a profit or attracting customers. Instead the focus was to be uncompromisingly on challenging and radical art.

Seiji still had the Midas touch. Taking huge risks and engaging in idealistic and uncommercial cultural activities, he only enhanced Seibu's reputation. Thanks largely to Seibu's patronage, contemporary art was becoming a more and more powerful force in society, and more and more people flocked to the museum's exhibitions.

Behind his idealism Seiji was as shrewd as his father. He could see which way the country was moving, and it coincided with his own long-term aims and ideals. His cultural projects were part of a grand plan to overhaul the whole image of the stores that made up his empire.

Mitsukoshi, the *grande dame* of department stores, had a long-established name and a three-hundred-year history behind it. It was a bastion of tradition, class and snobbery, all matters of great importance in Japan. Seibu, on the other hand, was an upstart, flaunting its youth and newness. Its success was the result of an enormously complex variety of factors—the democratization of society brought about at the end of the war, the slow disintegration of the traditional, all-powerful family structures, and Japan's gradual awakening to what was happening in the world outside. It was a movement that was still very new. Seibu did not merely recognize it and tap into it; Seibu was at the very heart of it, helping it to grow.

For young people, Seibu was the promised land. It was staffed by people in their twenties and thirties, who would never have been able to find such responsible positions in any other Japanese company. They had money, exposure and the freedom to do whatever they liked. They had the huge resources of Seibu behind them. Their designs, posters and ad campaigns were seen by large numbers of people. Yet they were encouraged to be creative, daring, avant-garde rather than commercial. They were paid, in fact, to do exactly what they wanted.

It was a policy that could easily have led to disaster. Instead it paid off a hundredfold. Seiji's instincts seemed to coincide exactly with the spirit of the age. Seibu—which gradually came to take over the torch from Parco—became a seedbed for creative talent, identified with the height of fashion, with the most avant-garde design, and with the most memorable and quirky advertising. Advertising as a creative form, in fact, was nurtured at Seibu. One of Japan's most famous names, the copywriter Shigesato Itoi, began his career at Seibu.

Itoi was responsible for the clipped slogans that came to epitomize the style of Seibu. *"Oishii seikatsu*—delicious life" was one of the slogans for 1982. The poster showed the wistful face of Woody Allen, in traditional men's kimono, kneeling on a cushion, peeking out from behind a scroll on which is written "Delicious life" in large childish characters.

Leaders of the British retail trade went to admire and learn from

Seibu's design and layout, the television screens on every floor, the changing themes behind the marketing. One, impressed by the crowds of people, said that Seibu "had the air of cash registers ringing." Another commented that Seibu made Harrods and Bloomingdale's look Stone Age.

More than ever before, Seiji was the public face of Seibu. When people heard the name Seibu, they thought of the department store. In an article published in *Newsweek* in 1976, it was Seiji's distribution group that was described as "the nucleus of the Tsutsumi family fortunes," and Seiji, not Yoshiaki, who was the main subject of the article. In a way he had reclaimed the empire.[2]

For all its glitter and dazzle, Seibu was also making money. In September 1982 Seiji finally achieved his aim: that month Seibu Ikebukuro passed Mitsukoshi to become the top-selling department store in Japan, with sales of ¥3.74 billion (roughly $15 million) against Mitsukoshi's ¥3 billion.

Mitsukoshi's decline was not purely the result of Seibu's brilliant marketing; in fact, Seibu's fortunes had been tied to Mitsukoshi's in a rather convoluted fashion for some years.

Around 1970, when Seiji was on his way to Chicago to negotiate with Sears Roebuck, he attended a U.S.-Japan financiers' conference in Washington, D.C. There he found himself sitting next to a man named Yoshiaki Sakakura. Seiji had heard a lot about Sakakura. He was one of the top men at Mitsukoshi, with a reputation as one of the best businessmen in the retail trade. It was also common knowledge that he was in the middle of a power struggle with a man named Shigeru Okada. Both had graduated from the prestigious Keio University and both, from the moment they joined Mitsukoshi, had been tipped as future presidents of the company. Sakakura was a quiet, solid, immensely talented businessman, who could be relied upon to ensure high profits as well as good sales. Okada, a heavyset man with an arrogant tilt to his eyebrows, was a far more showy character. Deferential to his seniors, he instilled terror in his subordinates, barking orders at them in the rough language of the *yakuza* underworld. He did, however, have a streak of brilliance. In 1968 he took over as the manager of the Ginza branch of Mitsukoshi. The Ginza is Tokyo's most elegant street and Mitsukoshi was located at the crossroads, on a piece of land that later, in the boom years of the eighties, was to become famous as the most expensive piece of real estate in the world.

There, in the equivalent of London's Mayfair or New York's Fifth Avenue, Okada decided to go all out for high sales. He installed a McDonald's right at Ginza crossing, directly opposite Wako, purveyor of eminently refined ladies' fashions. He set up a beer hall on Mitsukoshi's venerable roof. And he had the store decorated in the latest psychedelic style. Loyal customers were horrified. "Can this really be Mitsukoshi?" they asked. As for Sakakura, he was quoted as saying disparagingly, "Okada's business is completely hollow; there's no substance in it!"[3] But despite the complaints, customers poured in. Sales at the Ginza branch soared.

Sitting side by side at the financiers' conference in Washington, Seiji noticed with approval that Sakakura was taking all his notes in English. Such a grasp of languages was evidence of the man's ability. The two chatted. Freed from all the prying eyes that surrounded them in Japan, they had time to get to know each other. In the Japanese way, they steered clear of business talk. It was far too early for such things; instead they simply made friends. They enjoyed each other's company. Together they strolled around Washington and went to pay their respects at Kennedy's tomb.

There was one question that Seiji wanted to ask. In the course of conversation he said casually, "Are you staying on at Mitsukoshi?" There had been rumors that Sakakura might leave.

"When the time is right I was thinking I might escape" was the answer.

In April 1972 Okada was promoted to president of Mitsukoshi Ltd. There was a lavish reception at one of Tokyo's top hotels. Two hundred members of the press attended and Okada's face, wreathed in smiles, was on every television channel and in all the papers. Exactly a year later, in April 1973, Sakakura left.

Sakakura was an old-fashioned man and a man of honor. Under Japan's lifetime employment system, it was highly irregular to leave one's position at all; and certainly, having done so, it would be considered most improper to join a rival store. The correct course was to leave the retail trade completely. Seiji watched with interest. He was sure that Sakakura was the perfect man for Seibu. Seiji himself was much vaunted in the business world for his instinct as a headhunter and his skill at making good relationships and getting the people he wanted. He knew that he had to bide his time. If he moved too quickly he would lose his prey.

Some months after Sakakura's departure, a friend of Seiji's, a leading financial journalist, dropped in to see him. It was the journalist who brought up Sakakura's name.

"Have you come across a guy called Sakakura?" he inquired.

"Yeah," said Seiji cautiously.

"He quit Mitsukoshi, you know."

"Looks like it."

"Why not take him on?"

Seiji didn't need to be asked. "You think so too!" he exclaimed.

"Seibu needs him," the journalist asserted.[4]

With the journalist acting as intermediary, the two met and began discussions. Seiji had to ask Sakakura three times before he finally put aside his scruples and agreed to come over to Seibu. Seiji also paid a courtesy call on Okada to inform him that he was planning to recruit his ex-colleague.

"As you've come to tell me, it's okay by me," Mitsukoshi's president conceded.

In 1974 Sakakura joined Seibu department stores as vice president. After a short time, Seiji promoted him to president.

Initially, together Seiji and Sakakura made the perfect team. Seiji was the ideas man. He was perpetually coming up with dazzling schemes and exciting new strategies. The reshaping of Seibu's image, the focus on everything that was new, youthful, high fashion, avant-garde—all this was dreamed up by Seiji. But it was Sakakura, the pragmatic businessman, who made it happen and who ensured that the store also made a reasonable profit. In fact, the record sales of 1982 were thanks largely to Sakakura's good husbandry.

Over the years, Sakakura's relationship with Seiji cooled. Company insiders give different versions of the story, depending on their allegiance. The version perpetuated by the Japanese press and the many malcontents who left Seibu puts the whole business down to Seiji's capricious personality. Everyone agrees that Seiji was a superb headhunter. He had an unparalleled knack of spotting executives with exactly the talents that Seibu needed. But after some years his enthusiasm would cool. Many people, according to one version of events, were invited to join Seibu—journalists, television executives as well as business figures. Ten years later most of them had left. In the case of Sakakura, the two men were diametrically opposed in almost every respect in their approaches to business. While Seiji was an idealist, perpetually inventing new strategies, Sakakura was a conventional businessman, pragmatic and down-to-earth. Under his presidency the emphasis at Seibu changed from sales to profits and the company flourished, but inevitably the two approaches were bound to clash.

Within the company the story is very different. Sakakura, they say, was far from the great businessman he was made out to be. Seiji gave him a chance to prove himself, but he was simply not up to the job. He was lazy, he would fall asleep in the middle of a conversation, he was always taking time off to play golf, he ran up huge expenses. Seibu did well simply because the economy was strong. Moreover, say the company insiders, while the malcontents who left obviously broadcast their dissatisfaction, there were many more who stayed on until the end of their careers.

No doubt the reasons for Sakakura's resignation were many and complex. In any case, in 1984, ten years after he joined Seibu, he left. Just as he had done when he left Mitsukoshi, he announced that he was retiring from the retailing industry, but a few months later he was offered the position he had coveted from the very start: president of Mitsukoshi.

Sakakura is still the president of Mitsukoshi and also head of the department stores association. After his departure Seibu remained the top-selling department store for several years, with Mitsukoshi relegated to second place. In 1990 Seibu Ikebukuro's sales amounted to ¥432 billion ($2.98 billion) while the main Mitsukoshi store had sales of ¥315 billion ($2.17 billion).

Throughout his career, there were always those who questioned Seiji's methods. In Western terms his business style of hiring and firing would be scarcely worthy of note, but in the stolid Japanese business world, where lifetime employment and the old-school-tie network remained the norm, it caused outrage. In the seventies and early eighties, though, the dissenting voices were few. Seibu was booming, and while businessmen might look askance at Seiji's lackadaisical attitude toward profits, in the eyes of artists, designers, copywriters and fashion people he could do no wrong. To quote the designer Eiko Ishioka, "He was a hero businessman, a very rare businessman who could marry art and commerce."

He had, after all, no reason to restrict himself to pure retailing. In a broad sense the retailer's job was simply to serve the consumer. If the consumer wanted insurance, for example, why should he not be able to buy it in the supermarket along with his weekly shopping? So Seibu moved into the insurance business. The Seibu Allstate Life Insurance Company Ltd. started in 1975, not long after the oil crisis, as a joint venture with Sears Roebuck. To begin with, there were just two employees at the Japanese end. Their first task was to persuade the Ministry of Finance to grant them a license to trade. Given that Seibu had no experience whatsoever of the insurance business, the ministry was reluctant. It was only after a mountain of documents had been delivered that permission was finally granted. The two employees expanded to ten, five in Japan and five in Chicago, and together they set to work to develop an insurance system that would relate to the needs of the Japanese consumer.

As more and more Seibus, Parcos and Seiyu Store supermarkets opened all over the country, the scope of Seibu's operations continued to broaden. There were exclusive tie-ups with Sotheby's, Liberty and Habitat. Family Mart, a new chain of small local self-service "convenience stores" opened, providing groceries and everyday necessities until late at night.

There was also a credit-card operation, Seibu Credit, developed in conjunction with Sears. At the time the country had almost entirely a cash economy. No one used checks, salaries were paid in envelopes bulging with cash, and while corporations could approach banks for financing, there were very limited facilities for the individual borrower. It was a system appropriate for a country where funds were limited, but as the economy grew, it became clear that people needed more sophisticated ways of organizing their money. Seiji was one of the first to realize that credit cards could be successful in Japan. The Seibu Card was introduced in 1982 and was an instant success.

There was one occasion, however, early on in these years, when Seiji stepped too far beyond the bounds of retailing. Kunio Fukumoto, the friend who had frequented the geisha houses of Yanagibashi with him, used to say that he was "dancing the cancan on a hot frying pan." It began when Seibu acquired an interest in a piece of government land in Ikebukuro.

Ikebukuro was never a particularly salubrious part of town. One of its grimmest landmarks was Tokyo's central prison, Sugamo Prison, a gray sprawling complex of buildings where the wartime prime minister Hideki Tojo and his fellow class-A war criminals were incarcerated and eventually hanged. As the area began to change and shoppers replaced the gangsters and lowlife who had roamed its streets, the local business community became concerned about the proximity of the prison. It was not the kind of image that the business community wanted to promote.

In 1971 the prison was torn down. This left a gaping expanse of land, owned by the government and ripe for development. There was considerable debate about what should be done with the land. Should it be put to recreational use or taken over by business interests? Seiji came up with a winning scheme. What Ikebukuro needed was a cultural center, a complex of buildings housing theaters, museums, galleries and a concert hall. To make the project commercially viable, there would also be offices, a department store, an exhibition hall and a hotel. One of the buildings for the complex would be a skyscraper, Ikebukuro's first; with sixty floors it would be a landmark, the tallest building in the whole of Japan. It was a stunning idea. In the late eighties "cultural villages," much as Seiji envisioned, mushroomed all over Japan. But at the time there was nothing like it.

The plan had its detractors. According to company insiders, Yoshiaki was far from pleased to hear about it. In symbolic terms, it was almost a deliberate affront. Yoshiaki's headquarters, the offices of Seibu Railways, were in Ikebukuro, near the station. It was as if Seiji were building a castle of his own, sixty stories high, to loom over Yoshiaki's. There were other points. Seiji was planning a hotel; yet hotels were Yoshiaki's area of business, not his. In purely practical terms the project was questionable. Who on earth would want to stay in a hotel in the windy wastelands of east Ikebukuro? Yoshiaki made a public statement that he was strongly opposed to the plan.

Nevertheless Seiji pushed ahead. A consortium was formed made up of banks and various companies including Seibu, all of which held shares in the land. The details of what happened next are unclear. At some stage after the sudden shock brought about by the oil crisis, the banks and business circles who were supporting the project lost confidence in it. It was too big, too ambitious; and Seiji, as the kingpin of the whole project, simply did not have the landholdings to support the vast loans he required.

Seiji, always quick to recognize when a project was not going to work, decided to pull out, but this was very difficult. Many companies were involved, not merely Seibu, and a great deal of money had already been invested. The project was far advanced.

Once again the only solution was to turn to Yoshiaki. Whether he liked it or not, he too was involved. The banks and commercial interests had given their support because of the Tsutsumi name.

Yoshiaki, say company insiders, was very angry. He was put in a position where he could not refuse, yet Seiji had not consulted him before he began the project and he had been opposed to it from the very start. Reluctantly he agreed to take it over. There is a rumor that has circulated widely within the companies that, in exchange, he made one condition. He wanted Seiji's word that he would keep away from the hotel business from now on. Seiji, it is said, agreed.

In the end the project was completed by a new consortium that included Japan National Railways and Mitsubishi, with Yoshiaki as the ultimate controlling power. The sixty-story Sunshine 60 building opened in 1978, a monolith towering over the sleazy streets of east Ikebukuro. It was indeed the tallest building in Tokyo, with views out to the pristine pyramid of Mount Fuji on the horizon, until it was overtaken in 1991 by the new Metropolitan Government Buildings. The rest of the Sunshine City complex—despite its name, a rather bleak, windswept collection of buildings, reminiscent of London's Canary Wharf—was all much as Seiji had planned it. Besides a theater, a museum and a concert hall, there was also a planetarium, an aquarium and the World Import Mart, where goods from around the world were exhibited. There was even a hotel—the Sunshine City Prince Hotel, one of Yoshiaki's Prince chain.

Given the speed with which Seiji expanded his empire, it was hardly surprising that from time to time he should stumble. What was amazing in those golden years was not that he had the occasional fall but that for all the risks he took he fell so seldom. He danced on, performing his cancan on a hot frying pan, seemingly invincible.

Like any leading Japanese businessman, he had his share of love affairs. Nevertheless, his marriage remained a very happy one. Asako was strong, dependable, beautiful and independent, and the two often appeared in public together. But, as Seiji once said laughingly to one of his oldest friends, "If you don't like women you're not human."

The paparazzi, the gutter press, followed him like piranhas, convinced that he had his father's blood in him, but he was very skillful at keeping his affairs discreet. Only the smallest scraps of gossip ever emerged.

Like many powerful men, he is said to have a penchant for actresses. Around the mid-seventies his name became linked with an actress called Mayumi Ozora. Thirteen years younger than he, she was a sweet-featured and lively woman, with deep black hair and very white skin. Pretty rather than beautiful, she had a softly rounded face, large eyes that looked at you with a direct and humorous gaze, and a curving mouth with a full sensual underlip. She also had the independence of spirit that he has always valued in women and was deeply committed to her career. She frequently appeared in television dramas, on stage and in films.

The Seibu staff first began to speculate about a relationship when Seiji suddenly demanded that his stores should stock oolong tea and extolled its health-giving properties. Ms. Ozora, it transpired, loved oolong tea. Once or twice the two were seen together in the streets of Kyoto and were overheard addressing each other in familiar rather than formal language. In the closed world of Japanese society the tiniest nuance—the tone of voice, the sort of language used—is enough to make people speculate about a relationship. And from time to time the paparazzi managed to catch them together. Once one of Japan's leading gossip magazines published a photograph of the pair entering a condominium, he with his right arm around her.

Seiji in his novels was far more outspoken about his sexuality. The busier he became with his work, the more he seemed driven to write. Each of his novels was written when he was reaching a pinnacle of his career. *In the Season of Roaming* came out the year after the groundbreaking new Seibu opened in Shibuya. And in 1983, the year after Seibu Ikebukuro became the country's top-selling department store, *A Spring Like Any Other* was published.

Like *In the Season of Roaming*, *A Spring Like Any Other* was an

I-novel, full of revelations about the author's innermost feelings. As in much of modern Japanese literature, its introverted angst-ridden musings are fairly inaccessible to the Western reader and come across poorly in translation. One reviewer, writing in the *Japan Times*, described the English translation as

> an impressionistic collage of deadpan reminiscences, snatched, as it were, by the narrator, between board meetings and business breakfasts. . . . The book is eerily free of irony; the wet sand of prevarication and diffidence which comprises Junzo's [Seiji's] narrative is without guile. There is no climax to the novel. The title, like the narrator, is in no way disingenuous; the spring really was just like any other, if anything somewhat duller than most, and one is left to ponder just why the book was written in the first place.[5]

Nevertheless, among Japanese reviewers the book was well received and won a literary award, the Taiko Hirabayashi Prize, in 1983.

Despite the fictional names, nearly all the characters in the novel were easy to recognize: the mild, concerned, middle-aged company president; the dreadful father who even after his death cast an influence over the entire family; the mother, romanticizing the memory of the husband who had caused her such pain all her life; the sister who had fled to Paris to escape the loathsome, untrustworthy husband.

Only one character was ambiguous: Ritsuko, the fictional Seiji's lover. In the novel, the company president is unmarried. Ritsuko, his mistress, is the editor in chief of an art magazine and a spirited, independent woman. Yet, as a lover, she becomes childlike, coquettish, dependent. Seiji writes of her distinctive body odor, of the way she nuzzles up against him, of the games they play together. He crawls around on his hands and knees while she rides him like a horse. She pees in front of him while they are in the bath together. But is the character modeled on Seiji's wife, Asako, on Mayumi Ozora or on another woman—or is she an amalgam of several? Surely, even in Japan, would it not be unthinkably indiscreet for a happily married man to write even a fictionalized account of a love affair with another woman?

In *A Spring Like Any Other* Seiji writes, "Father was continually at the mercy of an intense yearning that sex could not satisfy, no matter how often he changed partners or how many encounters he had." Seiji's own life, in contrast, was uncomplicated and quite conventional. His marriage was a happy one. And his friendship with Mayumi Ozora, too, seems to have been a stable one that lasted many years. Until quite recently Ms. Ozora from time to time attended the opening of new stores. And, coincidence or not, she appeared in the Italian comedy *Oh Napoli!*, staged in April 1993 in the Ginza Saison Theater, one of the keystones of Seiji's cultural empire.

In his novel Seiji quotes the fictionalized Kuniko as saying that since she can't find one ideal man to satisfy all her needs, she may as well go out with three men at the same time and combine their good points. While Seiji was building his empire in Japan, Kuniko in Paris was leading the life of a princess. The Japanese gossip magazines that followed her there referred to her as Princess Tsutsumi.

Sometime before the oil crisis of 1973, when Kuniko was in her mid-forties, an opportunity arose that must have seemed like the answer to everything she had ever dreamed about. At the time the French government was promoting tourism in the Languedoc and subsidies were available for developing resorts and hotels. Kuniko's plan was to restore a two-thousand-ton ship, the *Lydia,* turn it into a shipboard casino and make it the centerpiece of a high-class resort near Perpignan on the Mediterranean coast, close to the Spanish border. Besides the casino there would be a hotel with two hundred rooms and a block of two hundred forty luxury holiday apartments. Thanks to her marriage she had French citizenship and for several years had been making investments in France on behalf of the Seibu group. A casino, surely, would be the perfect investment opportunity. On her next visit to Japan she spoke to Seiji about her project.

While Kuniko, steeped in French culture and values, saw casinos as the epitome of sophistication and glamour, to the Japanese in the early seventies gambling smelled of nothing but the racetrack. Seiji was concerned to raise the image of Seibu, not to lower it by investing in a gambling house. He was also doubtful about the financial viability of such a project. Kuniko's resolve, however, could not be shaken. With her talent and connections, surely a casino could only be a glittering success. In the end Seiji gave way and his Seibu retail group invested ¥3.5 billion in the project.

Casino Lydia opened in 1974. The cream of French society attended the opening, surrounding the roulette tables with wit and laughter while Kuniko, effortlessly chic in silks and pearls, presided. For the young Japanese woman alone in an alien society it was an extraordinary achievement.

But for all its glamour, Casino Lydia turned out to be a financial disaster. Once again Seibu's activities were bedeviled by the oil crisis. Off season the casino was deserted. The hotel was often half empty and one hundred of the luxury apartments remained unsold. Finally the casino was forced to close.

Then, around 1976, another opportunity arose. Once again Kuniko was filled with excitement. It seems that the mayor of Trouville-sur-Mer, on the Atlantic coast of Normandy, was eager to encourage development projects to attract visitors to the town. One proposal was to renovate the municipal casino. For Kuniko this was the perfect project. Sparkling with ideas, she got a license to manage a casino and planned a lavish development to include a restaurant, a luxury hotel and a nightclub.

But such a project needed investment. When the architects' plans were ready, once again Kuniko flew to Tokyo to persuade Seiji to help her. For Seiji it must have been an impossible situation. On the one hand, he was closer to this wayward sister of his than to any other member of his family. Yet, as the owner and president of a huge concern with many thousands of employees, he could not afford to become involved in a project that he was convinced would fail. It was a terrible dilemma—and one that eventually inspired him to write *A Spring Like Any Other*. An underlying theme of the novel is his attempt to reconcile the private man and the business leader, the quiet reflective poet and the president of the retail group.

In the end his responsibility was clear. Despite the inward pain it caused him, he informed his sister, "You're free to go ahead if you choose, but only if you sever all ties to the company."[6] Regardless of her brother's lack of faith in the project, Kuniko resigned her position as the head of Seibu's Paris office forthwith. She approached banks in Japan, asking for a loan, but without the backing of the giant Seibu concern they were unwilling to lend her money. In the end she sold her villa and her stocks and shares—everything that had been left to her as her part of the inheritance. With nothing left to tie her to Japan, she went back to Paris.

At first it seemed as if Seiji had been wrong. With her own funds as collateral she borrowed 6.5 million francs from French banks and poured the money into the restoration of the casino. When it was completed it was truly spectacular. On the night of the opening in the spring of 1978, European nobility, Hollywood stars and American magnates were in attendance. Kuniko, tiny and delicate, greeted her guests clad in mink.

In the first year the casino made a profit of three times the original investment. But all Kuniko's business ventures seemed to be jinxed: in October 1979 her company was declared bankrupt. Somehow the casino had accumulated debts of 2.6 million francs and her staff of 120 had not been paid for the last month. Worse still, Kuniko was arrested by the Trouville police, taken into custody and questioned for several hours; that night the woman who so loved luxury slept in a police cell.

"I was not afraid," she whispers in her mouselike voice. "It was like being in a cage at the zoo. It was very exciting. I was surprised—but not afraid. My only fear was what Seiji would think."

The following day Seiji paid her bail of 150,000 francs and she was released. Her passport, however, had been confiscated. Back in Paris she discovered that her flat had been ransacked and all her documents taken.

It was the worst time in Kuniko's life. "I lost all my money," she says softly. "I lost everything I owned. I lost my honor. I lost—but I didn't go under. In the end it was a good experience."

Poor Kuniko found herself entirely alone. All the so-called friends who had showered her with flowers and invitations no longer wanted to know her. As for Seiji, he refused to have anything to do with her. Kuniko wrote to him again and again but he would not answer. And he no longer put money into her bank account.

Once again Seiji was torn between his feelings as a brother and his duty to his company. There was a grave danger that Seibu might be implicated in Kuniko's disgrace. That was to be avoided at all costs. Besides, Kuniko had acted directly against his advice.

Kuniko was desperate. She began to sell her furs and her jewelry, but everyone knew she was bankrupt and she was often given a poor price. There were days when she lacked even the metro fare to take documents to court. Sometimes as she walked along she looked for money on the ground.

For a year there was silence. Then one day she found five thousand francs in her bank account. Seiji had finally relented. Another ten thousand francs arrived, then twenty thousand. Yoshiaki too helped her out. Despite the two brothers' dislike of each other, she had always understood and loved both of them. She was not involved in any rivalry that might exist between the two of them.

It was not until 1981 that Kuniko's case finally came to court, with Seiji paying her legal fees. It was a long and complicated procedure. In the end Kuniko was acquitted of all charges and ordered to pay only 150,000 francs to cover a technical violation of the commercial code. In fact, she had already paid the 150,000 francs as bail.

That same year, 1981, the Socialists under President François Mitterrand came to power in France. In the aftermath of their victory there was an investigation into some cases of corruption under the old regime. Evidence emerged suggesting that Kuniko had been used as a scapegoat. She had been a victim from beginning to end. She was totally innocent. Finally her name was cleared and her reputation restored.

The Sleeping Lion Wakes
Yoshiaki's Story 1964–1978

My grandfather reared my father. Ever since he was young, he had great expectations of him. He invested in him, threw away his honorary position in the village and his business as a linen collector, and died at the age of 74. So my father received his grandfather's 74 years of experience. Add to that his own 75 years and you have 150 years. When you add my age, 50, to that 150, that makes 200 years of experience. That is the power of the Seibu Railway Group. We have three people's ways of thinking. If you look at this, you'll understand what a secure foundation my business has.

YOSHIAKI TSUTSUMI

In Oshita, "Seiji Tsutsumi vs.
Yoshiaki Tsutsumi"

On Tuesday, March 1, 1966, the limousines began to arrive at the Tokyo Prince Hotel from midmorning. The guests who stepped out, clad decorously in formal black kimonos and morning suits, included the most wealthy and powerful in the nation.

The emperor's brothers, Prince Takamatsu and Prince Mikasa, were there with their consorts, representing the imperial family, together with Princess Yasuko, the emperor's sister. Former prime minister Kishi, Yasujiro's old colleague, who had been forced to resign when riots stopped Eisenhower's visit, arrived, a little older and shakier than before. In attendance were the chairman of Keidanren (Japan Federation of Economic Organizations); Shigeo Mizuno, Seiji's friend and mentor; Noboru Goto, the son of Yasujiro's old enemy Goto the Thief; the chancellor of Waseda University; and the commander in chief of the American naval forces in Japan. Cabinet ministers, members of the Diet, presidents of banks, mayors, prefectural governors, actors, actresses, musicians, diplomats—everyone was there. In fact, the only people who were not there, as one magazine wrote, were the emperor and his family. "If by some chance there were an accident, the entire nation would come to a standstill!"

The occasion for this splendid gathering was the marriage of Mr. Yoshiaki Tsutsumi to Miss Yuri Ishibashi, daughter of Mr. Tokutaro Ishibashi of Mitsui and Company.

Nearly two years had passed since the fateful day when the twenty-nine-year-old Yoshiaki, plump-faced and boyish still, had been plucked from the shadows to be chief mourner at his father's funeral. From then on he had been on his own. The whole vast empire of land, railways, hotels, buses, golf courses and ski resorts was his and his alone.

While Seiji had already made his mark in both the business and the political worlds, Yoshiaki was largely unknown. In business he was a child still, far too young and inexperienced to take over the reins of such a vast organization. His father's last command to him—confirmation if confirmation were needed that Yasujiro saw Yoshiaki as his successor—had been to do nothing for ten years. For those ten years he should leave the running of the company to the old men, the presidents and vice presidents and managers who had been with Yasujiro all his life and functioned almost as an extension of him. Yoshiaki should study and observe until he had mastered every detail of the company's operations. Above all, he should start no new business. In ten years the situation would have changed. Then would be the time to decide the proper way to move.

"It's okay to fail now while I'm alive," the old man used to growl. "But don't fail when I'm dead!"[1]

It is rumored that one of the first things Yoshiaki did after his father's death was to seek out the many children Yasujiro had sired. When he found these half brothers and sisters, the story goes, he paid them large sums of money to forestall any claims to the inheritance and asked them never to reveal that they were Yasujiro's children. People say that many of them work to this day in both Seiji's and Yoshiaki's companies, some in high positions. In the years after Yasujiro's death, those who did business with Seibu used to say to one another, "Whether you turn to the left or the right, there's a drop of the chairman. You have to be careful what you say in the Seibu Group."[2]

As the inheritor of the Seibu empire, Yoshiaki turned for advice to his father's friends. One of these was the prime minister, Hayato Ikeda. People have said that it was Yasujiro who ensured Ikeda's rise to power. Whether or not that is the case, it is certain that he was a friend and mentor to the prime minister in his last years.

At the time Ikeda was in ill health and was shortly to resign. Yoshiaki used to visit him and his family in their summer villa in the coastal resort of Atami. There he would mull over his future with Ikeda, listening respectfully while the prime minister expounded on the current political and economic state of the country. He remained close to the family and continued his visits after Ikeda died in 1965. On one of these occasions, according to Ikeda's widow, he told them that he was to be married. His bride-to-be, he said, was "the daughter of an ordinary businessman. My mother approved of her and chose her for me and I complied."

Yuri Ishibashi was really far more than the "daughter of an ordinary businessman." Her father was a leading figure in Mitsui and Company, deputy director of the overseas facilities department, and the Mitsuis were one of the most powerful and venerated clans in the country. The Tsutsumis, after all, were upstarts. They had money, but they lacked history and class. In the highest reaches of Japanese society—the old aristocrats who, although they had lost their titles, still formed a small exclusive community—they were regarded as nothing more than parvenus. No matter how much wealth and power they accumulated, it was only through marriage that they could enhance their status.

More than anyone else it was Tsuneko, Yoshiaki's mother, who chose Yuri. The girl had studied tea ceremony with her; and she had every quality that made her suitable to be a bride of the Tsutsumi family.

Both the family and Yoshiaki have always been very protective of her. After the wedding she never again appeared in public, and few of Yoshiaki's friends have ever met her. Those who have, among them the irrepressible Hoshino, the boyhood friend with whom Yoshiaki used to roam the hills of Karuizawa, say that she is very quiet. She is petite, gentle, soft-spoken, a pretty woman with shoulder-length wavy hair. She dresses modestly, in quiet colors. She has, in fact, all the qualities of the ideal Japanese wife.

People said that it was the most splendid wedding in all the years since the war. The ceremony itself was a private affair, for the family only,[3] followed by several receptions, one for people close to the bride and groom—relatives, friends, their old schoolteachers—and one for the family's vast network of business connections. The main reception was held in the Providence Hall, the banqueting hall of the Prince Hotel, with its chandeliers, deep-pile carpet and walls glimmering with gold leaf. As the guests entered, they passed a Japanese garden of raked sand, with gnarled pine trees and a dazzling display of flowers—delicate pink cherry blossoms in full bloom, peach blossoms, tulips and daffodils. There was even a small pond, with rocks and a bamboo pipe balanced on a fulcrum. An endless stream of water trickled into the pipe, which filled until it was brimming, then tipped over to hit the rock below it with a dry *tok* sound. It was the epitome of tea-ceremony elegance. Music was provided by leading members of the NHK Symphony Orchestra, one of the country's finest, and the master of ceremonies was a famous television personality. A representative of the cabinet read out congratulatory telegrams from the prime minister, Eisaku Sato, and the grand old statesman and postwar prime minister Shigeru Yoshida.

"It was the biggest wedding I'd ever been to," remembered Hoshino from Karuizawa. Among the thirteen hundred distinguished guests, Yoshiaki had not forgotten to invite his childhood friends. Takashi Yokota, whose mother had been so impressed by Yoshiaki's command of the tea ceremony, was there. He recalled the press of people—so many that instead of sitting down to eat, guests helped themselves from a buffet. The cuisine was French, as is usual at grand society weddings in Japan; along with small stands along the walls where sushi chefs sliced raw fish there was freshly made tempura and steaming bowls of noodles.

No one ate much. Yoshiaki, stiff and solemn-faced, stood in the reception line to greet his guests, wearing a formal black men's kimono, endlessly bowing. His bride, in the traditional way, appeared in a succession of sumptuous multilayered silk kimonos, richly embroidered in red and gold. Then both disappeared to change into a morning suit and white wedding gown with a flowing train for the cutting of the cake.

It was an awesome display of wealth and power, a chance for the family to introduce the new leader of the Tsutsumi clan and for the guests to pay their respects. Seiji undoubtedly was present; at the time he was the central figure in the empire, acting as regent during his brother's minority. None of Yoshiaki's old friends, however, could fail to be aware of one notable absence. It was Misao who stood in the reception line bowing, Misao who made the speech of thanks. "If the chairman was still alive, he would have been so happy today," she said, beaming, tiny and elegant in her black kimono.

Tsuneko had been left at home. Officially Yoshiaki was registered as the third son of Misao, Yasujiro's legal wife. There was no place for the woman in the shadows, even at her son's wedding.

For both the mother and the son it was the most bitter of experiences. Hoshino mused, "He had to endure this complexity of his family. . . . Emotionally I think he wanted to share his celebration with his own mother."

It was as if Yoshiaki had been swept up into a role he had had no part in choosing. He was to marry a woman chosen not by himself but by the family. Yet, emperor though he was, he did not even have the power to enable his own mother to be present on his wedding day. There was only one consolation: in marrying Yuri he was pleasing his mother. It was Tsuneko who had chosen her.

Many people have spoken about Yoshiaki's devotion to his mother. While Seiji was perpetually tormented by doubts that Misao was not really his mother, and Kiyoshi's life had been ruined by his father's callous treatment of the woman who bore him, Yoshiaki experienced no such suffering. His life was much simpler. Of all Yasujiro's recognized sons, only he and his two brothers had been brought up by their real mother.

Tsuneko showered her sons with love. She devoted her life entirely to them, but they in their turn could not but be aware of her sadness and frustration. Throughout her life she was doomed to be always three steps behind Misao, and could never escape the humiliation of being the mistress. Even after Yasujiro's death she still had to be hidden, she could never appear in public. For Yasujiro she had given up her youth. People have speculated that, had he lived longer, Yasujiro would have divorced Misao and made Tsuneko his legal wife. His death deprived her of ever discovering if that was so. The one great compensation was her children. As it became clear that Yoshiaki was to be his father's successor, she must have felt that finally her suffering had been vindicated.

Yoshiaki could not change his mother's status. Misao was still the official wife, and presided at official functions, but after Yasujiro's death he did everything he could to make Tsuneko's life as happy and as comfortable as possible. He had a new house built for her on the land in Takagi-cho, much grander and more spacious than the simple wooden house where he had grown up. And with Yasujiro gone, she no longer had to wear simple clothes. She had her hair permed, she wore brighter colors and she spent more time visiting her friends.

But the sadness remained. On the day of Yoshiaki's wedding, she called a friend and sobbed, "I bore that child, I brought him up—why can't I go to his wedding?"[4]

While Seiji, freed from his father's constraints, was spinning out a spectacular mini-empire, dazzling society with his flashy new stores, expanding into new areas, appearing on television, publishing poetry and novels, Yoshiaki remained far from the public eye, watching and waiting, obeying his father's command. The economic boom of the late sixties came and went but still Yoshiaki bided his time.

According to one of his earliest biographers, Koki Eikawa, he once said to him with a wink, "Eikawa-*san,* if a beautiful woman were lying close to you naked, would you be able to hold back and do nothing?"[5] The young man was bursting with ideas and had practically limitless resources at his disposal. While his father was still alive he had made a start on many projects—the skating center at Karuizawa, the beachside pool at Oiso, developing remote mountain areas into ski resorts or golf courses. But for ten years he had to put aside his ambitious plans and do nothing.

There was much to study. Yasujiro had been a one-man band, and kept a tight grip on his empire. Yoshiaki had to master the financial situation of each company that made up the group—which ones were making a profit, which were in the red. "When my father died, I had no idea how much profit the group was making. It took five years for me to grasp our financial affairs perfectly," he once said.[6] Besides the practical workings of each company, he had to become *au fait* with the networks of human relationships within the companies. Of the stubborn old men, the vice presidents who ran each section, which of them held real power? Out of loyalty to his father they would support him. How could he maintain their respect and bind all these disparate people and groups together? How was he, as a young man in Japan's very hierarchical society, to persuade these old men to change their ways and do something new?

For the first few years he allowed the empire to run on automatic. There were projects begun in his father's time that had to be completed—areas being developed, land purchases under negotiation, hotels being built or in the planning stage. In these years it was the group of five that took responsibility. Shojiro Kojima, the husband of Shukuko, Yasujiro's eldest daughter, was the president of Seibu Railways, as he had been before Yasujiro's death. Both Seiji and Yoshiaki were vice presidents. Yuji, Yoshiaki's youngest brother, fresh from the University of California at Los Angeles (UCLA) with a Beatles haircut, took on the hotel side of the business at the age of twenty-five. Juro Morita, Kuniko's despised ex-husband, ran Seibu Chemicals.

There was only one area of activity that was beyond Yoshiaki's control—the Seibu department stores. This was growing at an alarming rate, disproportionately to the rest of the business. Yoshiaki felt that Seiji was taking unacceptable risks, and he did not want the entire empire to be endangered by his brother's wild ambitions. As he once said, "I don't think about how to expand my business. I think about how to avoid bankruptcy."[7]

By 1970 the cautious Yoshiaki was convinced that Seiji's section of the business was too unpredictable. That year, on Yoshiaki's initiative, the empire was split into two. Juro Morita joined Seiji's side, taking with him the Seibu Chemical Company.

The "sleeping lion," as the press dubbed Yoshiaki, was beginning to stretch his limbs. In 1972 Shukuko's husband, Shojiro Kojima, died of cancer. Shukuko was sixty-three by then and Kojima must have been close to seventy. Rather than appointing a new president of Seibu Railways, Yoshiaki took it over himself. He was now president of the Railways as well as of Kokudo Keikaku, the real estate arm of the empire.

Then came the oil crisis of 1973. While many other property companies were caught up in a fever of land speculation, Yoshiaki had not been seduced by Tanaka's grandiose plans to rebuild the Japanese archipelago. Yasujiro's old rivals and business associates watched his inactivity with dismay. "If Yasujiro had been alive, he would surely have been buying land," said one. "Just as we thought—the second generation is no good!"

The oil crisis proved them wrong. While other companies were going to the wall, Yoshiaki's empire remained buoyant. And with Seiji's empire in danger of collapse, Yoshiaki stepped in to rescue him.

Until that moment the Japanese business community had largely concurred with public opinion: Seiji, with his dynamic expansionist policies and his trendsetting new stores, was the real inheritor of Yasujiro's mantle. But after Seiji's near disaster the most powerful businessmen changed their allegiance. They agreed that it was Yoshiaki who was the force to be reckoned with.

In 1974—ten years after Yasujiro's death—Japan was still in the grip of deep recession. Companies were going bankrupt, employees were being laid off, businesses had reined in their expansion plans.

Then the sleeping lion awoke. Yoshiaki's ten years had been far from wasted. He has always said that he plans ten years into the future, and in this period of inactivity, as well as consolidating his father's work, he had also laid the foundations for many future developments. There was one small project, close to his heart, that he had initiated, despite his father's strictures. Not long after Yasujiro's death, the old Kokudo Keikaku head office was torn down and a new one built in its place.

Yasujiro's headquarters had been the big house in Hiroo, which Seiji had inherited. The Kokudo head office had been a purely functional building, old, shabby, without a lift. It was, however, in a spectacular location. It was in Harajuku, in the area that had been transformed by the Olympic Games. Here Yoshiaki had a splendid new headquarters built as the nexus of his vast and growing empire. The new building was four stories high, with broad windows looking over the shaded groves of the Meiji Shrine. The fourth floor was given over entirely to the chairman's palatial quarters and featured, according to one source, a Western toilet and hot running water, still luxuries in the Japan of the late sixties.

This was Yoshiaki's palace and within it he ruled supreme. Here he instituted a code of conduct designed to reinforce his authority and to unify his staff, to mold them into one big family.

Whenever Yoshiaki arrived or left, his staff would be lined up at the entrance, bowing respectfully until the car was out of sight. This in itself was not unusual. Many old-fashioned company chairmen and *yakuza* godfathers demand the same display of respect. But there were other, more startling rules.

For a start, smoking was even more strictly forbidden than it had been in Yasujiro's day. There were no ashtrays anywhere in the building. In the Japan of the late sixties, when every virile businessman began a meeting by placing his packet of cigarettes on the table in front of him, this was an outrageous rule to enforce.

More outrageous still, in the eyes of modern Japanese, was the way in which women were treated in the company. When visitors arrived they were ushered into a meeting room. Every half hour during the course of the meeting, a young girl, neatly dressed in a red blazer and tie, would slip discreetly into the room. Dropping to her knees beside each guest, she would place a cup of green tea or coffee on the table before them, whispering *"Dozo,"* best translated in this context as "Your tea, sir." To older Japanese, this was no more than a charming courtesy, reminiscent of the tea ceremony and the gracious days when ladies knelt to greet you at their door. To younger people, it was abhorrent, the epitome of the authoritarian, male-chauvinist way in which Yoshiaki ran his empire. Many angry column inches have been devoted to the subject of "women serving tea on their knees at Kokudo."

Having set up his citadel, Yoshiaki was ready to make his first moves, but instead of stepping out to become a public figure like Seiji, he preferred to operate, initially at least, from the shadows.

The first signs that the lion was stirring came from an unexpected quarter of the empire. In Yasujiro's time the hotels, like the department store, had been an unloved appendage of the enterprise. In the course of his land purchases, Yasujiro had inadvertently become the owner of several country inns as well as the grand palaces of the ex-princes. Obviously these had to be put to use, but although guests enjoyed staying in the palaces and a few modern annexes were added, Yasujiro was loath to invest much money in what was really no more than an offshoot of his real estate business. The hotels were, in fact, so insignificant a part of the empire that, after the old man's death, they were handed over to the youngest member of the family, Yuji.

By the time Yuji was born, in 1942, his father was already fifty-three. And although the disputes that split the family were still to come—Kiyoshi's disinheritance, Seiji's long rebellion against his father and Kuniko's final flight to France—they happened in Hiroo. Yuji grew up very quietly in the humble wooden house in Takagi-cho with his mother, the gentle Tsuneko, and his two brothers.

Whereas the second of Tsuneko's sons, Yasuhiro, was a quiet withdrawn boy, Yuji was a sunny, open and handsome child. As the baby of the family, there was practically no chance that he would ever inherit the empire. As a result he grew up free of the pressures and responsibilities that weighed upon his brothers.

While Yasujiro watched over Yoshiaki's training every second of the day, yelling at him if he wasted soy sauce and hitting him to drive home a point, Yuji was allowed to go free. He enjoyed the type of liberal education suitable for the son of a rich family. To round it off, Yasujiro even sent him to the United States, where he studied marketing at the business school of UCLA. It was the kind of education designed to produce a sophisticated member of the elite with the easy charm and relaxed attitudes of an American—not at all the qualities required of a Japanese businessman and prospective heir to an empire.

Yuji still remembers his reprobate old father's shock when Yasujiro came to visit him at UCLA and discovered that the dormitory was co-ed. "He was a very traditional man," he commented in an interview, smiling.

Yuji's studies were cut short by his father's death when he was twenty-two. As the youngest son, he knew that he would inherit little. Yoshiaki, however, took on the role of father to his younger brothers and made sure that both received powerful positions in the empire. Yasuhiro became president of Toshimaen amusement park while Yuji was given a post in Seibu Railways. Then, in 1967, when Yuji was just twenty-five, Yoshiaki made him first director and then president of Prince hotels.

At the time the hotels were a very minor division of the mammoth Seibu Railways Company. Yoshiaki's plan seems to have been to divide the empire into sections and allocate a different section to each member of the family, under his overall control. In this way even previously undernourished sections could expand and flourish and the whole empire would prosper. He wanted to groom Yuji, it seems, to be the hotel man of the family. Brimming over with youthful energy and enthusiasm, Yuji flung himself into his new task. At the time, as he said in an interview in *Business Week* magazine in 1973, the hotels were sadly neglected. "I found the facilities all very bad and employee morale rather low. . . . If they got through every day without some accident, they were happy."[8] The first move, he decided, was to free them from operating under the yoke of the Railways, to make them into an independent enterprise.

Yoshiaki was worried at the prospect, in part because of his brother's extreme youth. In the end, however, he let him have his way, on condition that he kept the hotels in the black.

In 1971 the Prince hotels became an independent operation. But long before then, Yuji had already set about an ambitious program of expansion and development. He took on new staff, including a Canadian as manager of overseas development; in those days it was revolutionary to take on foreign employees, particularly in positions of responsibility. He started expanding and improving existing hotels, and he set about negotiations for new projects, including hotels to be built in Toronto, Los Angeles, on the islands of Maui and Tahiti and in Fiji. It was the first time since the disaster of the Los Angeles store that any part of the Seibu Group had considered expanding abroad.

No matter what Yuji did, Yoshiaki was always at his shoulder. In many ways the two brothers could not have been more different. Yoshiaki had inherited not only his father's mantle but his values and attitudes. He insisted on maintaining control over every part of his empire, and he accepted without question all the traditional Japanese values, in which hierarchy and respect for one's elders were central tenets. Yuji, on the other hand, with his democratic American education, was beginning to chafe under his brother's heavy-handed paternalism. Yoshiaki treated him more like a wayward son than an equal, though younger, brother.

The first of Yuji's new developments was a splendid modern building at the Takanawa Prince Hotel. The hotel stood in the grounds of what had been Prince Takeda's estate. The prince's beautiful Japanese garden, with its pond and teahouse and paths winding among woods, was still intact. His palace served as a wing of the hotel, while the old prince himself, quite happy with the arrangement, lived in what had been the stables, and was allowed to use the palace for entertaining guests.

No expense had been spared in designing the main hotel building, a massive twelve-story block. There were five hundred rooms, banqueting halls, luxury suites and a swimming pool.

The day before the grand opening, Yoshiaki arrived to inspect the new wing. He strode into the lobby, glaring around him while the staff stood nervously at attention in two long lines. Every last detail, they thought, had been attended to. Their shoes were polished, their buttons were gleaming, and there was not a speck of dust anywhere. Yoshiaki got no farther than the lobby. His glance fell to the spotlessly clean carpet. He stopped, jabbed a finger at the carpet and roared, in his father's high-pitched voice, "What's this? Yuji! Change it—all of it!"[9]

When Yoshiaki spoke, no one argued, and no one dared ask why he objected to the carpet. That day there was panic at the hotel. All the carpeting in all the five hundred rooms, the lobbies, the restaurants and the banqueting halls was torn up and replaced in time for the opening the following day.

The new wing of the Takanawa Prince Hotel opened in 1971, the year after the two empires separated. After that, new hotels began to open one after another. In 1972 a Prince hotel opened in Sapporo. In 1973 two hotels opened, one in Karuizawa and one in the resort of Shimoda. And in 1974, while the rest of Japan was still reeling from the oil crisis, a splendid new four-hundred-room hotel opened in Toronto at a cost of billions of yen. But while Yoshiaki was the final authority behind the projects, it was Yuji who was in the spotlight.

He was a glamorous figure, astonishingly young to be the president of a Japanese company, a strikingly handsome man, even-featured with a generous mouth and large eyes. By far the best-looking of all the brothers, he wore his hair fashionably long and dressed with impeccable style. *Business Week* described him as "a samurai in a Pierre Cardin suit" and wrote that his Prince hotels were the most aggressive performers of the entire Seibu Group.[10]

Yuji's triumph was to be short-lived. It was probably inevitable that a rift would develop between the two brothers. Their characters were too different. Besides, Yoshiaki wanted to ensure there was no one in the company who might threaten his control or question his authority. The breaking point turned out to be Yuji's marriage.

At the time it seemed a brilliant match: Yuji was one of the most eligible bachelors in Tokyo and his bride was the glamorous blond American heiress, Lynette Himmelman, the daughter of the then president, later chairman, of Westin International Hotels of Seattle. It was a union of two great families and, for the Prince hotels, a very useful alliance.

In 1972 Yuji brought his bride back to Tokyo and the two set up their home in the exclusive Nishi Azabu district. They soon became familiar figures in Tokyo's most glittering social circles. Lynette was tall, spectacularly beautiful and very American, a whirlwind of energy. She adored dancing, parties and dinners, where she could show off her magnificent wardrobe. In the world of Tokyo high society—of princes, aristocrats, scions of great families leavened with the small community of Westerners who had settled and worked in Tokyo in the early seventies—she was enormously popular.

Yoshiaki, however, was less than charmed. As a traditional Japanese, he was highly suspicious of "international marriage," as mixed marriages are termed in Japanese. He was uncomfortable with the idea of an American woman becoming part of the great Tsutsumi clan. Suppose something happened to Yuji—the American woman might inherit the Prince hotels and the family would lose them. To make matters worse, Lynette was overpoweringly American. Where Japanese wives were expected to know their place and to be deferential and obedient, she was outspoken and aggressive. She dared to criticize the Prince hotels, saying that they lacked charm. She objected to the carpets and curtains and offered to choose new ones. And she spent much of Yuji's money on turning their home into a glamorous American-style residence.

Yuji was put into a very difficult position, torn between his paternalistic elder brother and his equally forceful wife. And no doubt the pressures on any mixed couple living in Japan added to their problems. Yuji, in his own country and in the middle of his large and powerful family, was under a very heavy obligation to conform, while Lynette was disappointed to discover that the proper place for a Japanese wife was in the home. In the end the couple divorced. Lynette moved to Paris, taking their two children with her. Yuji remained, but his position was becoming more and more untenable. Yoshiaki did not need anyone else to run his empire for him. In an interview with *Newsweek* in August 1976 Yuji said, "I would foresee a time when Yoshiaki won't need me anymore."[11]

That time came far more quickly than Yuji could have anticipated.

Before the year was out it was announced that Yoshiaki Tsutsumi was now the president of the Prince hotels. Yuji was demoted to vice president with special responsibility for overseas developments and was sent to Canada to manage the Toronto Prince Hotel. In effect he had been banished: he seldom returned to Japan.

In an interview Yoshiaki once confessed that when he was young he was not interested in the hotel business at all. "I thought it wasn't the sort of work a man should do," he said. The grand old statesman and former prime minister Shigeru Yoshida, however, had persuaded him that he was wrong. "Even if you can do the job of company president, you can't easily be a hotel manager. It's as difficult as that!" he told him.[12]

By 1976 Yoshiaki was ready to take this new line of business seriously. Thanks in large part to Yuji's enthusiasm, the hotels were now an attractive and viable part of the empire.

At the age of forty-two Yoshiaki had maneuvered himself into a position in which, like his father, he was the master of his kingdom. There was no one to question his supremacy, no one to make mistakes. He was now the president of Kokudo Keikaku, Seibu Railways and Prince hotels, as well as a plethora of smaller companies. At the apex of the pyramid was Kokudo Keikaku, primarily a holding company, which held the bulk of the shares in all the other companies.

He had borne the burden of his responsibilities well. He was in the prime of life, a heavy, well-built, powerful man with the physique of a boxer. While his contemporaries were beginning to run to fat, he was in perfect condition, strong and well-muscled. In some ways he was a handsome man; he had a certain brute power that gave him an unmistakable presence. While Seiji's gentle round features showed the delicacy and sensitivity of the poet, Yoshiaki had the chiseled square features of a sportsman, a stubbornly jutting jaw and large mouth often compressed into an expression of samurai determination and unshakable will. If caught unawares his face had a gloomy cast, and he was seldom seen to smile.

He was a father now. The gentle, retiring Yuri had borne him three children: two sons, Masatoshi, born in 1970, and Hirotoshi, born in 1975, and a daughter, Chika, born in 1973. And every day, no matter what business he had to attend to, he always made time to drop in on his mother, Tsuneko.

Yoshiaki has always claimed that he did no more than follow the path that his father had laid down. He told the journalist Inose Naoki:

> My father's teaching was, first, number one, borrow money, and next buy land. By which he meant, once you've bought land you've done 99 percent of your business. My job is simply to put paint on my father's work—he already did 99 percent of the job. But if I only did that, the business would not progress, so in order to perpetuate the Seibu group I buy land for the future. My father's rule was always never to touch manufacturing. I just follow my father's way.[13]

Yasujiro had built his empire on land. By the time Yoshiaki came to inherit, land prices, in Tokyo in particular, were inflating at a breathtaking rate. Every year he became richer and richer, simply through the rise in the value of his property. He had the princes' magnificent estates in Tokyo, land in other cities, land so deep into the countryside that it took hours to get there. He had such enormous holdings that when he needed cash, he could borrow as much as he liked. He had no need for other collateral.[14]

Yasujiro had bought the land; Yoshiaki put it to use. As soon as his ten years of enforced inactivity came to an end, he began to unveil new projects, one after another. As Hoshino, his boyhood playmate in Karuizawa, put it, "For the first ten years after his father died, he was meditating what he wanted to do. Then suddenly he wanted to do everything. Like a flower he bloomed so quickly."

Deep in mountain country or at the side of lakes, the scaffolding came down to reveal modern luxury hotels, towering edifices of glass and concrete with banqueting halls, restaurants, shops, all the appurtenances of a top-class Japanese hostelry. New golf courses, ski runs, skating rinks and swimming pools appeared. Where Yasujiro had built up a small local business, Yoshiaki was turning it into a vast nationwide concern.

Yoshiaki's specialty was what he called "zone development." In the cities it was easy. As his father had done, he used the princes' old palaces as hotels and gradually began to embark on a program of hotel building. Several modern hotels had been built for the Olympics, but Tokyo still lacked a network of hotels for the executives, mainly Japanese, traveling from city to city on business.

Some of the Prince hotels were in rather eccentric locations. After all, the place was dictated not by where travelers might want to stay but simply by the fact that Seibu happened to have land there. One, the grandly named Yokohama Prince Hotel, was built on what had been the estate of Prince Higashi-Fushimi, high on a windswept bluff several miles outside the city. The palace itself was still intact, a splendid Art Deco confection in the Japanese style, that had once looked out over the tranquil waters of Tokyo Bay. But in the postwar years the shoreline had been transformed into a factory belt, a wasteland of spindly chimneys belching smoke.

In the countryside the problem was far more severe. Seibu owned vast tracks of undeveloped land, far from anywhere, unsuitable for farming or building factories or housing developments. Often the people who lived in the area were desperate. There was no work. Young people were leaving and moving to the cities.

Yoshiaki was a sportsman. He looked at the soaring snow-covered peaks and saw magnificent skiing country. He looked at the plains and woodlands around the foothills and saw lush green golf courses. Surely these were the perfect leisure activities for a nation of people who had money to spend but little time to spend it, who liked their leisure to be structured and usefully employed? Admittedly few people as yet had any leisure, but Yoshiaki was confident that he could achieve the same miracle he had with his indoor rink in Karuizawa and his beachside pool in Oiso. Once the facilities were built, people would come.

Yoshiaki built his first ski resorts in the last years before his father died, one at Manza in the mountains near Karuizawa, one in an area of spectacular jagged peaks above a tiny village called Naeba in central Japan. At that time skiing, like golf, was largely a rich man's sport, although in the countryside where the snow was ten feet deep in the winter, farmers used skis simply to get around. Yoshiaki's ski slopes were for ordinary office workers from Tokyo, not luxurious but functional. There was no après-ski, none of the glamour surrounding Alpine ski resorts. These were ski resorts for dedicated skiers.

Little by little Yoshiaki built up the facilities in particular areas, or "zones." It was not enough simply to drive out to the mountains for a day to ski, the skiers needed somewhere to stay. So, a few years after the first ski course at Naeba, in 1967, a small hotel opened there. As the facilities improved, more and more people came to ski. In 1970 a luxurious multistory new wing was added and the hotel became the Naeba Prince Hotel. By 1975 the facilities were so good that the Japan rounds of the FIS (International Skiing Federation) World Cup were held there.

One problem remained to be solved. Naeba's splendid Prince Hotel, with its restaurants and coffee shops and wide-windowed bedrooms looking out on the glistening white slopes outside, was used only during the winter. In summer it was deserted; with so much money invested, this was manifestly a waste. The solution was to find a way to bring customers to Naeba in the summer. In 1976 the Naeba Prince Hotel golf course opened, followed by tennis courts and a swimming pool.

In the years that followed, more ski slopes opened and wing after wing of the hotel. Where there had once been nothing but the lonely village of Naeba, sheltering in the lee of the mountain, there was now a vast hotel with seven towers, of which the tallest was more than twenty floors high, with a total of more than three thousand rooms. Naeba itself had changed from a small village of thatched houses into a resort consisting of rank upon rank of concrete tower blocks. And the mountains, which had once been closed and silent, were thronging with holidaymakers.

Once again Yoshiaki's instincts had been proved right. The trains were full of students and young office workers toting skis. Skiing was a bigger craze than anything that had gone before, and with it came the age of leisure Yoshiaki had anticipated. A whole leisure industry came into being, spearheaded by Seibu.

Seibu was always acknowledged as the leader. No other company could match their assets or access to capital. As they built more and more resorts, their expertise and experience grew. Mayors of small towns deep in the mountains would come to Yoshiaki, begging him to develop their area, to bring tourists and business and jobs to their part of the world. Seibu offered a complete package. They built ski slopes, hotels, restaurants. They even provided transport—they had buses, taxis and car-hire companies.

The face of the Japanese countryside was being irrevocably transformed. Remote mountains that had been untouched for centuries were turned into ski slopes. Although there were some who grumbled that too much of the profits went to Tokyo, most people were grateful for the jobs and the new life that Seibu brought to the area. Villagers worked in the hotels or on the ski slopes, or turned their homes into inns for the huge influx of skiers, but gradually people were to become aware of what was being lost for the sake of profit.

Yoshiaki himself was never happier than when he was on site. He had spent his youth at his father's side, stomping about the building sites, fraternizing with the workers or yelling at them when they made mistakes, stooped over the drawing board planning new projects and coloring in the Seibu holdings in pink on Yasujiro's map of Japan. Like his father, he was a practical man.

From the moment he took over the empire, Yoshiaki's management style inspired comment. In every way possible he modeled himself on his father, but what in the old man had been colorful idiosyncrasies, leavened with a good dose of humor, in Yoshiaki turned into immutable rules of conduct. He became famous for his terse remarks on the subject of management and of how he ran his companies.

"I don't need employees with a fancy college education," he once snapped. "I want people who can do what I tell them."

In an interview he elaborated, "In my company, first off you work with your body, then you use your head. I don't need intellectuals. I want people with guts. High school leavers start their jobs thinking 'I want to work,' so they're flexible. College graduates need to be re-trained. The four years are a complete waste.'[15]

Like his father, Yoshiaki ran his vast empire entirely by himself. Anyone who was too clever was a potential rival and therefore a threat. While Seiji was famous for his skill in seeking out high-caliber executives and surrounded himself with a coterie of brilliant people, Yoshiaki stood alone at the very top of a pyramid of power. He was the only one who understood the way in which the whole empire worked. As he said himself, "Whether it's hotels, ski resorts or golf courses, there is not one employee who has as much experience as I have."[16]

Like Yasujiro, he liked to keep control of every last detail. He chose everything, right down to the carpets, the sofas, even the glasses and cutlery for his hotels. He vetted every member of staff at Kokudo Keikaku, and every decision was subject to his final control.

From his staff he demanded complete devotion. One of his maxims was "If you want Sundays off, don't be a manager in my company." "Even on Sundays the trains run, hotels and golf courses are open," he used to say with a snort. "If you want a holiday just because it's Sunday, you haven't got what it takes to be a manager. If you want a summer holiday, you might as well give up being a manager. Managers have no holidays."[17] On another occasion he said, "Managers are really laborers. They aren't owners. So they should be having meals at the company cafeteria rather than in special executive dining rooms."[18]

The downside to this policy was that he was always surrounded by lesser men, and sometimes he found himself almost in the role of headmaster trying to control a mob of unruly schoolboys. Although Yasujiro had struck terror in the hearts of his employees, nearly all were completely devoted to the gruff old tyrant. In Yoshiaki's case, it was purely a reign of terror. Maybe the problem was simply that times had changed. A style that had been right for the age of giants was an anachronism in the well-fed seventies.

To keep control of his empire, Yoshiaki was perpetually on the move. Before the skiing season began every year he would travel to his resorts and hotels, making sure that everything was in order. In the early days, as his boyhood friend Hoshino remembered, he used to go by train. He would inspect the facilities, then the managers in their black suits would escort him to the station and stand on the platform bowing solemnly until the train pulled out.

In later years Yoshiaki's trademark became his helicopter. His empire had grown so vast that much of his time was taken up simply with flying from place to place. Hoshino related with a grin that there was a room in the Karuizawa Prince Hotel that functioned as a watchtower. Every fine day a boy was posted there, watching the sky fixedly. There were four local helicopters. He had to be able to distinguish which was which. The second he spotted Yoshiaki's helicopter looming in the distance, he pressed a button. A bell rang and the staff all flew into a panic. They rushed around the hotel, checking everything, polishing buttons, looking for stains on the carpets, in fear and terror of the moment when the great man arrived. And in every one of his hotels, the table with the best view in the restaurant was always reserved for the one or two times in the year when Yoshiaki might drop in.

In many ways it was a lonely life. Ever since he became his father's successor, Yasujiro had warned him against having friends. "Don't make friends," he used to growl. "They just use you. And they're no use to you."[19] Even when he was a boy, his school friends remember that he was always very quiet. He never told them anything about his family or his background. And once they found out, they always kept a wary distance.

The more rich and powerful he became, the more isolated he was. His boyhood friends complained that he was always surrounded by bodyguards. If they wanted to see him, they had to call his secretary and ask very deferentially if they could make an appointment. "I feel sorry for him," said Yoshie Toshio, a friend from his school days with whom he used to go on photography expeditions. "He's trapped by his position. Even the prime minister can do as he wants—but he can't."

Many of his friends expressed the same sentiments. Yoshiaki was, it seems, a very ordinary man trapped at the center of a vastly complicated web. He was the kingpin, the emperor, and yet he had no real control over his own life.

Once some of his relatives were in severe financial difficulties. As a last resort they decided to turn to Yoshiaki and ask for help. When they tried to approach him they discovered that he was surrounded by impenetrable barriers of guards, secretaries and clerks. Finally, at a family gathering, they managed to get close enough to speak to him for a few minutes. He was, he said, distressed to hear of their plight, but there was nothing he could do. His money was not his own, it was all tied up in the company. And he could use company money only to invest in land, to yield a profit.

Trapped in the middle of this vast web of money, spending his days commissioning hotels, ski resorts and golf courses at a cost of billions of yen, Yoshiaki lived a life of almost obsessive frugality. He lived, in fact, exactly like the son of a poor peasant from Shiga. Admittedly in Japan it is considered very poor taste to display one's wealth, but even among his peers Yoshiaki was legendary for his parsimony.

He was once photographed showing off a hole in the sole of his shoe that had been mended with black tape.

> My late father was very strict [he said]. He used to hit me if there was any soy sauce left in my dish. "What did you take so much for? Can't you even work out how much you need?" If I accidentally let the bath water overheat it was truly terrible. Well, in the old days it was like that in every household, wasn't it?

Even now, he said, he couldn't bring himself to waste a single piece of paper in his memo pad. If he went out to photograph hotels or ski slopes, it was a real struggle to bring himself to take in the roll of film to be developed if he hadn't used every single frame. And, rather than throw out his old shoes, if the uppers were in good condition he would have the sole mended and continue wearing them.

As far as his business was concerned,

> altogether there are more than seventy companies and 30,000 employees—and not a single one, after he's been to the toilet, uses more water or paper hand towels than he needs! If someone takes a whole bowl of rice when he's not really hungry and leaves some in the plate, and I see it, that's the end for him.[20]

Likewise in his hotels he would wait an extra year before putting in new carpeting, bathrobes, sheets or furniture. And when he did change the carpets, he would have the old ones cut up and used in the staff quarters.

On one occasion Yoshiaki ordered a cup of coffee at a Prince hotel. He tore open a packet of sugar and poured the contents into his cup. The packet contained eight grams of sugar, and when he had taken as much as he wanted, there were still two grams left inside. Clearly the packets were unnecessarily full. Sugar was being wasted. He called the hotel manager and from the next day all the packets of sugar in all the Prince hotels contained just six grams.

For many years after he had inherited the empire Yoshiaki continued to live very modestly in Takagi-cho, where he had grown up. There were two houses there, large by Japanese standards but in no way luxurious, crammed in side by side, one for his mother, Tsuneko, and one for himself and Yuri. Then, around the end of the seventies, he moved Yuri and the three children out to Oiso, the exclusive resort on the coast where he had designed a beachside pool years before in his student days.

The house to which they moved had been the mansion of the elder statesman Shigeru Yoshida. It is not clear when the house came into the possession of the Tsutsumi family. For years Yasujiro had coveted it. Over time he had snapped up choice pieces of land in the resort, including the seaside villa of another great statesman, the preeminent leader of the Meiji era at the end of the last century, Hirobumi Ito. But Yoshida's mansion and the estates that surrounded it remained the most desirable of all.

Finally the Yoshida family must have fallen on hard times. Yoshida's son and daughter arranged the sale, on condition that the Tsutsumis left the house exactly as it was. But of course, as Yoshida's daughter, Mrs. Aso, says, once it was sold, it was sold. In Yasujiro's time the house remained untouched, but Yoshiaki made major changes.

The mansion was a perfect fortress, practically inaccessible by road. There was a river behind and the sea in front forming a natural moat. The house itself was surrounded by dense forest. Yoshiaki had two atomic-bomb shelters built in the garden, and twice a week, on Wednesdays and Saturdays, arrived by helicopter to visit.

For the children it was a strange, isolated childhood. Yoshiaki, it was said, was terrified of kidnappers. As his children grew up they were seldom allowed outside the house, and when they went out they were always accompanied by bodyguards.

The presence of the family in the big house was, of course, a great source of gossip in the area. Neighbors have touching stories of the famous Mr. Tsutsumi attending sports day at the local Oiso school.

You ask if he's unusual—Mr. Yoshiaki is pretty much like everyone else, just an ordinary kind of man. My son and Mr. Tsutsumi's elder boy were in the same year at Uminohoshi nursery school, and on sports day the family from the big house brought tatami mats and packed lunches just like everyone else and came to cheer their child on. Mr. Yoshiaki took part in the parents' tug of war and the relay race. They're just ordinary people. From outside it looks really grand, it's an incredible house, but the people that live there are ordinary.[21]

Yoshiaki's indulgences always had some relationship to his work. He still loved sports, and he had found a way to turn what he loved into his work. His skiing was at a professional level, and he always tried out new ski slopes himself. When eventually he decided to break away from his father's path and venture into a new line of business, the area he chose was sport.

Playing for Power
Yoshiaki's Story 1978–1984

The worst thing for us staff is having to go to matches. There's ice hockey of course, and then last year we had to start rooting for the Lions as well. Whenever there's a game, if there aren't enough supporters they send us. Whether it's a holiday or working time makes no difference. We don't get expenses, we're half-forced to join the Lions' fan club, and we have to pay the ¥1000 membership fee out of our own pockets.   PRINCE HOTELS EMPLOYEE
                              In Manabe, "Conquering the Sports World"

It was January 1, 1978. At the hilltop cemetery outside Kamakura, the annual New Year's ceremony was taking place. Just as they had done every year since Yasujiro's death fourteen years before, five hundred top Seibu executives were gathered in the big marquee erected over the old man's tomb. They stood silently, row upon row of them, all in black, arranged in blocks according to company. The sides of the tent rippled in the icy wind. To the east, the first flush of dawn was sweeping up the sky, turning it pale apricot.

The huge bronze bell tolled six. As the last reverberation died away, the burly figure standing on the steps in front of the tomb began to speak.

"The wind blowing against the sides of the tent is the voice of the chairman speaking from heaven, saying 1978 will be a tough year," he declaimed in his high-pitched tones, his voice muffled by the roaring of the wind.[1]

As he did every year, he exhorted his men to work their hardest, harder than ever before. Last year had been tough, this year would be tougher still. There was no room in the company for slackers. Then he announced his New Year resolutions. This year, he declared, he was going to build a brand-new baseball stadium—in Tokorozawa.

No doubt the Seibu executives, who were strictly trained, heard the news without reaction. No doubt they stood impassive until the toasts were over, the chairman had left and the merrymaking could begin. But then one by one people had to speak up and voice their misgivings.

Until a young American named Horace Wilson handed his students a bat and a few balls in the early years of the Meiji era and began to teach them the rudiments of the game, baseball was unknown in Japan. Team sports were a totally new concept. Until that time the Japanese had practiced only martial arts, one-to-one combat sports like judo, kendo and sumo. These were training in the arts of war, designed to transform the body, forge the mind and build up the fighting spirit. They were taken with the utmost seriousness, and there was virtually no concept of sport for fun and relaxation.

The Japanese quickly developed a passion for baseball. They followed the rules strictly, but in spirit it was transformed into a martial art. The players became warriors, bonded together with their teammates like a group of samurai battling for their feudal lord. They were committed to a team for life, and their training was as rigorous as for any martial art.[2]

All over Japan children could be seen out in the road with baseball caps, gloves and bats, practicing with the utmost seriousness. And whenever there was a baseball match, crowds of spectators turned out.

Yoshiaki was in the business of drawing crowds. His indoor rink and beachside pool had been successful because crowds of people had come. Now he had another brainstorm. He would build a baseball stadium—the best in Asia, with the most up-to-date facilities. And, judging by the success of all his other projects, once he had built it, people would come. Even though there was no resident team, they would come simply to enjoy the facilities.

Building a stadium was a fine idea. What worried everyone was the location. Tokorozawa is to Tokyo as Croydon is to London, Flushing is to New York or Walnut Creek to San Francisco. It began life as a small country town well outside the limits of the city, on the edge of the western hills. Farmers from the countryside took their vegetables there and sold them to the local merchants, who transported them by boat up to Tokyo. It was also known as the birth-place of Japanese aviation. The first airport in Japan had been built there in 1910.

When the great age of railways arrived toward the end of the last century, the people of Tokorozawa were among the most enthusias-tic. They lobbied for a railway and, with the help of government sub-sidies, ended up as the junction of two. As fate would have it, the two railway lines that crossed at Tokorozawa were the Musashino Line and the Seibu Line. Both were later bought by Yasujiro.

Tokorozawa would have remained the most nondescript of sub-urbs had it not been at the junction of the two Seibu lines. Yasujiro, as was his policy, bought up land around his railway lines and began to develop it. Yoshiaki bought more. By his day most of Tokyo was heav-ily developed, but Tokorozawa was still on the edge of the country-side. The air was fresh and there was plenty of space to expand. By this time Seibu owned 5 percent of all the land in the town. Yoshiaki de-cided to make it his capital, and Tokorozawa began to turn into Seibu City. A golf course appeared, a specially designed heliport for Yoshi-aki's helicopter, bus lines and apartment blocks owned by Seibu Rail-ways. The head office of Seibu buses moved to Tokorozawa, and Seiji built a Seiyu supermarket at the station. Some of the people of Toko-rozawa found that they were living in Seibu apartments, traveling on Seibu buses, shopping in Seiyu supermarket and, when they went into Tokyo, taking the Seibu railway. Then, when they got there, they shopped at the Seibu department store at the Ikebukuro terminus.

Tokorozawa was still in the middle of nowhere. Despite Yoshi-aki's efforts, there was very little reason for sophisticated Tokyoites ever to go there. His new plan was brilliant in its simplicity. A base-ball stadium would be the perfect way to entice people onto his trains and out to Tokorozawa.

His staff was convinced that the plan would fail. All the baseball teams already had stadiums. They would never agree to play in an out-of-the-way place like Tokorozawa. Even his friends were worried. Several leading politicians advised him against the project. "At the time, I told him he'd better give it up," said Yoshiro Mori, a member of the lower house. "But he said, 'It's all right. I'll show you how to manage pro baseball. Without a doubt I'm going to make a profit—just keep quiet and see.' "[3]

When Yoshiaki made a new plan, he never explained the reasons for it to his directors. He simply announced it. At the board meeting after that New Year's Day announcement, he confronted the doubters.

"Each of you—take a guess," he demanded. "How long will it take to make a profit?" No one dared answer straightaway.

"I won't change my plan, no matter what you say. So make a guess!"

They all faltered out their answers: "Three years," "Six years," "Eight years."

"Note down the figure you just said. Later we'll get the answer!" snapped the great man.

He himself had no doubts. In front of the whole meeting he asserted categorically, "From the very first year we'll make a profit."[4]

Yoshiaki was, of course, proved right.

Work on the stadium began early in 1978, and a year later it was complete. The grand opening was on April 4, 1979. Everyone agreed that it was by far the best stadium in Japan. Crowds turned out just to marvel at it. For a start, the location was spectacular. It was set a few miles outside Tokorozawa, framed by hills and leafy woodland, right beside Lake Tamako, where Yasujiro had built his first railway line, the Tamako Line, back in 1925. Yoshiaki built a branch line out from Tokorozawa to serve it. As it happened, the car park was very small and conditions on the road very crowded, so most people ended up buying tickets and taking the Seibu Line.

The stadium itself was large and expansive, designed with the comfort of the spectators in mind. There was seating for thirty-seven thousand—not the usual cramped seats but broad seats, comfortably angled, imported from the United States, plus an expanse of grassy turf where several thousand more fans could spread out blankets. Behind the luxurious box seats was a clubroom where members could watch the match over a Chinese meal, while miniskirted waitresses served them cocktails. The players too enjoyed the most modern facilities, with several practice fields, a weight-training area and comfortable dormitories where they all lived.

Initially the plan had been that the stadium would house the company's amateur team, the Prince team. (Most large companies in Japan had amateur baseball teams; there was nothing unusual about that.) Well before the stadium was finished, however, Yoshiaki had a visitor, Choho Nakamura. He was a businessman who used to work in the Diet as the secretary of Nobosuke Kishi when he was prime minister. Nakamura was also the owner of a professional baseball team, the Crown Lighter Lions.

The Lions had had a checkered history. Like every professional baseball team in Japan, they were owned by a large company, the eponymous Crown Lighter Corporation. In Japan almost everyone follows professional baseball with frenzied devotion. Millions turn out every year to watch the matches of the Japan Series and practically everyone follows it on television. But from the point of view of the owners, professional baseball was simply a form of public relations and a tax write-off. Each team carried the company name. The oldest and most popular team in the country, the Yomiuri Giants, based in Tokyo, was owned by the Yomiuri newspaper and television conglomerate, while their traditional rivals, the Osaka-based Hanshin Tigers, were owned by the Hanshin private railway corporation. Whenever the team played and particularly when it won, the company name was broadcast all over the media. As Yoshiaki had observed in the case of ice hockey, it was far cheaper than advertising.

The Lions were based in Fukuoka, on the southern island of Kyushu. In the late fifties the franchise had been held by the Nishitetsu Corporation, owners of buses, trains, a hotel and a department store. The Nishitetsu Lions, as they were known then, had been one of the highest-scoring teams in Japan. For three years running they beat the Giants, traditionally the country's strongest team, thanks to the mighty arm of their legendary pitcher, "Iron Man" Inao.

In those days the team members were famous for their hard-drinking lifestyle. They had girlfriends in every city and spent their evenings in the geisha houses. But then times became hard. By the time Crown Lighter bought the franchise, the team had sunk to the bottom of the second league. Year after year they came last. They no longer provided useful advertising. In fact, they were costing the company money.

On the face of it, Nakamura's proposal was far from attractive. Yoshiaki, he argued, was building a ballpark, but he had no professional baseball team. How could he draw crowds to his stadium if he had no team of his own? He would have to rely on persuading other teams to play there.

The Lions were running out of money. Crown Lighter wanted to sell the franchise. Admittedly they were the worst team in either of the leagues; but as part of the deal Nakamura promised to throw in Suguru Egawa, a wild and idiosyncratic young man who was the most explosive pitcher to appear for many years.[5]

Yoshiaki was dubious. Setting aside the question of the team's competence, if he uprooted the Lions and moved them to Tokorozawa, the people of Fukuoka would have no team at all, while Tokyo would have five professional baseball teams, all competing against one another.

In the end he bought the franchise for ¥1.1 billion (just over $5.2 million). The Crown Lighter Lions moved to the Tokorozawa stadium, and from the 1979 season onward, when the stadium opened, they were known as the Seibu Lions.

Despite Nakamura's promise, the wild young pitcher Egawa managed to avoid being drafted into the worst team in the league. Ignoring all the protocol of the game, he made a deal with the famous Giants and eventually joined them. The baseball world was scandalized. Egawa went on to become the nation's best pitcher. Yoshiaki was bitterly disappointed. He had never before failed to get something he wanted.

When Yoshiaki bought the Lions, even his most devoted admirers scratched their heads. Surely this time Tsutsumi had made a mistake. In 1979 Japan was reeling from the second oil-price shock. Admittedly, by then the Japanese imported less oil from the Middle East and as far as possible dealt directly with the oil-producing countries rather than using the international oil companies. But still, there was 8 percent inflation and no growth that year. Yet Tsutsumi was spending a billion yen on the worst baseball team in the league. This was also the year that Kuniko's casino in France went bankrupt. Journalists writing in the weekly magazines were quick to point out that while Yoshiaki had plenty of money to buy a baseball team, he had none to spare to save his sister.

The stadium made a profit from the very first season. The Lions, in fact, lost all twenty-one games that they played, but the crowds came anyway. They took the Seibu Line out to the ballpark, they bought tickets, they ate, they drank, they spent money on pennants, caps and balls. Just as Yoshiaki had anticipated, if the facilities were good enough, the team's record would be irrelevant.

For all his strictures, Yoshiaki was far too ambitious a man to tolerate a losing team for long. It would never do for a company like Seibu to be represented by the worst team in the league.

Most of the team owners treated their teams as just cheap PR. The players did their best, of course. They were, after all, Japanese. By American standards they practiced insanely long hours, even on the day of a big match. But the teams were usually in the red. And even if they lost a match, ultimately it didn't matter, just so long as they continued to play and people continued to buy the company's products. It was more important, in fact, to be popular than to win. When the Yakult Swallows beat the ever-popular Giants one year, Giants fans were so incensed that sales of Yakult yogurt plummeted. The manager was hastily instructed to make sure that his team never committed such a faux pas again.[6]

Yoshiaki was different. First he required his team to function like a business. They were to be self-supporting and they were to make a profit. Second, he required them to win. He already had the best stadium in the country; now he wanted the best team. And he was willing to do whatever was necessary to produce it.

In the United States there is nothing unusual about this attitude, but in Japan it was revolutionary. Somehow it seemed unethical for a baseball team to make a profit. In effect, Yoshiaki was the first person to take baseball seriously as a sport. He set about building up the Lions like an American major-league team.

He began by hiring a general manager who also functioned as field manager, a man named Nemoto. Nemoto was effectively the managing director of Seibu Lions Incorporated, one small company within the giant Seibu conglomerate. From time to time Yoshiaki issued an order or passed on an instruction. But in general, once he had appointed his manager, he left the running of the team entirely to him. Nemoto was an experienced and popular manager, widely known in the baseball world. He was also nearly as stubborn as Yoshiaki; the two often clashed. His first job as general manager was to sign players. The Lions were the least popular team in the less popular of the two leagues. What was needed was a star, a player who would draw crowds of fans to the Tokorozawa stadium. Nemoto knew the very person. He did a swap and took on one of the stars of the Hanshin Tigers, a big, hefty, very popular catcher called Koichi Tabuchi.

The next stage was to form a team around Tabuchi of the best players available. This, however, was not so easy. No matter the size of Yoshiaki's bankroll, it was not enough simply to offer big salaries.

In Japan new players are taken on every year from the high school and college baseball teams. Talent scouts work throughout the season, watching out for the best young players. Usually several teams spot the same player and bid for him. In order to prevent the rich teams from getting all the best players, there is a draw. Whichever team wins the draw takes its pick of players. The players are bound by contract to the team for a year.

This system was not good enough for Nemoto. It was too chancy. He wanted to be certain of getting the best players. So Seibu devised a variety of methods to ensure that they got the players they wanted. Nemoto had a formidable team of scouts. When they spotted a good player, they would advise him to make it known that he was not interested in going professional and to give up playing for the year. Eventually the other teams would lose interest and the player would be passed over in the draft. As a further enticement, the young man might be offered a job in the Prince hotels. He would spend a year or two playing with the Prince amateur baseball team, then sign a contract with the Lions. Once he joined the Lions, he would find that his salary was far higher than that of the players in any other team—a strong incentive to stay on.

Eventually, for all Yoshiaki's power, the baseball world began to voice criticisms of his team's methods and Nemoto returned to more orthodox ways of recruiting players, but by then he had achieved his aim. The Lions already had the best players, and they were by far the strongest team.

Having acquired the players, the next step was to forge them into a team that would win every time. For that, another man was needed. Nemoto's specialty was in building up manpower. He remained general manager but took on as his field manager a man named Tatsuro Hiroka who was, according to most baseball commentators, quite simply the best manager ever in Japanese baseball history.[7]

As for Yoshiaki, his contribution was short and to the point. He wanted his team to win. Even though they had started at the bottom of the league, he wanted them to come first. It was no good relaxing when they reached third or second place. He would be satisfied only when they came first.

On one famous occasion after Hiroka had moved on, Yoshiaki called the manager of the day, a very famous ex-Giants catcher named Masaaki Mori, into his office. The Lions were at the height of their glory. That season they had won every game so far. Though there were still several more games to play, Mori came in to report that they were on course for the pennant. In front of the assembled television cameras, Yoshiaki said, "It looks good. But is there a chance you could still lose the pennant?"

Mori, a large, gentle, bluff man, laughed. "It's possible; but it isn't very probable."

"As long as it's possible, then we can't relax yet, can we?" snapped Yoshiaki.

Shamed in front of the nation, Mori flushed red.[8]

Baseball fans watching their televisions were aghast. Mori was a national hero and a household name, yet to Yoshiaki he was a mere employee who could be publicly humiliated at will. This event contributed largely to Yoshiaki's growing reputation for overweening arrogance. He seemed to have no concern at all for public opinion.

With Hiroka as field manager and Mori as head coach, the Lions were molded into an unbeatable team. Hiroka devised a training program for each player, but they were also—barely imaginable in a Japanese company—allowed days off. Even though Yoshiaki hardly ever interfered, every player knew that he was there, expecting them to win.

That same year, one fine afternoon in the autumn of 1982, just four years after the Crown Lighter Lions left Fukuoka to become the Seibu Lions, the team that had always been bottom of the league surprised everyone by winning the Japan Series. In Nagoya, where the game took place, there was nearly a riot. The police had to be called in to control the fans of the home team, the Chunichi Dragons, who were hurling rocks and bottles onto the field.

Thereafter the Lions were practically invincible. There were one or two shock defeats. After they failed to take the pennant in 1986,

Yoshiaki asked Mori in front of the television cameras whether he intended to stay on as manager. When Mori said yes, Yoshiaki replied grimly, "Well, in that case I suppose you can." This exchange, too, did nothing to increase Yoshiaki's popularity.

Apart from that the Lions always won. No one disputed that they were the best team in Japan. People complained that they were boring to watch because they played to win, not to entertain the crowd. Instead of playing hard, hitting the ball high into the air as the more flamboyant players did, they often didn't hit it at all. They "sacrifice bunted"; they simply let the ball hit the bat and drop to the ground, then raced to second base while the first-base catcher was running to field the ball. Their play, in fact, was just like Yoshiaki's management style. They were cautious, they took no risks, they were not flamboyant, nor were they interesting to watch—but they won every time. People said they played baseball as if they were wearing blue suits. Again, like Yoshiaki, even though they always won, they were not loved. They could dislodge the Giants from their place at the top of the league, but they could never dislodge them from the hearts of the Japanese people.

Thanks to Yoshiaki, however, Japanese baseball had been transformed. The balance of power had changed. The Giants could no longer sit back and assume that they would win every time. The despised Pacific League now dominated professional baseball.

In the 1990s, the Daiei supermarket chain, Seiji's great rivals, bought a baseball team, renamed them the Daiei Hawks and relocated them in the southern city of Fukuoka, which had been the Lions' home. The Hawks are the only team that offers the Lions any threat. They too are run like a business. To house them Daiei unveiled a gleaming modern stadium with every possible facility, including a futuristic retracting roof, which far outstrips the stadium in Tokorozawa.

Yoshiaki had one other small achievement. When he turned the Seibu Lions into the nation's top baseball team, he effectively reclaimed the name of Seibu. People still thought of the department store when they heard the name Seibu, but they also thought of the Lions.

This, say insiders on Seiji's side, was the beginning of the friction between the brothers. Yoshiaki's people always declare that there is

no friction. But they invariably preface their remarks by saying em-
phatically that it was Yoshiaki who was his father's chosen successor;
Seiji's business is completely different and has nothing to do with the
Seibu empire. To quote one of Yoshiaki's spokesmen:

> Yoshiaki Tsutsumi is the successor of Yasujiro—he continues the
> family line. Seiji is separate, starting a new line.
>
> Seiji says he gave up the inheritance by himself—but he took part
> in the student movement. . . . It would be dangerous to pass the
> company to someone who had been in the student movement. Seiji
> now says he gave up the inheritance. It depends on how you look at
> it. Actually Yoshiaki was chosen.

Certainly both brothers were not going to let any putative rivalry
interfere with business. It obviously paid to emphasize the link between the stores and the team. The logos of the Seiyu supermarkets
and Seibu department stores were blazoned on the scoreboard at the
Tokorozawa stadium. The Lions all wore the department-store logo
on their left sleeves, and every time the Lions won the Japan Series,
the stores celebrated with a huge sale. "Only Seibu does this—Mitsukoshi and Isetan don't have sales when the Lions win," Yoshiaki's
spokesman insisted, determined to play down rumors of rivalry. "If
the relationship [between the brothers] was bad, they wouldn't do
it." In fact it was virtually the only area of cooperation between them.

Buying the Lions franchise was the first brand-new business that
Yoshiaki had engaged in since he became master of the empire; until
then he had simply built on the foundations his father had laid. There
were many who had been colleagues of the old man who were keeping a keen eye on his progress, watching to see whether the son
would measure up to his father's achievements.

When the old man died, the question everyone asked was which
of his sons would inherit his political mantle. Yasujiro had been one
of the members for Shiga for forty years. He had been a pillar of the
conservative establishment, a key figure in the Liberal Democratic
Party. Since its formation in 1955, with the backing of the business
community, the LDP had kept a firm grip on power. The veneer of

democracy continued, with regular elections and a vociferous opposition; but few people seriously thought that the opposition had the remotest chance of taking over.

After the funeral, it became clear that neither son had any intention of going into politics. Yonosuke Miki, who had been Goto's biographer, had followed the family's fortunes with interest. Perhaps, he speculated, it was because they had seen their father's mistakes. He had used his political position to further his business at the expense of his own popularity. "They're aware of the disadvantages of being hated," said one of Yasujiro's longtime enemies, interviewed by Miki.[9] And they had witnessed his final discomfiture, in the last election not long before his death, when several of his supporters were arrested for corruption.

But as his sons they had a duty to settle all their father's affairs. One of the most urgent was finding a suitable candidate to run for his constituency in Shiga. In the world of Japanese politics such a matter could not be left to chance or to the vagaries of the electoral system. A candidate had to be found who had the proper network and connections, who would support the proper faction and who was acceptable to the most powerful members of the faction and the party. At some stage he would of course run for election; but, in the usual Japanese fashion, a consensus had to be reached beforehand.

Seiji set about the search. He began by asking the advice of one of the most powerful men in the LDP. Eisaku Sato was the brother of former prime minister Kishi (he had been adopted into a different branch of the family and therefore had a different surname). He was himself to become prime minister later that same year, 1964, when Ikeda retired. Within Japan's so-called democracy, real power was in the hands of a very small circle.

Sato recommended two men, both of whom fulfilled the basic condition of coming from Shiga. One was a man whom Seiji knew well. Shun Aoyama was a distant relative of Misao. He had been Sato's secretary and had recently retired from the Ministry of Finance. The other was a man named Ganri Yamashita, at the time working as chief of the tax bureau in Hiroshima.

Next Seiji turned for advice to Yasujiro's old friend, the ailing prime minister Ikeda. In the course of conversations, he brought up the name of the second candidate, Ganri Yamashita.

The old man slapped his thigh. "What? Is he from Shiga? Tsut-sumi, my boy—he's your man! None better!"

Cheered by this recommendation, Seiji paid a call on Yamashita. He found him to be, he later wrote, "for a civil servant, an excep-tionally unassuming man."[10]

In 1964 Yamashita was forty-four. He had been working at the tax office for seventeen years, under the overall authority of the min-ister of finance, Kakuei Tanaka, later to become prime minister and, famously, to be disgraced in the Lockheed scandal.[11] A prudent man, Yamashita considered Seiji's offer for several months. Then, unex-pectedly, he dropped in on Seiji one day. He had decided, he said, to take up his offer. In fact, he had already handed in his notice at the tax office.

Seiji was impressed. The date of the next election had not even been decided, yet Yamashita had already taken the risk of giving up his career. Surely this was a man of integrity.

The next hurdle was to drum up the support of the Tsutsumi-kai, the Tsutsumi Society, Yasujiro's support group. Seiji went down to Yagiso village, in the middle of windswept rice fields where his father had been born. But the village elders who had been behind Yasujiro nearly all his life were loath to transfer their allegiance to someone they didn't know. If it had been one of Yasujiro's boys, they would have supported him to the death. But a new man . . . Some of them were town councillors and would happily have run for election them-selves, had they been able to get the backing of the party. So Seiji turned for help to one of the most powerful men in the party, Ya-mashita's old boss, Tanaka.

There are various extravagant stories about how Tanaka secured the allegiance of the Tsutsumi Society. According to one version, he called up several leading members of the society and invited them to Tokyo for a meeting. There he entertained them in one of the most expensive restaurants in town, with a bevy of pretty young girls. Then, at the height of the merrymaking, suddenly the room cleared. Tanaka, a rough-spoken politician, swung onto his knees, bowed humbly and said, "Actually, honored sirs . . ." The village elders were flabber-gasted. Why on earth was the illustrious secretary general of the Lib-eral Democratic Party, whom none of them had had the good fortune even to meet before, treating them with such untoward respect?

Actually, said Tanaka, his language peppered with honorifics, Ganri Yamashita wanted to represent Shiga. "I wonder if he might not be able to be of some use to your honored selves." Then, reverting to character, he bawled, "Hey, Yamashita!" The paper doors that formed one wall of the room slid open. Yamashita was waiting there. He came into the room, bowed and introduced himself. The village elders were more and more astonished. With immaculate staging, Tanaka bowed out; the sliding doors along another wall opened, and there were their revered master's sons, Seiji and Yoshiaki, kneeling side by side.[12]

The story is no doubt apocryphal. Still, by one means or another, Tanaka succeeded in securing the support of the Tsutsumi Society. In the general election of 1967 Ganri Yamashita was returned as the member for Yasujiro's old constituency in Shiga. He has remained in politics ever since. At one time he was considered a likely candidate for prime minister, and long after Tanaka himself had disappeared from the political world, Yamashita continued to be known as the only remaining member of the Tanaka faction in the Diet.

Thus the matter of the succession was decided. Ganri Yamashita took on Yasujiro's political mantle while Seiji and Yoshiaki concentrated on building their businesses.

No one would dispute that business and politics are closely intertwined in Japan. As one leading financial journalist puts it, "If you don't use politicians, you can't expand business these days in Japan— that's basic." Businessmen provide politicians with funds, politicians provide businessmen with information. If you wish to develop a department store, a hotel or a ski resort, you need licenses and permissions and the cooperation of leading political figures in the area. And it is always useful to hear that a certain area is slated for development, preferably several years before development starts, when land prices are still low.

Thanks to Yasujiro, both Seiji and Yoshiaki had a powerful network of contacts. Both were far too clever to restrict their support to any particular party. It was important to retain good relationships with everyone who might one day be in power. From time to time they pulled a few strings behind the scenes, but both avoided taking on any direct political role.

As Yoshiaki's power began to emerge and his ability became apparent, his father's old colleagues and his own political connections started to urge him to consider running for election. Gradually he was developing a formidable political network. His friends included former prime ministers, the present prime minister and prime ministers to come, as well as the leading behind-the-scenes power brokers of the governing Liberal Democratic Party.

Besides the men who had been protégés and friends of his father, all of whom recognized him as the acknowledged heir, Yoshiaki also had his own network. There were friends from Waseda University who had gone into politics. One was Tsuruoka, his old friend from college days, who had helped with the Karuizawa skating center and had worked for Seibu for a short time before leaving to join the Clean Government Party. Another was Noboru Takeshita, until the early 1990s the most powerful backstage operator in the LDP and prime minister from 1987 to 1989. There were people who were linked, as Yoshiaki was, to the sports world, a connection that was strengthened in 1977, when he became chairman of the Japan Gymnastics Federation. And there were many others to whom he provided political donations and help of various kinds.[13] Takeo Fukuda, for example, the leader of the Fukuda faction, who was prime minister from 1976 to 1978, had a room set aside for him at the Akasaka Prince Hotel that he used as his office. After some years Takeshita, an opponent of his, complained to Yoshiaki about this. Fukuda was removed from the hotel and instead a small office was built for him on the grounds.

As early as 1971, Tanaka, who was shortly afterward to become prime minister, urged both brothers to enter politics. The occasion was a reception to celebrate the opening of Yamashita's new office, held in the splendid banqueting hall of the Tokyo Prince Hotel. Seiji, said Tanaka in his speech, should stand for the national constituency of the upper house; Yoshiaki should stand for the local constituency of the upper house;[14] while Yamashita would represent the family in the lower house.

Both brothers chose not to run. It was said that Yoshiaki was well aware that he would not become prime minister if he was a member of the upper house.[15]

After that, whenever a general election was approaching, representatives from various factions visited the Kokudo Keikaku headquarters and asked Yoshiaki to run on their behalf. But he always refused. People began to suspect that he had a plan of his own. Around 1976, when he had emerged from his ten-year period of silence and had building projects all over the country, he confided in an old friend of his, another Waseda graduate, a financial journalist named Yasuo Hariki. He needed, he said, another five years to complete all the projects now under way. Then he would have done all he wanted to do in the business world, and would be ready to turn his attention to politics. "I'll devote myself wholeheartedly to the country. I believe that is the way a man is supposed to live."[16]

Those next five years, 1976 to 1981, were a period of prolific activity. New hotels opened on the princes' estates that Yasujiro had bought and in resorts in the mountains. Mountain areas turned into ski resorts, foothills turned into golf courses. Even before the Seibu Lions won the Japan Series for the first time, Sosuke Uno, who was one of the members for Shiga, as Yasujiro had been, and who was to become prime minister for a brief three months in 1989, noted with approval Yoshiaki's revolutionary approach to baseball. Here was a man not hidebound by the conventions. Maybe he could transform politics in the same way. Surely this was the kind of man who should be leading society.

> Now is the time that we need to select our course in both politics and economics [Uno was quoted as saying]. It's a time when if we make a mistake in steering our course it would be a disaster. In the coming times Japan will need someone like Yoshiaki-*san* who distinguishes clearly between black and white. In his baseball team, he boldly thrust aside narrow-minded ways. In the same way he can secure our country's future. Young though he is, Yoshiaki-*san* is a great man.[17]

Throughout the political and journalistic worlds there was speculation. Was Yoshiaki planning to run for election and form a faction of his own? If he did so, he undoubtedly had the power and political connections necessary to become prime minister.

As one Diet member put it, "If you want to take power, you can't do it from the upper house, you have to be in the lower house. Moreover, unless you're in your forties by the time you become a minister it'll be too late, there won't be time. If he moves right now, given the scale of his influence he can aim at being prime minister."[18] In 1981 Yoshiaki was just forty-seven. The timing was perfect. He even had his constituency ready-made. He had no intention of ousting Yamashita from Yasujiro's old constituency in Shiga. Instead he would run for Tokorozawa, a constituency that he had practically built himself.

There were many other rumors, all of which told the same story. Whether or not in the end Yoshiaki chose to enter formal politics, his power in the political world was extraordinary. It was said that a month before Fukuda formed his cabinet in 1976, Yoshiaki knew both that he would be the next prime minister and the exact date that it would be announced—hardly surprising, considering that Fukuda had his office in Yoshiaki's Akasaka Prince Hotel. And there is another persistent rumor that when Prime Minister Masayoshi Ohira suddenly died in 1980, it was Yoshiaki who took control. It is said that he quickly collected younger business leaders to form a support group for Zenko Suzuki, and persuaded his political contacts to back him. The LDP members met in one of the Prince hotels to discuss the matter, and in the end Suzuki was selected. Yoshiaki later became one of his advisers.

After his long period of inactivity, by 1981 Yoshiaki seemed unstoppable. Everything he turned his hand to was a success. He often said, "If Father had lived a little longer, he would have been prime minister."[19] Was he planning to put his father's spirit at rest by achieving the same goal himself?

IV

Rival Empires

The Mysterious Deaths of the Two Mothers
1984

My life is a journey, fording a great river with my poet's heart.
My poems are exhausted, the blossoms are falling.

MICHIKO OTOMO (MISAO TSUTSUMI)

In 1983, on the last Saturday before Christmas, there was a party at the Takanawa Prince Hotel. It was held in the old French-Italianate château that had been Prince Takeda's palace in the years before the war. The palace was as magnificent as ever. In the evening, framed by the clear December sky, the stonework still glimmered silver-gray and the intricate copper fretwork edging the mansard roof caught the last rays of the setting sun. The hefty stone porch was still there, though from the colonnaded balcony at the back the visitor could no longer look across to the tranquil waters of Tokyo Bay. Instead, beyond the wooded gardens of the hotel there were towering office blocks and distant cranes outlining the bay.

The first guests began to arrive around six-thirty. The gentlemen were in tails, the ladies in elegant evening gowns or demure kimonos. There were actors, actresses, singers, business leaders, old wealth, new wealth and many ambassadors. Over the years the annual Seibu party had become more and more famous. To receive one of the coveted invitations was a final stamp of success.

Receiving her guests at the door was a slender elegant woman clad in an Yves Saint-Laurent gown. Misao was in her early seventies, yet she had changed remarkably little from the days when Yasujiro had first become entranced with her patrician beauty. The empress dowager of the Seibu kingdom was still a beautiful woman, charming and gracious.

When Yasujiro died, Misao was fifty-six, and one of the most powerful figures in the Seibu kingdom. She was a key member of the Tuesday family meeting, when all important business decisions were made. She was the president of the Tokyo Prince Hotel. And, as the wife of the ex-Speaker and one of the country's leading business magnates, she had an impressive network of friends and connections throughout the political and business worlds.

After Yasujiro's death, she continued to live in the big house in Hiroo. Seiji lived nearby, in another house that he had had built on the grounds.

She painted, she did pottery; she had an electric kiln in the family villa in Karuizawa. And, as she had done in Yasujiro's last years, she spent many hours in the garden. She tended the plants, strolled the paths or stood, as Yasujiro used to, on the stone bridge, looking into the dark waters of the pond. And she composed tanka, 31-syllable poems in the classical style, about the flowers, the birds, the seasons and her own feelings. She published volumes of poetry—by 1981 she had published nine volumes—under her pen name, Michiko Otomo; and she organized a tanka society and edited its monthly bulletin, *Shiju* (Purple Jewel).

All this was in addition to her work. Though tiny and fragile, she was as formidable as ever. Where once she had devoted herself to her husband's business, now she did all she could for Seiji. She was constantly present, just as in Yasujiro's day she had been ever at his side.

In meetings she could be fiercely assertive. Some British businessmen, in Tokyo in 1969 to organize British Trade Week, met her when they came to have talks with Seiji in his capacity as acting head of the whole Seibu empire. This was in the days before the empire split into two, when Yoshiaki was still unknown and Seiji was the public face of Seibu. Misao attended the meetings. By then she had reached the age when Japanese women are no longer required to be docile and subservient, even on the surface. She expressed her opinion with considerable force. "A very strong personality," remembered one businessman, while another, less tactfully, commented, "A real tartar!"

To the younger staff she remained a motherly figure, their supporter and ally, as she had been in Yasujiro's time. She often visited the stores, kept in close contact with staff members and would take them out for lunch and listen carefully to what they had to say. When an art exhibition opened she was always at the reception, smiling and bowing, immaculate in kimono or Yves Saint-Laurent, her favorite designer. Free now to use her time as she pleased, she acted as an unofficial fashion adviser to Seibu department stores. She loved going abroad. Once or twice a year she visited Milan, Paris, Montreal or New York to report back on the latest fashion developments there. But the high point of her year was undoubtedly the party.

No one can remember exactly when the custom of the Christmas party began, but it was several years after Yasujiro's death, around 1973. It quickly became a fixture in everyone's social calendar. Other companies took up the idea and began to have parties of their own, but none ever matched the glamour of Seibu's.

As one regular guest says, all the interesting people in town were there. Sometimes Akio Morita, the outspoken chairman of Sony, put in an appearance, sometimes the doyenne of fashion designers Hanae Mori. Politicians and presidents of banks mingled with ambassadors and the head of the American Chamber of Commerce. Eitaro Yoshioka, the man most responsible for organizing the details of the party, had worked in the film industry before he joined Seibu. He ensured that there were always plenty of colorful personalities and famous faces from film, theater and television thronging the rooms.

Most unforgettable of all was the unabashed extravagance of the evening. Each guest received a gift. There were Hermès ties for the gentlemen and scarves for the ladies, in the days when Hermès was available in Japan exclusively from Seibu.

Then the guests disappeared into the melee. The rooms in the palace had been turned over to different purposes. In one venerable chamber, under embossed oak beams and chandeliers, there was a floor show with an orchestra, featuring the most popular chanteuse of the day. In another there was a magic show. The antechamber to the right of the main entrance was the dining room, with a buffet of rich and elaborate dishes, French and Japanese. The room to the left was hung with dark drapes and given over to a Las Vegas–style casino. There were roulette wheels and card games, and thousands of yen in play money to gamble with. But the prizes were real and the croupier made sure that everyone won.

At the end of the evening, everyone gathered in the main drawing room and sang carols while Misao held a candle aloft. For that night she was the queen of the whole glittering assembly.

The last time that Misao appeared in public was at another party, held to celebrate the opening of Seiji's most spectacular department store yet.

Seiji had achieved nearly everything he wanted to achieve. There was just one more goal still to be attained. Seibu would never be considered a first-class department store until it had a branch in the Ginza. Until then, no matter how substantial its sales, no matter how stylish and influential it might be, it would never be more than a local store. It would always be at the wrong end of town.

In Japan small towns christen their shopping malls "the Ginza" in the hopes that the glamorous name will give the place an air of luxury. When Westerners arrived in Japan in the second half of the nineteenth century, bringing with them their technology, fashion and Western ways, the Ginza in Tokyo was the first place to take on the veneer of Westernization. The rest of the city was still a maze of narrow streets barely wide enough for a ricksha and crammed with wooden houses. But the main street of the Ginza had pavements, gaslights (the first gaslights in Japan) and brick buildings with colonnades and balconies. Young people in search of the latest extravagances—exotic Western items like suits, hats, spectacles, tables or chairs—roamed its stores or lounged in its coffee shops.

By the seventies and early eighties the area was beginning to take on a distinctly middle-aged air. While young people promenaded up and down Shibuya's Park Avenue, strolling into Parco and Seibu and the boutiques that surrounded them, the Ginza had become the place where wealthy dowagers bought their pearls, gold and expensive *haute couture*. Shops like Wako epitomized the Ginza. Everyone adored its window display, but few could afford to venture inside to examine the luxurious French fashions. Still, no matter how much the area changed, the name never lost its magic. Every great department store had a branch there, including Mitsukoshi with its vulgar McDonald's franchise right on Ginza crossing. Only one store was missing: Seibu.

To establish a store on the Ginza was no easy matter. The first problem was land. Every inch of space on the Ginza was already crammed with shops, restaurants, offices and theaters. In addition, land in the Ginza was prohibitively expensive and becoming more so by the day.

Around 1975 the *Asahi* newspaper announced that it would be moving to new offices outside the Ginza. There was a flurry of excitement in the department store world. The *Asahi* offices were on a prime piece of land, a few hundred yards to the north of the main Ginza crossing, served by both a railway and a subway station. The space was a little small; but together with the Nichigeki theater next door, which was also up for redevelopment, it was the perfect site for a department store. It was, in fact, the last remaining site in the whole of Tokyo suitable for building a first-class department store.[1]

The land was available not for sale but for rent. The *Asahi* newspaper and the Nichigeki theater realized the value of what they had to offer, and the deposit and rent for the land were extremely high. First Seibu, then other department stores—Sogo, Isetan, Goto's Tokyu, even Mitsukoshi—all put in a bid. One by one the other stores dropped away. Finally it was agreed that the Hankyu chain would take the land belonging to the Nichigeki theater. As for the *Asahi* land, two contenders were left: the Sogo chain and Seibu.

For five years the rivals put in their claims while the newspaper magnates deliberated. No matter how long he had to wait, no matter what the cost, Seiji was determined to hold out. He had many opponents. The small shopkeepers in the Ginza were afraid that Seibu, notorious for its "crazy expansion," would transform the image of the Ginza just as it had transformed Ikebukuro and Shibuya, and drive them out of business.

Finally the *Asahi* announced its decision. Seiji's persistence had paid off. Whether it was connections or simply the fact that Seibu was a better store than Sogo, he got the land. He had to make one major concession, however. To mollify the Ginza shopkeepers, he had to agree not to use the name Ginza in the title of his shop. He had hoped to call his new store the Ginza Seibu. Instead he had to make do with Seibu Yurakucho, after the nearby railway station.

Seibu Yurakucho opened on October 6, 1984. It was different from anything that Tokyo had ever seen before. It was small, so small that many retailers doubted that it was possible to make a profit. But Seiji was an expert at making use of limitations. He had never attempted to make a store that sold everything that any customer could possibly want to buy. He had always sold select merchandise for a select clientele. In Seibu Yurakucho he took this principle even further. Not only were there no kitchen goods, there were no electronic goods—no computers, no cassette players, no videos—and there was no toy department. Instead there were designer clothes and jewelry, chosen with the emphasis on luxury, quality and youth. On the sixth floor the discerning shopper could roam between racks of Giorgio Armani, Gianfranco Ferre, Donna Karan and Issey Miyake. On the seventh there were labels to which Seibu had the exclusive distribution rights in Japan—Hermès, Yves Saint-Laurent, Jean-Louis Scherrer.

It was the eighth floor that was the most revolutionary of all. What was on sale was not things but information and services. Shoppers could invest in gold, silver or shares listed on the Tokyo Stock Exchange. They could buy property in Japan or abroad. On impulse they could take out a loan or a mortgage, arrange an insurance policy, book a plane ticket or a holiday or buy a house.

Once again Seiji had shown that he had his finger on the pulse of the age. Other department stores had provided some of these services, but Seibu Yurakucho went further. The goods on sale were secondary; what was on offer was a lifestyle.

The building itself, which housed both Hankyu and Seibu department stores side by side, was all glass and mullions (it was called the Mullion Center) and mirrored faceted surfaces. Up on the top floors, a culture area with cinemas and an assembly hall, there were escalators on which one could see endless images of oneself reflected over and over again in the walls and ceiling of this glittering gold world.

With his store on the Ginza, Seiji had reached the apotheosis in the world of department stores. It was exactly twenty years since his father had died, and in those years he had proved himself. The name of Seibu was on everyone's lips, and when they spoke of Seibu most spoke of the department store.

Misao shared in Seiji's triumph. At the opening party she welcomed the guests with her radiant smile. She had brought Seiji up; she had been a great source of support and affection throughout his childhood and his tormented relationship with his father. And she, above all, must have shared in his humiliation when his father denied him the inheritance.

Finally, through his own efforts, he had reversed his destiny. Misao's satisfaction must have been as great as Seiji's that day.

Less than two weeks later she was dead.

In fact, although no one at the party suspected it, Misao had been taken ill two days before. She was taken to the hospital complaining of stomach pains and released just in time to be present at Seiji's celebration.

A few days later she was in the hospital again. She had an operation for stomach cancer, but the operation was unsuccessful and the cancer spread. On the sixteenth her condition became critical and at four o'clock in the afternoon of November 17 she died.[2] The cause of death was recorded as heart attack. Had she lived another week she would have celebrated her seventy-seventh birthday. It was almost as if she had willed herself to stay alive long enough to see Seiji's triumph.

The funeral was held two days later. According to Misao's wish, it was by Seibu standards a small gathering, held in Hiroo. All the family were there—Seiji and his sons, Yoshiaki and his brothers, Tsuneko and other relatives—and two or three hundred of the staff who had been with the company longest and had known Misao best. Kakuei Tanaka attended not as a politician but as a longtime friend of the family, to light a stick of incense before the portrait of the deceased.

The ceremony was a quiet, dignified one, befitting the widow of the ex-Speaker and *grande dame* of the Seibu empire. On the altar, there was a photograph of Misao, framed with white chrysanthemums, with a single orchid in a vase behind it.

From there the family went on to the crematorium. Misao's ashes were buried in the hilltop cemetery in Kamakura, just below Yasujiro's majestic tomb at the very top of the hill. A black marble gravestone marks the spot, inscribed simply with the two characters "Misao Tsutsumi." On another slab is engraved one of her poems.

A week later, on the day that would have been Misao's birthday, Yoshiaki and Tsuneko went to have a quiet dinner together in a restaurant in Akasaka, an area famous for its exclusive restaurants, hidden behind high walls. According to one company insider, there had been a family quarrel at the funeral, and the mother and son wanted to talk it over.

Tsuneko was seventy-one. While Misao had retained her cool elegance, Tsuneko had grown into a warm, motherly woman. Her youthful prettiness had disappeared, but she was still as sweet-natured as ever. She was plump, down-to-earth and overflowing with kindness. All the children adored her. Both she and Misao had always tried to treat all the children as their own.[3] It was their love for all of them, no matter who their mothers really were, that kept the family bound together.

All her life, Tsuneko had kept a few steps behind Misao. Now finally she might be able to step out of the shadows, to enjoy something of her son's reflected glory. Misao was no longer there to keep her in second place.

The mother and son sat in the restaurant, talking quietly together. From time to time a kimono-clad waitress slid open the door to the room and came in on her knees to place a dish of raw fish or some simmered vegetables, exquisitely carved, on the table in front of them. The restaurant's speciality was *kaiseki,* tea-ceremony cuisine, an appropriate choice for Tsuneko, who so loved the womanly arts of tea ceremony and flower arranging.

Suddenly Tsuneko complained of a headache. There at the restaurant she collapsed. An ambulance was called and she was rushed to the hospital. Yoshiaki was distraught. For two days, he never left her side. He canceled all his business appointments. He had no rest or sleep.

Tsuneko never recovered consciousness. After two days in a coma, at 7.30 P.M. on November 25, she too died. The cause of death was recorded as brain hemorrhage.

It was little more than a week since Misao's death.

Later, when he was interviewed, Yoshiaki said of Tsuneko:

There's only one word for it—she was kindness itself. Mum wrapped everything up warmly, she listened to people's silly stories and cheered them up. She always took all the burden on herself. Because I had a mum like that, I could respect my father. For a start, even when my father was tough on me, she always said "I'm the one who's wrong" and took all the blame on herself. She never spoke ill of anyone. Even when someone was causing problems she always said "He must have had a good reason for doing that" or "I'm sure he didn't mean badly" and interpreted everything in a good way.[4]

No one could fail to notice the proximity of the two deaths. It was as if the two women's lives were so closely intertwined that they could never be separated. It was the saddest of ironies that even on her last journey Tsuneko had followed a few steps behind Misao.

Yoshiaki made no attempt to conceal his grief. He wept openly. He walked around like a man in a daze. For years he had played the tyrant. Ever since his father had told him that he was to be the successor, he had taken on all the attributes of an emperor. His employees quaked before him. He demanded unquestioning obedience and public displays of respect. While the public might be shocked by his arrogance, the country's most powerful men saw him as a future leader of the nation.

But somewhere behind the mask of the iron-willed emperor the boy who had cycled the hills of Karuizawa was still there. His friends from his school days spoke of him as someone trapped inside a role not of his choosing. When his mother died the mask slipped, at least for a few days.

The day of Tsuneko's funeral, November 28, was cold and clear. A few autumn leaves still tinted the trees.

That day curious spectators turned out just to look at the crowds lined up at the ancient red-lacquered gates of Zojoji, one of Tokyo's most venerable temples. Zojoji's spacious grounds stretched alongside the Tokyo Prince Hotel. Both had once been the lands of the Tokugawa shoguns until Yasujiro bought them after the war. The

Tokyo Prince Hotel had been the Tokugawas' cemetery, and Zojoji had been their family temple.

While Misao's funeral had been a quiet family affair, Yoshiaki ensured that Tsuneko's was spectacular. In life she had never had the recognition she craved; at least on this one occasion he could demonstrate his love for her. Eight thousand arrived to pay their last respects to the gentle mother of the emperor of Seibu. The queue, ten people deep, stretched out of the gate and around the block. Inside, the air was heavy with incense and the altar was blanketed with white chrysanthemums.

Yoshiaki and his two brothers, Yasuhiro and Yuji, led the mourners. There were relatives, members of staff, politicians, leaders of business and industry, artists, entertainers and actors. In the front row were three former prime ministers: Kakuei Tanaka, Takeo Fukuda, whose office was in the Akasaka Prince Hotel, and Zenko Suzuki, whom Yoshiaki had helped to establish in power. Next to them were three more men who were to be the leading players over the next few years: future prime ministers Noboru Takeshita and Kiichi Miyazawa and their rival power broker Shintaro Abe. The prime minister of the day, Yasuhiro Nakasone, put in an appearance in the middle of the ceremony. It was an awe-inspiring display of strength for the Seibu empire.

There was only one speech. Yoshiaki, his head bowed and his eyes puffy, said a few words. His usually high-pitched voice was hoarse. "I've been so busy with my work, I haven't been able to do my duty for my mother. But today all of you have generously gathered here for her funeral—so in the end I managed to do something for her. . . ."[5]

Yoshiaki was the lord of the Seibu empire, but he lacked the power to accord his mother the last respect. Once again the ordinary man and devoted son was trapped by his position. Even in death, Tsuneko was still the mistress. It was not proper for her to be buried even in a corner of the great cemetery that Yasujiro had built on the hill in Kamakura. Instead her ashes were sent back to Niigata, where her father's family came from. Like a girl who had never been married, she was buried not in her husband's but in her father's family temple.

For weeks afterward Yoshiaki confessed to being still shaken.

When New Year's Day came round, for the first time since Yasujiro's death there was no dawn ceremony on the hilltop in Kamakura. "Mum died—so it can't be a happy new year," he said.[6] From then on, he vowed, he would be a different man.

That same year that the two mothers died there was a third death. Unnoticed and unannounced, Seiji's real mother too passed away, according to one company insider. An era had come to an end, in the lives of both the brothers. The last of the older generation had gone. There was no longer anything to bind them together.

The Age of Gold
Seiji's Story 1984–1991

I brought back to mind the look of Father's eyes. . . . A long-forgotten hatred welled up inside me. Are you still grading me after you're dead? I thought. Then let me tell you, my grade is zero. I'm damned if I'll be measured by your standards. TAKASHI TSUJII
A Spring Like Any Other

After Misao died, Seiji had one last Christmas party. It was held not at the Takanawa Prince Hotel, Prince Takeda's old palace, but in the sparkling new Seibu in the Ginza. It was every bit as splendid as Misao's parties had been. The guest list was the same. Ambassadors and the nation's political leaders mingled with singers, actresses and fashion designers. On each floor of the store there was a lavish buffet, loaded with different foods from all over the world—cheeses on one floor, beef on another. All the guests received gifts and there was a casino with extravagant prizes.

But the atmosphere was wrong. The hotel had been crowded and intimate; the store was too large and brightly lit. And everyone felt the absence of the empress dowager, greeting her guests with her radiant smile. That was the last party. After that Seiji brought the custom to an end.

Seiji was nearing sixty. He was now one of the most powerful men in Japan and probably the country's most famous business tycoon. His stores stood for everything Japan was proud of—the coming of wealth and luxury, the making of a society that could rival the West. The manufacturing companies had created the wealth. Seibu showed them how to spend it. It embodied the vision of its founder—to raise the quality of life in Japan.

For all his power and influence, in person Seiji remained an unexpectedly modest man. He was small, birdlike, ebullient, bursting with nervous energy. His round face was still boyish and so was his puckish grin and unbridled enthusiasm. In interviews he sat perched on the edge of his chair, taking notes, thinking hard before answering. Whereas Yoshiaki projected a tough, manly image, Seiji's public persona was gentle, almost feminine.

In many ways he was the exact antithesis of the archetypal Japanese businessman. For a start, he was bad at golf. And instead of spending his time adding up the account books and worrying about profit and loss, he was happiest talking about poetry. Westerners who met him described him as a Renaissance man. He was warm, charming, unexpectedly forthright and extremely cultured. No matter what the subject—Picasso, Debussy, flowers or sixteenth-century Europe— he had an extraordinary depth of knowledge and always had some new insight to contribute. Wherever he went, he always had a book in his hand. On long plane journeys, he preferred to fly Aeroflot, where he would not meet anyone he knew and could sit peacefully, reading. He read with great care, underlining key sections, and kept a card index of books he had read.

In the business community he was a maverick, an outsider. For all his success, he sat on few of the committees that marked the pinnacle of acceptance in Japanese business society. While Noboru Goto, the son of Yasujiro's old enemy Goto the Thief, was soon to take up the post of head of the Japan Chamber of Commerce and Industry, and other business leaders aspired to be chairman of Keidanren, Seiji was unlikely to be offered such socially prestigious posts. He was careless about maintaining the established hierarchies. He mixed with students and young people, listening as intently to their ideas as to those of his fellow business leaders. He was comfortable with foreigners, and in the most formal of situations he was liable suddenly to laugh and crack a joke.

No matter how busy he became, he always maintained his double life, as poet and businessman. Late in the evening, after three or four engagements, he would retreat to his study, lined with books to the ceiling and hung with one or two Paul Klees, and write for several hours. Sometimes it seemed that the poet Takashi Tsujii played a larger part in his nature than the businessman Seiji Tsutsumi.

At home Asako provided a solid foundation for his life. She was forty-six when the mothers died, and had grown, if anything, more beautiful as the years passed. She still had the large candid eyes and laughing smile of her youth, the sweet gaiety and warmth of the young woman who had once been a geisha. Tiny and chic, she favored French designers, as Misao had done, and played the role of society hostess with effortless assurance.

For years she had devoted herself to her sons. Koji was now twenty-six and had already joined Seibu, while Takao was a solemn-faced schoolboy of fourteen. Finally Asako had time to herself. She was far too vibrant a woman to sit at home doing nothing. She loved to be out in the midst of people, talking and laughing, so Seiji gave her a bar to run on the ground floor of one of his newest and sleekest stores. This was her domain. She oversaw the choice of spirits and the menu and there was a table reserved where she could entertain friends and chat with customers. She also went back to dancing, taking up a traditional and very stylized form of dance called *jutamae*.

After the death of the two mothers it seemed that there was no longer any holding back. Seiji was still involved in Yoshiaki's Seibu empire and still on the board of Seibu Railways. He attended board meetings, though it was said that in recent years his appearances had become less and less frequent. It was alleged that when he did attend he usually started arguments. To Yoshiaki, whose word was supposed to be law, this was intolerable.[1]

In 1986 it was announced that Seiji was stepping down as managing director of Seibu Railways. Various reasons were given, such as that the Railways needed a managing director who could devote himself full-time to the job and that Seiji was already too busy running his own businesses. Nevertheless the fact remained that after thirty years the last link had been cut that bound Seiji to the Seibu empire which his father had founded.

The previous year he had changed the name of his own business empire from the Seibu Retail Group to Seibu Saison. When the two empires split in 1970, Seibu Railways held a large proportion of shares in the department store. But by 1985 the stores held 100 percent of their own shares. Seiji's name had disappeared from the list of directors of Seibu Railways. Seibu Railways had disappeared from the list of shareholders in the Seibu Retail group. The two empires were now completely separate.

When he announced the new name of his group, Seiji explained the reason for the change. For many years he had been engaged exclusively in retail, but now the group had begun to diversify. It was no longer appropriate to keep the name Retail. Instead he chose the French word *saison*, to express a poetic awareness of the passing of the seasons.

Even before the mothers died Seiji had begun to expand into radically new areas of business. It started when a man called Shoichiro Okada came to ask him for help. Okada's father was of the same generation as Yasujiro and, like him, had made his fortune out of land speculation. The two had known and liked each other. On several occasions Okada had bought land right next to Yasujiro's. And, just as Yoshiaki had done, he built hotels and golf courses on it. His business, in other words, was identical with Yoshiaki's.

After Yasujiro's death, Okada's company, Taiyo Development Corporation, fell into difficulties. He was one of those, like Seiji, who bought land when Prime Minister Kakuei Tanaka announced his plan to rebuild the Japanese archipelago in 1972 and who found himself the owner of land worth far less than he had paid for it when the oil crisis struck. By the time his son came to take over the company in 1982, it was burdened with enormous debts.

For Seiji it was an attractive proposition. Despite the debts, which were rumored to amount to as much as ¥35 billion ($140 million), the company was the owner of some fine stretches of land—near Yokohama, on the northern island of Hokkaido and in Hawaii.

So Seiji agreed to take it over. He bought the stocks, paid off the debts and set to work to improve and develop his new properties. Not only had he stepped into Yoshiaki's area of business but he had also acquired properties that were right next to Yoshiaki's and in direct competition. Up in Onuma in Hokkaido, Seiji's newly acquired Onuma Taiyo Hotel was only a few minutes' drive from Yoshiaki's Onuma Prince Cottages. And both catered to golfers and skiers.

There was also a rumor that although the brothers had agreed to discuss all their business activities with each other, Seiji had failed to inform Yoshiaki of his proposed takeover of Taiyo Corporation. The first Yoshiaki heard of it, it was said, was when it was reported in the newspapers.[2]

The takeover of Taiyo, it transpired, was just the beginning. By now Seiji was committed to empire building on a grand scale. His "crazy expansion" was taking him into areas where no retail enterprises had ever gone before. Over the next few years he staged a succession of spectacular business moves. He forged links with another hotel chain, which gave him an interest in several Japanese-style inns. He bought the Kyoto Royal Hotel, a large hotel in the center of the old city of Kyoto, which had been in financial difficulties. And in partnership with Japan National Railways he was responsible for the planning and design of a small hotel called the Edmont. He formed a joint venture with Club Med to build the first resorts in Japan and another with Yamaha to develop marine resorts. He also took over an old trading firm called Osawa Shokai that imported sportswear.

On the surface he had turned into just another businessman. His admirers in the artistic community watched with dismay. He seemed to have lost his vision. Perhaps, as Eiko Ishioka has suggested, he just got bored. "The same person can't keep up the same power for three decades," she said.

The press had a different explanation. Ever since the division of the empires back in 1970, rumors had been rife that there was, at the very least, an unspoken agreement between the two brothers not to step into each other's territory. Now they watched gleefully as Seiji pushed deeper and deeper into Yoshiaki's sphere of business. Even if this was not deliberate provocation, at the very least it showed a careless disregard for the supposed agreement he had made with his brother.

The stories began from the moment that the mothers died. Most were unsubstantiated rumors. According to one, Seiji incurred Yoshiaki's wrath by begging to sit next to him at Tsuneko's funeral so as to allay suspicions that there might be a feud between them. Yoshiaki responded with fury. They were not schoolboys, they were grown men in their fifties! They had no need even to suggest such things.

Officially there was no feud. The days when Pistol Tsutsumi and Goto the Thief could carry out their dispute in full view of the public had long since passed. Seiji and Yoshiaki were modern sophisticated Japanese men, and as such could not be seen to quarrel in public.

There were no fights or public displays of anger. But in fact, the feud was common knowledge. Off the record, insiders within Seiji's empire were happy to confirm that the brothers seldom, if ever, met and that there was much bad feeling between them; they also offered harsh criticism of Yoshiaki and his high-handed style. The brothers themselves, however, covered their tracks with such care that there was very little concrete evidence. The press could only deduce the state of their relationship from their business activities and from hints and subtle implications.

One small though clear manifestation of the quarrel had to do with the Seibu credit card. The Saison card, as it was now known, was widely accepted in many stores and most major hotels, including the prestigious Okura and Imperial. There was just one major hotel chain that categorically refused to accept it: the Prince hotels.

The brothers were beginning to feel hounded by the press. Both denied vigorously that there was any bad blood between them. In interviews Yoshiaki maintained, very reasonably, that the two empires were completely separate, what Seiji did was no concern of his, and that the two had little to do with each other.

"We don't see each other much," he was quoted as saying. "From time to time he drops in for lunch, but we just chat. When we were kids, Seiji-*san* liked studying, he read a lot. We didn't play together." As for their companies, "We have an adult relationship. The department store and us, it's not like America and the USSR, it's like the American-Japanese relationship."[3]

As the rumors of brotherly rivalry grew stronger, Seiji became visibly irked by questions on that topic. Once he exploded, "*I* didn't make a mistake—*he* made a mistake. He has all this land, all this money. . . . If you have so much, it's a big worry!"

In Japan there is a very sharp demarcation between one's private feelings, *honne,* and one's public face, *tatemae.* No matter what you do or what you feel in private, the most important thing is just that—to keep it private. Keeping up appearances, maintaining face, are vital if society and business are to continue functioning smoothly. What the Tsutsumi brothers were doing wrong was that they were failing to keep their emotions where they belonged—behind locked doors.

Hot on his heels, the press attributed everything Seiji did to his urge to outdo his brother. But he was far too clever a businessman to let himself be driven by a single emotion. There were more complicated forces at work.

Japan by the mid-eighties was a very different place from what it had been even a decade before. While the countryside changed more slowly, in Tokyo the pace of change was frantic. The burning creativity that had characterized the seventies had passed. Eiko Ishioka and all the young talents who had made Parco into the nucleus of the decade had moved on. In Tokyo at least, no one could doubt that they were rich.

One thing creating new millionaires was the accelerating price of land. Those who happened to have land in Tokyo found themselves richer by the day. Another was the Plaza Accord of 1985. In international terms it was barely noticed. But in Japan it created a minor revolution. The yen was allowed to float freely against the dollar. Overnight the dollar tumbled and the price of imported goods practically halved. In dollar terms everyone was twice as rich as they had been the day before.

Mercedeses, which had been beyond most people's pockets, became commonplace. The streets were full of Rolls-Royces, Jaguars, the odd Ferrari Testarossa. People wore Chanel suits to go shopping. Students in trainers queued around the block to buy necklaces at Tiffany's in Mitsukoshi. It was the age of the two-hundred-dollar cup of coffee, when people dropped in to the gold shop on the high street to invest in a few bars. Besides wearing gold, you could buy gold lipstick or gold nail polish, eat salad or sushi scattered with flakes of gold dust, or indulge in a gold massage.

For years the Japanese had been a nation of savers. Now their children were learning how to spend. According to the new ethic, if it was not expensive, it was not worth buying.

Seiji, of course, had seen all this coming. His Seibu stores had nurtured a taste for luxury long before most Japanese dared even to covet it. Once only Seibu and Parco sold the latest French fashions. Now there were designer boutiques crowding the high streets of every provincial city. While Seiji's empire grew larger and larger, expanding in new and unprecedented directions, Seibu rolled on with a momentum that seemed unstoppable. Its ventures for the eighties were speciality stores on a grand scale, exploring the furthest reaches of technology. Long before the high-street stores had caught up, Seibu was already moving on.

In 1985, the year after the mothers died, Seibu's store for the space age, the "megatronic" Seibu, opened in Tsukuba, Japan's Science City. It was housed in a "smart" building and populated by robots. The window blinds were opened and closed by electronic sensors, the shelves were wired to keep track of which goods were running low, and when a food item passed the sell-by date the price automatically changed. The robots were three feet high with painted eyes and metallic samurai haircuts. They trundled up and down the aisles, wheeling shopping trolleys, following a signaling device attached to the shopper's belt.

Then came stores with names like Wave, Seed and Loft, offshoots of the Seibu empire. Wave was a vast music emporium, the largest in Tokyo, incorporating the latest technology. There was a computerized record reference section, a recording studio, a computer-graphics lab and a cinema, besides floor upon floor of records, tapes, videos and books. The first Wave occupied a windowless slate-gray building in the youthful disco-filled district of Roppongi. The bar where Seiji's wife, Asako, presided, Raintree, was on the ground floor. The second Wave was in Shibuya.

By now Shibuya, which had started out as Goto's fortress, was indisputably Seibu City. Seibu and Parco between them had coaxed it into the modern age. It was a temple to gilded youth, one of the most sophisticated parts of the city. Park Avenue, which had once been known as Ward Office Road, had sprouted rose trees and benches. Elegant young men with ponytails and overcoats several sizes too large for them promenaded up and down with chic young women, dressed from head to foot in black, on their arms.

Besides Parco, at the top of the slope, their promenade took them past Wave and a sleek gray granite building, ten floors high, called Seed. Seed was the seed of fashion to come. It was clothes for the sophisticate sated with designer fashion, for the individualist in a nation of conformists. Its ten floors stocked exclusive designer labels—not the great names, the safe bets that everyone bought, but obscure designers, both Japanese and Western.

But the store that inspired the most devotion, that seemed to embody the spirit of the age, was Loft. When its doors opened, young people flocked to shop there. It was a cult store on a grand scale. It was based on the most decadent of premises. It was a store for a generation that had everything it could possibly want. Surveys done toward the end of the decade revealed the worrying information that a sizable proportion of young people could think of nothing whatsoever that they wanted; they already had absolutely everything. Their elders called them *shinjinrui,* "a new species of human being," and wondered what would become of Japan when these spoiled youngsters, who were interested in little besides fashion and brand names, took over the country.

Loft was a grand jumble of goods that no one had ever wanted because they had never thought of them before. Like the loft of a house, it was full of unexpected finds, from a "rock television" (a television set into a rock) to a fax machine that doubled as a camera. The latest high-tech gadgets were on display, sleekly styled in shades of gray and black, along with expensive imported designer items—antique Rolexes, Alessi kettles, Bugatti watches.

Seiji had been preparing for the age of luxury long before it began. Now it was obvious that the age of mad spending, of obsessively acquiring goods, was reaching its peak. He had done all he wanted to do in the realm of retail, and he could see as clearly as Yoshiaki that the age to come would be the age of leisure. If he did not move on he would be left behind.

In interviews he commented with quiet pride that his was the only retail business that had managed to diversify, to adapt to new conditions and a new age. He explained his aim: to provide absolutely everything that touched on the consumer's life, to accommodate the consumer's every requirement.

The consumer did not want only to shop in department stores. He might want to travel, to take out a mortgage, to buy insurance, to invest in stocks and bonds; all that he could do at Seibu. As his lifestyle changed, so the company needed to change, too. What the consumer required next was hotels, designed with all the flair for which Seibu was famous.

The business world murmured darkly that the Seibu Saison concern was balanced over an abyss of debt. Sales were high. Most years Seibu Ikebukuro remained the highest-selling department store in the country, but the interest that the company had to pay on its debts was so vast that profits were always precariously low. According to one source, in 1985 Seibu and Mitsukoshi had roughly even sales. On sales of ¥568.4 billion ($2.38 billion), Mitsukoshi showed a profit of ¥7.2 billion ($30 million). Seibu recorded sales of ¥474.9 billion ($1.99 billion). But its profits were disproportionately small, a pitiful ¥354 million ($1.5 million).[4]

The only way that the company could keep afloat was by expanding more and more, growing larger and larger. Yet the larger it grew, the more its foundations shook. While the economy remained buoyant, there was no problem. But if ever there were a slump, as there had been at the time of the oil crisis, the whole edifice would be at risk. Still, it was the age of gold. It was a time for flamboyance, not caution.

One cold March evening in 1987 the city's most glamorous and influential people gathered to celebrate the opening of a spectacular new hotel. For a few moments the pavement was awash with peacock-bright gowns and kimonos and discreet dark suits, before the guests vanished through the automatic doors and up the plush pink staircase.

Rumor had it that Yoshiaki's henchmen were stationed in the café across the road, taking photographs as the guests went in.

For the past year everyone had been curious about the hotel that Seibu Saison was building on the Ginza. It was not that hotels were a rarity. In recent years there had been a spate of hotel building. Yoshiaki, for one, had opened a succession of Prince hotels, each designed by one of the country's leading architects, on prime sites across the city.

But this one was different. For a start, it was right on the Ginza. There had never been a hotel on the Ginza before. Even before the name was decided, everyone knew the address: 1-1 Ginza, the best address in town. Secondly, when the press and the curious tried to see it, they were turned brusquely away. Unlike the other Tokyo hotels, which were open to all comers, this one was to be small, luxurious and very, very exclusive.

Like everything Seiji did, the Seiyo Ginza reflected his own personal vision. Whenever he traveled abroad, he always stayed in small intimate European-style hotels, where the staff knew each guest. But

in Tokyo there was no hotel to suit his taste. They were all imper-
sonal, many-floored American-style hotels with glittering chandeliers,
thousands of rooms, banqueting halls and a lobby the size of a railway
station. Westerners who visited Tokyo complained that there were no
hotels that they really liked.

Seiji had originally been shunted into retail; but that had little to
do with his own tastes and inclinations. In the early days, when he
had believed himself to be the heir to the Seibu empire, he had taken
a keen interest in leisure and hotels. He had worked with Misao on
the Tokyo Prince Hotel, and when Yasujiro died the Tokyo and the
Haneda Prince were allocated to him as part of his portion.

Several times he had tried to enter the hotel business but each
time he had been foiled. First he had to sell the Tokyo and Haneda
Princes to Yoshiaki to help repay the crippling debts of the Los Angeles store. Then, when he tried to build a hotel in Sunshine City, on
the site of Sugamo prison just outside Ikebukuro, the project came to
grief and he had to turn to Yoshiaki to bail him out.

Company insiders say that when Yasujiro planned his first modern
hotel, the Tokyo Prince, he had wanted to build a hotel to rival the
best in the city, the Okura and the Imperial. The Prince hotels were
not that. They were functional hotels designed to yield an excellent
profit; they were not lovingly planned to be the finest hotels in the
city. In the Seiyo Ginza, Seiji planned to build the hotel that his father had wanted. It was almost a rebuke to his brother.

When a piece of land became available at the far end of the Ginza,
he snapped it up. For many years a theater had stood on the site, and
he planned to incorporate it into his hotel complex. Just as Seibu Yurakucho, the Seibu in the Ginza, had been the ultimate department
store, this would be the ultimate hotel.

The Seiyo was different from anything that Tokyo had ever seen
before. It was not huge, glittering and crowded with people. It did
not advertise its presence. It was not full of ladies taking tea. Instead
it was small, intimate and very discreet. The entrance was hidden
around a corner, off the main Ginza shopping street, with smiling
doormen in gray suits to discourage the casual visitor. The reception
area was like the lounge of a very stately private home, with chintz
sofas and leather-topped desks. The rooms, a mere eighty of them,
were nearly all suites.

It was the last word in luxury. The most decadent suite was said to be modeled after the French actress Catherine Deneuve's bedroom and featured a canopied bed, silver fox quilts and a bathroom of black marble. In another there was a bed draped with black mink. The guests had a choice of seven sorts of pillow, which ranged from feathers, down or artificial pearls to tiny ceramic balls (to improve circulation). There were sheets of Egyptian cotton, feather-light duvets and huge bathrooms equipped with television and steam room. The chef, from one of the best French restaurants in Tokyo, had studied with Roger Vergé in France. The cellars were stacked with the finest French wines. Seiji wanted only the best of everything.

Once he was discussing room charges with the manager, a man called Tokuya Nagai. Nagai, trying to keep up with Seiji's grand vision, made the bold suggestion that the junior suites should be priced at the outrageous rate of ¥90,000 ($620) a night. Too cheap, said Seiji, make it ¥100,000 ($690).

It was the sheer price of the Seiyo that took it into the realms of legend. It was the most expensive hotel in Tokyo, possibly in the world. Hollywood stars who used to stay at the Okura or the Imperial changed their allegiance. Elizabeth Taylor and Dustin Hoffman could be seen in its breakfast room. Japanese journalists, barred from tramping through its dining rooms, were skeptical. How could such a hotel, they asked, ever recoup its costs? Every other hotel in Japan made its money through banquets, wedding receptions and shopping arcades, but the Seiyo was far too grand for such vulgarity. Instead it relied on high room rates from expense-account Western executives and VIPs. But even before it opened, the dollar had begun to tumble against the yen.

If he was worried, Seiji gave no sign. The Seiyo served to raise the image of the Seibu Saison group yet higher. If it had to be subsidized by other companies within the group, so much the worse.

Seiji made two key appointments when he planned the Seiyo. One was the manager. With his famous instinct for finding the right man for the job, he went to New York to recruit Tokuya Nagai. Nagai, a florid, ebullient man of forty, had caused a stir in the Japanese press when he was offered the plum job of manager of the Waldorf Towers, a job normally held by elderly Anglo-Saxons, not youthful Japanese. He was charmed by Seiji. Here was one of Japan's most powerful tycoons, yet when they met, instead of grunting disdainfully as befitted his status, Seiji smiled his puckish smile and said, "I'm Seiji Tsutsumi. Very honored to meet you!"

Nagai's job was to help in the planning of the hotel and to run it on a daily basis. But the hotel also had to have a president, to work out the details of Seiji's original plan and put them into practice.

In 1984, when the mothers died, Seiji was already laying down the plans for his new luxury hotel. That year Yuji, who had been based in Canada for the last eight years, flew back to Japan to attend his mother's funeral. Seiji had always had a soft spot for the youngest member of the family. When Yuji married the American heiress Lynette Himmelman, despite Yoshiaki's opposition, it was Seiji who stood by him. He too had had to suffer the family's disapproval when he married, because of Asako's less than respectable background as a geisha. Besides, as a modern man and international executive, he had no particular objection to foreigners.

Yuji had been away from Japan for a long time. Ever since Yoshiaki had ousted him as president of Prince hotels, he had been living in Canada, managing the Toronto Prince Hotel. Two or three times a year he was able to get back on a business trip.

At the funeral the two half brothers talked. There was a gap of fifteen years between them—Yuji was forty-two at the time of his mother's death—but in many ways their personalities were close. Yuji was as personable and softly spoken as ever. Seiji, who enjoyed the company of foreigners, doubtless felt comfortable with his North American ways and easy charm.

From the events that followed, it seems likely that their conversation encompassed business. Seiji must have told him something of his dream to build the best hotel in Japan. Yuji for his part was perhaps tiring of his exile. Here was a magnificent opportunity—to create the most luxurious hotel in Japan, using all the facilities of the Seibu Saison group, with money no object.

There was one stumbling block. Yuji was Yoshiaki's blood brother, not Seiji's. Yoshiaki had treated him harshly; he had always played the role of stern father in his dealings with Yuji. But still, it would not look good for the family if Yuji were to move to Seiji's camp.

Less than a year after the mothers' deaths, the Prince hotels made a surprise announcement. Mr. Yuji Tsutsumi was resigning from the company and from his post as president of the Toronto Prince Hotel in order to devote himself to managing his two restaurants in Canada. It was, they said, a decision he had made of his own accord. There were rumors that he had handed in his notice six months earlier but the matter had been kept secret.[5]

Another year passed. On December 1, 1986, the Seibu Saison group unveiled its project to build a luxury hotel in the Ginza. The president was named as Mr. Hiroaki Takahashi. One of the nine directors was Yuji Tsutsumi.

Later, once the Seiyo opened, the manager, Nagai, confirmed what everyone had suspected. Yuji was the real president of the hotel. As the Americanized Nagai put it, the Seiyo was Yuji-*san*'s baby.

Seiji was famous for poaching top executives from rival companies, an activity regarded as most unsportsmanlike in Japan, but it was the first time he had ever snatched anyone from under Yoshiaki's nose, let alone his own brother. For years he had avoided direct confrontation with Yoshiaki and his huge empire, but now he was not going to hold back any longer. Yoshiaki, it seemed, was no longer family but a competitor.

Yuji's defection to the rival camp occasioned surprisingly little comment in the Japanese press. The grand master of Tsutsumi watchers, Toshiaki Kaminogo, in his book *New Seibu Empire,* quoted various anonymous people. Some were critical of Seiji for fueling discord between the blood brothers. There was a rumor that Yuji had brought staff with him from the Prince Hotel over to the Seiyo. And there was criticism of Yuji, who was the only person who was close to both brothers and might have bound the two sides together.

As far as possible the family tried to play down rumors of increasing friction between the two sides. Kaminogo quotes Yoshiaki as saying that he had no quarrel with Yuji. "Whenever he comes to Tokyo, he always stays in my house in Azabu. I rented it to use as a company house and from the start I let my brother have a section of it. There's always a place for him there. Whenever he visits, he comes to the office to get a key."[6]

There were those who argued that all this talk of rivalry was far from bad for business. No matter which side Yuji was on, he was part of the family concern. The family's holdings as a whole formed a vast octopuslike group, spreading its tentacles further and further across Japan. If Yasujiro had wanted to be sure that his empire would grow after his death, he couldn't have found a better way than by fanning the rivalry between his sons. The result was an empire twice as big as it would otherwise have been. The pink patches on the old man's map were growing larger and larger, until they threatened to blot out half of Japan.

Then Seiji's empire building moved on to a totally different scale.

The late eighties in Japan were a euphoric time. The country seemed unbeatable. By 1989, when presidents George Bush and Mikhail Gorbachev declared the Cold War officially over, Japan had become banker to the world. It was the world's largest creditor nation with assets of $350 billion worldwide, while the United States was the world's largest debtor with debts of $650 billion.[7]

Japanese companies were willing to part with sums that seemed totally outrageous. Suddenly international art dealers discovered that the Japanese were willing to pay unprecedented prices. It began in April 1987, when the Yasuda Fire and Marine Insurance company bought a version of Vincent van Gogh's *Sunflowers* for $39.9 million, more than twice the asking price, and came to a climax when Ryoei Saito, honorary chairman of Daishowa Paper Manufacturing, paid $82.5 million for van Gogh's *Portrait of Dr. Gachet,* the highest price ever, in May 1990. Saito also snapped up a Rodin sculpture at a bargain $1.6 million "for my backyard."[8]

While the West complained bitterly of unfair trading practices, Western companies went cap in hand in search of Japanese investment. The Japanese invested in foreign stocks and bonds; between 1985 and 1989 their net purchases totaled $433 billion, more than the annual economic output of Spain. They invested in factories abroad—direct investment rose from $6 billion in 1985 to $45 billion in 1989.[9] They also began to realize that their yen could buy them a stake in worlds which they had only ever been able to admire from afar.

Sony's purchase of Columbia Pictures and Mitsubishi's purchase of the Rockefeller Center were still to come when, late in 1987, Seibu Saison announced a joint venture with the Rockefeller Group to buy the Old Course country club in St. Andrews, Scotland. They were already involved in a hotel venture with the Rosewood Group and had made a business link with the Rothschild Group of France.

There is an apocryphal story about what happened next. It is said that a small, soft-spoken Japanese businessman dropped into the Inter-Continental Hotel in Manhattan and took a quick look around the lobby. "Very nice," he said, and left. The next day he returned—and bought the whole chain.[10]

In the autumn of 1988 Seiji called a press conference. He had an announcement to make: the Saison Group had gone global. He had signed a deal with the British conglomerate Grand Metropolitan to take over the Inter-Continental Hotels Group. At a stroke the group had become the owner of ninety-eight luxury hotels worldwide, and he was poised to expand even further. In the next few months he planned to establish new hotels, in locations better suited to Japanese tourists, including two or three in Japan itself. Japanese, who were traveling abroad more and more, would be able to stay in a Japanese-owned hotel and settle their account with their Saison credit card.

The most startling part of the announcement was the price: $2.15 billion. It was one of the largest overseas acquisitions made to date by a Japanese company.

Many people shook their heads. Far from being a stroke of genius, the deal, they said, had been an act of supreme folly. Tsutsumi had gone too far this time. He had paid well above the odds. The Inter-Continentals were massively overpriced, and the group had taken on a crippling burden of debt in order to make the purchase.

"Tsutsumi brothers in all-out war," shrieked the headlines. "Saison parts from Seibu." In comparison with the ninety-eight luxury Inter-Continentals scattered around the globe, the fifty-six Princes were nothing but a chain of local business hotels. The press pointed, too, to the fact that in the contract with Grand Metropolitan, the Seibu Saison group was referred to simply as the Saison Group. The name Seibu had disappeared.[11] It seemed that Seiji had cut the last link with the empire his father had built. The question was whether he had been so blinded by his urge to outdo his brother that he had brought his own empire to the brink of ruin.

Within the group the takeover caused a furor. People who have now left the company allege that the decision was made by Seiji and Yuji alone, without consulting the other directors of the group, who had been out of the country when the purchase was made, attending a meeting in Chicago with Sears Roebuck. On their return Seiji presented them with a *fait accompli*. He had had to keep the negotiations secret because of the nature of the purchase, he said. He then explained why he had made the purchase and what his plans were.

In fact there were excellent reasons for the takeover of the Inter-Continentals. The retail boom was over, and Seiji had already made the decision to move into the leisure industry. Many other Japanese companies were entering the global market. As he said in an interview, "We are in the hotel business and our customers are travelers. Travelers need hotels wherever they go, be it London or Stockholm. . . . A global hotel chain was necessary for our group to promote its hotel business."[12] The hotels would also give the group a series of bases worldwide from which to carry out its trading operations.

A company insider who is close to Seiji added a more personal note. Yasujiro had wanted to build not merely the best hotel in the country but the best hotel chain. The Prince chain was far from that. Seiji wanted to fulfill his father's dream. "We didn't have the funds to build it—so we went out and bought a chain," said the insider.

As for the price, it seemed that even there Seiji had not been as reckless as everyone had initially thought. Certainly the price was steep. But there had been other groups who bid higher still, though in the end they were unable to raise the capital.[13] In at least one case—a bid by Scandinavian Airline Systems (SAS) and a Canadian real estate company—Grand Metropolitan rejected the offer because they feared that the bidders would dissect the chain and sell off the hotels individually.[14]

The real question was whether a minnow had tried to swallow a whale. At one bound the Saison group had vastly increased its size and scope. But did it have the resources to pay for it?

Seiji had established a company called Saison Holdings, with Yuji as chairman, to deal with overseas investments. From the companies within the Saison Group, Saison Holdings raised a total of $750 million; $1.4 billion remained to be found. This was provided by a consortium of Japanese banks led by Daiichi Kangyo, Seiji's main bankers. There was one condition. The loan was to be repaid within two years, by December 1990.

The transaction had barely been completed before Saison Holdings was in need of more money. There were old hotels in the chain with facilities in need of repair. The information system had to be updated, and Seiji was eager to embark on a program of further expansion. The Inter-Continentals were weighted toward Europe and America. They needed more hotels in southeast Asia to cater to Japanese tourists.

Many people advised caution. It was beginning to seem as if the boom in property prices had peaked. The most sensible course, rather than establishing new hotels, would be to sell off sections of the chain. Seiji was not to be convinced by such doomsaying.[15] He had always chosen the most aggressive and positive path. And up to now his daring and ambition had always paid off—or nearly always.

So Saison went back to the banks and negotiated an extra loan of $200 million with an extension of the repayment date to five years. They also turned to SAS, which in April 1989 bought a 40 percent stake in the hotels for $500 million. And with the extra $700 million, within a short time the Inter-Continental Hotel chain had grown from 98 to 110 hotels.

It was around this time that observers began to notice a growing malaise in the group. Over in Seibu department store a group of ten young people were engaged in cultural promotions. One was a young man named Kunihiko Yoshimeki. With a budget of $5 million and complete freedom to spend it, he was in charge of organizing the launch of a new line of products called Tokyo Creative, commissioned from the country's leading designers. He planned events in venues all over Tokyo. There was performance art in a warehouse in one corner of the city, an exhibition of work by the country's leading avant-garde artists in a gallery in Seibu Shibuya and a spectacular multimedia event occupying a large section of the Yurakucho Seibu.

As it had for many people, Seibu had given him his break and far greater opportunities than he could have had in any other company in Japan. But from the beginning he had reservations about the way the company was run. The cultural activities that he organized seldom seemed to make a profit. The writers and artists were paid; but Seibu often made a loss. Despite Yoshimeki's prompting, Seibu never even kept artistic rights.

By 1988 everyone was beginning to suspect that Seibu might soon be in financial trouble. The head of Yoshimeki's department quietly advised him and his colleagues that it might be sensible to look for another job. In the end eight out of the ten members of the group left. Seibu had been such a treasure-house of talent that the great advertising houses Dentsu and Hakuhodo were waiting to snap them up.

Yoshimeki remains a great admirer of Seiji. But there were others whose exit was less graceful. One was Tokuya Nagai, the ebullient ex-manager of the Waldorf Towers, whom Seiji had recruited to manage the Seiyo Ginza Hotel.

It is not at all clear why Nagai was asked to leave. According to Seiji's supporters, it was an example of Seiji's ability to be as tough as any Western manager and to sack senior executives whom he found to be inefficient. He had made a huge investment in the Seiyo, and it had not produced the returns he was expecting. Nagai's story is rather different. There were, it seems, many areas in which he clashed with Yuji, his immediate superior. He had grave misgivings about the purchase of the Inter-Continentals; he tried to convince Seiji that they were not a highly rated chain. He was unhappy at the prospect that the Seiyo would be the flagship for the chain. He wanted it to remain independent. And no doubt his brash Americanized confidence made it difficult for him to behave with the deference which, in the long run, Seiji expected.

For all his brilliance at tracking down the right man for the job, there was a fatal flaw in Seiji's headhunting skills. Unlike Yoshiaki (whose dictum was "I don't need men with a fancy college education, I need people who do what I say"), he unerringly selected people who were at the very top of their field; but such people by definition had minds of their own. In many cases, it seemed, there came a point where Seiji began to feel that they were challenging his authority. Dark stories began to surface about the autocratic way in which Seiji ran his business.

Within the company Seiji was the voice of God. It was his company. No matter how much it grew, it remained his private concern, the vehicle of his inspiration. Someone who later left the company recalled the first time that he ever participated in a meeting with Seiji. He had been looking forward to a discussion of policy. There was a long table down the center of the room, he remembered. Lined up around the table were the top directors of the company. Mr. Tsutsumi was always ten to fifteen minutes late. Until he arrived there was casual chat. When he came in and took his seat, the atmosphere became hushed and formal.

One of the directors had a presentation to make. Then Seiji called for comments. Mr. A, whose area was in no way connected with the topic under discussion, apologized and said that he would have to do some research before he could say anything.

Seiji thrust a finger at him imperiously. "Do better, A!" he shouted. *"Baka!* Idiot!"

"When you meet Mr. A outside the conference room, you bow," said the ex-employee. "He's one of the managing directors of the company. But inside the conference room, he was just a schoolchild. Mr. Tsutsumi was like a teacher! . . . I expected real discussion. What I saw was ceremony—just Mr. Tsutsumi's one-man accusation play. I was very, very disappointed."

On another occasion, a new Seibu department store was at the last stages of planning. There was one section of the ground floor that it had been very difficult to fill. Various restaurants and stores had been approached to set up a shop there, but all refused. Finally the planners contacted a Chinese restaurant that had had a branch in the Ikebukuro store for years; almost as a favor the restaurant agreed to set up a stall in this unpopular corner.

At the last meeting before the store opened, Seiji was enraged. "Who decided to put a low-grade Chinese restaurant here? Change it!"

The directors explained unhappily that it was too late. There was no time to make major changes.

"Who was responsible for this?" Seiji bellowed.

For five long uncomfortable minutes there was silence. Finally Mr. B said, "I am responsible for this plan." In fact he was not responsible, but as the most senior person present he felt obliged to take the responsibility.

"Stand up!" yelled Seiji. "Stand over there!"

For the rest of the meeting, Mr. B stood at the side like a naughty schoolchild. Seiji had one last word for him.

"Who do you think gave you the chance to work as top management? You owe me for becoming promoted to managing director at Seibu department store. I promoted you!"

Shortly afterward, after twenty-five years of service, Mr. B left.

The ex-employee left too. In fact, he says, "Then everybody left Mr. Tsutsumi!"

Toward the end of the decade, even Seiji was becoming aware of the disadvantages of his management style. His closest associates agree that he "had that top person's disease," and friends of his remark that he knew perfectly well he was a tyrant—unlike Yoshiaki, who was a tyrant without even realizing it. His supporters, however, are quick to assert that although there were those who left the company, many remained until the end of their careers, and some of those who were sacked were incompetent or had some fatal flaw.

The problem was that the Saison Group was inseparable from Seiji Tsutsumi. In meetings Seiji gave up throwing ashtrays and banging desks, but the managing directors still tried to work out what he thought and what he wanted. Meetings were still not so much meetings as announcements from God. The group stood or fell by Seiji. If he made a mistake, the whole group suffered.

"It's impossible to control so many companies," said Seiji in an interview in 1990. "The Saison Group is made up of twelve independent core companies with twenty or thirty subsidiaries. Whenever something happens in those companies, the newspapers always write, 'The Saison Group and its representative Seiji Tsutsumi . . .' So my name is always coming up on bad as well as on good occasions."

For some time Seiji had been talking about retirement. The Saison group represented his vision, but in the last few years it had grown so rapidly that it was difficult for one man to control it. Maybe the time for vision had passed. Maybe it was time to step down and allow more prosaic men to take over.

The Emperor
Yoshiaki's Story 1984–1991

My father, the founder, always said, "Do something for the world," "Do something no one has done before." I'd like to go back to the beginning and try again, in that spirit. I've followed my father's teaching faithfully for twenty years, ever since he died—but then, before I realized it, I'd gone against it. If my father were alive he'd say to me, "In the matter of the Olympics you struck without thinking, you pitched in too far."
YOSHIAKI TSUTSUMI
In Taniguchi, *Yoshiaki Tsutsumi and the Olympics*

While Seiji briskly returned to work and set about organizing a Christmas party at the bright new Seibu in the Ginza after the mothers died, Yoshiaki mourned his mother for months. In an interview in January 1985, a few weeks after her death, he appeared in a softened, chastened mood.

Last year was a bad year because my mother died. . . . For several days after Mum died I felt completely cut off from my work; I had time to think. At that time I felt very keenly, "from now on I have to try to be like Mum, to try as hard as I can to be a better human being." Right now is an important turning point for me. I thought I have to develop human virtue and decide whether to carry on being harsh, as I used to be, or to be more easygoing.[1]

Around the same time a journalist named Shigeki Manabe spent two weeks with Yoshiaki. His plan was to observe the great man in action, to follow him wherever he went and record whatever he did or said.

On the first day he met up with him at the Prince Hotel in Manza, in mountain country not far from Karuizawa. Yoshiaki was standing at a table, examining a large plan. He looked up when Manabe came in.

"*Yaa, irasshai,*" he exclaimed, his voice as always surprisingly high-pitched for such a burly man. "Welcome!" His next words were "I'm still in shock from my mother's death. I'm working, but my heart's still in mourning." For a moment, writes Manabe, he looked very sad.

Manabe was instantly won over. Such openness—and to someone who was not just a complete stranger but a prying journalist.

The next day, well before dawn, the phone rang in Manabe's room in the hotel. It was Yoshiaki.

"I'm going to the bath," he said. "Want to come?"

Rubbing the sleep out of his eyes, Manabe grabbed his *yukata,* his bathrobe, and rushed out of his room and down the steps. It was an outdoor bath, a natural hot spring set in the rocks at the bottom of the valley, below the hotel.

In the changing room he met Yoshiaki.

"Let's go," said the great man. "Watch out—the stones are slippery!"

One behind the other, naked except for a tiny towel, they stepped out into the freezing December dawn. The icy rain stung their bare shoulders like needles. Padding along, shivering behind the master of the Seibu empire, his breath turning to steam, Manabe admired his broad shoulders and well-muscled back. The man was pushing forty, but there was not an ounce of spare flesh on him.

Later, relaxing in the steaming water, they gazed at the view. The sky had cleared by now, though there was still mist rising like smoke from the crevices in the hills.

"Too bad," said Yoshiaki, examining the sky. "Looks like the snow's going to be late this year. But it might snow today. I hope so."

At that moment, writes Manabe, he didn't seem at all like the chairman of a large and powerful group of companies. He was just an ordinary guy, a keen skier, like everyone else.[2]

By then it was difficult to imagine that Yoshiaki was just an ordinary man. People wrote of his legendary skills as a manager and even more of his legendary assets. He—or at least his company—was said to own one sixth of all the land in Japan, and to have assets equivalent to the entire national budget.

Kokudo Keikaku, the core company of the group, housed in its spacious offices overlooking the Meiji Shrine in Harajuku, was—and is—a "black hole," an accounting mystery. Very few of Yoshiaki's companies were listed. After all, he had no need to list his companies in order to drum up funds from shareholders. He could borrow as much money as he could ever need from the banks with his lands as security. In 1985, in a very sympathetic article, the *Shukan Asahi* magazine estimated "from financial data from financing companies" that the total land assets of Yoshiaki's companies exceeded ¥10 trillion (about $42 billion) in value. In comparison, Seibu's ancient rival, Goto's Tokyu Group, had land assets worth a tenth of that, a mere ¥1 trillion ($4.2 billion). Mitsubishi Real Estate had slightly more, while Mitsui Real Estate had lands valued at only ¥200 billion ($837 million).[3]

Such assets equaled power. From time to time articles appeared suggesting that if Yoshiaki were to enter politics, he could easily become prime minister. But he was already fifty, it was getting late. And he had still made no sign that he wanted the post. Perhaps, as one Tsutsumi-watcher suggests, he had concluded, quite accurately, that to enter politics costs a great deal of money and that politicians have little real power. Perhaps he had decided that he was better off wielding power from the sidelines.

But there was another factor involved: Yasuhiro Nakasone.

Nakasone became prime minister in 1982. In many ways he was the exact antithesis of Kakuei Tanaka, though in order to gain the position he had had to make an alliance with the great power broker. Where Tanaka was a self-made man and a rabble rouser, perpetually wiping sweat from his round shiny face, Nakasone was a gentleman, cool and aristocratic. For a couple of years Nakasone held on to power by delicately manipulating the various factions within the Liberal Democratic Party. Then came a couple of blows that knocked Tanaka out of the picture. The first was the verdict in the Lockheed trial. In October 1983 Tanaka was found guilty of receiving bribes and sentenced to four years in prison (though he was immediately freed on bail pending appeal). Then, in 1986, he suffered a severe stroke. The rambunctious godfather figure who had dominated the political scene for more than ten years was reduced to a mumbling old man in a wheelchair.

Tanaka had been a friend and mentor to both the Tsutsumi brothers. Nakasone was somewhat outside the mainstream of factional infighting. He held on to power largely for a reason that had never had much import in Japanese politics before: he was enormously popular with the electorate. Tall, statesmanlike, he could communicate on equal terms with the world's leaders. Famously, he was on "Ron-Yasu" terms with President Reagan. And when it came to photo sessions at summit meetings, instead of being bustled ignominiously to the end of the line, as previous Japanese prime ministers had been, he stood in the middle, next to Reagan.

Yoshiaki had always been careful to keep on good terms with the leaders of all the different factions. Nearly everyone, no matter what their political color, held their fund-raising parties and political conferences at the Prince hotels. There was just one political figure with whom Yoshiaki did not see eye to eye: Nakasone. Of course all these alliances and hostilities remained well below the surface. Still, it is perhaps clear that in the early eighties the climate was not really conducive to Yoshiaki's entering politics.

Instead he concentrated on building up his business empire. By 1985 there were twenty-seven splendid Prince hotels—most of them sparkling new multistory towers—twenty-two other inns and hotels, twenty-four golf courses and nineteen ski resorts.

Ten years before, Yoshiaki had said that when he finished the building program he was engaged in then, he would enter politics. In fact, of course, he never really finished. By the time one batch of building projects was completed, new ones had come up.

Yoshiaki was very meticulous about which projects he accepted and which he turned down. He insisted that the local populace must all unanimously request Seibu's presence before he would agree to start work in the area. And if the local officers approached any other developers, Yoshiaki would reject their application.[4] It was all completely proper and aboveboard. Seibu never began developing any particular area without the invitation of the local governors. Yet the net result was that every year the Seibu empire grew inexorably larger. The pink patches covered more and more of the map of Japan.

Sometimes Seibu was invited to buy land that was not available to anyone else. One case that attracted some controversy was that of the Takaragaike Prince Hotel in Kyoto.

Yasujiro, the old peasant from Shiga, had always harbored a yearning to expand his business to Kyoto. From Shiga, in the Japanese heartland, you could gaze across the shimmering waters of Lake Biwa and imagine the temples and palaces of the ancient capital on the opposite shore. For the merchants of Shiga, the ultimate stamp of success had always been to storm the aristocratic old capital, to set up business in Kyoto.

It was one ambition that Yasujiro never achieved. His landholdings were all in Tokyo and the northern half of the country. No doubt Yoshiaki, the dutiful son and heir, wanted to fulfill his father's last wish. It also made sense to begin to expand his territory into central and southern Japan.

In 1983 the decision was made to hold the next economic summit, in 1986, in Japan. The Kyoto city elders—the Kyoto Chamber of Commerce and the city's business leaders—very much wanted it to be held in their city. Admittedly Tokyo was the government and business capital of the country, but Kyoto had been the capital for a thousand years, and it was still the spiritual capital and home to everything that people thought of as Japanese. In order to offer a viable alternative to Tokyo, they had to have a conference center and a luxury hotel, suitable to house the leaders of the world's most powerful countries. But the Kyoto conference center was located in the foothills to the north, far from the city center. There were no suitable hotels anywhere nearby.

There was, however, plenty of land—rolling forest-covered hills dense with birds and shrilling cicadas. It was a national park, owned by the city and designated a protected zone, and not available for sale or development. Clearly this was an appropriate time to waive the regulations and to invite the country's leading developer to build a deluxe hotel. Furthermore, the city elders were well aware that on their own they had little chance of persuading the government to hold the summit in their city. If they were to ally themselves with Yoshiaki's renowned political clout, they would greatly increase their chances.

It is not entirely clear whether the city elders approached Yoshiaki or whether there were some overtures from his side. In any case, the end result was that he was able to buy 8,400 *tsubo* (7 acres) of fine woodland in the Takaragaike area, close to the Kyoto International

Conference Center. The average price of land in that area was ¥1 million ($4,200) per *tsubo*. Kyoto City sold the 8,400 *tsubo* to him for a mere ¥290,000 ($1,220) per tsubo, a third of the price.[5]

From Yoshiaki's viewpoint it was certainly a bargain, though there are some who allege that the deal was in no way unusual. Yoshiaki by now had such powerful connections, say these sources, that Seibu was routinely able to buy normally unavailable government land at vastly discounted prices.[6]

Work on the new Prince hotel began in August 1984. Seibu employed one of the country's top architects, Togo Murano. He designed a doughnut-shaped hotel with a central courtyard. The conference halls were on the ground floor and there were seven floors above. But Nakasone had still not decided where the summit was to be held. Yoshiaki, it is said, went to see him and asked him unequivocally to hold it in Kyoto. Nakasone refused to commit himself. Then, at the last minute, he announced that the 1986 economic summit would be held in Tokyo. It was almost a deliberate slight. It seemed that so long as Nakasone remained in power, Yoshiaki's famous political clout would be blunted.

Although Yoshiaki had failed to get the summit to Kyoto, the episode was not a total failure. He was the owner of a tract of valuable land in the middle of a national park, and there was now a Prince Hotel in Kyoto.

As a prime minister, Nakasone cut an impressive figure. Under his leadership Japan became a major player on the world stage, operating on equal terms with the Western powers. Even in the delicate matter of trade, he managed to create a good relationship with the United States. Then, just as his statutory two two-year terms in office were coming to an end, he called a general election. The LDP had a landslide victory and he was given an extra year in office.

Still, he could not remain prime minister forever. Noboru Takeshita, Shintaro Abe and Kiichi Miyazawa, respectively, headed the three strongest political factions. Of the three, Takeshita and Abe were political strongmen of the old school and formed a natural alliance. Takeshita, short and unprepossessing with a large head and cheerful smile, had taken over the largest faction from the old power broker Kakuei Tanaka and therefore had the greatest number of supporters behind him. Abe, taller and bespectacled, was said to be closest to Yoshiaki. As for Miyazawa, he was far more of an intellectual, a liberal and progressive thinker. In the tradition of Nakasone, he had specific policies to offer on national and international matters. Unsurprisingly he was a political long shot. Also unsurprisingly, he was a friend of Seiji. The two had met many years before, when Seiji was acting as Yasujiro's secretary in the Diet and Miyazawa was a young up-and-coming Dietman. They remained close friends, and Seiji supported and participated in many of Miyazawa's projects.

Miyazawa very seldom met up with the other two "new leaders." One occasion was Tsuneko's funeral. Another was in 1984, when Yoshiaki invited all three to a game of golf at his course in O-Hakone.

In Japan politics is a matter of Byzantine intrigue. Decisions are almost invariably made behind closed doors. As a result, journalists spend much of their time constructing elaborate theories out of whatever tiny scraps of information may emerge. When two politicians are seen together, that may signify an alliance. As for golf, no one ever plays golf simply for recreation. A game of golf is always an opportunity for networking, negotiating or shifting allegiances.

As far as the press was concerned, it was a major coup for Yoshiaki to bring the three rival contenders together. The function of the game must surely have been to mediate between the three, they surmised. It also showed that, even in the Nakasone era, Yoshiaki still had unequaled power.[7]

Yoshiaki himself denied any such analysis. In an interview with Shigeki Manabe—the same Manabe who had shared a bath with him a few years before—he said that the aim of the game was just "to improve everyone's relationship." For people in the business world, he went on, it made little difference who became prime minister. That was a matter for the politicians.

> The politicians' method is, they each make their own factions, then try and make their leader prime minister. That's natural, but from our point of view, it really doesn't matter much who the prime minister is. So it's unlikely that people in the business world will poke their noses in much, it's not necessary. Again, we don't have much power and if we try and wield influence it'll look bad in others' eyes;

no one's stupid enough to do something like that. But there must be a few people who try and make it look like that, because they want to show off their power.[8]

Yoshiaki, for one, had no need to show off his power. As a Japanese businessman of the most traditional variety, he understood perfectly the need to maintain a harmonious surface, to say the proper thing at the proper time. The press would not have expected him to do otherwise.

The more Yoshiaki's empire grew, the closer the press followed his every move. While Seiji skillfully cultivated the journalistic world, doing his best to ensure that he was portrayed as a mild-mannered man of literature—he was, after all, building a business in which image played a crucial part—Yoshiaki was a man in his father's mold. He wanted to get on with his business. He didn't like the prying eyes of journalists, and he made no attempt to conceal the fact. He agreed to interviews as seldom as possible. But the more he shied away from public view, the more he fueled the speculation and suspicions of the press. As a result he quickly gained a reputation for supreme arrogance. As one highly respected figure in the journalistic world put it, "He's a very, very arrogant man. Men are unhappy when they're with Mr. Yoshiaki!"

While the serious press restricted themselves to reports and interviews on business matters and analyses of his entrepreneurial genius, the gutter press imposed no such limitations on themselves. In Japan the weekly and monthly magazines are packed with all the stories that the serious press felt it was inappropriate for the public to know, leavened with a good-sized dose of scurrilous supposition, rumor, scandal and sheer invention.

The serious papers, on the other hand, are so anxious not to offend the powers that be that they turn a blind eye on anything remotely questionable. Many stories appear only in the gutter press simply because serious journalists are afraid to dirty their fingers.

In 1987 Nakasone's term of office finally came to an end. According to the Japanese system, it was up to the faction leaders—each of whom was the representative of a block of Dietmen who in turn represented the electorate—to decide who would succeed him. Accordingly, the months before Nakasone's resignation were full of secret meetings and rumors of alliances, counteralliances and cutthroat treachery as the three prime-ministerial hopefuls—Takeshita, who headed the largest faction, Yoshiaki's favorite Abe and Seiji's friend Miyazawa—battled it out.

One of the most persistent rumors was of the involvement of the Tsutsumi brothers in the selection process. The first to intervene was Seiji. He offered his own home as the venue for a secret meeting between Miyazawa and Abe. If the two were to form an alliance, they might be able to muster more votes and therefore more power than Takeshita.

Until then Yoshiaki had kept his distance. He had been careful to show equal favor to all three candidates. Rumor has it that it was Seiji's involvement that drove him to show his hand.

What happened next is pure speculation. Yoshiaki and his spokesman have always denied it. The story goes as follows.

By October 19 the situation was critical. The contenders would have to come to an agreement within a few hours. That morning all three met in a room in Yoshiaki's Akasaka Prince Hotel. Then, around noon, Miyazawa left and Abe and Takeshita continued their negotiations.

Meanwhile their aides waited impatiently in the adjoining room. Suddenly the phone rang there. Keizo Obuchi—who has since become very prominent in Japanese politics and had been close to Yoshiaki since he was his junior in their Waseda University days together—took the call.

The caller was Yoshiaki. He had inside information, he said. If Abe and Takeshita could not decide which of the two should be prime minister, it would be left in the hands of Nakasone. And in that case, Nakasone would undoubtedly choose Miyazawa. According to the story Yoshiaki added the words, "I'll bet all my assets on that!"

Obuchi relayed the information to the two candidates. What aroused their suspicion and makes the story less credible is that Yoshiaki would surely have been the last person to know what Nakasone was thinking.

The information was false. Some people say that Nakasone intended to back Abe, others that he intended to back Takeshita. Certainly as Yoshiaki well knew, he had no intention of backing Miyazawa. The effect of the rumor, which Yoshiaki allegedly put about, was to scare Abe and Takeshita into coming to an agreement. It neatly destroyed the perilous alliance that Seiji had been trying to set up between Abe and Miyazawa. Indeed, it had as much to do with the hostility between the two brothers as with the political process.[9]

Most important, it was also a way of indicating that although Yoshiaki was closest to Abe, on this occasion, in order to keep Miyazawa out, he was willing to throw his considerable political weight behind Takeshita, the more powerful of the two.

Whether or not the story of the telephone call is true, the candidates quickly reached agreement. Nakasone officially made his choice: Noboru Takeshita. It was an obvious one. Takeshita was the head of the largest faction. There are those who say that it was precisely because Yoshiaki had indicated that he would back Takeshita that he got the job.

Yoshiaki has always maintained that the whole story is patently absurd. "I couldn't have bet all my assets," he said to the journalist Shigeki Manabe. "You have to have someone to bet with." As to the telephone call, "maybe you should check with NTT [the Japanese equivalent of AT&T]!"[10]

More seriously, in another interview he commented:

My relationships with [the "new leaders"] are broad and shallow. If they were narrow and deep, we would put too many demands and expectations upon each other. Business and government are two very different entities, and business people should meet government people only in a private capacity independent of their business activities. At present the political and business communities are too close.[11]

The most piquant part of the story, the part that everyone remembered, was Yoshiaki's offer to bet all his assets. For by then people were well aware that his assets were far, far greater than anyone had ever suspected. In June that same year, 1987, *Forbes* magazine had published its annual list of the world's billionaires. For the first time ever *Forbes* found more dollar billionaires in Japan than in the United States, twenty-two in all. Heading the list, with an estimated personal fortune of $21 billion (equivalent to the gross domestic product of Israel) was the world's wealthiest man: Yoshiaki Tsutsumi.

Thrust unwillingly into the limelight, Yoshiaki professed himself amazed with *Forbes*'s findings. "I have no comment to make on that dollar figure" was all he would say. Analysts were quick to point out that the figures were tempered by many factors. Most of Yoshiaki's supposed fortune was based on the landholdings of his companies—and everyone knew that the price of land in Japan was still rising. Another tempering factor was the volatile Japanese stock market. Lastly, the yen had recently doubled its value in dollar terms. But even taking all those factors into account, if *Forbes*'s calculations were correct Yoshiaki was still several times wealthier than the richest American, Sam Moore Walton, a relative pauper with a mere $4.5 billion in assets.

In order to arrive at their conclusion, *Forbes* had had to probe deep into the black hole that was Kokudo Keikaku's accounts. They began with the assets, mainly landholdings, of all the different companies that made up Yoshiaki's empire, and assigned a value to the land based on current market prices. Then they investigated what percentage of each company was held by Kokudo Keikaku, the core company of the group. It was known that Yoshiaki owned 40 percent of Kokudo Keikaku, so from this they could work out the value of his assets.

It was, said the company spokesman, all nonsense. It was the company that was rich, not Yoshiaki. He just received a salary. And besides, the whole complicated edifice of calculations was based on the value of land. Once this fell, so would Yoshiaki's supposed fortune.

One question that *Forbes*'s investigations left unanswered was: Who owned the remaining 60 percent of Kokudo Keikaku? There were rumors that Yoshiaki owned this, too—which would take the value of his assets into astronomical figures.

There was another anomaly that came to light once the spotlight was turned on Yoshiaki and his businesses. It seemed that the company owned by the richest man in the world paid no corporate taxes.

In an article published the previous year, two Japanese journalists had analyzed Kokudo Keikaku's accounts. Each year the company had a good-sized operating income. In 1986 it was ¥4.5 billion (nearly $13 million). But it was a healthy, growing company, so, rather than using its income to invest in new landholdings, hotels, golf courses and ski resorts, it borrowed large amounts of money from the banks. Once depreciation of assets had been taken into account, plus interest repayments of debts, the company's taxable profits each year came very neatly to zero. While listed companies had to produce a profit to satisfy their shareholders, Kokudo was unlisted and could afford to keep its profits tiny. "This," said an analyst, "is a company that is trying to erase its profit, not trying to make a profit!"[12]

It was all perfectly aboveboard, a matter of clever accounting. But to the public it didn't look good.

Company spokesmen argued that as an expanding business they were bound to be in the red. It was not a matter of deliberate policy. Besides, although they didn't pay corporate tax they paid other taxes—local taxes, for example.

Of course Yoshiaki paid taxes on his private income. In 1986 he paid a not inconsiderable ¥218 million ($1,290,000 at the exchange rate of the time), which implied that his income was a little less than double that.[13]

One mystery was how he spent it. Traditionally in Japan there are two areas in which men spend their wealth. One is political influence. The other is women. According to an old Japanese saying, "All great men are also great lovers." Yoshiaki was no exception. However, unlike his father, he did all he could to keep his indiscretions as far as possible from the vulgar eyes of the press.

If Yoshiaki saw his women as anything other than recreation, he never communicated that to anyone else. One of his closest friends compared him to a butterfly, flitting from flower to flower. "I tease him about it," he said. As Yoshiaki grew more and more wealthy and powerful his name became linked with some of the country's most beautiful and adored actresses. But there are no stories of mad obsessions or grand passions. If there was a great love in his life, he kept it very secret.

The one area in his life where Yoshiaki was driven by passion was sport. He loved skiing and golf. Whenever he had the time, he tried out the new ski slopes in his resorts and designed golf courses himself. He followed the fortunes of the Seibu ice-hockey team closely; in fact, he more than anyone else had been responsible for making ice hockey popular in Japan. And he was the owner of the country's top baseball team, the unbeatable Lions.

By the late eighties, a quarter of a century since he became the master of the Seibu empire, Yoshiaki had established a formidable power base in the world of sport. He was the chairman of the skiing and skating federations, vice president of the Japan Amateur Sports Association and member of the Japanese Olympics Committee (JOC). He was rumored to be the most influential person in Japanese sport.

At the time Japanese sport was in crisis. Ever since the great Tokyo Olympics of 1964, the standards of athletics had been declining. In 1988, at the Seoul Olympics, Japan took just four golds and a miserable fourteen medals in all, while among Japan's Asian competitors, South Korea took thirty-three medals and China twenty-eight. In every other area Japan seemed unbeatable: the economy was booming, incomes were rising. Only in sport, it seemed, was the country lagging behind. The results of the Olympics were a great blow to national pride.

That same year the JOC met to pick their candidate city for the 1998 Winter Olympics. The choice was Nagano, a small, sleepy town deep in the Japan Alps, an hour up the line from Karuizawa, where Yasujiro had laid the foundations for his empire.

The sporting world had two key tasks. One was to raise the level of sport in Japan and in particular to raise the standards of Japanese athletics. The other was to do everything possible to ensure that the Winter Olympics of 1998 went to Nagano. What was needed was a powerful leader, someone with the ability to raise the necessary funds and the strength and charisma to turn a group of losing athletes into a winning team. The choice was obvious: the man who owned and ruled over one of the country's most efficient business enterprises, whose baseball team won the pennant practically every year without fail and who was in 1988, for the second year running, listed in *Forbes* magazine as the richest man in the world.

Initially Yoshiaki turned down the job. He had, he said, his own business to run, and he had no time to take on an extra position.[14] At the time the JOC was part of the Japan Amateur Sports Association. It was essential to make it into a separate foundation free to control its own fund-raising and training program. Thanks at least in part to Yoshiaki's powerful political and business connections, in July 1989 the JOC was recognized as an independent body. Even before the process was completed, Yoshiaki was unanimously voted in as chairman.

From the beginning he ran the JOC as if it were one of his own companies. He barked orders, he chose personnel. He had succeeded in transforming the Lions because he had treated baseball as a business. Now he intended to do with same with the JOC. In interviews, he said that the JOC's aim was "to win as many medals as possible in the Olympics."[15] That meant improving the performances of the athletes, and for that he needed a far larger budget—multiplied by ten, from ¥2.3 billion ($16.7 million) a year to ¥20 billion ($145 million). Now that the JOC was independent, many businesses that wished to contribute would be able to do so. As a start he installed leaders of the business community as trustees of the JOC and set up negotiations with competing advertising companies.

A few months after he took on his new duties as chairman of the JOC, Yoshiaki had a visitor. Juan Antonio Samaranch, president of the International Olympic Committee (IOC), had presided over the transformation of the Olympics from an idealistic but bankrupt festival of sport into an enormously profitable business venture. The shrewd, gnomelike seventy-year-old Spaniard was eager to meet the legendary and reclusive Japanese tycoon, who was said to be the richest man in the world. Moreover, there was business to discuss. One of the Japanese IOC members had retired and the IOC had asked the JOC to propose some candidates to take over his post, but the matter had not yet been decided.

The richest man in the world prepared an appropriate welcome for the most powerful man in sport. Yoshiaki hosted a magnificent reception in the banqueting hall at the New Takanawa Prince Hotel, built on land that had once been the gracious estates of Prince Kitashirakawa.

Later, in a small tea-ceremony room in the grounds, four people met: the grand master of the Urasenke school, Soshitsu Sen, who conducted the ceremony and passed round bowls of foaming green tea, and three guests—Yoshiaki, Samaranch and Yoshiaki's personal interpreter. In his book *Yoshiaki Tsutsumi and the Olympics,* sports journalist Gentaro Taniguchi reports the gist of the conversation.

Samaranch, he writes, suggested that Yoshiaki himself should take on the job of IOC member. One of the rules of the IOC was that members should be able to speak English. On this count Yoshiaki failed, but Samaranch was prepared to waive the rule and accept Yoshiaki together with his interpreter. The IOC was, after all, Taniguchi comments, a club of the rich and well-born, and who better to join it than the world's richest man? Yoshiaki declined. The JOC had already proposed Shun-ichiro Okano, he said, and he had his support.

Many Japanese observers, watching Yoshiaki's progress through the world of sport, predicted that in the future he could rise to be president of the IOC. That, they whispered, was the prize that he was after.

The first hurdle was to ensure that Nagano was awarded the Winter Olympics of 1998. Nagano was a small, dingy, old-fashioned town three hours by train from Tokyo. While its nearest neighbor, Matsumoto, boasted a glorious castle surrounded by a lily-covered moat and streets ablaze with neon signs, Nagano was dark and quiet. Pilgrims went to visit the ancient temple, Zenkoji, but apart from that it had little to recommend it. Neighboring Niigata, which had been the constituency of the old power broker Kakuei Tanaka, had a bullet train and motorway connecting it with Tokyo (including an enormous bullet-train station for the tiny village where Tanaka was born). Nagano had neither. It was an inconvenient, inaccessible place.

It was, however, surrounded by some of the grandest and most spectacular mountains in Japan, the Japan Alps, making it the perfect place for a network of ski resorts. Yoshiaki had begun to buy up land and develop the area several years before. One of the cornerstones of his empire, Karuizawa, was only an hour down the line. The logical place to develop was the Shiga Highlands, mile upon mile of gorse-covered plateau and rugged peaks more or less between Karuizawa and Nagano. There he built large modern hotels in the valleys and shaved the hillsides of trees to make ski runs.

Another developer too had a special interest in Nagano. More than a hundred years before, Yasujiro's hated enemy Keita Goto had been born in a small farming village not far from the city. So the Tokyu Corporation, which he had founded, had also moved into the area. They concentrated on the Hakuba region, at the foot of snow-covered mountains on the other side of Nagano City. There they too built hotels and ski slopes.

Twice before, Nagano had competed to be chosen as Japan's candidate city for the Winter Olympics, but on each occasion it had been beaten. Now finally it had crossed the first hurdle. There were those who whispered that Yoshiaki had used his famous political clout to make sure that Nagano won. But, as his spokesman quite accurately pointed out, Seibu's ski resorts dominated almost all the contending cities. With 70 percent of all the skiing areas in Japan, Seibu could hardly lose, no matter which area was chosen.[16] Apart from that, the rival Tokyu conglomerate had almost as large a stake in Nagano as Seibu and stood to benefit nearly as much.

It was notorious, however, that Nagano and its surrounding skiing grounds were badly served by road and rail. If Nagano became Japan's Olympic candidate, it would force the government to make it a priority in their transport plans. There would have to be a bullet train, motorways, even an airport in place before 1998.

The citizens of Nagano were overjoyed when their city was chosen as Japan's candidate to host the Winter Olympics of 1998. There were hundreds of volunteers to help prepare their bid for the final vote, which would take place at the IOC meeting in Birmingham, in 1991. One small but vociferous group, however, was very strongly opposed to the Olympics. In October 1989, just after Samaranch's visit to Yoshiaki, there was an election for mayor of the city. Besides the incumbent, Mayor Tsukada, who had worked hard to promote Nagano's bid, there was a mystery candidate. Noriko Ezawa, a thirty-year-old local woman, stood on a platform of opposition to the Olympics. If the games came to Nagano, she argued, there would be untold damage to the environment. The unspoiled Nagano mountains would have to be devastated to build new ski slopes, and animals and birds would be driven from their native habitats.

When the votes were counted, Mayor Tsukada had the vast majority: 103,000 out of a total population of 350,000. Noriko Ezawa, however, had a surprising 15,406. More than 10 percent of the turnout had chosen to vote against the Olympics.

The JOC and the Bidding Committee pooh-poohed the objectors, since the overwhelming majority of the electorate supported the Olympic bid. But meanwhile the opponents to the Olympics had discovered an unacceptable development plan. Soaring behind Yoshiaki's ski slopes in the Shiga Highlands were two spectacular unspoiled peaks, Mount Iwasuge and Mount Ura-iwasuge ("behind Iwasuge"). Nagano needed many and varied ski slopes if it was to host the Olympics. In particular, it would be advantageous to plan a "compact Olympics," with all the alpine events taking place in the same area. It made sense to clear the virgin forest on the slopes of one of these mountains to make way for a downhill ski course.

Ezawa, her husband, Masao, and their supporters were incensed. The mountains were a national park. They were home to the Japanese serow, a sort of antelope, and Asiatic black bears. The golden eagle, of which there were only forty pairs left in Japan, lived there. And there were butterflies, dragonflies and many rare varieties of plants. Moreover, there was already a perfectly good downhill ski course in the area. But it happened to be in Happo-one, in the Tokyu-dominated area of Hakuba.

As far as the protesters were concerned, it was perfectly obvious that Tsutsumi's real intention was to concentrate the Olympic developments in his own area, to take advantage of the bid for the games to build up his own resorts. No matter which of the two mountains was chosen, the nearest hotel of Olympic standards was the Shiga Highlands Prince. If everything went ahead as planned, Yoshiaki would end up profiting whether or not Nagano won the Olympics. If he was hoping to stage the Olympics as a corporate moneymaking venture, that would be scandalous.

To mollify the protesters, the Nagano Olympic Bidding Committee established an environmental subcommittee, which produced reports and issued bland statements about how important it was to protect the environment. The Bidding Committee by now had settled on Mount Ura-iwasuge, declaring that there would be less environmental damage there. But the Ezawas were not to be deflected. They took their protest to the World Wildlife Fund of Japan, which in March 1990 submitted a letter to the governor of Nagano Prefecture. The matter would be taken to the international World Wildlife Fund and then to the IOC, it said. If a new course was not chosen, Nagano would have little chance of winning the Olympics.[17]

Earlier that same month, in his capacity as chairman of the JOC, Yoshiaki had presided over his first major sporting event, the Asian Winter Games. One of the first events was the short-track speed skating. As the youthful South Korean winner, thirteen-year-old Kim So Hee, stepped up to the winner's stand, out of the loudspeakers set up around the stadium came the stirring notes of the Mongolian national anthem. Horrified, the officials rushed to change the tape. This time—worse still—it was the North Korean anthem that boomed out across the stadium. It was only at the third try that the correct anthem was played. The days that followed were dogged by a succession of highly embarrassing blunders. The announcers introduced one South Korean athlete as North Korean. Then, in the 10,000-meter speed-skating event on the fourth day, officials signaled to the Japanese competitor that he had one lap to go, when in fact he had two. It all showed an unacceptable lack of preparation.

None of this was directly Yoshiaki's fault, but, as the chairman of the JOC, the final responsibility was his. Together with the mayor of Sapporo, where the games were being held, he had to go to the South Korean embassy to offer humble apologies to the ambassador. It was a few days after this that the letter from the World Wildlife Fund arrived on his desk.

Then came yet another protest. This time it was led by a fiery young man named Kaoru Iwata, an ex-journalist who had settled in Karuizawa and been elected to the town council. His complaint was about a golf course that Seibu was planning in the hills above his house. If a course was built there, he said, the weedkillers and fertilizers would filter down into the water supply of those who lived below and contaminate it. He collected fifteen thousand signatures of local people who were opposed to the course. But Seibu pushed on with its land purchases regardless of the fact that the town had not given its permission. Finally Iwata put in a complaint to the Tokyo District public prosecutor's office, special investigation department.

It was the first time that Yoshiaki had ever found such obstacles in his path. There had been murmurs of complaint before, over the matter of the land for the Takaragaike Prince in the north of Kyoto, for example, but he had always kept strictly on the right side of the law. No one had ever been able to pin anything on him.

There was nothing for it but to back down gracefully. On April 5, two days after Iwata submitted his complaint, in an exclusive interview with the *Asahi* newspaper, Yoshiaki, in his capacity as chairman of both the JOC and the Ski Association of Japan, announced that the JOC had decided not to go ahead with its plans to construct a new downhill course on Mount Ura-iwasuge.

Nagano's bid for the Games could go ahead only with the full support of the people, he said. "When I compared the disadvantages of holding part of the alpine events outside Shiga Heights against the problems in bringing the Winter Olympics to Nagano while there is opposition, I felt that the latter was bigger."[18] He also privately agreed to give up his plan to build a golf course in the area above Iwata's house.

It seemed that the problems had been solved. The matter was ended. But a week later there was an announcement that shook the sporting world. After only nine months in office, Yoshiaki had decided to step down as chairman of the JOC. On the surface the reason for his resignation was to take responsibility for the embarrassing mistakes that had marred the Asian Games. As a man with businesses of his own to run, he had not been able to give the job the time it required. "I'm afraid I have put you to much trouble," he said. "A part-time president, as long as he has other jobs, can serve better by quitting his post. It is better that I hand over the post at an early date."[19]

The press could not fail to notice the timing. The tabloids—the weekly and monthly magazines—ever eager to see the arrogant Tsutsumi humbled, had taken up the Ezawas' and Iwata's cause with great enthusiasm. Even the serious press had begun to question Yoshiaki's true motivation in working for the Olympics. He suffered, as his spokesman put it, "much misunderstanding." The best way to bring the chorus of criticism to an end was to resign.

For the JOC and the people of Nagano it was a blow. Yoshiaki's successor was the one-time Olympic swimming star Hironoshin Furuhashi. But everyone feared that in losing Yoshiaki, with his political strength and his undoubted ability to deal on equal terms with the IOC members, Nagano had lost its chance of hosting the Olympics. Yoshiaki, however, had not withdrawn from the battle: he had simply retreated from the front lines to a position where he felt far more comfortable. Once again he was operating in the shadows. And he still retained his position as honorary chairman of the Nagano Olympic Bidding Committee.

The vote to decide which city would host the Winter Olympics of

1998 was due to take place at the ninety-seventh session of the IOC in Birmingham in June 1991. The two favorites to win the bid for the Winter Olympics were Nagano and Salt Lake City, Utah. Of the two, Nagano had the edge because the Winter Olympics had not been held in Asia for twenty-six years. Besides, the Summer Olympics of 1996 had been allocated to Atlanta. It would not look good for the United States to host two Olympics in a row.

There were, however, huge disadvantages to Nagano's bid. Whereas Salt Lake City already had all the necessary facilities and infrastructure to host an Olympics, Nagano didn't even own the necessary land; if it won the vote, it would need to secure the land to build a stadium, an Olympic village, new ski slopes, skating rinks and a bobsled-luge track. All this would be extremely costly; and uses would have to be found for all the facilities after the games were over. Worse, road and rail connections between Tokyo and Nagano, and between Nagano and the nearby areas where the Olympics would be held, were very poor. And there was not a single hotel in the city that was up to international standards.

Nagano's answer to all this was simple. Whatever was needed, they would build it. They had the enthusiasm of their citizens and the booming Japanese economy behind them. In fact, long before the vote was taken, work began on Olympic highways to link Nagano to Shiga Highlands and the Tokyu-dominated resort of Hakuba.

In May, a month before the crucial meeting in Birmingham, the IOC president, Juan Antonio Samaranch, arrived in Japan to see the World Table-Tennis Championships. There he attended a grand reception to celebrate the full independence of the JOC from the Amateur Sports Association, held at the New Takanawa Prince Hotel. During the celebrations he presented the party's host and his new friend Yoshiaki Tsutsumi with the Gold Olympic Order. The IOC explained that Yoshiaki had given exceptional service to the Olympic movement. But there were many who questioned what exactly he had done to deserve such an honor.

Two days later, on the invitation of the mayor and governor of Nagano, Samaranch set off on a special chartered three-coach train for the mountain city. According to one source, it was a splendid old upholstered imperial train.[20] According to another, it cost the city of Nagano ¥2.4 million (nearly $18,000).[21]

Three people accompanied him on his journey: the mayor, the governor and Yoshiaki Tsutsumi.

No one knows what was discussed on the train. According to the old-hand sports journalist Taniguchi, with his vaunted access to inside information, Yoshiaki and Samaranch had a private conversation through Yoshiaki's interpreter. Samaranch had two proposals to make. He asked the richest man in the world to contribute to the Olympic Museum, which Samaranch was planning to build in Lausanne, Switzerland. The sum he suggested, according to Taniguchi, was $13 million. Yoshiaki reportedly was willing to cooperate and agreed to do what he could to persuade Japanese corporations too to contribute. The IOC president also suggested a business venture. Perhaps Seibu might be interested in extending its resort-development activities to Barcelona, Samaranch's home city?[22] It seemed likely to become an unbeatable alliance.

On June 11, 1991, the IOC convened in Birmingham. The citizens of Nagano, desperate to win the vote, sent a huge delegation. Besides the official Nagano room in the Hyatt Hotel, they also rented Highbury House, a splendid house in the Birmingham suburbs. Here they wooed visiting IOC members with a tea ceremony followed by a luxurious dinner of sashimi and deep-fried tempura. Noriko Ezawa's husband, Masao, was there too, with six other protesters. As far as they were concerned, Yoshiaki had outmaneuvered them on the matter of the downhill ski course on Mount Ura-iwasuge. Once he had given in on that one issue, the press had lost interest in them and their protest. But it was the Olympics that they were opposed to, not merely the ski course. Every day, while the IOC members feasted, the protesters stood on the gray, damp street outside the International Convention Centre, chanting and waving banners proclaiming NO OLYMPICS IN NAGANO.

There was one notable absence: Yoshiaki Tsutsumi, honorary chairman of the Nagano Bidding Committee. As one observer put it, "He likes to wield power—but not to be seen wielding it."

The all-important vote was on the evening of June 15. On the other side of the world, in Japan, it was the small hours of the morning. But the grounds of ancient Zenkoji temple in Nagano were jammed with people, anxiously scanning the enormous television screens that dominated the compound. At 3:30 A.M. Samaranch's gnomelike face appeared, blown up to giant size.

A hush fell over the temple grounds. In Birmingham, six thousand miles way, Samaranch unfurled a small piece of paper.

"Nagano," he proclaimed.

The crowds screamed with joy. *"Banzai!"* they shouted. "Nagano! Nagano!" Kimono-clad women beat drums and in the city center the bidding committee smashed open a keg not of the traditional sake but of water. "We have to be modest," said a local official.[23]

By voting for Nagano, IOC members had avoided the risk of any accusation that they always favored the United States. Yet in order to win the vote, the Bidding Committee had spent the astronomical sum of ¥2 billion, about $14.5 million, well over three times as much as any other bidding city. Where had the money come from? Where had it gone? Did the rest of the world see Japan simply as a moneybag, prepared to buy anything, from a van Gogh to the Rockefeller Center or the Olympics?

And Nagano's bid had consisted largely of promises. With each month that passed, estimates of the ultimate cost of all the building works multiplied. Besides all the sporting facilities in and around the city, Nagano was to have a bullet train, with a stop at Karuizawa, where the speed skating was to be held. The bullet train would stop very conveniently right outside the Karuizawa Prince Hotel. There would be several motorways cut through the mountains to Nagano, with slip roads linking to Karuizawa. And the airport in the neighboring city of Matsumoto would be modernized to take jet planes.

The people of Nagano were not complaining; one result, however, of Yoshiaki's brief venture out of the shadows and into the light was that he now had enemies. They were not powerful, they were not numerous, but they were able to feed the tabloid press with plenty of material.

The press had not failed to notice Yoshiaki's involvement in the Olympics, nor the fact that his resorts in Nagano and Karuizawa would benefit very substantially from the improvements and the rise in the value of land. After the Olympic bonanza a spate of articles appeared in the weekly and monthly magazines, though the serious press remained silent.

> There is no mistaking the fact that [Tsutsumi] is one of the behind-the-scenes wire-pullers concerning the running of the Nagano

Olympics [wrote one journalist]. If the government constructs a Shinkansen bullet-train line and highways for the sake of the Nagano Olympics, the value of golf courses, ski grounds and hotels scattered all over Nagano prefecture will go up. And his company is most likely to benefit the most from the Nagano Olympics.[24]

The years passed. The media furor died down. And, despite fears that, as the economy hit a downturn, Nagano might not be able to complete all the facilities in time, work went ahead steadily on the building projects. The city of Nagano and the Nagano Olympic Committee are confident that all the facilities will be in place by 1998.

However, sources within the organizing committee say that whenever the JOC is required to make a decision on marketing or any other matter, there is always a delay. When the final decision is reported, although his name is never mentioned, all parties appreciate that this is what Tsutsumi wants.

In June 1993 the splendid $55 million Olympic Museum celebrated its opening in Lausanne. Yoshiaki did not attend. One striking feature was a wall of bricks, each engraved with the name of a corporation that had made a donation toward the building of the museum. At the top of the wall of sponsors were two bricks, side by side. In the entire wall these were the only two engraved with the names of individuals rather than company sponsors. One read "Juan Antonio Samaranch"; the other, "Yoshiaki Tsutsumi."

Achieving Peace
1989–1993

Along the deserted street
a white horse walks away,
head drooping, silently.
The lord of the castle is not on the horse
and the stone monument stands there, silent, in bright sunlight.

TAKASHI TSUJII
A Stone Monument on a Fine Day

As 1988 crossed into 1989, as the year of the dragon ended and the year of the snake began, life in Japan seemed to be in a state of suspended animation. The usual raucous end-of-year parties were canceled or, if they were held at all, were hushed, somber affairs.

Emperor Hirohito was dying. At the age of eighty-seven, after a reign that had lasted sixty-four years, from the militaristic buildup before World War II to the prosperity of the eighties, the old man who spent his last years pursuing his interest in marine biology was on his deathbed. Every day the front page of the newspaper carried a detailed description of his condition—his pulse rate, the state of his jaundice, his intake of liquid food, his bowel movements. It was an inglorious end for the man who had once been styled the Son of Heaven.

On Saturday, January 7—conveniently timed, just after the New Year's holiday—the chief cabinet secretary made the long-expected announcement. His Majesty the Emperor had passed away.

There were many conflicting responses. While older people and people from outside Tokyo journeyed to the imperial palace to put their mark in the volumes of condolences open there, younger people—the *shinjinrui,* the "new breed," the children of the age of gold—professed utter indifference. The day of the emperor's funeral was a public holiday, but instead of lining the route to watch the cortege go by, many simply took it as an excuse for a day off work.

When Akihito, four hours after his father's death, accepted the imperial regalia—the seals, the sword and the jewel—instead of using the archaic language reserved for the imperial family, for the first time ever the emperor addressed the nation in modern standard Japanese.

For some time the imperial officials pondered the proper name for the new era. Finally they settled on Heisei, "Achieving Peace." A new batch of calendars was printed for Heisei I, the first year of the Heisei era.

At first it seemed as if the era of achieving peace was to be a continuation of the golden years that had led up to it. Japanese corporations were snapping up everything from golf courses in California to Impressionist masterpieces. Sony bought Columbia Pictures. Sales of gold and diamonds boomed. Schoolgirls queued up to buy Louis Vuitton handbags; a poll of women shoppers revealed that their favorite designers were Chanel and Ralph Lauren; and the sales of Mercedes-Benzes multiplied to such an extent that the 1991 model was introduced months ahead of schedule. The media wrote of the "Heisei aristocrats," people who had grown rich simply on the rise in land and stock prices. And the price of land continued to soar.

In 1989 *Forbes* found forty-one dollar billionaires in Japan; in 1990 there were forty. Each year the same name topped the list. In 1989 Yoshiaki's assets were estimated at $16 billion, in 1990 at $15 billion. The variation in the figure depended as much as anything on the relative strength of the yen and the dollar.

Seiji's name appeared in the list too, lower down, with assets estimated at more than $1 billion. By now the small grubby department store out in the backwoods of Ikebukuro had grown into a sprawling empire. While Yoshiaki's empire was like a pyramid, with the great man at the top, his iron hand controlling an organized, cohesive set of enterprises, Seiji's was the product of bursts of brilliance and impetuous acquisitions. It was like a tree with many branches, growing further and further from the central trunk.

Besides the Seibu department stores, the Parco chain, the Seiyu supermarkets and the Inter-Continental hotels, now 110 strong, there were holdings in real estate, town planning, restaurants, food wholesaling, import of luxury goods, the insurance and credit-card sections of the empire and a fleet of helicopters. There was a company, inherited from Yasujiro, manufacturing fertilizer and another making tofu. All in all there were about 130 different businesses, spread across development, leisure, hotels, finance and food.

Seiji presided over the whole thing from his office on the forty-eighth floor of the Sunshine Building in east Ikebukuro, part of the Sunshine City complex that he had been developing when the first oil shock put a stop to his most ambitious plans. There he sat in his luminous white office, tastefully furnished with a thick pile carpet, a crescent-shaped black glass table and chairs upholstered in black leather. Around the room were scattered *objets d'art* and paintings by his favorite artists, with a white slashed-card abstract by Lucio Fontana dominating one wall. On a clear day he could look out across the jumble of dusty roofs, narrow streets and mushrooming high-rise buildings, stretching to the horizon in every direction. On rainy days, as he writes in his autobiographical novel *A Spring Like Any Other,* he was utterly cut off from the world outside, floating in a sea of milky-white cloud.

Late in the evening, after several receptions, he would go back to the house where he lived with Asako. The doormen would rush to open the big gates as his car swung in. There he would retire to his study and write for two or three hours. In all he probably slept four hours a night. He was entering his sixties now, although he still retained the boyish round face, pixie grin and buoyant energy of his youth.

In an interview on Belgian television, filmed in 1990, Seiji spoke of his student days, when he had rebelled against Yasujiro and everything he stood for:

> I felt if I didn't overthrow my father I couldn't overthrow authority. However, I do now feel that it was a kind of love that I felt for him. Now, as I find myself at the same age as my father, I realize that there were things that he wanted to say that he couldn't say, and I realize that it wasn't so easy for him either. So there is a certain amount of nostalgia that I feel for him.

Asked about the inheritance that his father left him, he replied:

> I refused it. So all that was left to me was to take the position of
> manager of this little old general store in Ikebukuro—which was at
> the time a small shop, in a perilous state, likely to go under at any
> minute. So in that sense I didn't receive any material heritage or in-
> heritance from my family—and I thought that because I had severed
> these family connections I had got away without any spiritual inher-
> itance either. But thirty years later, I realize that my father's influ-
> ence was not so easy to escape.[1]

Just as Yasujiro had wrestled with the question of who was to be
his successor, so Seiji now found himself up against the same
problem.

His eldest son, Koji, the child of his first marriage with Motoko
Yamaguchi, was now in his thirties. After his parents separated, while
he was still a small child, Seiji had taken him to live in the big house
at Hiroo. He was six when Yasujiro died. Photographs show the old
man and the small child in the garden with Misao, and American
generals in uniform crouching down, beaming, to shake hands with
the little boy.

Compared with Seiji's childhood, Koji's was uncomplicated. He
grew up to a life of privilege, as the son of one of the wealthiest and
most powerful families in the country. From the time he was a small
child, he was fascinated by the world of films. Some of Yasujiro's old
male secretaries used to take him to the cinema and recall that he particularly loved the Godzilla monster movies. While he was still a university student he was taken on at the offices of Haruki Kadokawa, a
poet, publisher and film producer who was an old friend of Seiji's and
something of a legend in Japan.[2] There he learned the basic principles
of filmmaking and helped to produce science-fiction and fantasy films
with titles like *Dirty Hero* and *The Great War of Magic and Fantasy*.

When Koji graduated he joined the Seibu department stores.
Seiji, who had always had a hankering to direct films himself, created
a special film-producing section for him, called Cine Saison. At
twenty-nine he was promoted to be a director of the department
stores. It seemed he was being groomed to take over as Seiji's
successor.

He had grown into a rather handsome, bespectacled young man, with something of Misao in the evenness and balance of his features. Like Seiji—indeed, like nearly every member of the family—he was quiet and reserved. In photographs he is always solemn and unsmiling, giving nothing away. But, like Seiji, given the opportunity to talk about a subject he loved—in his case, films—he would burn with passionate enthusiasm. On one occasion he happened to see a silent black-and-white film made by a young unknown director named Kaizo Hayashi. Against everyone's advice, he insisted on working with him. Together they created a film called *Zipangu* that was a surprise success.

Koji was a pleasant, talented, unexceptionable young man. But he lacked the hunger that drove Seiji. He was certainly no businessman. If he had inherited anything of Seiji's gifts, it was his creativity.

From the moment he stepped into society the tabloids were on his heels, watching out for any hint that he might have inherited his father's and his grandfather's predilection for women. For years he skillfully evaded them. He was simply a serious, quiet young man who loved films and filmmaking. Rumors began to circulate that he was gay. But then stories appeared that suggested that he was not as quiet and serious as he seemed. The revelations began when he was thirty-two. Sources within the film world hinted that he had been seen with a glamorous young pinup girl named Kumiko Takeda. By Western standards it was all utterly innocuous; the two were, after all, both single. But in Japan, the very fact that they were single made the liaison all the more startling. Suppose the heir to the Seibu Saison empire were to choose a pinup as his first bride . . . The tabloids were gleeful. "Revelation of relationship between the Prince of Seibu Stores and curvaceous idol Kumiko Takeda," screamed the headlines.

Kumiko was famous for her lovely heart-shaped face, cascade of wavy locks and above all for her spectacular bust. She had begun her career by winning the Tokyo University Heartthrob Competition at the age of thirteen. She was full of chatter and unrestrained laughter. The two apparently met at a party to celebrate the completion of a film he had been working on.

Koji asserted firmly that the two were just good friends and eventually the rumors died away, but even the suspicion of such a frivolous and unsuitable relationship added to the doubts about whether he had the ability to take over the vast unwieldy empire that his father had created.

Seiji was beginning to talk more and more about retirement. In an interview in 1990, he was asked whether he had ever thought of quitting business and devoting all his time to literature.

"Often," he replied. "Even now. After all, my companies are doing well and I'm becoming old. I may quit much earlier than many people suspect."[3]

Still, when the announcement came, it was a shock to nearly everyone. On Saturday, January 12, 1991, a headline appeared in the *Asahi* newspaper. The English version read, "Giant Saison Retail Group head Tsutsumi to retire." Unlike most Japanese chairmen, who remain in their positions into their dotage, he had chosen to step down to make way for a new generation

He had decided, moreover, to go against the Japanese tradition of keeping the business in the family. He made his intentions regarding his son very clear. "The enterprise is a public institution," he said.[4] "I will not have my son inherit it automatically. If Koji remains at the department store, people around him might favor him. . . . He also says that he's willing to work anywhere, so I will ask that he distance himself [from the store]."[5]

Instead the responsibility would pass to a collective leadership. The era of the lone owner manager frantically juggling the various parts of the vast complex empire was over. "It is not desirable for one man to control the group like a dictator."[6] The whole Saison Group would be divided into six divisions, reflecting the diverse areas it encompassed: retailing, wholesale distribution, foreign trade, financial services, property development and restaurant management.

As for Seiji, he was not exactly retiring. He would no longer hold the title of all-powerful "representative" of the group, but he would remain as adviser. He was not, in other words, actually loosening his hold on the reins. He was merely moving to a backseat. In Japanese politics, at least at the time when the Liberal Democratic Party (LDP) dominated, prime ministers—like Kakuei Tanaka—were often far more powerful once they had completed their period of office and were operating from the wings. In the same way it seemed likely that Seiji would remain as powerful as ever.

The question everyone asked was "Why?" Seiji was sixty-three, in

Japanese terms very young to abdicate as chairman. He had made it clear in interviews that he was no longer much involved in the day-to-day operations of the group and that he was grooming the next generation of leaders. But why had he chosen this particular time to make his exit?

In the press there was a fever of speculation. Seiji himself gave as the reason a series of accidents that had befallen the Asahi Koyo helicopter corporation in the last few months. Asahi Koyo was one branch of the Saison group. That August one of their helicopters had crashed in the sea off the coast of Okinawa, killing four people, including the pilot. The funeral was barely over when another crashed, causing three deaths. In all there had been nine accidents in the past year and a half, and twenty-two deaths. It was reminiscent of the fires that had bedeviled Seibu department stores in the early days. The Ministry of Transport ordered an inquiry and concluded that the cause of the accidents was the company's policy of putting profit above all else. There is a long tradition in Japan of the chairman of a company resigning to take responsibility for some corporate failing or disgrace. Seiji commented that it had become impossible for him to monitor all of the group's activities.[7]

But what was the real reason? Many people suspected that Seiji's spectacular empire—the trendsetting department stores, the luxury hotels—was on the brink of disaster. Far from leaving of his own accord, he had been pushed out. As one commentator put it, it was either him or the whole concern.

By now ugly fissures were becoming more and more evident in the business. With huge debts and small profit margins, Saison depended for its continuing existence on a booming economy. The tiniest tremor opened vast cracks. In early 1990 there had been a stock market collapse in Tokyo. Interest rates rose and immediately the Saison Group, with its overwhelming debts, was in difficulties.[8]

Many people dated the beginning of the end to the purchase of the Inter-Continentals. It had been a magnificent gesture but it had loaded the business with an intolerable debt. To make matters worse, having once made the purchase, Seiji immediately increased the loan in order to expand yet further. There were those who saw it as a Pyrrhic victory in Seiji's battle to outdo Yoshiaki. He had finally achieved what he wanted, and built an empire not only infinitely more stylish but also every bit as weighty as his brother's, but in the process he had brought himself and his business to the very edge of ruin.

According to one scenario, it was Saison's bankers, Dai-ichi Kangyo Bank (DKB), who applied the pressure. One Tokyo-based economist was quoted as saying, "Seiji had no choice but to step down when DKB threatened to cut Saison's line of credit. How else can Saison continue to expand?"[9]

Whatever the reasons, in the months that followed it became apparent that Seiji had bowed out in the nick of time. Maybe with his family's famous prescience he had foreseen the trouble that was in store. Or maybe, as he himself said, he simply retired because it was time to retire.

By now everyone was beginning to talk with apprehension about an economic downturn. The stock market collapse of early 1990 had been one of the first omens that Japan's economy had reached its limits, though, compared with the recession that was ravaging many countries in the West, it was still in reasonably good health. Land and stock prices began to fall and profits too took a downward turn. Suddenly it was possible to find an empty taxi late at night or to get a table at a French restaurant without booking ahead. As bankruptcies and unemployment rose, as overtime decreased, everyone collectively tightened the purse strings. It was no longer fashionable to be fashionable. Instead of designer labels, people took to wearing jeans. When asked how he spent his evenings, one famous fashion leader who had made his name designing extravagant bars and nightclubs said that he now went home and read a book.

Above all, people stopped buying luxury goods. Diamonds were left on the shelf, sales of Mercedes-Benzes decreased. No one any longer worried about owning the very latest refrigerator or the most advanced state-of-the-art audio and video equipment.

Now, as the taste for luxury ebbed, Seibu's sales plummeted. The other department stores suffered, too, but Seibu, which had always relied on huge sales to pay back the interest on its huge debts, suffered most.

To make matters worse, the role of the department stores within the Saison Group had been to subsidize the development of the other, less sturdy branches of the tree. The hotel side of the empire continued to lose money.[10] Many of the Inter-Continentals were in the Middle East, and the Gulf War of 1991 hit business very hard. It was the worst crisis the group had ever faced.

Seiji by now had appointed his successors: Sueaki Takaoka, the chairman of the Seiyu supermarket chain; Toshio Takeuchi, the president of Credit Saison, the credit-card arm of the empire; and Shigeaki Wada, the president of Seiyo Food Systems. All three were close to him. Takaoka, an ex-journalist, had been a friend of his when they were students together at Tokyo University, while Takeuchi and Wada had both joined the company as young men. Takeuchi had been one of Seiji's first graduate appointments, back in the days when new entrants had to go trembling on their knees to greet Yasujiro.

None of the three had absolute power. By appointing three instead of one, Seiji had ensured that he would retain the ultimate control, acting as a buffer between them. The three met with him nearly every week and consulted him on every important policy matter. He had indeed merely taken a backseat. Still, the poet and dreamer had been replaced at the front of the company by men in suits.

Then the details of a scandal began to emerge. One of the furthest-flung sections of Seibu department stores dealt in medical equipment. They took orders from hospitals, took short-term loans from financing companies and purchased imported equipment like X-ray machines, scanners and kidney machines. Japan has large hospitals, and in addition many doctors run their own small hospitals packed to the beams with the latest gleaming machinery, so there was plenty of demand.

There were also opportunities for making deals on the side. Somewhere in the middle of the eighties three managers from the Medical Equipment Division at Seibu put their heads together with the president of Pasco, a firm importing medical equipment. Together they came up with a fiendishly complicated scam. It involved using Seibu's name plus forged orders from hospitals to get money from financing companies that the plotters would then use to play the stock market. In those high-flying days they never doubted that their speculations would be successful. They would then pay off the loans and the scam would never come to light.

For several years these activities went undiscovered. But as the economy slowed, many scandals came to light, particularly in the securities industry. In August 1991 Pasco's speculative schemes all came to grief. Together with another medical import firm, which was also involved in the scam, they went bankrupt.

Seibu quickly discovered that its managers were implicated and sacked them. But over the next few months more and more grisly details leaked out. Finally, in June 1992, the public prosecutors moved in. Two of the three managers, the two presidents of the import firms and another employee of Pasco were arrested.

For Seiji the scandal had profound repercussions. As in every corporate disgrace, a sacrificial victim was required. In order to cleanse the company's image, a very senior figure would have to "take responsibility."

Initially Seiji still manipulated the strings, but the balance of power was changing. The puppets were beginning to assert themselves. Seiji had already ceded much of the real control over the Seiyu supermarkets to the new chairman, the white-haired ex-journalist Takaoka. Takaoka became effectively the leading figure within the Saison Group and set to work to restructure the debt-ridden Inter-Continental hotels. Now Seiji was voted out as the chairman of Seibu department stores, and the tough-talking, square-jawed Wada, whom people spoke of as a "shogun type," was installed in his place. Rumor has it that Wada accepted the job only on condition that Seiji was prohibited from any decision-making whatsoever in the stores.[11]

The old regime was not yet over. All three men still felt great affection and respect for Seiji. He was also the largest individual shareholder in the Saison group. Takeuchi, the genial, soft-spoken president of Credit Saison and the third man in the triumvirate, said, "His opinions are the best. He has a long and deep experience. He has the best judgment." But still, it was clear that the new, harsher conditions of the times required new approaches and new men.

With the business finally in other hands, Seiji had time to focus on other interests. For a start there was politics. His friend, the thoughtful and intellectual Kiichi Miyazawa, who had been squeezed out in the leadership race with Abe and Takeshita a few years before, now took his turn as prime minister. He was voted in in November 1991. Reportedly, for six months before the crucial decision, Seiji met with politicians and businessmen and asked them to give their backing to the Miyazawa cabinet.

Often he acted informally as Miyazawa's adviser. He was also on the board of many powerful committees—the Japan Committee for Economic Development (Keizai Doyukai), the Economic Planning Agency, the Foreign Ministry's Southwest Asia Forum, the cultural promotion council at the Agency of Cultural Affairs, and others. He went to India and Burma as a member of the economic delegation of the Southwest Asia Forum and took part in the Angkor Wat rescue mission in Cambodia.

For years the powerful and wealthy business leader Seiji Tsutsumi had coexisted uneasily with the poet Takashi Tsujii. Around midnight every night the mask of Tsutsumi had been cast aside and for a few hours the tormented poet was allowed to emerge. His poems explored the dichotomy.

> As we continue living
> Obscurities accumulate.
> What I feared in those days—
> Becoming a member of the elite—
> Made me vomit.
> All the same, of course,
> I was searching for another elite.
> Why have things come about as they have?
> Somewhere I have made a mistake,
> My two eyes haven't focused as one.[12]

In interviews Seiji spoke of the way in which a phrase or an idea for a poem would suddenly bubble up in the middle of a board meeting or a conference. If he had the chance he would scribble it down. Otherwise as soon as he got home he would make a note of it—"that is, if I remember it. If I don't remember it then I consider it unimportant. Important things are not forgotten easily."[13]

Now there was time to think and write. Seiji began to ponder his next major writing project. Perhaps it was simply the passage of time, but as he had grown older and more successful, gradually the torment of his relationship with his father and the final humiliation when he was denied the inheritance faded into the past. Now he decided to write a biography of his father.

Well before he announced his resignation, he began work on a memorial hall for the old man. The main Hiroo house was torn down. In its place a truly enormous modern building appeared, with a huge heavy roof and enormous gables. In Japan, where most people live in homes that have been likened to rabbit hutches, it was breathtaking.

In front were flower gardens and a fountain. At the back, the glorious old garden remained where Yasujiro used to stroll, with its stone bridge and pond shaped like Lake Biwa and exuberant foliage. Inside there were reception rooms where Seiji entertained visiting diplomats and dignitaries, offices and the memorial hall.

The most striking thing about the memorial hall was how empty it was. There was a bust of Yasujiro. There was a model of the house in Yagiso village where Yasujiro was born. And there were photographs documenting Yasujiro's career, focusing on cultural developments, town planning and the department store. Even the photographs were sparse. It was Yasujiro's career minus the real estate business, the railways and the hotels—which left very little. There was a photograph of a monument Yasujiro had erected to Yoshida and six other political leaders whom he admired, but none of his own tomb in Kamakura.

In creating this memorial hall, Seiji was finally acknowledging his roots. Monstrous though he had been, Yasujiro had also been a great man—and Seiji's father. Perhaps the shadow that he had cast over his son's life had lifted at last.

In 1993 a strange item arrived on the desk of every manager of every branch of Seibu department store and Seiyu supermarkets. It was a bust of Yasujiro. To go with it there was a plinth, a little over three feet in height, with instructions and a diagram showing how the bust should be set on the plinth and where it should be placed: in the manager's office, on the left-hand side of the desk.[14]

It was uncannily reminiscent of the photograph of Yasujiro that hung, smiling benevolently, in every office of every company of Yoshiaki's great Seibu empire, from the offices of the hilltop cemetery in Kamakura to the most obscure hotel in the most remote corner of Japan. It was almost as if the Saison Group were out to match Yoshiaki's veneration of the old man, to take him back as their patron saint.

Or perhaps, now that Seiji had retired the group was free to acknowledge the common roots that bound the two empires.

Over in the splendid offices in Harajuku, overlooking the wooded grounds of the Meiji Shrine, the incense never ceased to burn beneath the huge portrait of Yasujiro. And every night, throughout the snow and ice of winter and the sultry heat of summer, two men carried out the vigil at Yasujiro's tomb, ringing the great bell at dusk and dawn and tidying the lawns around the black granite tombstone. There was always a long list of hopefuls waiting to carry out the nightly watch.

Yoshiaki, seven years younger than Seiji, was far from ready to think about retirement. According to the Japanese way of reckoning, he would have his sixtieth birthday in 1993. He was still a fine figure of a man. When he was together with his old school friends the contrast was striking. While they were paunchy and balding, he was still trim and youthful, square-jawed and sharp-eyed, every hair in place. On the rare occasions when he managed to snatch an hour with a friend, he liked talking politics. "He likes to bet who'll be the next prime minister," said one. He was careful about his health. He had never been much of a drinker, and as he grew older he cut down on drink and shed a few pounds. But he seldom had the chance to shed the role of master of the Seibu empire.

Some people spoke of him as the "emperor who has no clothes." There were endless stories—of red carpets spread in the Prince hotel lobbies when he was expected to arrive; of manuals sent to members of staff on precisely how their children should phrase their letter of thanks to the great man after they received their annual book token from him; of staff seeking advice on whether or not they should look at him when he stepped down from his helicopter. It was said that before he went abroad members of staff would travel the whole route to ensure that if he traveled down a certain road at a certain time the sun would not be in his eyes.

An old man in Karuizawa who had known Yoshiaki since he was a little boy said wistfully that the old Mr. Tsutsumi, Yasujiro, had been more human. "He had failures," he said. "We felt closer to him."

As for the present Mr. Tsutsumi, "He has this big empire. He's the richest man in the world." Yasujiro had been a familiar figure in the village, stomping around the building sites, waving his stick, whereas Yoshiaki from time to time would descend from the heavens in his helicopter, "like a god." The villagers would be waiting like suppliants to talk to him. If the road needed widening or they wanted to discuss the matter of the new bullet train, they would appeal to him. He was like a feudal lord.

There was one crucial matter that had yet to be decided: the successor.

Yoshiaki's eldest son, Masatoshi, had had a pampered childhood. He had grown up on the coast at Oiso, in the splendid mansion that had once belonged to the old statesman Shigeru Yoshida. Once or twice a week his father would descend from the sky in his helicopter to join in the family picnics or the school tug-of-war.

In an interview just after Tsuneko died, Yoshiaki said that he had no intention of forcing his son to be his successor. "It's not that kind of age anymore. Being company chairman is no fun! I don't want to inflict all the trouble I have to suffer on my son." He remembered how his own father used to beat him, even when he was only the runner-up successor and Kiyoshi and Seiji were still in line in front of him. He had no intention of subjecting his son to that. In fact, he said with a grin, "My wife takes care of the children. It's better if the father doesn't have too much contact with them!"[15]

But, he added, if his son wanted to become his successor, he was sure the loyal company men would give him all their support.

So as a boy Masatoshi was left free to do anything he liked. There was just one condition. After he finished university he would have to settle down.

He grew up rather a wild boy. Those of Yoshiaki's friends who met him spoke critically of him. "Useless boy," said one disapprovingly. "Never studies, very spoiled." Masatoshi was no intellectual but, like Yoshiaki, he was a superb sportsman. In the winter he perfected his skiing technique. In the summer he went surfing. Then, at sixteen, he discovered skateboarding. By the time he started university, he was already a member of a professional team. Yoshiaki had a skateboard rink built for him at home.

Wild though he was and lacking in social graces, young Masatoshi Tsutsumi was undoubtedly one of the most eligible bachelors in the country. He was heir presumptive to an unimaginably vast fortune, and moreover, it was said, his father held the entire Liberal Democratic Party in the palm of his hand.

Yoshiaki was rich, he was powerful. But the aristocracy (who, although they had lost their titles, still formed a self-perpetuating upper stratum in society) looked down their well-bred noses at him. He was eternally doomed to be dismissed as new money, nouveau riche. The only way to rise was by creating new family links through marriage. As Masatoshi reached adulthood, rumors began to circulate that Yoshiaki had his eye on the highest prize of all.

Over the years Yoshiaki had been careful to maintain the special relationship that his father had built up with the imperial family. Each year when the heat of summer became too intense, the emperor retreated to the hills of Karuizawa. There, just as he had done when he was the young prince Akihito, he stayed in the Edwardian-style villa that had once, many years ago, belonged to his great-uncle, Prince Asaka. It was now the Sengataki Prince Hotel, part of Yoshiaki's Seibu empire. Despite the name, it was not a hotel at all but the emperor's summer palace. He stayed there courtesy of Seibu.

There were other links. The emperor's sister, Princess Takako Shimazu, had a post as adviser to the Prince hotels. And the Prince hotels had partial responsibility for providing the catering at the imperial guesthouse. From time to time, holidaying in Karuizawa, Masatoshi met the emperor's youngest child, the sweet and innocent Princess Sayako. As it happened, the two were almost exactly the same age. While he was enjoying his last years of freedom, mixing with surfers and skateboarders, she was being prepared for a new world in which she might have to marry a commoner. Technically, she had no choice, given that the aristocracy and minor princes had all been abolished. Her mother, Empress Michiko, who had been born a commoner herself, took her shopping, taught her to cook and once even took her on a train.

For years rumors linked the two young people. As personalities, the two could not have been more different, but that was irrelevant. Marriage was a union of families, not of individuals.

Then, in 1993, Crown Prince Hiro won the hand of the girl whom he had long been pursuing, Masako Owada. Only one of the emperor's children remained unmarried. The spotlight turned on Princess Sayako. At first it seemed that Masatoshi was the main candidate. The all-powerful Imperial Household Agency, which deals with the affairs of the imperial house, refused to comment, a clear sign that the matter was under discussion. But there were many people who said that it would not be right. There were too many scandals in the Tsutsumi history—too many women, too many dubious deals. It would not do for the imperial family to make such an alliance.

At some high level a decision must have been reached. By the end of the year, when articles appeared naming potential candidates for Princess Sayako's hand, Masatoshi was absent from the list. All the young men were of noble stock. None of them were skateboarders.

Times had changed. In the past, when Pistol Tsutsumi and Goto the Thief stomped about the land carving out empires for themselves, it mattered little what the public thought. They were feudal lords. The peasants might grumble, but they had no say over what their masters did. Many people complained that Yoshiaki was made too precisely in his father's mold. He comported himself like a feudal lord, behaving as if Japan were his own private fiefdom. A word in the ear of his powerful friends and he could buy a piece of land at a discount price or build a ski run on an unspoiled mountain in the middle of a national park. But in the modern age such behavior could not go unnoticed. The word that everyone used for Yoshiaki was "arrogant." He showed a high-handed lack of concern for public opinion. He broke no laws; he could not be accused of corruption. But in the 1990s image was important. And, fairly or unfairly, Yoshiaki was unquestionably unpopular.

Everything was thrown into relief by the continuing economic downturn. Prosperity had bred content. From time to time scandals surfaced, of which the most notorious had been the Lockheed scandal, but the dirt was always quickly whisked away and business went on as usual.

By the beginning of 1992 it was becoming obvious that the economic slump was not going to go away. It had been assumed that, like the oil shock of 1973 or the worldwide stock market crash of 1987, Japan would ride it out with its usual panache and emerge triumphant, even stronger than before. Instead, the situation became more and more grave. Land and stock prices continued to fall, growth declined. For ordinary people, who had grown accustomed to luxury, life was becoming tougher. There was plenty of goods in the shops, but far from buying designer clothes, people were now shopping in discount stores. Everyone knew of bankruptcies, and it was harder and harder to find work. Until now, unemployment had been practically unknown in Japan.

Finally even the government, which had been publishing optimistic reports, had to concede that this could no longer be called a downturn. This was a recession.

In the past Yoshiaki's vast landholdings and cautious management strategy had buffered him against the more violent swings of economic fortune. Building a hotel or a ski resort entailed a commitment of years. It was not a business where he could suddenly apply the brakes or make a change of course to accommodate some new economic circumstance. He had always planned ten years into the future.

Then profits began to fall. In the early days of the downturn, people had taken advantage of the slowdown to go on holiday. The ski resorts continued to bustle, but as money became tighter, business began to slow. Corporations were no longer prepared to lodge their executives in the luxury Prince hotels. Fewer people had the spare cash to go skiing. In 1992 Seibu Railways, the only sizable section of Yoshiaki's Seibu empire to be listed, showed a mammoth drop in profits of 92 percent. The following year profits plunged again, by 73 percent.

The bitterest blow of all was the land tax. Passed in 1992, it was a holding tax on land that was owned and used for commercial purposes. No one knew exactly how much land Yoshiaki and his companies owned—rumor had it that one sixth of the entire landmass of Japan was his. Much of it, however, was tracts of hill and woodland not yet put to commercial use.

In the end Seibu Railways' land-tax bill came to ¥3.7 billion ($29.6 million at the exchange rate of the time). A few other companies paid more. Given Seibu's gravely diminished profits, it was a crippling blow.

None of this, however, could be taken to suggest that Yoshiaki and his Seibu empire were in difficulties. Seibu Railways was the empire's main publicly listed company. It nearly always showed low profits. But behind it was Kokudo Keikaku, recently renamed Kokudo, the core company. Even if Seibu Railways was going badly, no one knew the state of Kokudo's accounts. It remained a mystery, a black hole.

And still the empire continued to expand. In addition to the hotels and ski resorts and golf courses, the railways and amusement parks, the new dinosaur park that opened in 1993 near the Seibu Lions stadium, there were also hotels in Hawaii, Toronto, Australia's Gold Coast, Penang, Singapore and Alaska, and building projects in Barcelona (Samaranch's city) and eastern Europe. There was no sign of applying the brakes.

And despite the country's economic troubles, Yoshiaki was still, according to *Forbes,* the richest man in the world. In 1993, after a detailed investigation, the magazine pronounced his dollar assets to be $9 billion. As always, the figure was based on the assumption that, as publicly stated, he owned 40 percent of Kokudo. The owner or owners of the remaining 60 percent remained a mystery.

But sources close to the family confirmed what many people suspected: in reality Yoshiaki himself was the sole owner of the entire empire. If that was indeed the case, far from being in difficulties, on paper at least he was worth the astronomical sum of $22 billion.

Epilogue

On June 21, 1993, news broke of an extraordinary new development. "Seibu Railways and Saison in business tie-up," trumpeted the front-page headline in the highly respected *Nikkei* (Japan Economic Journal). The English edition was more explicit: "Tsutsumi brothers bury the hatchet."[1] For years the press had followed the brothers' fortunes relentlessly, interpreting their every move in terms of duel-to-the-death rivalry. Now, judging from their business activities, it looked as if finally there might be a truce.

It was not quite the last thing anyone had ever expected. For years, whenever Saison was in difficulties, there had been rumors that Yoshiaki might step in to help it out or even take it over. And there were those who asserted that no matter how huge Saison's debts became, the banks would always continue their support because of Yoshiaki's enormous assets. Even though the two groups were utterly independent, in the end the relationship could not be denied.

The biggest factor was Seiji's retirement. The staff at Kokudo was harshly critical of Seiji, while at Saison the employees weighed in with tales of Yoshiaki's arrogance and meanness, and the way his companies never paid tax. By all accounts the two brothers never met or communicated in any way, but the acrimony was restricted to the brothers themselves. Many of the older staff had joined when the two empires were still one, so they had been colleagues for years. When the empires split they remained in touch. The new men at Saison, the triumvirate who had taken over power on Seiji's retirement, were all from that generation. They had nothing against their counterparts on the other side. They had also inherited one last dream of Seiji's: satellite television.

Even in retirement Seiji's vision continued to drive the Saison Group. In his last years as chairman he turned his attention to the most exciting developments in what was for him a new area: the media.

Seiyu, which had started out as a supermarket chain, joined forces with Robert Redford's Sundance Institute in the United States and began making films. It also independently produced several films, one of which, Mitsuo Yanagimachi's *Fire Festival,* won the Golden Palm at Cannes in 1985. Seiji took a keen interest in the whole process and checked the screenplays before shooting began. Seiyu was also involved in a business venture with NHK, the Japanese broadcasting corporation, to start a new company to buy and sell films and television programs. There were interests in high-definition television, satellite and cable.

The next step was obvious. Saison needed a broadcasting channel of its own. It was a development that would open up infinite possibilities—from cultural programming and news broadcasts to advertising and TV shopping. In 1993 the opportunity finally arose. Plans were announced to launch a new broadcasting satellite, BS4, which would allow for new television channels. Takaoka, the white-haired chairman of Seiyu who was now the most powerful figure in the group, had begun his career as a journalist. He shared Seiji's enthusiasm for broadcasting. But everyone knew that the driving force behind the project was Seiji. In an interview in the *Nikkei* (Japan Economic Journal), Seiichi Mizuno, Seiji's brother-in-law and the vice president of Seibu department stores, was quoted as saying, "Mr. Tsutsumi's business determination is as strong as ever."[2]

Saison was determined to go ahead with the satellite project, but the cost was daunting. Altogether the group would need to lay out more than ¥100 billion (about $900 million) for broadcasting equipment and software. For any company it would have been a huge commitment. But in the case of Saison, still battered by financial problems, it was breathtakingly ambitious. That year Seibu department stores had reported a loss for the first time since its founding in March 1940, and Mitsukoshi took over as the country's top-selling department store.[3]

The obvious solution was a joint venture—and, with Seiji's retirement, the door was now open for an alliance that had never been possible before.

It was not as outrageous as it seemed. Yoshiaki's Seibu Group had been broadcasting the Lions' baseball games on TV Saitama, based in the Lions' home city of Tokorozawa, for some time. Saison too had an interest in TV Saitama. The two empires complemented each other perfectly. Saison could provide arts and cultural programs while Seibu would cover the sporting side.

It was Takaoka who contacted his old friend and colleague Iwao Nisugi, the president of Seibu Railway. The two began negotiations, and in June 1993 they were ready to make an announcement.

They also settled another small irritant that company insiders referred to as the last battle. The Prince hotels still routinely refused to recognize the Saison credit card. It was an absurd anomaly. Now that the fire had gone out of the quarrel, it was time to rectify the situation. Nisugi and Takaoka agreed that henceforth the Saison card would be accepted in the Prince hotels.

In interviews Takaoka insisted that the cooperation between the two groups was strictly limited to broadcasting and credit cards. But the media gleefully treated the whole thing as a rerun of the American-Soviet détente. Just as America was helping Russia, so the railways had to support the department stores.

Seiji remained as noncommittal as ever. He was retired, he said very properly. It had nothing to do with him; though he encouraged, of course, any plans to expand the business. As for whether he would be talking directly to Yoshiaki, "He is the owner, but I have retired, so it would be strange if I went to see him. If it can be decided at the administrative level, that will be fine."[4]

Meanwhile, triggered at least in part by the economic downturn, there were seismic realignments in the Japanese political scene. There had been a series of spectacular scandals, resulting in the downfall of the most powerful political godfather in the land, the manipulative Shin Kanemaru. No one could fail any longer to be aware of the vast sums of money that oiled the political system. Several members of the Liberal Democratic Party (LDP), anticipating the growing public disgust, broke away to form their own factions. On July 18, 1993, following a vote of no confidence in Kiichi Miyazawa's government, there was a general election. To everyone's surprise, the breakaway factions, together with some of the opposition parties, were able to form a coalition large enough to oust the LDP. It was the first time the LDP had been out of power for thirty-eight years. The new prime minister, Morihiro Hosokawa, began the uphill struggle to push through bills to reform the political system and boost the failing economy. It seemed a minor revolution. Tentatively people spoke of *perestroika,* though, as some pointed out, the new rulers were in many ways more rather than less conservative than the old LDP.

Both the Tsutsumi brothers, predictably, had links with the new government. Yoshiaki's ties with Hosokawa went back to the mid-eighties, when the handsome young aristocrat became governor of Kumamoto, in the central part of the southern island of Kyushu. Yoshiaki wanted to develop the splendid countryside at the foot of volcanic Mount Aso, inland from Kumamoto, and Hosokawa was eager to bring jobs and money to his area.

With Seibu's expertise in resort development, the plan was to turn the area into an international resort, the "Karuizawa of Kyushu." A large hotel and golf course appeared in the lush green countryside at the foot of Mount Aso and work began on marine development on the coast. The two men became friends. From time to time they went skiing together. Hosokawa was quoted as saying that "Yoshiaki-*san* is a rough skier."[5] And in the summer, when Hosokawa was staying at his family villa in Karuizawa, he sometimes played tennis with Yoshiaki.

Seiji had sat on the Kumamoto Twenty-first Century Group, the informal advisory council that Hosokawa set up when he was governor. The group included leading figures from the arts—a theater director and the avant-garde architect Kisho Kurokawa—with Seiji as a representative of the business world. But once Hosokawa became prime minister, Seiji altered his allegiance.

The very fact that Yoshiaki was close to Hosokawa was indication in itself that Hosokawa was far from liberal. Ironically the new leader of the ousted LDP, Yohei Kono, was actually much more of a liberal than the "new prime minister for the new age." In the past he had left the LDP in protest against money politics to form an opposition party, the New Liberal Club, though he later rejoined. Kono followed in the footsteps of Seiji's old friend, the intellectual and progressive Miyazawa. He was the new leader of his faction. Early in 1994 it was revealed that Seiji had set up a support group for him. Once again, each in his own characteristic way, the Tsutsumi brothers had positioned themselves on opposite sides.

Despite all the hopes that had been invested in it, Hosokawa's government lasted less than a year. Hosokawa was succeeded by Tsutomu Hata, the former finance minister and one of the leading power brokers behind the coalition government. Hata was a member for Nagano and an old friend of Yoshiaki's. His hold on power, however, seemed more tenuous than ever, and in fact after less than two chaotic months the coalition government was toppled by an unprecedented alliance of the Socialists and the conservative LDP, with the leader of the Social Democrats, Tomiichi Murayama, in the unlikely position of prime minister. In reality, despite the token presence of the Socialist prime minister, power was firmly back in the hands of the LDP; it was business as usual.

Shortly afterward, the economy took an upward swing. It appeared that Japan was finally moving out of recession.

A few months earlier Yoshiaki had made one of his rare public appearances. The occasion was the opening of the Makuhari Prince Hotel, a triangular fifty-story edifice dominating the newly developing area of Makuhari, just outside Tokyo. The glittering banqueting hall was crowded with men in dark suits. Jowly politicians, representatives of every party and every faction, joked with heavyweight figures from business and industry, while actresses and singers flitted among the crowd. The Seibu Lions were there in force, tall and athletic, together with many familiar faces from television and theater.

In the center of the throng, standing out among all the dark suits, was a trim, youthful figure. That day Yoshiaki chose to appear in an elegant suit of the palest silver gray. Surrounded by television cameras, the most powerful people in the land stood in line, waiting to speak to him. While they bowed he greeted them with a gracious inclination of the head and a few words, until his assistants stepped in and ushered them away. It was ample demonstration that far from courting the politicians, they were eager to court him.

Nearly a century had passed since Yasujiro left Yagiso, determined to keep his promise to his grandfather, to make the Tsutsumi house an honorable house. Each of his sons inherited a part of his personality and his genius; people said that if you put the two together, you would have Yasujiro. Each, in turn, built two very different empires, which touched on nearly every facet of life in Japan. But both, like their father, remained mavericks, in some way outside the mainstream of Japanese society.

What role would the brothers take in the new changing Japan? Seiji was no longer a leading player. His Seibu department stores were struggling while he himself had taken a backseat—though in the classic Japanese way he continued to manipulate the strings of the men at the front. He had, however, carved out a new role for himself as a cultural figure; in 1993 he won his most prestigious award yet, the Jun Takami award for his poetry.

As for Yoshiaki, an interviewer once asked him what he would do after he retired. "Nothing," he replied. "I plan to stay active all my life." With the economy booming once again and many years of vigor ahead of him, it seemed that his fortunes could only continue to grow. And on the political front his network was so vast that practically the only certainty in an uncertain future was that no matter who took power, they would be a friend of his.

The biggest question mark hung over the next generation. No doubt Yoshiaki and Seiji would continue along the paths they had carved out for themselves. But who would be their heirs? Their children, it seemed, had not inherited the fire that drove Yasujiro and his two sons to build larger and larger empires.

Seiji had already handed over his business to others. But to Yoshiaki the Seibu empire was almost a sacred heritage, entrusted to him by his father. He held the reins, and the company was indelibly stamped with his personality. It seemed likely that as a stubbornly traditional Japanese man he would keep the business within the family. Perhaps he had already chosen his successor from among his sons, whether legitimate or illegitimate, and was grooming him to take over.

His heir would inherit unparalleled assets, an empire that was beginning to expand beyond the shores of Japan and a formidable political network. How would he choose to use it? Just as Yoshiaki had developed his inheritance in new directions, so his son too would need to move into new areas of business to suit the new age. Would he prove a worthy successor? Or would he fritter away his fortune? Would the old Japanese saying apply and the third generation be paupers?

The story was far from over. Japan was moving into a new phase of its history. As the world's second largest economy, Japan would inevitably be forced to play a larger and larger role on the world stage. No one could predict what the future would bring, though the Tsutsumis, with their famous foresight, probably had a shrewder idea than most. And it seemed more than likely that they themselves would have a large part to play in that future.

One thing was certain. Night and morning without fail, for as long at least as Yoshiaki was alive, the custom of the nightly watch would continue on the hilltop in Kamakura. Even as you close this book, two young men are earnestly sweeping the lawns around the graveled tomb of Yasujiro Tsutsumi. As the great bell tolls out across the valleys and the glimmering silhouette of Mount Fuji appears on the eastern horizon, one can imagine that the rough old peasant entombed there might allow himself a small smile of satisfaction.

Select Bibliography

Japanese-language sources

BOOKS

Asaka-miya-tei no aru.deko (The Art Deco of the Asaka Palace), Tokyo-to bunka shinkokai, 1986.

Chikui, Masayoshi, *Tsutsumi Yasujiro den* (The Story of Yasujiro Tsutsumi), Toyoshokan, 1955.

Eikawa, Koki, *Tsutsumi Yoshiaki no hasso* (Yoshiaki Tsutsumi's Concept), KK Besutoserazu, 1984.

Inose, Naoki, *Mikado no shozo* (Portrait of the Emperor), Shogakkan, 1986.

———, *Tochi no shinwa* (The Legend of Land), Shogakkan, 1988.

Kaminogo, Toshiaki, *Seibu Okoku* (Seibu Empire), Kodansha Bunko, 1985.

———, *Shin Seibu Okoku* (New Seibu Empire), Kodansha Bunko, 1987.

Katabami: Tsutsumi kaicho tsuito tobubetsu go (*Katabami* magazine: special edition in commemoration of Chairman Tsutsumi), No. 52, May 15, 1964.

Kobayashi, Kazunari, *Tsutsumi Yoshiaki: 12 oku en no tochi wo motsu otoko no jigyo senryaku* (Yoshiaki Tsutsumi: Business Strategy of the Man Who Has ¥1.2 Billion Worth of Land), Paru shuppan, 1985.

Manabe, Shigeki, *Tsutsumi Yoshiaki no keiei tamashii: Ju nen mae ni katsu* (The Management Spirit of Yoshiaki Tsutsumi: Winning Ten Years in Advance), Kodansha, 1986.

Nakajima, Matsuki, *Karuizawa hishochi 100 nen* (The Summer Resort of Karuizawa, One Hundred Years), Kokushokan Kokai, 1987.

Narishima, Tadaaki, *Seibu no subete* (All About Seibu), Nihon Jitsugyo Shuppansha, 1989.

Nihon no shozo: Kyu ozoku. Kazoku hizo arubamu (Portrait of Japan: The Old Imperial Families; Album of the Peers' Treasures), Mainichi shimbunsha, 1990.

Noma, Tsuyoshi, *Kyosei Tsutsumi Yasujiro* (The Great Yasujiro Tsutsumi), Waka Shuppan, 1966.

Oshita, Eiji, *Waga seishun no Waseda* (My Youthful Waseda), Shodensha, 1991.

Seibu vs Tokyu: Retto seiha e no tatakai (Seibu vs. Tokyu: The Fight to Control the Archipelago) edited by *Nikkei rizoto* (Nikkei Resort magazine), Nihon keizai shimbunsha, 1992.

Sezon no rekishi: henkaku no dainamizumu (History of Saison: The Dynamism of Revolutionary Change), edited by Tsunehiko Yui et al., Libroport, 1991 (4 vols.).

Shishi, Bunroku, *Hakone yama* (Hakone Mountain), Asahi shimbunsha, 1968.

Taniguchi, Gentaro, *Tsutsumi Yoshiaki to Orimpikku: Yabo no kiseki* (Yoshiaki Tsutsumi and the Olympics: In the Tracks of His Ambition), San-ichi Shoho, 1992.

Tsujii, Takashi, *Hoko no kisetsu no nakade* (In the Season of Roaming), Shinchosha, 1969.

———, *Itsumo to onaji haru* (A Spring Like Any Other), Kawade Shobo Shinsha, 1983.

Tsutsumi, Yasujiro, *Kuto sanju nen* (Thirty Years of Struggle), Sanko Bunka Kenkyujo, 1962.

———, *Shikaru* (The Scolder), Yuki Shobo, 1964.

———, *Watashi no rirekisho* (My History) from a collection of columns published in *Nihon keizai shimbun* between 1957 and 1969.

Yasuda, Shinji, *Tsutsumi Seiji: Seibu ryutsu gurupu wo kizuita otoko no hikari to kage* (Seiji Tsutsumi: The Light and Shade of the Man Who Built the Seibu Retail Group), Paru shuppan, 1985.

ARTICLES

Akimoto, Yasushi, "Akimoto Yasushi no 'shacho' ni natta 'shonen' " (Yasushi Akimoto and the "Boy" Who Became "Chairman"), *SPA*, March 21, 1990.

Aochi, Shin, "Goto Keita to Tsutsumi Yasujiro: jimbutsu raibaru monogatari" (Keita Goto and Yasujiro Tsutsumi: Story of a Rivalry), Chuo Koron, February 1956.

Aoki, Eiichi, "Seibu tetsudo no ayumi" (History of Seibu Railway), in *Tetsudo Pikutoriaru* (Railway Pictorial), issue 560, May 1992, special issue on Seibu Railway.

"Gicho fujin no meigi ryo. happyaku man en nari" (The Fee for Being Called Speaker's Wife—Eight Million Yen), *Sunday Mainichi*, August 8, 1954.

"Hassen nin sanretsu no osogi no asa. 'Hikage no mi' no mama itta haha wo miokuru Tsutsumi Yoshiaki shi. Seibu no teio ga miseta namida" (On the Morning of a Grand Funeral Attended by Eight Thousand People, Yoshiaki Tsutsumi Sees Off His Mother, Who Died Still "the Wife in the Shadows." The Emperor of Seibu Shed Tears), *Shukan Asahi*, November 1984.

"Hosokawa Morihiro: 'Saidai no jakuten' uyoku to kane" (Morihiro Hosokawa: Biggest Weak Point—Right-winger and Money), *Shukan Bunshan*, July 9, 1992.

"Hosokawa sori ga 'Seibu' ni ashi wo mukerarenai 'jisseki' " (The "Actual Facts" of Prime Minister Hosokawa's Obligation to Seibu), *Shukan Shincho*, October 21, 1993.

"Hyakkaten mo hoteru mo fushin: Tsutsumi Seiji no 'intai' wa tekizen tobo da" (Department Stores and Hotels Both Depressed: Seiji Tsutsumi's "Retirement" Is Really Flight in the Face of the Enemy), *Shukan Bunshun*, January 25, 1991.

"Jitaku tokusetsu rinku de kitaete zenkoku rankingu 7 kurai. Tsutsumi Yoshiaki shi no chonan. Masatoshi kun wa 'sukebo' meijin" (Seventh in the Country Trained on Specially Installed Home Rink. Yoshiaki Tsutsumi's oldest son, Masatoshi, is Skateboard Champion), *Friday*, August 10, 1990.

"Juichi miyake kyo riseki: gojuichi ho go shin-seikatsu e" (Eleven Imperial Houses Today Removed from the Registry: Fifty-one People to Have a New Life), *Asahi Shimbun*, October 14, 1947.

Kaifu, Takao, "Itan no tosho Seibu okoku Tsutsumi Yoshiaki no henshin 'chichi no kage' wo fukkiraseta 'haha no shi' " (Seibu's Yoshiaki Tsutsumi, Champion of Heresy, Changes. "His father's shadow" Washed Away by "His Mother's Death"), *Shukan Asahi*, January 18, 1985.

Kamibayashi, Kunio, "Waga Tsutsumi ichizoku chi no himitsu" (My Tsutsumi Family—the Secret of Blood), *Shukan Bunshun,* August 1987.

"Kechi fudoki: Kifu nante no wa dai kirai" (Record of a Stingy Climate: I Loathe Making Donations), *Asahi Shimbun,* July 19, 1987.

Manabe, Shigeki, "Moshin suru haken gundan no akilesu ken: Tsutsumi Yoshiaki no yabo 6" (The Achilles Heel of the Conquering Army with Its Powerful Leader: Yoshiaki Tsutsumi's Ambition 6), *Shukan Gendai,* July 2, 1981.

———, "Nagashima. Seibu wo tehajimeni supotsukai seiha e!: Tsutsumi Yoshiaki no yabo 2" (Conquering the Sports World Beginning with Nagashima and Seibu!: Yoshiaki Tsutsumi's Ambition 2), *Shukan Gendai,* June 4, 1981.

———, "Seikai rannyu de nani wo nerau no ka?! Tsutsumu Yoshiaki no yabo I" (What is He Aiming at by Breaking into Politics?! Yoshiaki Tsutsumi's Ambition I), *Shukan Gendai,* May 28, 1981.

———, "Tsutsumi Yoshiaki chokugeki!" (Yoshiaki Tsutsumi Direct Hit!), *Shukan Gendai,* date uncertain—end 1987.

Miki, Yonosuke, "Hakone yama kaitaku wo kisotta Goto Keita to Pisutoru Tsutsumi" (Keita Goto and Pistol Tsutsumi: Competitors in the Development of Hakone), *Zaikai,* February 26, 1991.

———, "Kessen Hakone yama" (The Decisive Battle of Hakone), *Chuo Koron,* August 1957.

———, "Zaikai saigo no kaibutsu no shi" (Death of the Last Monster in the Financial World), *Zaikai,* July 1, 1964.

Noda, Mineo, and Tadashi Koyama, "Futatsu no 'Seibu' wo eguru! Tsutsumi Yoshiaki vs. Tsutsumi Seiji no taiketsu ima shintenkai! Retto seiha e zemmen senso totsunyu" (Carving out Two Seibus! New Development in the Confrontation of Yoshiaki Tsutsumi vs. Seiji Tsutsumi! Rushing into Full-frontal War to Control the Archipelago), *Gekkan Hoseki,* October 1986.

Ohashi, Masaaki, "Eigakai yurugasu Pari no nihon musume" (Japanese Girl in Paris Shakes the Movie World), *Shukan Tokyo,* December 14, 1957.

Oshita, Eiji, "Seibu okoku no meishu wo uba e! Tsutsumi Seibi vs. Tsutsumi Yoshiaki—kotsuniku no zemmen senso" (To Snatch the Leadership of the Seibu Empire! Seiji Tsutsumi vs. Yoshiaki Tsutsumi—All-out Sibling War), *Gekkan Gendai,* December 1984.

" 'Purinsesu' Tsutsumi Kuniko-san shoshin no hibi" ("Princess" Kuniko Tsutsumi's Days of Heartbreak), *Sankei Shimbun,* November 25, 1979.

Sadaka, Makoto, "Ki ni kakaru 'hadaka no osama' no yukusue" (The Worrying Direction of the Emperor Who Has No Clothes), *Asahi Journal,* 1987.

———, "Seibu tetsudo gurupu" (Seibu Railway Group), *Asahi Journal,* 1987.

"Seibu okoku 'nazo no jotei' Misao-san wo okuru Tsutsumi Seiji famiri no igaina hyojo" (Unexpected Expressions on the Faces of Seiji Tsutsumi and His Family, Seeing Off the "Mysterious Queen" of the Seibu Empire), *Friday,* December 7, 1984.

"Seibu Sezon no purinsu Tsutsumi Koji shi to homan aidoru Takeda Kumiko no 'kosai' hakkaku" (Revelation of Relationship Between the Prince of Seibu Saison and Curvaceous Idol Kumiko Takeda), *Shukan Gendai,* July 7, 1990.

"Seibu tetsudo to Sezon ga jigyo kyoryoku: Yukidoke e no dai ichi bu" (Seibu Railway and Saison Business Tie-up: First Step to a Thaw), *Nihon Keizai Shimbun,* June 22, 1993.

"Soni-san ga eiga-gaisha wo baishu shita yoni, jibun mo eiga jigyo ga kongo okina pointo wo shimeru to omotte yatteiru wake desu" (Just as Sony Bought a Film Company, I'm Doing It Because the Film Industry is Going to Be Major), *Shukan Posuto*, February 16, 1992.

"Sosaisen ni katsuyaku shita 'Tsutsumi kyodai' no shohai" (Wins and Losses of the Brothers Tsutsumi Who Plunged into the Presidential Election), *Shukan Shincho*, 1987.

Tateishi, Yasunori, "PARCO seiko no makoto no kosekisha: Tsutsumi Seiji kyoki no keiei, dai yon bu" (The True Creator of Parco's Success: Seiji Tsutsumi's Mad Management, Part 4), *Shokun!*, August 1989.

———, "Seibu hyakkaten gurupu zankoku monogatari" (The Cruel Story of Seibu Department Store Group), *Shukan Gendai*, August 21, 1993.

———, "Tetsugaku naki bocho no yukue: Tsutsumi Seiji kyoki no keiei, dai san bu" (Direction of the Expansion without Philosophy: Seiji Tsutsumi's Mad Management, Part 3), *Shokun!*, July 1989.

Tsutsumi, Misao, "Jigyo no oni to tomoni sanjukyu nen" (Thirty-nine Years with the Demon of Business), *Fujin Koron*, 1964.

———, "Shikaru nushi wo ushinatte" (Losing the Scolder), Epilogue to *Shikaru* (The Scolder).

Tsutsumi, Seiji, "Rekidai sannin no shusho ni suikyo sareta hito" (The Man Who Was Recommended by Three Prime Ministers), in *Ningen. Yamashita Ganri* (Ganri Yamashita: The Person), *Ikkosha*, November 1967.

"Tsutsumi Asako-san. 30 sai no sugao" (The Unpainted Face of Thirty-year-old Asako Tsutsumi), *Josei Sebun*, October 23, 1968.

"Tsutsumi Seiji 'dokushin shugi' no zasetsu" (Collapse of Seiji Tsutsumi's Principle of Staying Single), *Shukan Bunshun*, October 21, 1968.

Yamanaka, Keiko, "Une Vie à l'étranger 3: Tsutsumi Kuniko: hanayakana seiko no kage ni" (A Life Abroad 3: Kuniko Tsutsumi: Behind the Bright Success), *La Seine*, 1990.

Yamashita, Tsuyoshi, "Tsutsumi Yasujiro-shi no haka wo meguru 'kaidan' " (Ghost Stories That Circulate the Tomb of Yasujiro Tsutsumi), *Hoseki*, September 1975.

TELECAST AND RADIO BROADCAST

Kono hito kono michi (This Man, This Road), recorded by NHK, April 1964.

Tsuma wo kataru (Talking About My Wife), broadcast on TBS radio, February 24, 1964.

English-language sources

BOOKS

Beasley, W. G., *The Rise of Modern Japan*, Charles E. Tuttle Company, Rutland, Vt., and Tokyo, Japan, 1990.

Behr, Edward, *Hirohito: Behind the Myth*, Hamish Hamilton, London, 1989.

Bergamini, David, *Japan's Imperial Conspiracy*, William Morrow and Company, New York, 1971.

Fewster, Stuart, and Tony Gorton, *Japan: From Shogun to Superstate*, Paul Norbury Publications, London, 1987.

Gayn, Mark, *Japan Diary*, Charles E. Tuttle Company, Rutland, Vt. and Tokyo, Japan, 1981 (first published 1948).

Horsley, William, and Roger Buckley, *Nippon New Superpower:* Japan since 1945, BBC Books, 1990.

Kosaka, Masataka, *A History of Postwar Japan*, Kodansha International, Tokyo and New York, 1972.

Minichiello, Sharon, *Retreat from Reform: Patterns of Political Behavior in Interwar Japan*, University of Hawaii Press, 1984.

Mishima, Yukio, and Geoffrey Bownas, editors, *New Writing in Japan*, Penguin Books, London, 1972.

Oka, Yoshitaka, *Five Political Leaders of Modern Japan*, translated by Fraser and Murray, University of Tokyo Press, 1986.

Packard, Jerrold M., *Sons of Heaven: A Portrait of the Japanese Monarchy*, Charles Scribner's Sons, New York, 1987.

Richards, Tom, and Charles Rudd, *Japanese Railways in the Meiji Period 1868–1912*, Brunel University, London, 1991.

Roberts, John G., *Mitsui: Three Centuries of Japanese Business*, Weatherhill, New York and Tokyo, 1973.

Stokes, Henry Scott, *The Life and Death of Yukio Mishima*, Charles E. Tuttle Company, Rutland, Vt., and Tokyo, Japan, 1975.

Seibu Group of Enterprises: Its Characteristics, Present Conditions and Future Prospects, Seibu, 1961.

Seidensticker, Edward, *Low City, High City: Tokyo from Edo to the Earthquake, 1867–1923*, Alfred A. Knopf, New York, 1983.

———, *Tokyo Rising: The City Since the Great Earthquake*, Alfred A. Knopf, New York, 1990.

Tasker, Peter, *Inside Japan: Wealth, Work and Power in the New Japanese Empire*, Sidgwick & Jackson, London, 1987.

Tsujii, Takashi, *Age of Disorder*, translated by Geoffrey Bownas, in Mishima and Bownas, eds., *New Writing in Japan.*

———, *Quiet Town*, translated by Geoffrey Bownas, in Mishima and Bownas, eds., *New Writing in Japan*, Penguin Books, London, 1972.

———, *A Spring Like Any Other (Isumo to Onaji Haru)*, translated by Beth Cary, Kodansha International, Tokyo and New York, 1992.

———, *A Stone Monument on a Fine Day: Selected Poems*, translated by Hisao Kanaseki and Timothy Harris, Libro Port, 1990.

Tsutsumi, Yasujiro, *Bridge across the Pacific*, Sanko Cultural Research Institute, 1964.

Vining, Elizabeth Gray, *Windows for the Crown Prince: Akihito of Japan*, Charles E. Tuttle Company, Rutland, Vt., and Tokyo, Japan, 1989 (first published 1952).

Waley, Paul, *Tokyo Now and Then: An Explorer's Guide*, Weatherhill, New York and Tokyo, 1984.

Waseda University: A photographic history of 100 years (1882–1982), Waseda University, Tokyo, 1982.

Whiting, Robert, *The Chrysanthemum and the Bat*, Dodd, Mead and Company, New York, 1977.

Whiting, Robert, *You Gotta Have Wa: When Two Cultures Collide on the Baseball Diamond*, Macmillan Publishing Company, New York, 1989.

Yoshida, Shigeru, *The Yoshida Memoirs,* translated by Kenichi Yoshida, Heinemann, London, 1961.

ARTICLES

Abe, Yoshibumi, "Saison Founder Wields Power Behind Curtain," *Nikkei Weekly,* March 23, 1993.

Allen, Mike, "Seiyu: A Dynamic Reassessment," Barclays de Zoete Wedd Research, July 31, 1992.

Bornoff, Nick, "Japan's Apostle of *Raifustairu* (lifestyle)," *Asian Advertising & Marketing,* June 1990.

"Bright Young President Pushing Seibu into Lead among Department Stores," *Japan Times,* June 17, 1960.

Hagiwara, Takao, "Business Rivals (10)," *Yomiuri,* March 22, 1966.

Hayabusa, Nagaharu, "The Tsutsumi Brothers, Feuding Magnates," *Japan Quarterly,* April–June 1988.

"Head of Saison Conglomerate Steps Down," *Japan Times,* January 14, 1991.

Horiguchi, Bob, "Inside the Weeklies: Why Didn't Millionaire Brothers Bail out Jetset Sister?," *Japan Times,* November 14, 1978.

"The Imperial Takeda Family (Distinguished Families of Japan 23)," *Mainichi Daily News,* October 2, 1991.

Ishii, Yohei, "Intercontinental Hotels: Too Big for Saison Group to Swallow?," *Tokyo Business Today,* March 1992.

Ishizawa, Masato, "Arrest of Seibu Executives Exposes 'Sales Supremacy' Strategy," *Nikkei Weekly,* July 4, 1992.

"Japan: The Young King of Prince Hotels," *Business Week,* October 13, 1973.

"Japanese Casino Proprietress Runs Out of Luck," *Japan Times,* October 26, 1979.

Kanise, Seiichi, "Joust of the Half Brothers," *Time,* November 21, 1988.

Kinmont, A., and K. Ohtsuki, "Railways Sector Research (9002): Seibu Railway," Credit Lyonnais Alexanders Laing & Cruikshank Securities, Japan, August 1988.

Kometani, Foumiko, "The Conversation: Seiji Tsutsumi," *Tokyo Journal,* January 1991.

Kuroda, Kazuo, "Rivalry of Tycoons: Two Railway Magnates Widely Recognized for Enterprising Spirit," *Japan Times,* October 18, 1958.

"Lax Management Played Big Role in Seibu Scandal," *Mainichi,* July 21, 1992.

Matsuzaka, Takeshi, "Tsutsumi Brothers Bury the Hatchet," *Nikkei Weekly,* June 28, 1993.

Menkes, Suzy, "The Pioneer Behind an Empire," *International Herald Tribune,* October 10, 1992.

Morikawa, Kathleen, "Celebrations are over for Nagano: Challenges Have Just Begun," *Asahi,* July 6, 1991.

Murata, Kiyoaki, "Japan's Biggest Real Estate Man," *Nippon Times,* April 6, 1954.

"New Diet Speaker is Known as a Successful Businessman," *Tokyo Evening News,* May 19, 1953.

Ogihara, Makiko, "Hotel Deal Revives Seibu Fraternal Rivalry," *Japan Economic Journal,* October 29, 1988.

Rubinfien, Elisabeth, "Family Rivals Build an Empire in Japan," *Wall Street Journal,* December 30–31, 1988.

Sato, Seichu, "Making Full Use of People," *Business Tokyo,* September 1987.

"Seibu Boss's Sister Indicted in France," *Mainichi,* October 27, 1979.

"Seibu Saison Boosts Hotel Business," *Tokyo Business Today,* March 1989.

Shoji, Kaori, "The Harder They Fall," *Business Tokyo,* September 1991.

Stokes, Henry Scott, "The Plight of Artists," *Asahi Evening News,* September 7, 1979.

"Strong Criticism of Tsutsumi Brothers," *Tokyo Business Today,* December 1987.

"Tourist Titans are Engaged in Running Battle for Power," *Yomiuri Japan News,* April 3, 1958.

"Tsutsumi Ceding Some Control in new Saison Setup," *Yomiuri newspaper,* January 13, 1991.

"Tsutsumi Stepping Down from Frontlines of Saison," *Tokyo Business Today,* February 1991.

Tsumiji, Takao, "7 Days a Week Makes an Executive," *Asahi Evening News,* May 8, 1985.

Webb, Peter, with Alan M. Field, "Family Fortunes: Rising Sons," *Newsweek,* August 23, 1976.

French-language sources

TELECAST

Antoine, Jean, *Seiji Tsutsumi, ou, Les Vertus de la fortune,* La Sept RTBF-BRT Cinéma et communication, en association avec FR3-Oceaniques, 1990.

Notes

Epigraphs

Yasujiro is quoted in Sadaka, "Seibu tetsudo gurupu" (Seibu Railway Group).
Yoshiaki is quoted in Oshita, "Seibu Okoku no meishu wo uba e!" (To Snatch the Leadership of the Seibu Empire!).
The last is an excerpt from Seiji's *Itsumo to onaji haru* (A Spring Like Any Other).

Prologue

1 Manabe, "Moshin suru haken gundan no akilesu ken" (The Achilles Heel of the Conquering Army with Its Powerful Leader).

PART I *The Patriarch*

General sources (for details, see bibliography):
Tsutsumi, Yasujiro: *Bridge across the Pacific; Kuto san-ju nen* (Thirty Years of Struggle); *Shikaru* (The Scolder); *Watashi no rirekisho* (My History).
Chikui, *Tsutsumi Yasujiro den* (Story of Yasujiro Tsutsumi).
Inose, *Mikado no shozo* (Portrait of the Emperor).
Kaminogo, *Seibu Okoku* (Seibu Empire).
Tsujii, *Hoko no kisetsu no nakade* (In the Season of Roaming).
Kamibayashi, "Waga Tsutsumi ichizoku" (My Tsutsumi family).
Minichiello, *Retreat from Reform*.

Chapter I *The Beginning*

1 Chikui, *Tsutsumi Yasujiro den* (Story of Yasujiro Tsutsumi).
2 Tsutsumi, Yasujiro, *Shikaru* (The Scolder).
3 Tsujii, *Hoko no kisetsu no nakade* (In the Season of Roaming).
4 Kamibayashi, "Waga Tsutsumi ichizoku" (My Tsutsumi Family). The quotation marks are Kamibayashi's.
5 Ibid.
6 Tsutsumi, Yasujiro, *Shikaru* (The Scolder).
7 Tsutsumi, Yasujiro, *Kuto san-ju nen* (Thirty Years of Struggle).
8 *Kono hito kono michi* (This Man, This Road).
9 Tsutsumi, Yasujiro, *Kuto san-ju nen* (Thirty Years of Struggle).

Chapter 2 *Escape*

1 Chikui, *Tsutsumi Yasujiro den* (Story of Yasujiro Tsutsumi).
2 Oka, *Five Political Leaders of Modern Japan*.
3 Tsutsumi, Yasujiro, *Watashi no rirekisho* (My History).
4 *Waseda University: A Photographic History of 100 Years*.
5 Tsutsumi, Yasujiro, *Bridge across the Pacific*.
6 Tsutsumi, Yasujiro, *Watashi no rirekisho* (My History).
7 Children were automatically the property of the father, produced in order to perpetuate the father's family name. In the case of divorce, the wife returned to her parents while the children stayed with the father.
8 Quoted in Inose, *Mikado no shozo* (Portrait of the Emperor).
9 Tsutsumi, Yasujiro, *Bridge across the Pacific*.
10 Tsutsumi, Yasujiro, *Watashi no rirekisho* (My History).

Chapter 3 *Breaking New Ground*

1 Kamibayashi, "Waga Tsutsumi ichizoku" (My Tsutsumi Family).
2 Inose, *Mikado no shozo* (Portrait of the Emperor).
3 Kamibayashi, "Waga Tsutsumi ichizoku" (My Tsutsumi Family).
4 Inose, *Mikado no shozo* (Portrait of the Emperor).
5 Nakajima, *Karuizawa hishochi* (The Summer Resort of Karuizawa).

Chapter 4 *The Women*

1 Tsutsumi, Yasujiro, *Shikaru* (The Scolder).
2 Tsutsumi, Misao, "Jigyo no oni to tomoni san-jukyu nen" (Thirty-nine Years with the Demon of Business).
3 Kamibayashi, "Waga Tsutsumi ichizoku" (My Tsutsumi Family).
4 Tsujii, *Hoko no kisetsu no nakade* (In the Season of Roaming).
5 Inose, *Mikado no shozo* (Portrait of the Emperor).
6 Ibid.
7 Tsutsumi, Yasujiro *Watashi no rirekisho* (My History).
8 Inose, *Mikado no shozo* (Portrait of the Emperor).
9 This was the cabinet formed after the assassination of Prime Minister Inukai and led by Admiral Makoto Saito; it included representatives of both parties.
10 Minichiello, *Retreat from Reform*.
11 Tsutsumi, Yasujiro, *Watashi no rirekisho* (My History).
12 Ibid.
13 Ibid.
14 Ibid.
15 Tsutsumi, Yasujiro, *Bridge across the Pacific*.

Chapter 5 *The War Years*

1 Tsutsumi, Yasujiro, *Bridge across the Pacific*.
2 Kamibayashi, "Waga Tsutsumi ichizoku" (My Tsutsumi Family).
3 "Gisho fujin no meigi ryo" (The Fee for Being Called Speaker's Wife).
4 Tsujii, *Hoko no kisetsu no nakade* (In the Season of Roaming).
5 Ibid.

6   Tsutsumi, Misao, "Jigyo no oni to tomoni san-ju-kyu nen" (Thirty-nine Years with the Demon of Business).
7   Tsutsumi, Yasujiro, *Kuto san-ju nen* (Thirty Years of Struggle).
8   Ibid.
9   Kaminogo, *Seibu Okoku* (Seibu Empire).
10 Tsujii, *Hoko no kisetsu no nakade* (In the Season of Roaming).
11 Ibid.

Chapter 6 *The Imperial Link*

1   Tsujii, *Hoko no kisetsu no nakade* (In the Season of Roaming).
2   Ibid.
3   Ibid.
4   Gayn, *Japan Diary.*
5   Seidensticker, *Tokyo Rising.*
6   "Ju-ichi miyake kyo riseki" (Eleven Imperial Houses Today Removed from the Registry).
7   Inose, *Mikado no shozo* (Portrait of the Emperor).
8   Ibid.
9   The House of Representatives, the equivalent of the House of Commons.
10 "Gen-miyasama no seikatsu shin sekkei" (The Ex-imperial Families' New Life), *Asahigraph,* March 17, 1948.
11 Unlike his father and grandfather, who attended the exclusive Gakushuin (Peers' School) only during their primary school years, on the occupation's orders Akihito became a regular student at the Middle School there, where Mrs. Vining, who was also his private tutor, gave classes. See her *Windows for the Crown Prince.*

Chapter 7 *The War of Hakone Mountain*

1   Miki, "Zaikai saigo no kaibutsu no shi" (Death of the Last Monster).
2   Aochi, "Goto Keita to Tsutsumi Yasujiro: jimbutsu raibaru monogatari" (Keita Goto and Yasujiro Tsutsumi: Story of a Rivalry).
3   Tsutsumi, Yasujiro, *Kuto san-ju nen* (Thirty Years of Struggle).
4   Miki, "Zaikai saigo no kaibutsu no shi" (Death of the Last Monster).
5   Ibid.
6   Miki, "Hakone yama kaitaku wo kisotta Goto Keita to Pisutoru Tsutsumi" (Competitors in the Development of Hakone).
7   Tsutsumi, Yasujiro, *Kuto san-ju nen* (Thirty Years of Struggle).
8   "Seibu Line Wins Battle for Road," *Japan Times,* Friday, March 17, 1961.

Chapter 8 *Elder Statesman*

1   The two main parties of the right after the war were Yoshida's Liberals, the successor to the prewar Association of Political Friends, and the Democratic Party, which had originated as Okuma's Progressive Party. As before the war, Yasujiro was a member of the Progressive/Democratic Party. The Socialist opposition was split into two, the left and the right, and there were also many smaller parties of every color.

2 Murata, "Japan's Biggest Real Estate Man." (The *Nippon Times* later became known as the *Japan Times*.)
3 "New Diet Speaker Is Known as a Successful Businessman."
4 "Gicho fujin no meigi ryo" (The Fee for Being Called Speaker's Wife).
5 Ibid.
6 Tsutsumi, Yasujiro, *Kuto san-ju nen* (Thirty Years of Struggle).
7 Ibid.
8 "House Speaker and Vice-Speaker Plan to Resign," *Nippon Times,* June 5, 1954.
9 "Speaker Explains Why He Did Not Use Judo," *Japan News,* October 1, 1954.
10 Tsutsumi, Yasujiro, *Kuto san-ju nen* (Thirty Years of Struggle).
11 *My Life Between Japan and America,* by Edwin O. Reischauer, John Weatherhill, Inc., 1986.
12 *Tsuma wo kataru* (Talking about My Wife), TBS radio.
13 Tsutsumi, Misao, "Jigyo no oni to tomoni san-ju-kyu nen" (Thirty-nine Years with the Demon of Business).
14 Tsutsumi, Yasujiro, *Bridge across the Pacific.*
15 Ibid.
16 Hayabusa Nagaharu, "The Tsutsumi Brothers, Feuding Magnates."
17 Tsutsumi, Yasujiro, *Bridge across the Pacific.*
18 "Tsutsumi to meet Eisenhower today," *Japan Times,* January 12, 1961.
19 Miki, "Zaikai saigo no kaibutsu no shi" (Death of the Last Monster).
20 Ibid.
21 "Tachiai enzetsu: junin to iro" (Speech Contest: Ten Men, Ten Ideas), *Shiga nichi nichi shimbun,* November 7, 1963.
22 "Doronuma no Tsutsumi ha ihan" (Tsutsumi Faction's Slough of Violations), *Shiga nichi nichi shimbun,* December 10, 1963.
23 Miki, "Zaikai saigo no kaibutsu no shi" (Death of the Last Monster).

PART II *The Sons*

General sources:
Tsujii, *Hoko no kisetsu no nakade* (In the Season of Roaming); *Itsumo to onaji haru* (A Spring Like Any Other).
Kaminogo, *Seibu Okoku* (Seibu Empire).

Chapter 9 *The Rebel*

1 Tsujii, *Hoko no kisetsu no nakade* (In the Season of Roaming).
2 Ibid.
3 Gayn, *Japan Diary.*
4 Antoine, *Seiji Tsutsumi, ou, Les Vertus de la fortune,* La Sept RTBF-BRT Cinéma et communication.
5 Ibid.
6 Tsujii, *Hoko no kisetsu no nakade* (In the Season of Roaming).
7 Ibid.
8 Ibid.
9 Ibid.
10 Ibid.

11 Kometani, "The Conversation: Seiji Tsutsumi."
12 Tsujii, *Hoko no kisetsu no nakade* (In the Season of Roaming).

Chapter 10 *Taking Flight*

1 Kometani, "The Conversation: Seiji Tsutsumi."
2 Ibid.
3 "Bright Young President Pushing Seibu into Lead among Department Stores," *Japan Times,* June 17, 1960.
4 Ibid.
5 *Seibu Group of Enterprises: Its Characteristics, Present Conditions and Future Prospects.*
6 Ibid.

Chapter 11 *A Very Ordinary Boy*

1 Akimoto, "Akimoto Yasushi no 'shacho' ni natta 'shonen' " (Yasushi Akimoto and the "boy" who became "chairman").
2 Inose, *Mikado no shozo* (Portrait of the Emperor).
3 Ibid.
4 Oshita, *Waga seishun no Waseda* (My Youthful Waseda).

Chapter 12 *Death of the Last Giant*

1 The name changed in 1960 from Asahi Chemical Fertilizers to Seibu Chemicals.
2 *Tsuma wo kataru* (Talking about My Wife), TBS radio.
3 *Kono hito kono michi* (This Man, This Road), NHK.
4 Griffin, Stuart, "Meeting the People: Misao Tsutsumi," *Mainichi Daily News,* April 14, 1964.
5 Tsutsumi, Misao, "Shikaru nushi wo ushinatte" (Losing the Scolder).
6 Hara, Hyo, "Tsutsumi Yasujiro shi wo itamu: Jo ni atsui 'jigyo no oni' "(Grieving for Mr. Yasujiro Tsutsumi: Warm-hearted "Demon of Business"), *Asahi Shimbun,* April 26, 1964.
7 Miki, "Zaikai saigo no kaibutsu no shi" (Death of the Last Monster).
8 Kaminogo, *Seibu Okoko* (Seibu Empire).
9 Antoine, *Seiji Tsutsumi, ou, Les Vertus de la fortune,* La Sept RTBF-BRT Cinéma et communication.
10 Yamashita, "Tsutsumi Yasujiro shi no haka wo meguru 'kaidan' " (Ghost Stories that Circulate the Tomb of Yasujiro Tsutsumi).

PART III *New Beginnings*

General sources:
Tsujii, *Itsumo to onaji haru* (A Spring Like Any Other).
Kaminogo, *Seibu Okoku* (Seibu Empire) and *Shin.Seibu Okoku* (New Seibu Empire).
Yasuda, *Tsutsumi Seiji: . . . hikari to kage* (Seiji Tsutsumi: The Light and Shade).

Chapter 13 *The Midas Years*

1   Interview with the author, 1990.
2   Stokes, *The Life and Death of Yukio Mishima.*
3   *Queen* magazine, January 1970, quoted in Stokes, *The Life and Death of Yukio Mishima.*
4   Kometani, "The Conversation: Seiji Tsutsumi."
5   Yasuda, *Tsutsumi Seiji: . . . hikari to kage* (Seiji Tsutsumi: The Light and Shade).
6   Antoine, *Seiji Tsutsumi, ou, Les Vertus de la fortune,* La Sept RTBF-BRT Cinéma et communication.
7   Kaifu, "Itan no tosho Seibu okoku Tsutsumi Yoshiaki no henshin" (Seibu's Yoshiaki Tsutsumi, Chairman of Heresy, Changes).
8   Kaminogo, *Seibu Okoku* (Seibu Empire).
9   Ibid.
10 Sadaka, "Ki ni kakaru 'hadaka no osama' no yukusue" (The Worrying Direction of the Emperor Who Has No Clothes).
11 Tateishi, "PARCO seiko no makoto no kosekisha" (The True Creator of Parco's Success).

Chapter 14 *The Oil Shock and Its Aftermath*

1   Shimomura, Mitsuko, "Hope for Better Times Is Ruled out by Tsutsumi," *Asahi Evening News,* February 20, 1976.
2   Webb et al., "Family Fortunes: Rising Sons."
3   Kaminogo, *Seibu Okoku* (Seibu Empire).
4   Ibid.
5   Sevenoaks, Tim, "Tsujii's *Spring* is far too ordinary," *Japan Times,* August 18, 1992.
6   Tsujii, *Itsumo to onaji haru* (A Spring Like Any Other).

Chapter 15 *The Sleeping Lion Wakes*

1   Kobayashi, *Tsutsumi Yoshiaki: 12 oku en no tochi wo motsu otoko no jigyo senryaku* (Yoshiaki Tsutsumi: Business Strategy of the Man Who Has ¥1.2 Billion Worth of Land).
2   Yamashita, "Tsutsumi Yasujiro shi no haka wo meguru 'kaidan' " (Ghost Stories that Circulate the Tomb of Yasujiro Tsutsumi).
3   In the traditional way, the ceremony was Shinto; weddings are usually Shinto, whereas funerals are Buddhist.
4   Kaminogo, *Shin Seibu Okoku* (New Seibu Empire).
5   Eikawa, *Tsutsumi Yoshiaki no hasso* (Yoshiaki Tsutsumi's Concept).
6   Ibid.
7   Kaminogo, *Seibu Okoku* (Seibu Empire).
8   "Japan: The Young King of Prince Hotels," *Business Week.*
9   Kaminogo, *Seibu Okoku* (Seibu Empire).
10 "Japan: The Young King of Prince Hotels," *Business Week.*
11 Webb et al., "Family Fortunes: Rising Sons."
12 Akimoto, "Akimoto Yasushi no 'shacho' ni natta 'shonen' " (Yasushi Akimoto and the "Boy" Who Became "Chairman").

13 Inose, *Mikado no shozo* (Portrait of the Emperor).

14 Kaifu, "Itan no tosho Seibu okoku Tsutsumi Yoshiaki no henshin" (Seibu's Yoshiaki Tsutsumi, Champion of Heresy, Changes).

15 Kaifu, "Itan no tosho Seibu okoku Tsutsumi Yoshiaki no henshin" (Seibu's Yoshiaki Tsutsumi, champion of heresy, changes).

16 Ibid.

17 Ibid.

18 Tsumiji, "7 Days a Week Makes an Executive."

19 Kaminogo, *Seibu Okoku* (Seibu Empire).

20 "Kechi fudoki: Kifu nante no wa dai kirai" (Record of a Stingy Climate: I Loathe Making Donations), *Asahi Shimbun*.

21 Kaminogo, *Seibu Okoku* (Seibu Empire).

Chapter 16 *Playing for Power*

1 Manabe, "Moshin suru haken gundan no akilesu ken" (The Achilles Heel of the Conquering Army with Its Powerful Leader).

2 Whiting, *You Gotta Have Wa*. Cricket was in fact played before baseball in the 1860s at the Yokohama Athletic Club but never caught on because a game takes too long.

3 Manabe, "Nagashima Seibu wo te hajimeni supotsukai seiha e!" (Conquering the Sports World Beginning with Nagashima and Seibu!).

4 Oshita, *Waga seishun no Waseda* (My Youthful Waseda).

5 Kaminogo, *Seibu Okoku* (Seibu Empire).

6 Whiting, *You Gotta Have Wa*.

7 Ibid.

8 Ibid.

9 Miki, "Zaikai saigo no kaibutsu no shi" (Death of the Last Monster).

10 Tsutsumi, Seiji, "Rekidai sannin no shusho ni suikyo sareta hito" (The Man Who Was Recommended by Three Prime Ministers).

11 Tanaka was arrested in July 1976 and accused of receiving $2.1 million in bribes from the Lockheed Corporation for promoting the sale of Lockheed's Tristar airplane to All Nippon Airways during his 1972–74 tenure as prime minister. The case dragged on for years, and Tanaka had no difficulty in being reelected four times during the proceedings. In 1983 he was fined and sentenced to four years' imprisonment, but he immediately appealed and was released on bail.

12 Kaminogo, *Seibu Okoku* (Seibu Empire).

13 Manabe, "Seikai rannyu de nani wo nerau no ka?!" (What Is He Aiming at by Breaking into Politics?!)

14 Under the prewar constitution, the upper house is held to consist of "learned and experienced persons" and representatives of professional interests. Of the 252 upper-house seats, 100 are elected from the nation at large, or national constituency, with the remaining 152 elected from local constituencies on the prefectural level.

15 Manabe, "Seikai rannyu de nani wo nerau no ka?!" (What Is He Aiming at by Breaking into Politics?!)

16 Ibid.

17 Ibid.

18 Ibid.
19 Ibid.

PART IV *Rival Empires*

General sources:
Kaminogo, *Shin Seibu Okoku* (New Seibu Empire).
Noda et al., "Futatsu no 'Seibu' wo eguru!" (Carving out Two Seibus!).
Taniguchi, *Tsutsumi Yoshiaki to Orimpikku* (Yoshiaki Tsutsumi and the Olympics).
Tsujii, *Itsumo to onaji haru* (A Spring Like Any Other).

Chapter 17 *The Mysterious Deaths of the Two Mothers*

1 Kaminogo, *Shin Seibu Okuku* (New Seibu Empire).
2 Ibid.
3 Tsutsumi, Misao, "Jigyo no oni to tomoni san-ju-kyu nen" (Thirty-nine Years with the Demon of Business).
4 Interview with Yoshiaki in *Shukan Sankei,* quoted in Kaminogo, *Shin Seibu Okoku* (New Seibu Empire).
5 "Hassen nin sanretsu no osogi no asa . . ." (On the Morning of a Grand Funeral Attended by 8,000 People . . .).
6 Kaifu, "Itan no tosho Seibu okoku Tsutsumi Yoshiaki no henshin" (Seibu's Yoshiaki Tsutsumi, Champion of Heresy, Changes).

Chapter 18 *The Age of Gold*

1 Kaminogo, *Shin Seibu Okoku* (New Seibu Empire).
2 Ibid.
3 Kaifu, "Itan no tosho Seibu okoku Tsutsumi Yoshiaki no henshin" (Seibu's Yoshiaki Tsutsumi, Champion of Heresy, Changes).
4 Noda et al., "Futatsu no 'Seibu' wo eguru!" (Carving out Two Seibus!).
5 Ibid.
6 Ibid.
7 Horsley and Buckley, *Nippon New Superpower.*
8 "Japanese Buyer of Renoir, Van Gogh Was Prepared to Pay Even Higher," *Asahi Evening News,* May 19, 1990.
9 Horsley and Buckley, *Nippon New Superpower.*
10 From the *New York Times* of October 1988, quoted in Bornoff, "Japan's Apostle of Raifustairu (Lifestyle)."
11 Ogihara, "Hotel Deal Revives Seibu Fraternal Rivalry."
12 "Seibu Saison Boosts Hotel Business," *Tokyo Business Today.*
13 Allen, "Seiyu: A Dynamic Reassessment," BZW Research.
14 "Seibu Saison Boosts Hotel Business," *Tokyo Business Today.*
15 Allen, "Seiyu: A Dynamic Reassessment," BZW Research.

Chapter 19 *The Emperor*

1 Kaifu, "Itan no tosho Seibu okoku Tsutsumi Yoshiaki no henshin" (Seibu's Yoshiaki Tsutsumi, Champion of Heresy, Changes).

2 Manabe, *Tsutsumi Yoshiaki no keiei tamashii* (The Management Spirit of Yoshiaki Tsutsumi).

3 Kaifu, "Itan no tosho Seibu okoku Tsutsumi Yoshiaki no henshin" (Seibu's Yoshiaki Tsutsumi, Champion of Heresy, Changes).

4 Ibid.

5 Noda et al., "Futatsu no 'Seibu' wo eguru!" (Carving out Two Seibus!).

6 Kinmont et al., "Railways Sector Research (9002): Seibu Railway," Credit Lyonnais Alexanders Laing & Cruikshank Securities.

7 Kobayashi, *Tsutsumi Yoshiaki, 12 oku en no tochi wo motsu otoko no jigyo senryaku* (Business Strategy of the Man Who Has ¥1.2 Billion Worth of Land).

8 Manabe, "Tsutsumi Yoshiaki chokugeki!" (Yoshiaki Tsutsumi Direct Hit!).

9 "Sosaisen ni katsuyaku shita 'Tsutsumi kyodai' no shohai" (Wins and Losses of the Brothers Tsutsumi Who Plunged into the Presidential Election), *Shukan Shincho*.

10 Manabe, "Tsutsumi Yoshiaki chokugeki!" (Yoshiaki Tsutsumi Direct Hit!).

11 Sato, "Making Full Use of People."

12 Noda et al., "Futatsu no 'Seibu' wo eguru!" (Carving out Two Seibus!).

13 Ibid.

14 Taniguchi, *Tsutsumi Yoshiaki to Orimpikku* (Yoshiaki Tsutsumi and the Olympics).

15 "Independence Is Goal of Olympic Committee," *Japan Times*, August 11, 1989.

16 Kinmont et al., "Railways Sector Research (9002): Seibu Railways," Credit Lyonnais Alexanders Laing & Cruikshank Securities.

17 Taniguchi, *Tsutsumi Yoshiaki to Orimpikku* (Yoshiaki Tsutsumi and the Olympics).

18 "JOC Drops Downhill Ski Course Idea in Nagano's Shiga Heights," *Asahi Evening News*, April 5, 1990.

19 "JOC Chief Tsutsumi Tenders Resignation," *Yomiuri* newspaper, April 13, 1990.

20 Taniguchi, *Tsutsumi Yoshiaki to Orimpikku* (Yoshiaki Tsutsumi and the Olympics).

21 "We Can Hear Yoshiaki Tsutsumi Laughing," *Shukan Bunshun*. June 27, 1991.

22 Taniguchi, *Tsutsumi Yoshiaki to Orimpikku* (Yoshiaki Tsutsumi and the Olympics).

23 "Nagano Wins Right to Host 1998 Winter Olympics," *Asahi Evening News*, June 17, 1991.

24 Chujo, Kazuo, "Tsutsumi Undermines Trust in the JOC," *Asahi Evening News*, January 12, 1992.

Chapter 20 *Achieving Peace*

1 Antoine, *Seiji Tsutsumi, ou, Les Vertus de la fortune*, La Sept RTBF-BRT Cinéma et communication.

2 Kadokawa's career ended abruptly on August 29, 1993, when he was arrested on suspicion of being the mastermind behind a cocaine-smuggling syndicate.

3 Kometani, "The Conversation: Seiji Tsutsumi."

4 Seiji was using the word "public" to mean not "listed" but "having a responsibility to its employees."

5 Abe, "Saison Founder Wields Power Behind Curtain."

6 "Head of Saison Conglomerate Steps Down," *Japan Times.*

7 "Tsutsumi Ceding Some Control in New Saison Setup," *Yomiuri* newspaper.

8 At the time the Saison Group's debt was estimated at $17.8 billion.

9 Shoji, "The Harder They Fall."

10 According to *Forbes,* July 22, 1991, the Inter-Continentals lost $63 million in 1989 and $26 million in 1990 and forecast a loss of $34 million in 1991.

11 Allen, "Seiyu: a dynamic reassessment," BZW Research.

12 From "A Life," in Tsujii, *A Stone Monument on a Fine Day.*

13 Kometani, "The Conversation: Seiji Tsutsumi."

14 Tateishi, "Seibu hyakkaten gurupu zankoku monogatari" (The Cruel Story of Seibu Department Store Group).

15 Kaifu, "Itan no tosho Seibu okoku Tsutsumi no henshin" (Seibu's Yoshiaki Tsutsumi, Champion of Heresy, Changes).

Epilogue

1 *Nihon Keizai Shimbun* (Japan Economic Journal), June 21, 1993; *Nikkei Weekly,* June 28, 1993.

2 "Seibu tetsudo to Sezon ga jigyo kyoryoku" (Seibu Railway and Saison Business Tie-up), *Nihon Keizai Shimbun,* June 22, 1993.

3 *Kyodo,* April 26, 1993.

4 "Seibu tetsudo to Sezon ga jigyo kyoryoku" (Seibu Railway and Saison Business Tie-up), *Nihon Keizai Shimbun,* June 22, 1993.

5 "Hosokawa Morihiro: 'Saidai no jakuten' uyoku to kane" (Morihiro Hosokawa: Biggest Weak Point—Right-winger and Money), *Shukan bunshun.*

Index

Permissions Acknowledgements

Extracts from the following are reprinted with the kind permission of the publisher: *Mikado no Shozo* (Portrait of the Emperor) by Naoki Inose, Shogakukan; *Seibu Okoku* (Seibu Empire) by Toshiaki Kaminogo, Kodansha; *Hoko no kisetsu no nakade* (In the Season of Roaming) by Takashi Tsujii, Shinchosha; *Kuto san-ju nen* (Thirty Years of Struggle) by Yasujiro Tsutsumi, Sanko Bunka Kenkyujo. Gratitude is also due to the following, from whose works the author has quoted: Shigeki Manabe, *Tsutsumi Yoshiaki no keiei tamashii* (The Management Spirit of Yoshiaki Tsutsumi); Gentaro Taniguchi, *Tsutsumi Yoshiaki to Orimpikku* (Yoshiaki Tsutsumi and the Olympics); Takao Kaifu, "Itan no tosho Seibu okoku Tsutsumi Yoshiaki no henshin" (Seibu's Yoshiaki Tsutsumi, Champion of Heresy, Changes), in *Shukan Asahi;* Kunio Kamibayashi, "Waga Tsutsumi ichizoku chi no himitsu" (My Tsutsumi Family—the Secret of Blood), in *Shukan bunshun;* Foumiko Kometani, "The Conversation: Seiji Tsutsumi," in *Tokyo Journal;* Shigeki Manabe, "Tsutsumi Yoshiaki no yabo 1, 2, 6" (Yoshiaki Tsutsumi's Ambition 1, 2, 6) and "Tsutsumi Yoshiaki chokugeki!" (Yoshiaki Tsutsumi Direct Hit!), all in *Shukan Gendai;* Yonosuke Miki, "Kessen Hakone yama" (The Decisive Battle of Hakone), in *Chuo Koron;* "Zaikai saigo no kaibutsu no shi" (Death of the Last Monster in the Financial World) and "Hakone yama kaitaku wo kisotta" (Competitors in the development of Hakone), both in *Zaikai;* Mineo Noda and Tadashi Koyama, "Futatsu no 'Seibu' wo eguru!" (Carving out Two Seibus!), in *Gekkan Hoseki;* Makoto Sadaka, "Seibu tetsudo gurupu" (Seibu Railway Group) and "Ki ni kakaru 'hadaka no osama' no yukusue" (The Worrying Direction of the Emperor Who Has No Clothes), both in *Asahi Journal;* Yasunori Tateishi, "PARCO seiko no makoto no kosekisha" (The True Creator of Parco's Success), in *Shokun!,* and "Seibu hyakkaten gurupu zankoku monogatari" (The Cruel Story of Seibu Department Store Group), in *Shukan Gendai;* Takashi Tsujii, *A Spring like Any Other;* Misao Tsutsumi, "Jigyo no oni to tomoni san ju kyu nen" (Thirty-nine Years with the Demon of Business), in *Fujin Koron;* and Jean Antoine, *Seiji Tsutsumi, ou, Les vertus de la fortune,* La Sept RTBF-BRT Cinéma et communication.

ABOUT THE AUTHOR

LESLEY DOWNER has written for several publications, among them *The New York Times, The Wall Street Journal, The Sunday Times, The Independent, Condé Nast Traveler* and *Travel & Leisure. On the Narrow Road,* her book about her travels in Japan, was made into a television documentary titled *Journey to a Lost Japan.* She lives in Tokyo and London.

ABOUT THE TYPE

This book was set in Galliard, a typeface designed by Matthew Carter for the Merganthaler Linotype Company in 1978. Galliard is based on the sixteenth-century typefaces of Robert Granjon.